CW00550581

Stressing Wachsmann

Edition Angewandte
Book Series of the University of Applied Arts Vienna
Edited by Gerald Bast, Rector

*edition:*ˈʌngewʌndtə
Universität für angewandte Kunst Wien
University of Applied Arts Vienna

Stressing Wachsmann

Structures for a
Future / Strukturen
für eine Zukunft

Klaus Bollinger, Florian Medicus,
Institute of Architecture
at the University of Applied Arts
Vienna and the Akademie
der Künste, Berlin (Hrsg./Eds.)

Birkhäuser
Basel

Contents/
Inhalt

Texts

"New materials, methods, processes, static and dynamic insights, planning, sociological givens have to be accepted." This is what Konrad Wachsmann wrote in his manifesto *Vom Bauen in unserer Zeit* (Building in Our Time). "Human and aesthetic ideas will receive new impetus from the uncompromising application of contemporary knowledge and expertise," he continued.

Preface

Gerald Bast

Building in our time has to follow the lead of state-of-the-art science and technology—is one way of paraphrasing that text from 1958. Throughout his whole lifetime Wachsmann endorsed an architecture that made scientific methods of experimentation and laws of automation his instruments. He is regarded as the pioneer of industrial building. For him architecture was an organized mass undertaking for which teamwork was absolutely essential. He advocated an all-encompassing rationalization of building—one that was ultimately to also find expression in a new form, i.e., function following form instead of "form follows function."

Today his ideas are particularly topical again. Digital means of manufacturing as well as logarithmic planning techniques dominate current architectural discourse. Conceptual considerations of industrial building from Wachsmann's time overlap with contemporary debates on algorithmic building. It thus makes sense to take a new look at architects and theoreticians such as Wachsmann—to critically examine them and to learn from their insights and achievements but also from their mistakes.

The radical changes taking place today require that we be wary about promises and respond to them with correlative and creative approaches to thinking. We need to explore new technologies in order to be able to use them in a progressive, visionary way. Stressing Wachsmann is an important contribution to showing how the history of architecture can be a key to understanding contemporary architectural debate as well as today's social challenges.

"And then, in an environment that still belonged entirely to the post-Victorian age, whereas I yearned longingly for the Zeppelin, who was to advise me and whom should I believe?"—Konrad Wachsmann on his childhood in *Selbstdarstellung*[1], 1973

After *Unbuildable Tatlin?!* (Springer Verlag, 2012) from 2013 onwards we worked on a further publication about our seminar work in which we examined unbuilt architecture icons of the 20th century: Friedrich Kiesler's *Endless House*. Produced in close collaboration with the Vienna Kiesler Foundation, this book (*Endless Kiesler*, Birkhäuser Verlag) was presented at MoMa in New York in September 2015. On that occasion it was Mark Wigley who asked us in which way we intended to continue this fine series. With our students from the Institute for Architecture we had produced a number of good seminar works (on Lissitzky, Melnikov, Mies van der Rohe, Wachsmann, Price, Domenig/Huth among others), but it was thanks alone to Mark Wigley's suggestion that we later examined the work of Konrad Wachsmann so intensively. At that time Wigley remarked how strange it was that Wachsmann, who was so diverse and internationally important, always surfaced only on the perimeter and was, in general, grossly underappreciated.

Since that warm evening in New York we, and thankfully many others with us, have worked on this book. We hope that it makes a comprehensive and appropriate contribution to filling a gap and to reevaluating Konrad Wachsmann, his work and his impact.

The Hangars

As a historical type, Konrad Wachsmann's USAF-hangar, which we examined in two seminars (*Advanced Structural Design*, 2012 and 2016; a number of selected works can be found in this book[→107–138]) is positioned at the end of what was indeed an exciting series of constructional experiments. Whereas for Karl Marx the locomotive was the symbol of modernism (and the wonderful and yet ambivalent infrastructure buildings of the 19th century can be understood in this context) from roughly 1910 onwards we see how the first civilian air flights and their daring protagonists appropriated this symbol. Franz Kafka, in Brescia, described this very aptly: "But now comes the apparatus with which Blériot flew across the Channel; no one said it, all know it. (...) In contrast everyone looks up to him, there is no room in any heart for any other. (...) Up here 20 meters above the earth a human being is captive in a wooden frame and battles against an invisible danger to which he has freely exposed himself."[2] Gravity could no longer be conquered just by more or less static "lighter than air balloons" but with noisy motors and their new speeds.[→1] It is certainly no coincidence that in the same year (1909) Marinetti in his *The Futurist Manifesto* sings of the "love of danger," the "beauty of speed" and "the gliding flight of the airplane, whose propeller rattles like a flag blowing in the wind and claps

The Future Was Everything
—
Konrad Wachsmann's USAF-Hangar

Klaus Bollinger, Florian Medicus;
Fig.: 1–11

like an applauding crowd."[3] It was also in 1909 that Fritz Wichert's fine text *Luftschifffahrt und Architektur* appeared, in which he sees monumental "gravity architecture" overcome by what was now the frontal value of the roofs. "The aircraft," Le Corbusier was later to write in 1922, "has mobilized inventiveness, intelligence and daring: *fantasy* and *cool reason*"[4], about which Peter Sloterdijk is also certain that: "anyone who does not want to talk about uplift, should remain silent about modernism."[5]

As the 19th gave way to the 20th century new, huge but generally lightweight, sophisticated shed structures for the construction and servicing of airships, initially attracting little attention, were erected in the form of functional industrial buildings, as well as a number of completely bizarre mechanical structure projects, whose daring quality still astonishes us today (Rainer Graefe's *Geschichte des Konstruierens* has a fine essay on this subject by Angelika Osswald and Berthold Burkhardt). At this point, mention should be made of the classic "airship sheds in Orly" by Eugène Freyssinet (1922–24, infilled reinforced concrete parabolic arches). In the second edition of *Vers une architecture* from 1924, in two photos from the building site Le Corbusier triumphally compares their colossal dimensions of 300×90 m and a height of almost 60 m with the nave of the Cathedral of Notre Dame (12 m wide, 35 m high).[*2] In 1933 *Hangar One*, designed by the German engineer Karl Arnstein, opened in Sunnyvale in California. Covering a ground area of 345×94 m and with a height of 60 m (arched steel trusses), it is still one of the largest shed constructions worldwide.[*3] Between 1935–38 Pier Luigi Nervi built an equally iconic hangar in Orvieto: a covered, barrel-vaulted shell made of a lattice of concrete beams that have a wonderfully delicate cross-section of just 110×15 cm, and with only three columns along the entrance side.[*4] In this context it is certainly particularly exciting that Nervi, like Eduardo Torroja in Madrid at the same time, initially tested these constructions using structural models and from this developed a patent for industrial precast construction methods (Pat. 377969, 1939; "Building system for making load-bearing frames for vaults, domes and general structural systems by means of elements made in the works and connected by reinforced concrete joints").[6]

While Freyssinet and Arnstein still built for what were called "rigid airships" i.e. large Zeppelins, whose heyday would end with the Second World War at the latest (the Hindenburg exploded in 1937), Nervi dealt exclusively with airplane hangars, which he self-confidently published in *Casabella* not as ingenious functional buildings but as fully-fledged contributions to architecture.

USAF-Hangar

In 1939, while still in France, Konrad Wachsmann had developed a "New method of construction for an Aeroplane Hangar (prefabricated, demountable, transportable).[7] As *President of the General Panel Corporation* of New York and commissioned by the *Atlas Aircraft Corporation* Konrad Wachsmann had developed an aircraft hangar, his *Mobilar Structure*[8], which was exhibited at MoMA in spring 1946[→5]; an important and, as was later to be shown, pioneering project. Only a few years later, more precisely at the end of 1949, Wachsmann was asked by Serge Chermayeff to come to Chicago in order to formulate a sound technical program for the *Institute of Design* (founded in 1937 as a "new Bauhaus" and therefore part of the Illinois Institute of Technology; Mies van der Rohe and Ludwig Hilberseimer were already there), which had run into difficulties following Moholy-Nagy's premature demise. "Two of what were certainly the most decisive discoveries of my life were made during my time in Chicago period," Konrad Wachsmann was later to recall: "I discovered the importance of team work and at the same time understood that it was necessary to rigorously combat the cult of personality). (...) This was the beginning of a journey that would lead me with my general theme, the industrialization of building to universities and architecture schools on almost all continents."[9]

In spring 1951 Wachsmann's institute, the *Department of Building Research* obtained, more or less by chance, an important commission to develop a "new method of construction for airplane hangars based on an invention by Konrad Wachsmann" (the *Mobilar Structure* already referred to) along with the substantial sum of, initially, $ 80,000. The contract between the US Air Force and the *Advanced Building Research* describes "the development of an airplane hangar designed of unusual dimensions and structural features in which the structure shall provide a new type of metallic construction which is suitable for any kind of structure, where speed of erection and dismounting of uniform standard parts, flexibility of layouts, large unobstructed floor areas, and unlimited accessibilities are desired. (...) This contract further requests an extreme reduction of the variety of parts and the simplicity of connections such that any structure so designed can be readily erected by members of the Armed Forces."[10]

In early summer 1951 Wachsmann started work with a group of older students and assistants in the rooms of the *Armour Research Foundation*. It quickly became clear to all involved that they were "tackling a problem that was not exactly simple. The right-angle was questioned, the aim was to decide upon a new concept of space. The junction and the spatial triangle as keys to working with three-dimensional structures opened up entirely new aspects to me."[11/→6] "Sometimes we worked day and night, seven days a week. We had also finished a large model which played an important role in the whole research and the evolution of the design, more important than drafting, since it was extremely difficult to visualize every angle of this three-dimensional structure."[12] After postponing it twice, Konrad Wachsmann was able to submit a first report in April 1952: "In fulfillment of our Contract, we have in the foregoing submitted a project consisting of forty drawings, many models, numerous photographs, and a report consisting of weight figures, cost estimates, and stress analysis."[13] Above all the conceived dimensions (a cantilever on both sides of 50 m, improbably delicate pyramidal columns) and the narrative quality of the model and the photographs provided the basis for the "inspiring character of the image" in the sense of an "incarnation of constructivist building"[14], as it is later flatteringly described in the book *Vision der Moderne—das Prinzip Konstruktion*.

Wachsmann concluded his summary in 1952 by writing that there was a shortage of time and money for very promising research work and that he would be happy to continue with further studies, if the US Air Force were to make further means available. Which it did: over the course of the next three years the military administration was to invest a total of nearly $250,000 in Wachsmann's research work.[15] This made it possible to undertake detailed studies of the connections,[→7] to build prototypes and also allowed for wide-ranging refinements, although the final questions about how to close the space, the roofing, and about the mechanics of the gates ultimately had to remain unanswered. The last large plans[→169–180] and a comprehensive description completed the project in 1954. A short time later (1955) the US Congress decided not to fund any further research work without a precise application in the form of a project and, for strategic reasons, to concentrate investment on underground hangars that were atomic bombproof.[16]

JOINTS

In 1963 an excited Reyner Banham was in top form when he wrote The Dymaxicrat, a hymn of praise to Buckminster Fuller. To much the same extent as he lavishes praise on Fuller's confidence and visionary greatness (while not dealing with tiresome details), Banham pokes fun at Robert le Ricolais and Konrad Wachsmann: "while Wachsmann has done little more than pursue certain problems of structural jointing with the same fiendish narrow ingenuity that other typical German genii have applied to clockwork mice and magnetic mines."[17] This impression should be vigorously contested, although admittedly, as regards the jointing problem, Banham was not entirely wrong: Wachsmann appears to have been almost obsessed by the details of joints and by connectors in general.[→8]

After Graham Bell's wonderful experiments German engineer Max Mengeringhausen (also a "typical German genius") developed his Mero space frame and the universal threaded nodes to which up to 18 tubes can be connected during the Second World War; the first, admittedly small-scale, use for transportable structural systems for the air force then followed. It was only in 1957 that he, or rather his Mero system, achieved a major breakthrough with the *Halle der Stadt von Morgen* at the Berlin Interbau. We can assume that Wachsmann already knew this impressively simple detail. Perhaps he also knew Robert le Ricolais' text *Les Tôles Composées et leurs applications aux constructions métalliques légères* from 1935, in which the lightweight, load-bearing outer skin constructions employed by progressive aircraft technology are recommended for the architecture of the future. Naturally, in *Wendepunkt im Bauen* (p. 133) Wachsmann shows Bell's viewing tower from 1907 with its prefabricated tetrahedra, as well as the Mero node, but as regards the latter without going into detail about its capacities and possible consequences.

As regards space frames it is not so much a question of the tubes or the elements that they are made from, but rather where and how they rest and how the joints are constructed. The Mero node is as simple as it is clever, although it is limited geometrically and consequently also in terms of form. Wachsmann's joint aimed at achieving more: the truly universal solution, total design freedom, as he writes: "The result of almost two years work on development was a universal joint that forms a ring around the main tubes from which the secondary tubes can radiate in all directions and in every combination and at every angle desired. This joint can take up to 20 construction tubes. This means almost unlimited adaptability to suit every geometric system, as because different strains can be imposed on the individual tubes, eccentric connections are also permissible."[18] But precisely there, where the decisive moment in his total rationalization should have lain, Wachsmann's multi-part joint mechanics were too complicated, the typification of the tubes and their cross-sections was ultimately unsuitable for a universal structure, the hangar's will to create form had grown beyond itself.

In fact, competent industrial architecture and other approaches to construction that were no less suitable existed at the same time as Wachsmann's, indeed, hangar structures had already been patented and built beforehand (see for instance *L'Architecture d'Aujourd'hui*, Nov. 1936[+9]) already patented and built hangar structures,[+10] as well as other approaches to construction that were no less suitable. But the way in which Konrad Wachsmann was able to combine existing ideas and elements with his own concerns, and in the process to enrich them, still distinguishes him clearly today. Under the given circumstances, exactly one hundred years after Paxton's *Crystal Palace*, a far more boring building could have been developed which, as a result, would naturally have been less able to inspire the dynamic ambitions of the industrial present and future. The USAF-Hangar itself, despite its uniqueness and intentionally iconic quality, was therefore more a narrative vehicle to prove the inescapable consistency of industrial building and the indispensability of work within and as a team. It was certainly a contentious symbol of its time (in this regard see Stefan Polónyi's critical review from 1961 on p. 97) but the constructive potency of the machine, the open methodology and Wachsmann himself represented an expanded and constantly expandable expression of *confidence vers une architecture.* For "suddenly it was said that with the hangar I had anticipated the feeling for space of the twenty-first century. Much to my own amazement I was then celebrated as a daring prophet of the culture of the future by even the most severe critics," a much-amused Konrad Wachsmann later recounted.[19/→11]

1   Wulf Herzogenrath (ed.), *Selbstdar-stellung—Künstler über sich,* Droste Verlag, Düsseldorf, 1973, p. 225.

2   Franz Kafka, *Die Aeroplane in Brescia,* Fischer Bibliothek, Frankfurt am Main, 1977, pp. 21f.

3   Filippo Tommaso Marinetti, "Manifest des Futurismus," in: Norbert Nobis (ed.), *Der Lärm der Strasse,* catalog Sprengel Museum, Hannover, 2001, p. 367.

4   Le Corbusier, "Ausblick auf eine Architektur," in: *Bauwelt Fundamente 2,* Vieweg Verlag, Braunschweig/Wiesbaden, 1982, p. 89.

5   Peter Sloterdijk, *Sphären III—Schäume,* Suhrkamp, Frankfurt a. M., 2004, p. 718.

6   See: Claudio Greco, *Pier Luigi Nervi,* Quart Verlag, Lucerne, 2008, pp. 179, 285. Nervis' patent from November 1939 outlines the use of steel pipe-trusses as well.

7   AdK, Konrad-Wachsmann-Archiv, Wachsmann 0300 Arbeitskopie.pdf.

8   See: *Vision der Moderne,* Heinrich

9   Klotz (ed.), Munich (Prestel Verlag) 1986, pp. 242f.

9   Konrad Wachsmann in Michael Grüning, *Der Wachsmann-Report,* Verlag der Nation, Berlin, 1986, p. 543.

10   AdK, Konrad-Wachsmann-Archiv, Wachsmann 0605 006 Arbeitskopie.pdf.

11   Konrad Wachsmann in Michael Grüning, *Der Wachsmann-Report,* Verlag der Nation, Berlin, 1986, p. 540.

12   Konrad Wachsmann, "Timebridge, Konrad Wachsmann: An Autobiography," AdK, Konrad-Wachsmann-Archiv, Wachsmann 2128, p. 199.

13   AdK, Konrad-Wachsmann-Archiv, Wachsmann 0605 051 Arbeitskopie.pdf.

14   Heinrich Klotz (ed.), *Vision der Moderne,* Prestel Verlag, Munich, 1986, pp. 16, 236.

15   See: N. M. Newmark, "Evaluation Of [sic] Aircraft Hangar Design, Report to General Mr. Eric H. Wang, 31 May 1952, III. Recommendations," AdK,

Konrad-Wachsmann-Archiv, Wachsmann 2090, pp. 14f.

16   See Konrad Wachsmann, "Timebridge," AdK, Konrad-Wachsmann-Archiv, Wachsmann 2128, p. 200.

17   Reyner Banham, *A Critic Writes,* University of California Press, Berkeley and Los Angeles, 1996, p. 94.

18   Konrad Wachsmann, *Wendepunkt im Bauen,* Krausskopf Verlag, Wiesbaden, 1959, p. 172. Of interest are also the calculations and physicals stress models of the joints by Frank J. Kornacker & Associates (Armour Research Foundation of Illinois Institute of Technology): *"Calculations on the Wachsmann Hangar, August to October, 1953, IV. Conclusions and Recommendations,"* AdK, Konrad-Wachsmann-Archiv, Wachsmann 600, pp. 30f.

19   Konrad Wachsmann in Michael Grüning, *Der Wachsmann-Report,* Verlag der Nation, Berlin, 1986, p. 541.

The Konrad-Wachsmann-Archiv was presented to the Baukunst-archiv (Architecture Archive) of the Akademie der Künste, Berlin (Academy of Arts) on April 14, 1999. The Akademie der Künste, Berlin had purchased it from his widow Judith Wachsmann after it had been stored for many years at the Huntington Library in San Marino (USA). The archive included a detailed list that had been compiled already in 1977, while Wachsmann was still alive, by Robertson Ward at the University of Southern California (USC) and encompassed four areas: "File 1," 22 boxes with written material and photographs; "File 2," two file cabinets with subject files and material related to Wachsmann's activities as professor at USC; "File 2," 23 boxes with written material and photographs. The fourth list gave an overview of the plans and drawings. The Academy also received material not documented in the list: books, newspapers and journals, photographs and written material as well as audio-tapes and films. The archive contains various model elements of Wachsmann's connecting node from the Packaged House System and the USAF-hangar. There are also photographs and plans from the early projects from his period working for Christoph and Unmack, a timber construction company in Niesky (1926–29) and material relating to various projects in exile (1933–41). The most extensive documentation is on the projects both realized and not realized in the United States. This includes mainly the Packaged House System, which he marketed together with Walter Gropius (1942–51) as General Panel Corporation and for various airplane hangars (Mobilar Structure), which was commissioned by the Atlas Aircraft Corporation (1939–45) and the United States Air Force (1951–53). Moreover, there are also manuscripts and photographs for the publications "Holzhausbau" (1930) and "Wendepunkt im Bauen" (Turning Point in Building) (1959) and manuscripts and photographs from lecture tours through Europe and Israel as well as Japan and Russia from the 1950s to the 1970s. In addition to private correspondence from the 1920s and 1930s the archive holdings include extensive correspondence with architects who worked internationally. Especially enlightening is the manuscript of his unpublished autobiography "Timebridge 1901–2001." Altogether, the holdings and the structure of the archive reflect how meticulous-ly Wachsmann went about documenting his entire work. This also gives an idea of his general working style.

Throughout his entire life Konrad Wachsmann remained a seeker and experimenter who never reached final results in his endeavor to turn building into a massively structured undertaking, while at the same time protecting environmental resources. At the end of his "Timebridge" autobiography he euphorically prophesized a new time beyond the year 2001: "The year 2001 will inaugurate the new epoch, so fantastically exciting. No period in the history of

Konrad Wachsmann
—
The Artistic Legacy of an Experi-menter at the Aka-demie der Künste, Berlin

Eva-Maria Barkhofen;
Fig.: 12–14

civilization has ever offered anything so promising, so humane, so effective, so intelligent and so meaningful."

The period covered by the Konrad-Wachsmann-Archiv contains written documents from 1920 to 1980, encompassing a total of thirty running meters of files, photographs and written material, ca. 2030 plans and drawings, 13 models and various individual model pieces, 100 audiotapes with original recordings from his talks, lectures and discussions as well as films documenting experimental projects. Today most of the holdings have been archived and can be accessed at the Architecture Archive of the Akademie der Künste in Berlin.

From Meditation to Mediation: Reclaiming Wachsmann's Legacy

Parsa Khalili; Fig.: 15, 16

I—A Critical Conservation

In secret and across distorted fields of architectural representation and practice, we witness Konrad Wachsmann's legacy even to this day; we are, in effect, unknowingly beholden to his quest to formalize and tame endless space. He provided an alternative medium to both modernism's heroic insistence on the monolithic qualities of concrete, but also to modernist claims to have solved the problems of architecture and its social utility through the fusing of dogma and ideology with built form. From the sublime images of the impossible volumes contained within his space-frames to relentlessly autocratic diagrams for his modular construction systems and joints, his obsessions knew no boundaries of scale or scope—or so the impression and the legend. As a result, he has been lost within the ambiguous terrain between failed techno-futurist[1] and pre-utopian urbanist[2]. He has escaped substantial critique or consideration because of the gratuitous focus by architectural historians on the failure of his *General Panel System* and the inability of architecture to position his relevance beyond the usual trappings of modernism's overall failure to secure for architecture a humanist project that would not devolve, through entropic indecision, to mere utility and functionalism.

The primary coordinates for a possible redemption of the lifework of Wachsmann from architecture's own extensively biased narrative(s)—notably the point of Tafuri's denunciation of operative critique—includes an investigation of microhistories on the subjects of industrialization and architecture, plus representation and construction. Out of necessity, such a redemptive re-reading would then require de-construction of the premise that Wachsmann's significance for modernism rests on some form of extending the potency of the Crystal Palace (1851), and the implicit belief that through technology a universal construction system might be found that could serve the progressive social agenda or new utilitarianism of modernism. Paradoxically, ridding Wachsmann's legacy of such ideology then becomes one means for understanding his role both in the failure of the modernist utopian project (a bias that justifies overemphasis on his own personal failures) and his role as humanist (never reducible to mere utility). If we remove the pure utilitarianist rhetoric defining his successes and failures, we find the key to reconstructing his legacy.

It is impossible to overlook the connection between the imagery Wachsmann produced and the explosive fallout of his aspirations on a new generation of post-war architects. The technical sophistication and intricacy of the systems he produced liberated young practices from the oppressive dogmas of professional obligations at the time and gave them the tools and language to radically engage and envision new utopian ideals, if not in some obscure revolutionary delusion, in the very least, at the level of imagery. The systems he envisioned, but never quite perfected, have both transcended cultural and geographical barriers but also done so continuously and iteratively over the second half of the twentieth century. Sociocultural shifts from one generation to the next have developed his project and legacy through a number of phases to the present day. Many of these periods are also notoriously "futuristic" in their own right, and it is that aspect of his humanist imagination that gets swept aside by too close a reading of the systems employed.

ii—Evolutionary Mutation

The immediate reception of his work was met with projects of "Radical Hyperbole." Yona Friedman's *La Ville Spatiale* (1960), Eckhard Schulze-Fielitz's *Space City* (1959), and Constant Nieuwenhuys' *New Babylon* (1959) all speculated on the impossible future of architecture liberated chiefly in its orientation (and obligation to gravity). The lightness and infinite reproducibility of the space-frame meant omni-directionality and growth, limitlessness in function and purpose, but most critically, in the intellectual underpinnings of the implication of a complete detachment from the ground itself—a symbolic erasure to the continuity of the architectural tradition as a whole. This "new beginning" liberated the utopianism of modernism from the ideology of modernism. The key was exuberance and fantasy versus sober technological utilitarianism, which of course is embodied in the ubiquitous mid-century modernism everyone then despised (and blamed on Mies et al.). Note that the "anti-capitalist" New Babylon had first been conceived in 1959!

Following this big bang comes a moment of respite from the wildness of speculation, ushering in an only slightly more sobering second phase of "Hyperbolic Functionalism," which urged a rethinking of Wachsmann within a more realistic framework. Kenzo Tange's *Tokyo Bay* (1960), Cedric Price's *Fun Palace* (1964), Archigram's *Plug-In City* (1964), and Kisho Kurokawa's *Agriculture City* (1960) reeled in some of the fantasy of the past decades and offered plausible, even if still extreme, provocations for new models of housing, recreation, and urbanity. These projects confined the space frame into manageable networks of systems and programs often conceiving of the discrete insertions first and propagating them up, out, and beyond second; this maturity reflected a shift from top-down to a bottom-up reticence of Wachsmann.

In its third phase of "Functional Visibility" the spaceframe became the framework—literally and metaphorically—for celebrating both advancements in and the reliance upon mechanical building systems and led to whole new systems that either ironized structure or fetishized it. There is no better example of this than Renzo Piano, Richard Rogers, and Gianfranco Franchini who furthered the utility of the space frame in the most vividly pragmatic sense for the most quotidian of uses in their *Centre Pompidou* (1971). With the specter of Friedman and Price in the periphery, the ubiquity of the space frame was filled with (and celebrates) the various building systems needed to create the undisturbed and unobligated openness of the interior. It was only because of this armature that space could be liberated—on all levels a stark contrast to the normative means and methods of construction at the time. In many ways Wachsmann's "structural logic" is an open-ended system; in its post-modern detour it was appropriated as part of an architectonic mash-up of modernist functionalism/utilitarianism and open-plan mischief by default. The latter is what permitted the avant-garde to appropriate him and the former is what permits this phase to give way to the next.

In its most contemporary manifestation, a nameless "Fourth Phase Drift," roughly analogous to what is called super-contemporary[3] in the art world, it could be argued that the ethos of Wachsmann has since been hyper-stylized, heavily-computed upon, and optimized in service to the contorted, twisted, and concealed structural logic of built work today. Without this reformulation the heroic projects of the digital era would have been impossible, if not, horrifically uneconomical. From Shoei Yoh's *Prefectura Gymnasium* (1991) to Coop Himmelb(l)au's *BMW Welt*[→60] (2001) to Zaha Hadid Architects' *Hedar Aliyev Centre*[→15] (2007) this drift may be read or tracked. The implicit ideology of this shift concerns the triumphalism of architecture's new forms of spectacle. It remains unclear whether Wachsmann was consciously assimilated on the architectural side of this cultural shift or merely complicit by having developed the means to construct what is effectively "spatial drift" as a mirror-state for hyper-capitalism.

Embarrassed by its own cliché and the dated image of industrial-era efficacy, megastructralist utopian armature, or reified building-systems apparatus, Wachsmann's techno-formalist idiom has most recently been forced behind the thin-shelled, aluminum cladding of architecture's vacuous, contemporary tectonic language. This language also exposes the notion of drift associated with the hyper-capitalization of architecture as ultra-commodity (built to embody capitalist drift itself).

III—Proto-humanism

Through tracing his legacy through a broader historical lens, what emerges is this line of transmission from the late 1950s to the 2000s of built and unbuilt work that assimilated Wachsmann's structural innovations, even if the work departs from his utopian agenda and wanders into a phased re-deployment in spectacular architectures that are all founded on one form or another of exuberance. For this reason, it is possible to say that another aspect of Wachsmann was jettisoned in the process, and that it is only one side of his legacy that has survived. The architectural historians, having painted Wachsmann as an unrepentant technologist, have thus in many ways facilitated the transfer of his legacy to architectural engineering, dropping along the way what was behind the modernist quest for industrial production and precision craft.

In the aftermath of his failed experiments, Wachsmann published his *Seven Theses*[4] (1957), as a way to resituate the idea of material processes within, not as a replacement to, architecture. As a manifesto, it tried to reposition the underpinnings of his broader ideological project, and yet only one point of seven is strikingly absent of any tectonic- or systems-related language such as science, technology, machine, tool, materials, processes, industrialization, scientific, automation, or industry. Within Article 7 we finally find Wachsmann's "Rosebud" on display, a subtle proto-humanism—and in direct opposition to the techno-determinism most have claimed as his legacy. Article 7 states: "Human and aesthetic ideas will receive new impulses through the uncompromising application of contemporary knowledge and ability."[5]

Across the arc of the periods mapped in this text and through various works that might be said to re-embody Wachsmann's idiom (however distorted by architectural historians), what was radical and proto-humanistic has since become parody, if not outright distortion. Saving Wachsmann from both therefore requires that *his* Article 7 be read against—and in parallel to—Article 7 of Austrian philosopher, Ludwig Wittgenstein's *Tractatus Logico-Philosophicus* (1922): "Whereof one cannot speak, thereof one must be silent." What we know now may be technically deduced, but what we do with it matters most.[6]

1   See Reyner Banham's unapologetic critique, "I complessi della prefabbricazione," in: *Casabella* 1986 Sept., vol. 50, no. 527.

2   See Kenneth Frampton "I tecnocrati della Pax Americana: Wachsmann & Fuller," in: *Casabella* 1988 Jan.–Feb., vol. 52, no. 542–543.

3   The term came into play in the 2000s originally to distinguish the media spectacle that overtook the art world at the time.

4   See p. 55 of this publication.

5   Konrad Wachsmann, "Seven Theses," in: Ulrich Conrads (ed.), *Programs and Manifestoes on 20th-century Architecture* (Cambridge, MA: The MIT Press, 1970), p. 156.

6   Wittgenstein and Wachsmann come within inches of one another on page five of Francesca Hughes, *The Architecture of Error: Matter, Measure, and the Misadventures of Precision* (MIT Press, 2014). Hughes conflates the logical-positivist universe of early Wittgenstein with the rationalist and scientific inclination of late Wachsmann—both in this case, according to Hughes, obsessed with precision to the point of *irrationality*. Criticism levied against Wachsmann's obsessiveness for most of his career.

Konrad Wachsmann was a non-conformist architect who planned almost obsessively into the future. Scientists have usually focused on his visionary technical designs and hardly ever taken a closer look at his personal life and his origins—in spite of the fact that his oeuvre and his influence can hardly be understood without considering his early biography.

Konrad Wachsmann was born on May 16, 1901 as the third of four children to the pharmacist couple Elsa and Adolf Wachsmann in Frankfurt an der Oder. The pharmacy was located in a Gothic town house, right on the market square, and the family lived one floor above it. His parents' strict adherence to tradition and their loyalty to the emperor made young Konrad protest against everything that had to do with duty and compliance. His father's early death in 1908 certainly influenced the young man's rebelliousness. As can be gleaned from his later notes, he abhorred school. After having to repeat a class two times and then cultivating social contacts in dubious inner-city circles in Frankfurt's poor neighborhoods, he was taken out of school. In April 1917 his mother brought him to the Münning cabinetmaker's shop where he began an apprenticeship and ultimately thrived here. Working with wood gave him the chance to acquire technical and artisanal skills and proved satisfying to him.[1] During World War One the shop mainly produced coffins. He himself says that on one day in 1918 he made a coffin, the lower part in the morning and the lid in the afternoon. He remembers that he would lower himself into the finished lower part at noon to take a break, pulling up his legs since the coffins were cut very small to save money. By Sunday he would have to bring his week's output on a hand-pulled cart to the military hospital. After completing his three-year apprenticeship Wachsmann passed his exam on March 31, 1920 and planned to finally fulfill his long-standing desire to study architecture. He felt drawn to the Bauhaus in Weimar; his mother, however, was not pleased with the socialist ideas and sent her son, now twenty years old, to Berlin to study with Bruno Paul at the Arts and Crafts School (*Kunstgewerbeschule*). There he was immediately overcome by his familiar dislike for the constraints of school. He left the Arts and Crafts School, after only one year, in 1922.

An unpublished letter from the 19-year-old to his mother shows how much he suffered from everything he was subjected to and against what he rebelled. Just the first sentences are absolutely crucial for understanding his later work: "Dear Mama! Only he who always does what he is supposed to knows how to live right, that is, he who always falls in line in the face of the inevitable and for whom being compelled to do something is always voluntary. I will never learn that."[2] That he elaborates on this ordeal for a further three pages gives pause to the reader. His relation to his mother and

Biographical Notes

"… only he who always does what he is supposed to knows how to live right …"
(Konrad Wachsmann)

Eva-Maria Barkhofen;
Fig.: 17–29

his sister was never a warm one. After leaving the Arts and Crafts School he kept himself going with occasional assignments, which usually emerged from his daily sojourns at the Romanisches Café on Potsdamer Platz. He would engage in lengthy discussions there with Bertolt Brecht, Else Lasker-Schüler, Erwin Piscator and other artists. He had no clue as to where life would take him. He was hired straight from the café table to construct film backdrops. He was only able to survive thanks to the support of a well-to-do Berlin aunt. It is not difficult to understand that his family did not approve of his life style. His mother decided to remove him from the detrimental influence. He was sent to Dresden to study at the Academy of Art with Heinrich Tessenow whose architecture he initially was inspired by. Once again he had trouble fitting in with the discipline of the teaching program and returned to Berlin in 1924. There he took on a job as a draftsman for Leo Nachtlicht. Here, too, he did not stay for long. He sought contacts with Hans Poelzig whose *Großes Schauspielhaus* fascinated him. Poelzig took him on as a student (*Meisterschüler*) in his studio. But the Golden Cage in which he sat at Poelzig's studio became constricting. Wachsmann wanted to get out of Germany. In 1926 he traveled to Holland to work with Pieter Oud. He was deported because he could not present the required residence permit. He traveled to Paris to Le Corbusier but could not afford to work for nothing. If his sister had not paid for his return ticket to Berlin he would have, in his own words, got lost in the streets of Paris. In 1926 Hans Poelzig got him a job with a wood construction company—Christoph & Unmack in Niesky (Lausitz, Brandenburg) where he for the first time flourished in his work. This job which lasted until 1929 was to provide the basis of all his later project ideas for pre-fabricated buildings and his notions of an automatized world.

His most important project at Christoph & Unmack was the construction of the wooden house for Albert and Elsa Einstein in Caputh near Potsdam, which was completed in 1929.

The turmoil of the war years led him as a refugee—he was half-Jewish—to various places in Europe but thanks to the help of Gropius and Einstein, he received a visa for the USA in 1940. Wachsmann could not speak a word of English except for a sentence that an English painter in Rome taught him: "a thunderstorm refreshes the atmosphere."[3] Walter Gropius tried to find a job for him but his lack of linguistic skills prevented him from teaching at the university. Gropius invited him to Boston. Since Marcel Breuer had just split with his office partner Gropius, Wachsmann was able to join in ongoing projects.

He told Gropius about the universal building system for prefab houses he had developed in Marseille, and showed him the 13 ketches he was able to salvage. Gropius was very taken by all of this. In the heating basement of the apartment building Wachsmann set up three drafting tables, with a revolving chair in the middle, so that he could work on all of them at the same time. In spring 1942 the model, sketched in 44 drawings, was ready to be built. He often had altercations with Ise Gropius since he would also sharpen his pencils on the white carpet of the bedroom. She said that someone like him should be locked away in a bird's cage with a grid on the bottom to catch all the scrap right away.[4]

Drawings, models, descriptions and applications for patents now existed for the General Panel but where was the money for their implementation to come from? Possible investors still had doubts about the success of the concept. Yet Wachsmann finally received a letter from an engineer at MIT and began to look for investors in June 1942. On parting Ise Gropius is supposed to have said: "You can only come back WITH your shield or ON your shield"[5], which is to say, either as a winner or a complete loser. In September of the same year he returned as a winner. The official founding of the General Panel Corporation was scheduled for September 12, 1942 to mark Wachsmann's arrival in the United States exactly one year before. Four months later a test house was completed with the help of German-language carpenters. A period of great success began.

From the end of 1949 onwards, Wachsmann embarked upon a teaching career at the Chicago Institute of Design. He who had always hated everything related to school delved into a new world and noted that he had no idea of teaching or design. And yet he was able to enjoy a successful career as a teacher and lecturer who, until his death on November 26, 1980, was able to propagate his ideas of flexible and prefab building structures to the world on hundreds of lecture tours.

In the last sentence of his autobiography Wachsmann summarized his life motto very aptly as follows: "My friends: The past is the past, the present is only in passing, but the future is everything."[6]

1   This and other details were taken from the unpublished biography: Konrad Wachsmann, "Timebridge, Konrad Wachsmann: An Autobiography," AdK, Konrad-Wachsmann-Archiv, Wachsmann 2128.

2   Letter to his mother, dated June 3, 1920, AdK, Konrad-Wachsmann-Archiv, Wachsmann 1077.

3   Konrad Wachsmann, "Timebridge," p. 153.

4   Konrad Wachsmann, "Timebridge," pp. 159f.

5   Konrad Wachsmann, "Timebridge," pp. 159, 160.

6   Konrad Wachsmann, "Timebridge," p. 164.

In late 1973 and early 1974 Konrad Wachsmann worked in Los Angeles on a series of handwritten and typed drafts of a major but ultimately unpublished text entitled *Manifest for the Evolution of Assembling the Artificial Human Environment between Time and Space.*[2] The 49-page manuscript by the 75-year-old expert in industrialized building finally dissolved the very idea of a building. It begins by declaring that: "Building is energy and motion in time and space." The form of structures, environments and societies has always been determined by the availability of energy. The relatively recent arrival of electrical energy dramatically transformed all physical, social and economic life by "triggering" the age of machines. Our planet/spaceship travelling in outer space is already covered by a "blanket of energy, of electrical energy which does not know boundaries of any sort" and nuclear energy is accelerating this undoing of limits. Solid buildings will inevitably give way to diaphanous "networks of points" in space that support temporary spatial configurations guided by computerized cybernetic feedback. Walls, floors, columns, doors and windows will be replaced by a new building technology "for which there was no word yet." The illusions of permanence sustained by traditional buildings will finally give way to the "perpetual adaptability" of a seemingly massless structure whose "porous" character would be reinforced by temporarily suspending dispersed thin horizontal surfaces within it as "planes of movement" and even more temporary vertical surfaces as "gleaming screens." These screens construct a sense of distance between people living within dense urban configurations. In reverse, the "television screen" reduces the distance for those living in more isolated settings. The built environment becomes a point cloud that supports endless temporary configurations of mobile screens that either create or remove the effect of distance. Space pulsates. Architecture as such doesn't appear. It is not missed.

This image of the near future resonates strongly with the vast megastructure spider-webs floating above the ground proposed by Constant Nieuwenhuys, Cedric Price, Yona Friedman, Eckhard Schulze-Fielitz, the Metabolists, Superstudio, and so many others from the late fifties to the seventies.[3] Yet it is important to note Wachsmann's major influence on all of them and the ways his project remained more radical.

What is crucial in the Wachsmann narrative is that the ability to wirelessly transmit and receive information reshapes the built environment. Information is not just the basis for more efficient and responsive design. It is a building material in its own right. Indeed, it is the ultimate building material. Television screens are never simply suspended within an existing environment. Rather, they engineer a whole new environment, as the *Manifest* insisted:

Konrad Wachsmann's Television: Post-Architectural Transmissions[1]

Mark Wigley; Fig.: 30–42

"He will always be intimately connected with his community and the world by energy waves which transmit information to him which he is free to accept or reject as demonstrated in a television screen. How much this affects the concept of the meaning and function of the house, the street, the community, the urban or regional system is obvious."[4]

Conventional buildings are dissolved by these energy waves along with the difference between buildings, society, economy and politics. What used to be thought of as a delimited building becomes a system of systems embedded within an ever larger set of nested systems. No line between building, street, city, community, and brain survives. The very idea of the designer and of designing gives way to interdisciplinary teams and ultimately the division between such expert teams and the inhabitants of cities gives way to a broader ecology of information exchange facilitated by computers. The gathering, updating, classification, storage, analysis, accessibility and exchange of information becomes crucial. The drawings of information systems by the Wachsmann teams were as detailed as those of building systems. Indeed, they were treated as building systems in their own right. Buildings, institutions, social groups and ideas had to be thought in the same way.→[54–56]

Architecture as traditionally understood is "optional" in such a world and yet Wachsmann insisted that a globally shared aesthetic would emerge as a kind of collaborative art work. The project to make architecture disappear is paradoxically an aesthetic project. Disappearance itself is a carefully designed event. The *Manifest* tries to visualize an architecture without limits, which is to say an architecture without architecture, for "wide open and free spaces of relatively unlimited dimensions and the superimposition of spaces in relatively limitless numbers" with an "unlimited supply" of energy. It even speculates that the electrical energy blanket that is wrapping the planet in a "wire-mesh harness" might soon be replaced by a network of orbiting satellites that will convert the energy of the sun and beam it to wherever it is needed in concentrated "wireless transmitted energy waves." Not only is all wireless transmission a form of environment-shaping energy wave, but energy itself, the raw material of the built environment, would become a wireless transmission. Wachsmann, like his close friend Buckminster Fuller, was ultimately a wireless architect or post-architect.[5]

Wachsmann's work was an obsessive form of systems research focused on material organization and assembly that therefore tends not to be read in aesthetic, philosophical, ethical or political terms— but it was these things more than any else.[6] The *Manifest* argued that the new availability of wireless energy that knows no spatial limit means, for example, that war becomes unnecessary but continuous political engagement is essential—as represented by the TV screen offering real-time information and the right to respond to it. Wachsmann insisted that the structure of government has to change, even in the responsibility of "the great task of information" to communicate with the widest possible public about the fact that the 20th century is just a preparatory phase to a new lifestyle and new social orders that have already been "triggered by the availability of new media of information such as TV for instance." In other words, television has to communicate its own ongoing effect in a socially transformative feedback loop. There is an intimate relationship between the dissolution of the limits of building, access to information, and political engagement.

As a refugee whose own personal life was determined by the need to escape the violence of a specific hateful prejudice magnified by the Nazis, and the murder of his mother, sister and nephew, along with millions of others, Wachsmann visualizes a society of the near future without any reference to race, gender, class, sexuality, religion, or nation. It is as if the thought that electricity doesn't know boundaries had become the basis for an idealistic image of a future society beyond the violence of limits, rejecting any permanent line but demanding permanent vigilance against singular authority figures, elites and mobs in a kind of techno-optimism that would surely shudder at the way information technologies and the supposed sharing economy are so efficiently nurturing the very same violence today.

Towards the end of the *Manifest*, Wachsmann offered a sketch of this world to come in the Air Force Hangar project, a building of "virtually unlimited dimension" done with students and colleagues in Chicago between 1951 and 1954. The project had a huge influence on the megastructure movement after its simultaneous extensive publication in the major international magazines in September 1954.[7] This architecture for a new post-war collectivity that was paradoxically designed to house war machines, but presented to be applicable to structures of any kind, was literally a "spider-web" network of countless interconnected metal tubes with a set of mobile thin screens acting in place of all the traditional elements of roofs, walls, floors, doors and windows. The structure seemed to defy gravity by cantilevering out and up dramatically on both sides. It floats like a cloud on a set of minimal see-through supports set so deeply in from its edges that the polemical horizontals of Frank Lloyd Wright and Mies van der Rohe seem insufficiently horizontal.

Magazine editors couldn't resist publishing the lacy images across the fold of two pages to capture the effect of a low-flying 805-foot long steel cloud that could be extended to any desired length. The network space-frame structure is by definition a three-dimensional web, and Wachsmann treated all structural systems as omnidirectional radiation patterns, but the project culminated in a massive horizontal statement. It is as if the anti-hierarchical politi-cal project is necessarily horizontal—literally reaching out to any neighbor, hypothetically to all neighbors, and widening the sense of community by putting everyone on the same level. The space-frame is first and foremost an attack on the vertical, dissolving all columns and walls to remove any permanent lateral division.

Many of the published photographs of the polemically intricate 17-foot long model of half the building show a few human figures on the ground. They are symbolically dwarfed beneath the vast horizon-tal net that is both a specific technological artifact, tuned to the task of sheltering aircraft, and an aesthetic image of the new network logic of the electrical and increasingly wireless world.

The Wachsmann *Manifest* presents the otherworldly Air Force Hangar as a continuation of the experimentation into industrialized building launched by Paxton's *Crystal Palace* in 1851—a building that was likewise conceived as a system of factory-made standard-ized metal elements that could be assembled on site in any combina-tion for any desired function without the traditional preoccupation with form. Paxton's 1848-foot long structure had already dissolved any traditional sense of walls and roof into a set of "points in space" and was the first vast horizontal spider-web of joints that dwarfed those who entered it. Through the very rigor of its technical and logical commitment to industrialization, it was, Wachsmann insists, an artwork, a visual representation of the still unseen reality of our networked world.

The attempt to develop a radical horizontality was already under way with the Mobilar Structure that Wachsmann developed in New York between 1944 and 1945 (having first sketched the con-cept in Grenoble after being released from the internment camp in 1939). It was simply a huge hovering horizontal plane, made of hun-dreds of interconnected 8-foot long steel tubes, with folding sets of self-supporting walls on motorized wheels that could take any con-figuration. Anything vertical was temporary. Even the four legs set deep within the limits of the horizontal web have their own web-like quality, as if they are just temporary extensions of the horizontal web that become ever thinner before lightly touching the ground plane and being stiffened by some barely visible cables. The struc-ture was again configured as a hangar for many aircraft (able to be expanded to any length to accommodate "dozens or hundreds of large planes"), and would become the basis of the first conversations with the Air Force in the Fall of 1950 and the resulting military research contract in the Spring of 1951 to develop an exponentially larger structure. But it was likewise offered for use in any kind of building, as the patent application in mid-1945 argued.[8]

An intricately detailed 8-foot long model was exhibited at the Museum of Modern Art in New York in early 1946,[9] and simultaneously featured on the cover of *Progressive Architecture* with photographs by Anna Wachsmann already showing a tiny dwarfed human figure.[10] Mies van der Rohe's successive projects for floating horizontals with barely visible supports (Museum for a Small City of 1942, Convention Center for Chicago of 1953–54, Bacardi Office Building for Havana of 1957, and National Gallery for Berlin of 1968) became so canonic that it is hard to realize how radical Wachsmann's project was at the time—without even a line of glass to define its outer limit. The two colleagues at IIT were good friends, spending "countless nights" eating and drinking together. Students recall that Wachsmann's required classes were even taught each week as gin-enhanced seminars in Mies' apartment and the two did extended road trips together. In 1952, Wachsmann compiled a 16-page survey on the recent work of Mies for *Arts & Architecture* and they worked together with students on a large low-flying space frame structure using the Air Force Hangar structural system that would evolve into the Convention Center that Mies did with three of the graduate students.

Yet the horizontals of Mies never had the same political ambition, being visually open but hermetically isolated glassed-in spaces in which the horizontal plane was heavier and represented a new monumentality, a new permanence rather than a new impermanence. Floating thin surfaces under the horizontal were an integral part of Mies concept, as exemplified by his Concert Hall collage in 1942 (done again with IIT students and not by chance superimposed on a photograph of the interior of the huge aircraft assembly building designed by Albert Kahn in 1937), but these flying surfaces typically take a permanently fixed position. Wachsmann literally put the surfaces on motorized wheels and enabled them to change configuration at will, defining new inner spaces or outer limits, or leaving the site altogether. Even the basic network structure is designed to be undone and reassembled in a different place or in a different form.

Wachsmann orchestrated a succession of projects whose point was to produce a new kind of extreme horizontal with optional mobile vertical elements below, at the edge, or outside (as exemplified by the student seminar workshops in Chicago in 1954, Tokyo in 1955, Salzburg in 1956, 1957, 1958, and Lausanne in 1959) and was theorized as such. The October 1955 lectures in Tokyo, for example, described the relentlessly horizontal project in which "man may try to subdue what today is so often emphasized in the vertical."[11] They predicted that columns "may so completely disappear that we finally may not notice them even if they are there," when there will be "only surfaces: opaque and translucent, none of them related to the structure." Even these surfaces will tend to "diminish to zero," becoming ever thinner, lighter, flatter, smoother planes. Matter itself would be "dissolved" into the smallest parts distributed around "points in space." Wachsmann's succession of models and drawings of lacy horizontal nets floating on the most minimal vertical elements tried to visualize this inevitable and desirable dissolution of all sense of mass into barely tangible radiant patterns.

Wachsmann had already associated the idea of porous lightweight reconfigurable modular structures supporting countless combinations of mobile modular surfaces with the question of energy and electricity in "Building for Modern Man," a March 1947 symposium of the world's most prominent modern architects at Princeton University.[12] The April 1948 lecture given both at UCLA and at the Institute of Design in Chicago (the first encounter with Mies), again pointed to the transformation of the entire political life of communities and of the state by electricity—adding radio and television sets to refrigerators and aircraft as models of industrialized construction that highlight how backward buildings were.[13] Over the next three decades, the call for a horizontal network of points and suspended surfaces energized by electricity became an argument about transistors, computers, wireless and television. Wachsmann's most influential book on structure, *Wendepunkt im Bauen* (The Turning Point of Building) of 1959, for example, not only called for "free space" without visible supports in which environment-defining surfaces are temporarily "hung" but talks about the fact that "any piece of technical equipment that transmits signals, words, tones or images," including television sets, enables the concept of the "universal room" capable of performing any function. Such a room could be shielded from its immediate surroundings, yet the same communication equipment would bring it "into closest touch with the outside world at any time, without being thrown open in the physical sense."[14] Electronic signals completely transform the way spaces function and how they interact. Structure is no longer the same

It was not about new media entering architecture but more about architecture having to lighten itself up to enter the already existing world of signals and electronics. Wachsmann kept insisting that the material world had already been revolutionized, and a conceptual revolution had to follow. The new energy-information flows triggered by electricity in the form of radio, telephone, television, airplanes, and engines had completely transformed the surface of the earth.[15] The tone was again not futuristic utopia but contemporary urgency. Only by catching up to the dramatic changes that have already happened could design position itself for whatever came next.

In a 1965 talk at the Aspen International Design Conference, Wachsmann had once again argued that the radical transformation triggered by electricity was just the beginning since "our buildings and our world" will look completely different in a wireless age in which energy is transmitted in electrical waves. The talk was basically an announcement that the new Building Research Division at UCLA was being set up to address this wireless challenge.[16] It was not by chance that Wachsmann's most emblematic project to realize an extreme horizontal for an electronic age, the ultimately unbuilt Civic Center for California City, got underway at the Institute just a few months later.

The project, developed by the team at USC from late 1965 to 1972 is more Mies than Mies. It is simply a thin horizontal plane hovering above the ground without any visible support. A lightweight, five-inch deep, 80×180 feet fiberglass-foam-fiberglass sandwich is suspended on a set of eighty parallel 1.25-inch thick steel cables in pairs spaced two feet apart horizontally and 1.5 feet vertically. The cables are stretched in massive tension between angled steel buttresses 192 feet apart and anchored 70 feet deep in the ground. The resulting structure is a hybrid of bridge and tent. Wachsmann insisted that the cables reaching out 16 feet beyond each end of the horizontal plane would not be visible, producing the effect of a flying carpet under which the city could continually reorganize its spaces in "essentially unlimited variations" as it evolved. Even the thin edge of the carpet would be barely visible until visitors went under it and they could anyway pass right through as if walking in a garden. The lack of any fixed vertical element was associated with political transparency and interactivity. The main city council chamber on the lowest level was always exposed from above, looking more like a sunken landscape element than a room, and easily able to be entered or observed from citizen's homes or wherever their TV was through a 111-foot-tall antenna that was a crucial part of the building's design. All council activity would be broadcast live on a low power local channel and the building itself was a kind of gallery in which activities, exhibitions, and archives were on continuous display. The structure was first and foremost an information machine.

It was as if the seemingly unlimited spaces of the Mohave desert, the dream of a new kind of city and citizenry and the promise of industrialization had coalesced in a single project. The horizontal expanse of the empty desert acted as the model of free space and the new city acted as the model of a self-aware community adjusting itself cybernetically through feedback. Wachsmann had first visited the site of the city in 1960, flying over it with its developer Nathan Mendelsohn (who had invited him to California ten years earlier to help convert the barracks of a military camp to private housing). Mendelsohn had been to Wachsmann's lecture that April at UCLA and Wachsmann was immediately very eager to be involved in the project, writing that he "became almost possessed by the idea that here lies a task which hardly could be overestimated."[17] Wachsmann proposed a massive involvement with every level of rethinking what a city can be in its organization, assembly and evolution— wanting to do regional studies and distribution plans for traffic, greenbelts, schools and hospitals along with developing materials, construction methods, environmental control and housing typologies, but above all to think of "the image of a new city, a city of our time" in the spirit of his lecture.[18] Mendelsohn offered "one entire nucleus of a community" to work on and Wachsmann was on a monthly retainer to think about it throughout 1961 but seemingly unable to come up with anything while concentrating on the English edition of *Wendepunkt im Bauen*.[19] Finally, after years of interruptions, the project for California City became just a single building— even it was to be the collective, administrative and representational heart of the city.

The work on the Civic Center didn't start until the end of 1965 but it moved quickly and the concept of welding a seemingly unsupported roof and a television antenna was already established when Mendelsohn and the city council visited Wachsmann's office at USC in February 1966 and went to dinner to discuss it further. The mayor formally commissioned the design a few days later, expressing the council's unanimous support for the ideas.[20] The first public announcement was promptly made in the March issue of *California City Sun*, stressing the double innovation of a floating horizontal plane and vertical television antenna. The high-tension cables supposedly "would not be seen by the naked eye, giving the effect of a gigantic floating roof" suspended over a sunken garden, and "shooting up into the sky over the roof would be a television tower for closed circuit purposes ... marking the first time this coverage would be available to any citizenry in the world ... we would participate via our TV screens. ... California City and its City Council coverage would become known from one end of the globe to the other."[21] A barely visible structure was to have the most visibility. In the same month, Wachsmann told the mayor about talking to engineers working on the technical problems of television and hoped to have a model and drawings by the end of April.

A final single photograph of the model complete with antenna posed against the back-drop of a photograph of the surrounding landscape became the standard image of the project. It was used, for example, in *California City a Success Story*, a 95-page booklet trying to attract people to join the city, describing the project as the "ultimate space" dreamed of as the "grail" of contemporary architecture:

"The purpose was to create a complete open space, neither disturbed nor penetrated by any kind of column or support either on the inside or at the perimeter of the building, to create, as it were an 'ultimate' space. Under the floating, tent-like cover spaces can be created as needed, increasing as the city grows."[22]

The same photograph and text was used when the project was published in detail in a survey of Wachsmann's work in the May 1967 issue of *Arts & Architecture*, with a photograph of the Civic Center's pattern of high-tension cables that captured Wachsmann's fascination with horizontal nets symptomatically forming the wrap-around cover of the magazine.[23] Other photographs in the issue showed the space with and without the internal elements to empha-size the extreme openness of the concept, magnified by the reflecting pool under the roof, the fact that the temporary internal divisions did not touch the roof and that the display panels for showing information to the public did not touch the floor. The television antenna and its supporting wires appear in the model photographs and many of the unpublished photographs simply look through the abstract, concrete-lined dip in the landscape along with the equally abstract white horizontal plane ghosting above it and the wires and mast of the antenna that even had highly detailed broadcast equip-ment modeled on its peak (which were ultimately cropped out of the standard image to hide the top of the background image of the surrounding landscape).

The antenna and its supporting cables precisely drawn into the main section drawing was the only constant in an otherwise unde-fined open system. Indeed, the openness of the horizontal was dependent on the antenna. After all, as later recalled, it had not been the buildings that interested Wachsmann and Mies on their extended twenty-two day road trip to California while developing floating space frames at the Institute in Chicago, but "those thou-sands of TV antennas on roof tops."[24]

Wachsmann treated the apparent lack of limits offered by tele-vision as a response to the original commission for "the most pro-gressive and advanced structure of our time ... a building pointing towards the twenty-first century" for a new city in "almost limitless perspective in scale"—as he wrote to the Mayor on the eve of the public vote in November 1967 whether to go ahead with the pro-ject—describing the structure as a symbol of all that is to come and its center of gravity:

"In the wide open environment I see a floating, protecting surface in space under which people can congregate ... an unlimited space ... a space as open as the enormous landscape, as open as the whole plan for the future city, as open as the future scope of this community."[25]

Television was a crucial architectural element in expanding this symbolic and practical openness. The letter went on to insist that "Television, including the transmission tower, which also shall carry telecamera and receiving antennas and amplifying equipment, is an integral part of the design concept of this building." A democratic belief in equal rights for all requires "a system of government which in its feedback function should not only take place inside a building of predetermined form but should embrace and radiate into each home of the whole city." This "lifeline of communication" enables the participation of all citizens in "the future development of their own environment." Political action is, for Wachsmann, by definition, environmental action. In reverse, shaping the environment is, by definition, political. This calls for continuous "information exhibits" in the building. Telephone recordings and tapes were to be treated as "resources of instant information" for exchange and decision-making between city council and citizens. The anti-building itself is primarily an information system.

Wachsmann could not attend the public meeting before the vote (the building being itself subjected to the democratic feedback it intended to facilitate) but in the very spirit of the project sent a taped media message saying it was a building for the 21st century that uses cables to produce "an effect of total space."[26] Newspapers again highlighted the integrated television tower,[27] and the success of the vote was announced a few days later, but the whole building would be redesigned more than four times, with countless engineering tests of mockups. A definitive set of drawings was not completed until December of 1970 and the project was once again put to a public vote, this time to approve the expenditure. Wachsmann ran yet another set of public meetings with the model, leading to a positive straw vote in April 1971 and then the formal final vote to go ahead in May.[28]

The final drawing set of December 1971 (detailing all architectural, structural, mechanical, and built-in furniture) went out to bid without the antenna included but with "FUTURE TV ANTENNA" marked on the electricity site plan.[29] The announcement in the December 1972 issue of *Architectural Record* that construction was about to go ahead and scheduled for completion in January 1974 used the usual model photo but with the antenna retouched out of the image.[30]

The anti-building posed at the end of architecture and the beginning of televisual politics finally didn't go ahead. But Wachsmann had become more committed to the architecture of television than ever. In fact, television had taken over.

In 1973 Wachsmann was again talking about an imminent wireless future (the transmission of electricity by waves, no longer having to pull wires through walls, transistorization, and computers ultimately replacing design teams) while yet again rejecting any distinction between physical structures and political-economic structures "tightly connected with social problems."[31] The traditional building industry and its designs "strapped into the straightjacket of architecture" have to be resisted by simultaneously engaging government and the whole society: "This can be done through the television screen for instance, a medium of communication not to be underestimated."[32] In the same year, Wachsmann was still hoping to realize his 1971 project for a new kind of interdisciplinary center, "an entirely new organism" devoted to every dimension of decision making and production in an age of industrialization—devoted, that is, like all his buildings, to "the multiplication of increments of bits of units shaped through electrical energy" as the catalog of a 1971 retrospective of his 30 years of work in the US put it when introducing the concept.[33] Wachsmann's unpublished autobiography, written in his final year, ends by talking about the fact that in this concept for what would ultimately replace the contemporary university—undoing the lines between disciplines and between the center and the public—his model for "the need for simultaneous information to and, vice versa, feedback from the general public by means of the best available communication media" was television: "It was television which had fascinated me from the beginning, not so much as a source of entertainment but more as a possibility for enlightenment."[34] Wachsmann ultimately realized that the new center would never happen but ended up writing a proposal for a TV series of 13 programs, thinking it would actually play the same role, then agreed to make a book that would be the basis of the TV series to be broadcast then available as a set of TV cassettes.

The epilogue of the autobiography manuscript symptomatically returned to the central Wachsmann argument since the late forties that "the introduction of electrical energy caused unimaginable consequences" leading to transistors, computers, nuclear and solar energy that will have their own unforeseen effects and call for political, social, economic, scientific, technological and artistic ideas to be "totally re-structured" in the 21st century. This ending echoed the early moment in the manuscript describing the summer house for Albert and Elsa Einstein in 1929 (with Wachsmann designing all its elements to be prefabricated in a factory then assembled on site). Wachsmann recalls having already understood the transformative impact electrical energy had on material techniques and therefore on society. Unlike Einstein, the 28-year-old designer was sure that this made the traditional concept of "architecture" irrelevant but didn't know yet what would replace it.

In the end, Wachsmann was never sure. Ever more inspired by television, the successive floating nets just concentrated on dissolving architecture as we know it, breaking it down into ever smaller parts and finally into radiant patterns of wireless signals. In a remarkable lifetime anti-architectural project that was too radical to be recognized as such, buildings became transmissions.

1   This essay is extracted from the forthcoming book: Mark Wigley, *Konrad Wachsmann's Television: Post-Architectural Transmissions*, Berlin, Sternberg Press, 2020.

2   Konrad Wachsmann, "Manifest for the Evolution of Assembling the Artificial Human Environment between Time and Space," unpublished manuscript dated 1974, final typewritten draft. AdK, Konrad-Wachsmann-Archiv, Wachsmann 2323, p. 1.

3   Mark Wigley, "Network Fever," in: *Grey Room* 04 (2001), pp. 82–122.

4   Konrad Wachsmann, "Manifest for the Evolution of Assembling the Artificial Human Environment between Time and Space," p. 68.

5   Mark Wigley, *Buckminster Fuller Inc.: Architecture in the Age of Radio*, Lars Muller, Zurich, 2016.

6   "Whereas design and planning are of secondary importance within the context of such work, aesthetics, philosophy and ethics play a vital and autonomous part." Konrad Wachsmann, introduction to "Studium im Team," in: *Bauen + Wohnen* 10, 1960, p. 351.

7   The Illinois Institute of Technology press release of the Air Force Hangar design was in September of 1954 and, in a choreographed publicity blitz, the project was featured in the same month with extensive model photographs in the September issues of *L'Architecture d'Aujourd'hui, Baukunst und Werkform*, and *Architectural Forum*, along with the October issue of *Werk*.

8   us Patent 2,491,882 submitted June 22, 1945, patented December 20, 1949.

9   "Museum of Modern Art Shows Revolutionary New Type of Steel Construction," MoMA Press release for exhibition of February 5 to March 6, 1946.

10   "Mobilar Structure," in: *Progressive Architecture*, March 1946, pp. 87–99.

11   Konrad Wachsmann, "Building in Our Time: Toward Industrialization of Structure, The Training-Research Process and Contemporary Concepts," manuscript dated 1955. AdK, Konrad-Wachsmann-Archiv, Wachsmann 460, p. 43.

12   Speaking after Walter Gropius, Wachsmann's presentation defined the limitations and possibilities for design in terms of energy, with electricity controlled by machines as the new form of energy that is redefining design, feeding mass production and standardization and producing new kinds of joints sustaining ever more lightweight structures in which the vertical surfaces play only a visual and acoustic role and "uncounted combinations of surface elements will create our surrounding world." Konrad Wachsmann, "Machine Energy: The Technique of Our Time," in: Thomas H. Creighton (ed.), *Building for Modern Man: A Symposium*, Princeton University Press, Princeton, 1949, pp. 46–48.

13   Konrad Wachsmann, "The Means for Design," text of talk in the Society and Design Seminar at Illinois Institute of Technology, Spring 1948, in: Serge Chermayeff Papers, Avery Drawings and Archives, Avery Library, Columbia University.

14   Konrad Wachsmann, *Wendepunkt im Bauen*, 1959, translated by Thomas E. Burton as *The Turning Point of Building: Structure and Design*, Reinhold, New York, 1961, p. 110.

15   "Through its advancing dynamic force and technology, electricity more than anything else, is changing the direction of world progress. Mass communication and information, such as the radio, telephone, and television, airplanes, engines and all things run by electricity, have completely changed the appearance of the surface of the earth. New communication methods and new education have created a new base." In: Konrad Wachsmann, "A High Level in Function is Indeed Beauty: Hiroshima Should be Made a Functional City," October 29, 1955. Wachsmann 2271. p.1.

16   Konrad Wachsmann, "To Build is Everything or Nothing is Built," manuscript of talk at 15th Aspen International Design Conference. AdK, Konrad-Wachsmann-Archiv, Wachsmann 1777.

17   Konrad Wachsmann, letter to Nathan Mendelsohn dated April 25, 1960. AdK, Konrad-Wachsmann-Archiv, Wachsmann 0513.

18   Konrad Wachsmann, letter to Nathan Mendelsohn dated June 27, 1960. AdK, Konrad-Wachsmann-Archiv, Wachsmann 0613.

19   Nathan Mendelsohn, letter to Konrad Wachsmann, undated but circa October, 1960. AdK, Konrad-Wachsmann-Archiv, Wachsmann 0613.

20   Letter from Mayor Jim Riley to Konrad Wachsmann dated February 28, 1966. AdK, Konrad-Wachsmann-Archiv, Wachsmann 1871.

21   "Eighth Wonder Here! Civic Center to Have 'Floating Roof,'" in: *California City Sun*, March 1966. AdK, Konrad-Wachsmann-Archiv, Wachsmann 1890.

22   *California City a Success Story*, undated publicity brochure. AdK, Konrad-Wachsmann-Archiv, Wachsmann 1890.

23   Konrad Wachsmann, "A New American City Hall," in: *Arts & Architecture*, May 1967, pp. 23–26.

24   Konrad Wachsmann, "Timebridge, Konrad Wachsmann: An Autobiography," unpublished manuscript, AdK, Konrad-Wachsmann-Archiv, Wachsmann 2065, p. 245.

25   Konrad Wachsmann, letter to Mayor Jim Riley, dated November 1, 1967. AdK, Konrad-Wachsmann-Archiv, Wachsmann 1871.

26   "Even though I am unable to be with you in person, modern science and technology has made it possible for me to talk to you anyway …" Konrad Wachsmann, transcript of taped statement for public meeting of November, 1967. AdK, Konrad-Wachsmann-Archiv, Wachsmann 1871.

27   "Noted Architect Named to Design Civic Center," in: *The Bakersfield Californian*, November 23, 1967. AdK, Konrad-Wachsmann-Archiv, Wachsmann 1887.

28   Before the vote, Wachsmann rehearsed his reasons for making a building that is really a "wide open space … undisturbed by any load-bearing wall or column … which in turn would be located in a wide open space" and gave a chronology of all the different tests and expert knowledge that had been necessary to realize it. Konrad Wachsmann, "Statement to City Council of California City," dated March 15, 1971. AdK, Konrad-Wachsmann-Archiv, Wachsmann 1872.

29   "Civic Center California City," final drawing set revised December 1971. Wachsmann 362.

30   "California City Civic Center,"
     Architectural Record, December
     1972, p. 41.
31   "Structures are not only physical
     phenomena but also ordering
     systems and resulting geometries.
     They are political and finance
     political systems which are tightly
     connected with social problems
     and capital investment, amortization,
     wages, etc." Konrad Wachsmann,
     "The Future between Space and
     Time," manuscript in German
     and English of a lecture given at
     the seminar on Industrialization of
     Building at the Technical University
     of Hannover on October 12, 1973
     AdK, Konrad-Wachsmann-Archiv,
     Wachsmann 2065, p. 8.
32   Ibid., p. 9.
33   Konrad Wachsmann, *Toward Indus-
     trialization of Building*, catalog
     text from exhibition at the Depart-
     ment of Architecture of the
     University of Southern California
     and the Graham Foundation for
     Advanced Studies in the Fine Arts,
     Los Angeles, usc, 1971, p. 1.
34   Konrad Wachsmann, "Timebridge,
     Konrad Wachsmann: An Autobio-
     graphy," unpublished manuscript,
     AdK, Konrad-Wachsmann-Archiv,
     Wachsmann 2065, p. 468.

For Konrad Wachsmann the essence of serial production was to be found in the process. It comes as no surprise that his perspectival drawings (from ca. 1953) of the so-called grapevine construction can be described as a notation, that is, a documentation of a form-creating process.[1] This project of Wachsmann's testifies to his search for a single universal connecting element that could be produced on an industrial basis.[2] Conceived as a basic building block of a dynamic structure, its modular character was to enable the construction of zero-g buildings. What makes this so fascinating today is that nature, in this case the grapevine, becomes a model. Wachsmann spoke of "standard three-arm dowser-like turned elements."[3] In connection with his arguably best-known project—the design of an airplane hangar out of steel constructions (1951)—reference is made to a "spider web-like structure" relating to a dynamic spatial syntax, as a hand-written note reveals.[4]

In the drawings Wachsmann used zoomed-in details of an overlapping modular structure. The part—indeed, each part—stands for the whole.

This principle will be described in the following as "cinematographic notation." We find it not only in the construction drawings but, first and foremost, in the sequence of architectural photographs—in many of his photographs used for publications and exhibitions as well as in those he took himself. On meeting Wachsmann Pablo Picasso is said to have exclaimed: "You talk as if you were a photographer yourself!"[5] Walter Gropius who observed Wachsmann photographing near Split in the 1930s (they didn't know each other yet at the time) was able to see the architect in the photographer "because of the way you photograph."[6] For the architect who displayed a bit of coquetry as an amateur photographer, photography and film served as an ideal "medium of documentation."[7] Wachsmann published several photography books—something that has hardly been noted in the literature to date.[8] It is all the more remarkable that this sequential principle found an echo in the 2010 retrospective of his work in Munich—as an exhibition concept.[9] In order to reveal the essence of his thought—i.e., the process dimension—the organizers decided to add screens with film montages to each of the architectural models in the exhibition. The idea was that it was only possible to see how he built and assembled, when up to thirty photographs were arranged one after the other, as was stated in a publicity film for this exhibition. Drawings and photographs from his working process were used in equal number for this cinematographic montage.[10] This appears extremely significant given the current discussions and reflections on the pictorial quality of architecture.[11]

In the mid-1930s three photography books by Wachsmann appeared—on Prague, Salzburg and Berlin, respectively.[12] In his

Konrad Wachsmann's Cinematographic Notation

Angela Lammert; Fig.: 43–48

later writings, exhibitions and publications he would again and
again return to his formative experiences from this period—to the
ribbed vaults of the Hradčany in Prague or the Gothic dual-spiral
staircase of the castle in Graz[13], showing how they could be compared to the dynamic connecting structures of a future architecture. In 1961, another photography book was published. Its title—
Aspects[→47, 48]—refers to these very experiences. This book begins
with a zoomed-in detail of a plastered staircase. The building itself
is for the most part cut off and only captured on the ground level.
The texture of the lines of the railing that are set diagonally in the
picture continues in the vertical struts of the body of the building,
resulting in an abstract play of zero-gravity linear systems of order.
On the following double page, one can only sense the ground on
which the buildings stand, which is structured by means of vertical
shadows; as isolated bodies they cannot be recognized in the shapes
depicted in the detail all the way to the edge of the picture. This
serial sequence of photographs culminates in two roof or tower constructions. It is, in other words, a visual statement that can only be
perceived successively in motion. Wachsmann wrote the following
about this photographic series: "Transformations or the overcoming
of the notion of finiteness on the wall seem to be a perennial challenge to dissect, structure, dissolve."[14] Elsewhere, the diagonal low-
angle shot of the church on the Capitoline Hill in Rom with a view
of a round window structured by means of tracery is juxtaposed
with a photograph in which the same tracery fills the front of the
picture. The filmic succession of various shots of a building, along
with the amassed photographic details, refers to the complexity of
the whole. By the same token, the detail is to be found in the
whole—a principle that recurs in his later search for a universal
element.

Wachsmann insists here on a subjective documentation—a
notation beyond that of indexicality. The camera becomes an
abstract, clarifying means of recording and conveying. A Gothic
cathedral, a structure, a building, a square or an entire landscape of
the past is what one longs to see only from angles that are amenable
to the present and not as what they really mean. Wachsmann was
interested in using photography to find a means to document certain structures or details in this sense and to visualize the ideas that
shaped things and to put them down. In his words: "If photography
is used, the result here, too, will not be objective documentation
but rather subjective transformation into an intended visual idiom.
Even the inanimate recording mechanism of a camera is unable to
render an object the way it is but only as the person using it is able
to see or wants to see (...) Whether this means of recording will
continue to meet even greater demands in the future is uncertain,
since film offers better possibilities. Film allows the object to be

circumambulated in its spatial relation or to be shown in its own movement."[15] Here he even went so far as to imagine the perspective of sound being included. To describe the machine as a tool of the new age in terms of a new approach to the notion of the original, he also resorted to the procedure of the photographic negative and positive.[16] In a manuscript, unpublished to date, from his estate, there is evidence that Wachsmann intended to produce an approx. 10-minute film.[17] We were unable to find this film in our investigation but the plan he had to make one certainly confirms the argument presented here.[18]

The cinematographic ideas of his photographic books can also be identified as a visual strategy in his 1959 publication, his best-known one, titled the *Turning Point in Building*. His photographs there serve as "moments, details, torsos, reflections of impulsive movements or thoughts on elucidating dynamic processes." Wachsmann was aware of this interplay in the sequence of the photographs.

The estate, located at the Akademie der Künste (Academy of Arts), also contains several unpublished photographs. I was already in their thrall when I was preparing the exhibition "Notation. Form und Kalkül in den Künsten"[19] (2007). Looking at the most recent research on the pictorial dimension of architecture, together with Wachsmann's photography books, it strikes me as essential to view them from a new perspective. I will sketch three in the following.

Zoom

In the photographs of modular constructions, details, close-ups and blurredness negatively impact the functional legibility. Their filmic effect of zooming-in and enlarging a fragment of the modular steel construction is so radical that it is no coincidence that they are among the unpublished photographs. For this very reason they are a nice discovery. In the sequential series of a perceptual process of architecture they are the opposite of the iconic single shot that is so widespread in architectural photography.

Various shots of the same model can also be found in his publication titled *Wendepunkt im Bauen* (Turning Point in Building). The successive perception resulting from the viewer's movement is less evident. Detail, frame and zoom recur, though, at various spots. On a double page of the photograph of an architectural model taken from up front, there is a juxtaposition of two detailed shots of the modular system: on the one hand, a close-up to visualize the force progression on the point of a support and on the other hand, a roof construction zoomed in on to show the main and lateral struts.[20] Both pictures were taken by his wife Anna Wachsmann and can be seen as an intimate reflection of their shared intellectual world. The effect of this sequence is augmented by placing one single photograph over a double page. The interplay and layering of shadows, light and structure appears to develop its own dynamic in the zoom shot of the detail. It is striking that this piece was titled "Glimpse into the landscape of a spatial structure." It was made by Harry Callahan, who worked together with Wachsmann in Chicago, and who, like Anna Wachsmann, was familiar with his basic principles.[21] The sequencing of photographs, which culminates in the enlarged shot of the detail of a spatial structure, dropping off on the edge, corresponds to a filmic zoom.

Dynamic Structure

Wachsmann implemented his concept of dynamic structure, not just by sequencing photographs, but also by arranging several similar modules of a picture format for his publications.

Here he often let professional object photographers take shots of the connecting elements as a module of dynamic structures. The photographs by Aaron Siskind (Institute of Design of Chicago) are particularly striking. The stacked elements of an articulated chain of a nodal point[22] recall the aesthetics of enlarged plant fragments made by Karl Blossfeldt in the 1920s. The intrinsic aesthetics of these photographs assumes, functionally speaking, dysfunctional traits, as the shot depicting five standard precision elements in the *Turning Point of Building* shows. The fragmentary detail taken from the structure of the construction systems only renders three of them in rhythmic repetition.[23] Today the concept of dynamic structures has resulted in the practice of digital animation in the design process and reconstruction. "Architecture becoming pictorial" (in the grapevine structure), recently produced by Christina Sumi, seems to lend itself particularly well to merging the representation of the emblematic dimension of architecture with the animation of bodily perception.[24] A spatiality that evolves in the situation is alluded to and simulated. Such an approach not only has potential to become a research tool, it can also, at times, erase the established distinction between building design and building execution.[25]

Team

Konrad Wachsmann's postulate that the necessary industrial manufacturing can only take place in team work is also reflected in hitherto unpublished photographs from his estate at the Academy of Arts in Berlin. Unlike his concept in which small working groups work in parallel on various subtasks, in these photographs the joint work of a team of architects can be seen, carrying a triangular construction made of rods. Not the process of building but the potential of a quick montage is staged. The photograph of the triangular construction without the actors seems almost utopian—with a building kit that is easy to work with. What is surprising is that even here a bird's eye view and a frontal view are employed. Architectural photography is not just the staging of something built or of the model but rather the notation of process and dynamic structure.

For the photographs he used in *Turning Point in Building* an entire institute, e.g., the Institute of Design, Chicago, is sometimes named as the photographer. Only the above-cited Harry Callahan, who was professor in Chicago, and Aaron Siskind are named specifically. This is also true of his wife Anna Wachsmann. It is thus not surprising that the bundle of photographs from his estate at the Academy of Arts was also largely inventoried as anonymous. It is in keeping with his idea of teamwork which, to put it ironically, he only did without if it was in his interest and in connection with his photography books. And this he would do with the flourish of an amateur photographer. It would however be worthwhile to take a closer look at the origin of individual photographs and their function in relation to his architectural concept. One thing, however, is perceptible in an initial characterization of this methodological approach: Notation in the architectural thinking of Konrad Wachsmann can mean photographic or cinematographic documentation of the form-finding process.

This fits in with the present discussion of the pictorial dimension of architecture, which revolves around three key notions. Semiotic picture concept, architecture as an immersive art aimed at the corporeal and architecture becoming a picture. It is not only about the impact of imagery or a phenomenological approach. Andreas Beyer, Matteo Burioni and Johannes Grave described the emblematic sign-like function of architecture as a conception of pictoriality which is bound to being conveyed by media via photography and film and a semiotic picture concept and is thus to be criticized.[26] Georges Didi-Huberman's polemics against the iconographic, art historical method, which he develops in his text "Was wir sehen, blickt uns an" (What we see, looks at us)[27], is applied by the authors to architecture in relation to a postmodern building practice. A further variant of this concept, which cannot to be elaborated on here and is less explicit, is to be found in the analysis of limited, expansive building phenomena such as the emergence of framed surfaces. A semiotic concept of architecture applied to a two-dimensional surface—often linked to an iconic photography of architecture—fails to take into account the spatial and immersive qualities of architecture as spatial art or as production of atmospheres. It also thus neglects their status created by the media. The opposition of two- and three-dimensionality is thus only the other side of the coin.

Against this backdrop, the focus on Konrad Wachsmann's oeuvre seems to hold potential that has yet to be appreciated in the discourse on the pictorial dimension of architecture. One should not just take a closer look at perceptual processes of images and thus of architecture as an image but also critically examine the intrinsic value of visual forms of thinking, the images produced or used by architects and thus the blurring of the lines between design and work. Walter Benjamin spoke of "borderline" architectural drawing.[28] "But it is the borderline case that in combing through the facts its key positions must be asserted as uncompromising as possible."[29]

1   Angela Lammert, *Bildung und Bildlichkeit von Notation. Von der frühen Wissenschaftsfotografie zu den Künsten des 20. Jahrhunderts*, Munich 2016.

2   Marianne Burkhalter, Christian Sumi (eds.), *Konrad Wachsmann and the Grapevine Structure*, Chicago 2018.

3   *Konrad Wachsmann auf dem Weg zur Industrialisierung des Bauens*, catalog for an exhibition in "Octagon" of the American Institute of Architects Foundation Washington D.C. March 1972 (German edition June 1972).

4   Konrad Wachsmann, *Hangar-Flugzeughallenkonstruktion*, in: AdK, Konrad-Wachsmann-Archiv, Wachsmann 410, p. 5.

5   Michael Grüning, *Der Wachsmann-Report. Auskünfte eines Architekten*, Berlin 1985, p. 322. The director of the Villa Massimo in Rome, Herbert Gericke, provided Wachsmann with his Leica 35 mm camera so that he could document his "unconventional view" of architecture. Wachsmann experimented in his lab with photograms, which he mounted in architectural photographs as a kind of compositional element, in: ibid., pp. 264–267. He used a long tele-objective and a special viewfinders. In: Konrad Wachsmann, "Timebridge, Konrad Wachsmann: An Autobiography," 1981, unpublished autobiography, AdK, Konrad-Wachsmann-Archiv, Wachsmann 2128, p. 86.

6   Ibid., p. 87.

7   Konrad Wachsmann, *Aspekte*, Krauskopfverlag 1961.

8   An exception is the second chapter of the publication by Otto Maier, *Die räumliche Syntax. Konrad Wachsmanns Beitrag zum Bauen in unserer Zeit*, Karlsruhe 1989. However, the focus here is on Wachsmann's notion of time and not his photographs.

9   Winfried Nerdinger in collaboration with Rainer Barthel, Richard Junge, Roland Krippner and Frank Petzold (eds.): *Wendepunkte im Bauen: Von der seriellen zur digitalen Architektur*, Munich 2010.

10   Wilfried Nerdinger 2010 in: https://www.youtube.com/watch?v=3rxEKZFL8zQ—accessed on May 20, 2018.

11   Andreas Beyer, Matteo Burioni, Johannes Grave, "Einleitung. Zum Erscheinen von Architektur als Bild," in: (ibid. ed.), *Das Auge der Architektur*, Munich 2011, p. 12. Angela Lammert, "Bildlichkeit von Architektur als Prozess," in: Ulrike Kuch (ed.), *Diaphane Architektur* (series: Jörg Gleiter (ed.), *Architektur Denken*), transcript, Bielefeld, 2018 (forthcoming).

12   Konrad Wachsmann, *Salzburg—Die Altstadt; Berlin—Unter den Linden; Prague*, Grieben Verlag Berlin 1934. See: Otto Mayer, *Die räumliche Syntax. Konrad Wachsmanns Beitrag zum Bauen in unserer Zeit*, Karlsruhe 1989. This travel guide was produced through the support of Victor Goldsmith and was a good source of income for Wachsmann who was unemployed at the time, in: Konrad Wachsmann, "Timebridge, Konrad Wachsmann: An Autobiography," 1981, AdK, Konrad-Wachsmann-Archiv, Wachsmann 2128, p. 82.

13   Konrad Wachsmann, *Wendepunkt im Bauen*, Verlag der Kunst, Dresden 1989, p. 28 and p. 195.

14   Konrad Wachsmann, *Aspekte*, p. 5. In keeping with this principle there are no photo or illustration credits and thus the architecture photographs cannot be assigned to Wachsmann.

15   Konrad Wachsmann, *Aspekte*, no page.

16   Konrad Wachsmann, *Vom Bauen in unserer Zeit* (lecture at the Hochschule für Gestaltung Ulm, December 1956), in: AdK, Konrad-Wachsmann-Archiv, Wachsmann 466, p. 3.

17   Konrad Wachsmann, "Die Zukunft aus Situationen zwischen Räumen und Zeiten" (10.12.1973, lecture at the TU Hannover), in: AdK, Konrad-Wachsmann-Archiv, Wachsmann 2065, p. 16.

18   GTA Zurich, Fritz Haller Archives

19   *Notation und Kalkül in den Künsten der Nachkriegszeit*, Hubertus von Amelunxen, Dieter Appelt, Peter Weibel (eds.) together with Angela Lammert, AdK, 2007.

20   Wachsmann, *Wendepunkt im Bauen*, p. 162.

21   Other photographs used by Callahan are cropped on the sides, accentuate with blurredness the hovering of the construction or they move it to the right-hand lower edge of the picture.

22   Ibid., p. 174.

23   Ibid., p. 177.

24   In: http://www.griffenenrightarchitects.com/projects/connection-points/ retrieved 4.4.2018. It is common to speak of the immersion effect in connection with computer games.

25   Bálint András Varga, *Gespräche mit Iannix Xenakik*, Zurich, Mainz, 1995, p. 29.

26   Andreas Beyer, Matteo Burioni, Johannes Grave, "Einleitung. Zum Erscheinen von Architektur als Bild," in: (ibid. ed.), *Das Auge der Architektur*, Munich, 2011, p.12.

27   Georges Didi-Huberman, *Was wir sehen, blickt uns an*, Munich, 2005.

28   Walter Benjamin writes in his first version of the text "Strenge Kunstwissenschaft" in 1931 with an eye on Carl Linfert's publication "Die Grundlagen der Architekturzeichnung" that architectural drawing is "a borderline case."

29   Quoted in: Walter Benjamin, *Kritiken und Rezensionen. Gesammelte Schriften*, vol. III, Frankfurt a. M., 1991, p. 367 ... Carl Linfert's publication appeared in 1931.

In 2016 Justin Vernon (Bon Iver), whom I greatly admire, said at a press conference that the best stories emerge "when you suspend your disbeliefs as much as possible."[1] That is also, somewhat surprisingly, not only the declared goal of this chapter, but of the entire book *Stressing Wachsmann*. Clearly, there have been and still are a number of "imponderabilities," to put it cautiously, with regard to the person, work and impact of Konrad Wachsmann. Were this not the case the history of architecture of recent decades would offer many more serious examinations of this "pioneer of the architecture of the 20th century," as Friedrich Achleitner called him; but not without adding and writing that Wachsmann would probably have preferred to be understood as a "pioneer of building."[2] This is, therefore, a further selective search for traces and nothing other than that! And so at this point I make an attempt to understand Wachsmann with his permanent optimism as regards existing industries and those yet to come, his weakness for geometrical structures in general and turning points in particular from the viewpoint of the at times materialist German language tradition and here I am happy to let William Faulkner contradict Konrad Wachsmann, who was generally so cheerfully optimistic[3] (in this regard see his 1956 lecture from page 55 onwards): "The past is never dead. It's not even past."[4]

The story of Wachsmann's central theory and interests was published in 1959 under the title *Wendepunkt in Bauen*. A fine book, the first edition of which can still be bought suspiciously easily and cheaply. But why "a" or indeed "*the*" turning point? Are there, in fact, such clear (the term is used here to mean generally accepted) turning points in history? In the mathematical curve discussion, there certainly are. There a turning point describes the point at which a function graph changes its direction or, to put it more precisely, alters its curvature. If applied to cultural history such turning points would generally be tied to certain dates, persons, and to successful or failed projects and events. But even then, are these not more like overlays, developments and displacements rather than genuine turning points? Was Paxton's *Crystal Palace* really such a clear, tangible caesura, was the *Bessemer process* one, and if so then when and for whom? In Peter Collin's *Changing Ideals in Modern Architecture* we find an appropriate sentence in this regard: "From 1750 onwards architects were motivated by a number of notions that had previously played little or no part in the formation of their ideals, and these new notions did not simply succeed one another as an evolutionary sequence; they were to recur continually, in various combinations and expressed in different ways, during the whole of the following two centuries."[5] Manuel De Landa says much the same: "But the resulting emergent structures are simply added to the mix of previously existing ones, interact with them, but never

On Turning Points

Florian Medicus; Fig.: 49–61

leave them behind as an earlier stage of development (although, perhaps, they create the conditions for their disappearance)."[6] A historical turning point is also always a theoretical construction, that
is like the critical reduction of history to just a linear graph. But,
of course, "turning point" sounds good and is catchy! Wachsmann's
long-standing friend Klaus Mann (who is mentioned fourteen times
by name in Grüning's *Der Wachsmann-Report*, which also has an
illustration of his grave in Cannes[7]) in 1942 called the second part
of his biography *The Turning Point*, however this was against the
background of his volunteering for the *US Army* which, the way I see
it, does not really help us any further ...

Konrad Wachsmann concludes the book *Wendepunkt im Bauen*
(published in 1959), which has already been referred to, as follows:
"But the objective question, which, beyond all other aspects, is ultimately dominant, about what is meant by the term "art of building"
must remain open. It is only when humanity is capable of recognizing
the environment as its own and can fully identify with it, that this
question will become clearly recognizable in all its complexity. The
answer will then emerge of its own accord."[8] Despite a considerable
effort and the requisite confidence here he does not seem entirely
certain about this prospect—neither as regards *Wendepunkt im
Bauen* nor the term "art of building" (and not architecture, it should
be noted!) This somewhat strange attempt to create a formal distinction recalls the wonderful and telling printing error in the book
Bauen in Frankreich—Bauen in Eisen—Bauen in Eisenbeton (1928)
by Sigfried Giedion (also a longstanding friend, mentioned 12 times
by Grüning). The title ARCHITEKTUR in heavy type should have
been followed by an important question mark, also in heavy type."[→49]
Between these two books there are thirty years of world events,
but nevertheless the decisive question about the complete implant-
ing of contemporary (industrial) structural forms in the classic
understanding of the art of building was still to "remain open," like
Giedion's earlier question as to "whether the limited term 'architecture' will survive at all."[9] In 1914 Antonio Sant'Elia had (with
Marinetti's help) voiced precisely the same consideration: "The calculation of material strength, the use of reinforced concrete and
iron make an 'architecture' in the classic and usual sense impossible.
[...] We have in fact, lost a sense of the monumental, the powerful
and the structural and have enriched our sensibility through a taste
for the light, the transient and the fast."[10] Whatever the case, the fact
that what the manifestos often and radically called for could not
materialize immediately in the sense of being directly implemented
(although Sant'Elia's and also Mario Chiattone's drawings are otherwise among the very finest!), that this often did not happen more
quickly is regrettable for the entire history of culture. But today it
is amusing to read Paul Scheerbart's *Glasarchitektur* from 1914; or

exciting to read El Lissitzky, who with regard to his Wolkenbügel[→50] or "Sky Hook" described in a completely self-evident way building materials that did not yet exist: "lightweight materials and those that offer good heat and noise insulation are envisaged for ceilings and partitions. Similarly, chemically processed glass that allows light to enter but screens the rays of the sun."[11] Excellent ideas— and that in 1925! Wachsmann's language, however, is not that of the young avant-garde—at the time of *Wendepunkt im Bauen* he was already in his late fifties—he was aiming for something rather different. In this sense the entire book, despite all its certainty, is calm and generally more cautious, which in my opinion is partly due to the somewhat overheated history of stone and iron in Germany from around 1820 onwards.

Stone and Iron

After training as a carpenter and cabinet-maker Konrad Wachsmann first of all studied with Tessenow in Dresden and subsequently, from 1924 to 1926, at the Kunstakademie in Berlin, and later described himself as a "master student of Hans Poelzig."[12] And in 1931, only three years after Giedion's book on France, Poelzig wrote as follows in his essay "Der Architekt": "What is architecture about? Certainly, it is about form and, in fact, symbolic form. Are the technical forms symbolic, can they ever be so? [...] The engineer takes an unswerving path, but his creations remain nature,—they don't become symbolic, they don't become a style. [...] The technical forms [...] are and remain calculated, unsymbolic and, the iron beams, even if gilded, do not lose the rigidity of their mathematical origins."[13] This seems somewhat odd, as together with, for instance, Julius Posener,[14] we strongly wish to start from the notion that architecture has always been about creating space in the sense of symbolic forms. And precisely this is what, with due caution, Wachsmann writes: "From the means of the time not only will a new aesthetic and a special language develop that uses previously unknown definitions of beauty, but also a new ethic of looking at art, as a symbol of a new epoch."[15] Both Poelzig and Wachsmann, however, and a number of others before them, refer here, consciously or unconsciously, to a German discourse that had been conducted with remarkable tenacity since the early 19th century.

Let us read what Arthur Schopenhauer in Berlin in 1820, at the same time as the far less amusing Hegel, attempted to teach in his *Metaphysik des Schönen* and elsewhere: "The attempts undertaken in our times, first of all here in Berlin, to make works of architecture in iron cannot fulfill the second purpose of good architecture, which is to reveal the nature of light, as the black colour of iron eliminates the effect of light, swallows it up. [...] However, iron buildings can certainly meet the first aesthetic purpose of architecture, to demonstrate weightiness, rigidity, cohesion, as they have those qualities in abundance. But precisely because in such (iron) buildings the pro-portion of both forces with regard to each other is different to stone, and because of the additional aspect of the tenacity of iron, the proportions that have been found to be the best for stone buildings and their parts cannot be directly applied to iron: therefore, to pro-duce fine architecture in iron it would be necessary to invent different columniations and rules. This cannot be illustrated by means of the monument, as unfortunately it is Gothic and Gothic architecture does not comply with my aesthetic theory. (*Suo loco.*)"[16] For constructions in iron "other rules must be found," which seems understandable and possible, but ought not to have taken a hundred years, especially as this indecisiveness led, above all in Germany, to a very unproductive stalemate.

Only a few years after Schopenhauer's failed attempts as a teacher Karl Friedrich Schinkel enthused about Thomas Telford's Menai Strait suspension bridge and on site he drew "the situation in order to record the colossality of the object."[17/→51] Schinkel also used very unfussy and elegant slender cast iron parts in the Palace of Prince Albrecht (1829). And indeed as regards Schinkel—Wachsmann described the respect for Schinkel as the common denominator between himself and Mies van der Rohe: "Although Mies was also influenced by Berlage and Wright, he could never properly free himself from Schinkel's gravitational field"[18]—he grew ill and died far too young and so, five years after his death, it was the lot of the otherwise unfortunate and inconsequential architecture philosopher Carl Gottlieb Wilhelm Boetticher in his eloquent speech *In Honour of Schinkel* to identify the future of the German art of building as lying in iron architecture: "In every way of building the concern is first of all the development of a structural force from the building material which is introduced as an effective principle to the system of sheltering. There are only three structural forces that can be used in building and, as technical language puts it, are embedded in the material as absolute, relative and reactive stability or as resistance to tearing, breaking or crushing."[19] Here Boetticher describes the three structural forces of compression (columns and beams among the Greeks), thrust (in arches and vaults, particularly in Gothic architecture) and tension, which however was devoted too little attention, for: "one can say that, in fact, it is iron which introduces into architecture the last of these three structural forces, still unused as a principle until this point."[20]

During his lifetime Arthur Schopenhauer was hardly listened to or read at all; equally, we can assume that Boetticher's speech in 1846 did not provoke a scandal or even mark a turning point. At a national level it makes a tangible difference whether the great proponent of beautiful and also modern architecture was for or against architecture in iron: in France Eugène Emmanuel Viollet-le-Duc (from 1814 to 1879), in Germany Gottfried Semper (from 1803 also to 1879); it is also these two who H. P. Berlage contrasted in 1904 as the two great theorists of the 19th century and the representatives of a "practical aesthetic." Berlage here turned away from Semper (and consequently Schopenhauer) and towards the "Gothicist" Viollet-le-Duc, "... as he understood that medieval art could in principle provide the right basis for the modern age; it is not founded on a purely constructional base but in a sense forms the thread between old and new, a thread that we must take up again at the right place."[21] At almost the same time as Viollet-le-Duc in Paris, Gottfried Semper, almost thirty years after Schopenhauer, followed the latter's assessment: "one thing is certain: iron and indeed every hard and tough metal, as a construction material used in accordance with its nature in thin rods and at times as wires, on account of its minimal surface [...] escapes the eye increasingly, the more complete the construction is and that therefore the art of building that exerts its effect on the mood through the sense of sight ought not rely on this, so to speak, invisible material, if the concern is the effects of mass and not just a lightweight accessory."[22]

Two years later Semper did not change his mind when, in autumn 1851, he stood in Paxton's *Crystal Palace* in which he saw the tendency to dematerialization, which ran contrary to his theory, irritatingly confirmed by this "glass-covered vacuum which suits everything that one wants to bring into it"[23] as he writes in a long essay addressed to "the German reader." But Gottfried Semper does not see here any factual caesura of the kind that, about one hundred years later, Konrad Wachsmann regarded as a proven fact: "the Crystal Palace can indeed be seen as a turning point made visible, through which the entire development of the history of building took a different direction. [...] Out of reason and logic, intuitively understanding the thought of the technical age, a new beauty arose of a kind that had never previously been recognized, assessed or felt. The Crystal Palace was an artwork."[→52]

Even through the experiences of the great World Expositions (particularly, of course, in 1889 in Paris, where, "the Galerie des Machines showed how a new material [steel] and a new way of thinking about structure produced new forms" (Jörg Schlaich[24]), German discourse was unable to agree on the recognition or normative incorporation of the engineering aesthetic in the fine art of building. "The beauty of the building systems," Richard Lucae, the architect of the Frankfurt Opera House, still said in 1870, "is based on the surplus of mass over and above the amount of material required to carry the load."[25] And that, if you please, is how it should remain!

France is different

And although in the intervening period a number of good minds had made serious efforts to establish a wider understanding of the art of building that was expanded by the "engineering aesthetic" (see, for instance, Joseph August Lux, 1910), even at the end of the 1920s this was still the great uncertainty against which Sigfried Giedion wrote. The "Frenchification," the open partisanship for Le Corbusier, Garnier and Perret in his book, was, naturally enough, criticized, whereby it was Le Corbusier who directed Giedion "to the sources of today's architecture: to the iron architecture of the 19th century, to the big World Expositions, where it appeared most visibly."[26] And despite—or perhaps because of—the trench warfare on the position of the classical École des Beaux-Arts and the increasingly more powerful engineering schools, a certain continuity in this matter can be noted in French history, which spans from the constructive rationalism (the Boullée students J.-B. Rondelet and J.-N.-L. Durand), to Labrouste and Viollet-le-Duc, to Eiffel and Contamin (with C. L. F. Dutert) down to Auguste Choisy, Tony Garnier, the Perret brothers (who, even though they came from the École called themselves "constructeurs" and not "architectes") and, of course, to Le Corbusier. His findings are clear: "The engineers also make architecture, as they practice calculations derived from the laws of nature and their works enable us to experience harmony."[27] In terms of theory and practice France tended to be open to the new, whereas England, despite the early iron buildings and Paxton, seemed far more cautious and also heterogeneous (the Arts and Crafts movement), while Germany was important only as regards its indecisiveness. To this extent although Giedion's France book was somewhat one-sided in its focus on the industrial use of iron and concrete, it was important due to its historically coherent summary and, ultimately, due to the optimistic outlook that "our time, too, will find a new building material that is homogeneous to its demands."[28] However, Giedion meant neither iron nor concrete in that respect, as those were known materials of the 19th and early 20th century that had already been tested adequately. To the extent that Giedion places something completely new in a still unknown space, he sees the first phase of modern architecture, in which classical architecture could still be separated from contemporary construction, as fulfilled and therefore completed.[29] Based on that assumption, something entirely new was now to be undertaken.

Wachsmann as a Turning Point

However, it was to take a further thirty years until this assessment, i.e. of a historic conclusion of the first modernism, was tangibly and comprehensively established. Through Sputnik 1 (1957) and later through Yves Klein's "Leap into the Void" the familiar spatial boundaries were dissolved, much like, in 1959, the Congrès Internationaux d'Architecture Moderne. At the same time an unusually large number of books on this theme appeared: in 1957 Eduardo Torroja's *Razón y ser de los tipos estructurales* (which appeared in

German in 1961 as *Logik der Form*) and Bruno Zevi's *Architecture as Space* finally in English translation; in 1958 then Henry-Russell Hitchcock's wonderful overview *Architecture: Nineteenth and Twentieth Centuries* and Jürgen Joedicke's *Moderne Baukunst* (dedicated to Curt Siegel!), in 1959 Konrad Wachsmann's *Wendepunkt im Bauen*; 1960 Leonardo Benevolo's *Storia dell'architettura moderna*; Curt Siegel's *Strukturformen der modernen Architektur*; Conrads' and Sperlich's *Phantastische Architektur*; Reyner Banham's *Theory and Design in the First Machine Age* (with the wonderful essay *Functionalism and Technology*), and the manifesto of Metabolism on the occasion of the *World Design Conference* in Japan.

In all of this Konrad Wachsmann plays, involuntarily, a double role. He is both protagonist and incomplete historical object of the attempted conclusion of an epoch. For instance: Benevolo mentions Wachsmann only in connection with Gropius and the *General Panel Corporation*, referring to him as a "pure researcher,"[30] the same, incidentally, applies—strangely enough—to the 1964 revision of Giedion's *Space, Time, Architecture*; Hitchcock and Banham do not mention Wachsmann at all. Joedicke remains politely neutral, but at least he prints two pictures of the USAF-Hangar. Conrads and Sperlich are similarly dispassionate. Curt Siegel remains sceptical: "to what extent it is possible to realize such daring projects (USAF-Hangar, author's note) as a mobile construction is unclear."[31/→53, 54]

There is something strange about the manner in which, during these years, Konrad Wachsmann was ignored (and later, too, for example in Banham's *Megastructure* or Dahinden's *Stadtstrukturen für morgen*). I assume that he and his central concerns had not been completely perceived and understood. For Wachsmann offered himself as a turning point and saw the New Building, detached from the actual (building) project, as a broad definition of communication. He wrote "perhaps it is only the thought, the idea in which this era can fully express itself, while the work itself is an act of the temporary condition and consequently its significance cannot lie in its permanence. [...] There are other goals through which the culture of the era to come will express itself, which can be achieved through different means, which civilization must strive for using its own strengths."[32] The new building material that Giedion writes about, appears in Wachsmann's oeuvre as the greatest possible development of the industrial and the mobile: communication and inspiration, as the explanation of idea and ideal, the playful development of contemporary, interdisciplinary models that are suitable for the future, which, however, do not inevitably lead to a tangible project or to a classic building.[→55, 56] In his seminars an apparently rigid structure of repetitive, condensed turning points leads to a total dissolution of the familiar and as a formative event, according to Žižek, to the "emergence of something new that undermines every stable scheme" and "therefore brings about a change of the framework through which we register the world and move about in it."[33/→57] During these years Konrad Wachsmann was more successful than almost anyone else as one who changes, or, to put it better, expands the framework. His well-documented seminars, his teamwork, whether in Chicago, Karlsruhe, Tokyo or Salzburg, had immediate consequences in the development of visionary systems and (mega)structures. It is therefore hardly surprising that Wachsmann, along with Cedric Price or Archigram, was the intellectual godfather of the young Metabolists (the invitation to Japan was extended in 1955 by Kenzo Tange; at the seminar itself Noboru Kawazoe, Kenji Ekuan, the current Pritzker prize-winner Arata Isozaki, Mamoru Kawaguchi, Hiroshi Sasaki, Kazuhide Takahama met each other;[34] "the ideas from this key meeting of East and West arguably filtered down into Metabolism five years later," writes Hans Ulrich Obrist[35]). Peter Cook later said: "Konrad Wachsmann was even more important to us than Bucky (Fuller)."[36] I also suspect that there was a certain influence on Louis Kahn through Anne Tyng and that without Wachsmann Kenzo Tange's *Big Roof* of the EXPO 1970[→59] would never have existed, or at least not in this form. The timelessly elegant building systems of Fritz Haller (a freelance staff member of Wachsmann's building research institute at the University of Southern California) should also be mentioned as well as contemporary traces, such as Coop Himmelb(l)au's wonderfully crazy BMW World in Munich.[→60]

Wachsmann's ideas and ideal images speak persistently about overcoming intellectual and spatial boundaries in new understandings of the terms, overload and cantilever through contemporary (construction) methods. We owe to Konrad Wachsmann both the industrial aesthetic expansion of the understanding of architecture (without in the process ever mentioning the word "architecture") and the idea of an entirely new, completely egalitarian interdisciplinary teamwork. Consequently, it would only be appropriate to separate the impact—and with it the significance—of Wachsmann from the material proofs and to measure these more by the number of restructurings that directly reference him and his method. Naturally, with all of this both caution and criticism are necessary, much did not happen as expected and some things went completely awry. In a more general overview, however, the dominant impression is that the figure of Konrad Wachsmann is ideally suitable both as a striking endpoint and starting point, and thus unites everything that comes at least close to a real historical turning point. Wachsmann was the endpoint of the long German history of stone and iron and, equally, the start of a new-born international optimism. "Everyone is an architect. Everything is architecture."[37] Hans Hollein, who attended the seminar, was to write in 1967; likewise and ultimately, Sigfried Giedion's previously mentioned title ARCHITECTURE! did not lack a question mark, but rather an exclamation mark. After all, a good story should try to suspend your disbeliefs as much as possible.

Postscript

I was fortunate to be able to buy a really lovely and reasonably-priced print by Konrad Wachsmann at Edward Cella's excellent Los Angeles Gallery. It shows a bearing part of the construction of the USAF-Hangar, and was produced in an edition of 50 prints. In this series there are other sheets and versions, whereby, naturally, one could immediately ask why Wachsmann, otherwise an unpretentious constructor, worked here as an artist. Whatever: next to the signature "Konrad Wachsmann" stands the date: 11.22.63[61]; at that time, I believe, Wachsmann, together with his young family was still in Genoa. That Friday was also the 27th birthday of my father, Gottfried Medicus.

After signing the print Wachsmann probably smoked a few cigarettes down at the harbor, while at 12:30 p.m. local time John F. Kennedy was shot, which was to prove to be a historical turning point in many ways.

1   Bon Iver, 22, A Million Press Con-
    ference, at https://www.youtube.
    com/watch?v=eNqCV fC4oj4,
    accessed on March 10, 2019.
2   Friedrich Achleitner, foreword to
    Michael Grüning, Der Architekt
    Konrad Wachsmann, Löcker Verlag,
    Vienna, 1986, p. 6.
3   Konrad Wachsmann, Timebridge,
    Konrad Wachsmann: An Autobiogra-
    phy, 1981, unpublished autobio-
    graphy, AdK, Konrad-Wachsmann-
    Archiv, Wachsmann 2128, pp. 340f.
4   William Faulkner, Requiem for a Nun,
    1950/51, Penguin Random House,
    London, 1996, p. 85.

5   Peter Collins, Changing Ideals of
    Modern Architecture, McGill
    University Press, Montreal (1965)
    1998, p. 15.
6   Manuel De Landa, A thousand years
    of nonlinear history, Swerve
    Editions, New York 2000, p. 271.
7   Michael Grüning, Der Wachsmann-
    Report, Verlag der Nation, Berlin,
    1986, pp. 574, 471.
8   Konrad Wachsmann, Wendepunkt
    im Bauen, Krausskopf-Verlag,
    Wiesbaden, 1959, p. 232.
9   Sigfried Giedion, Bauen in
    Frankreich—Bauen in Eisen—
    Bauen in Eisenbeton, Klinkhardt &

    Biermann, Leipzig/Berlin 1928, p. 6.
10 Antonio Sant'Elia, "Futuristische
    Architektur," in: Ulrich Conrads
    (ed.), Programme und Manifeste zur
    Architektur des 20. Jahrhunderts,
    series Bauwelt Fundamente 1,
    Birkhäuser, Basel, 2013 (2nd
    reprint), p. 32.
11 El Lissitzky, Proun und Wolkenbügel,
    Fundus Bücher 46, VEB, Dresden,
    1977, p. 82.
12 Otto Maier, Die räumliche Syntax,
    Dissertation bei Fritz Haller,
    Karlsruhe, 1989, p. 324.
13 Hans Poelzig, "Der Architekt" (1931),
    in: Bauwelt 27–28, 2009, p. 9.

14   Julius Posener, *Neuere Aufsätze*,
     Birkhäuser, Basel, 1995, pp. 55f.

15   Konrad Wachsmann, *Wendepunkt
     im Bauen*, Krausskopf-Verlag,
     Wiesbaden 1959, p. 232.

16   Arthur Schopenhauer, *Metaphysik
     des Schönen*, Serie Piper, Munich/
     Zurich, 1985, pp. 138f.

17   Karl Friedrich Schinkel in Julius
     Posener, *Vorlesungen zur Geschichte
     der neueren Architektur V, Neue Ten-
     denzen im 18. Jahrhundert – Das Zeit-
     alter Schinkels*, ARCH+ 69/70, p. 42.

18   Michael Grüning, *Der Wachsmann-
     Report*, Verlag der Nation, Berlin,
     1986, p. 534.

19   Carl Gottlieb Wilhelm Boetticher in:
     Julius Posener (ed.), *Schinkel zu
     Ehren*, Fröhlich und Kaufmann (no
     year), p. 19.

20   Carl Gottlieb Wilhelm Boetticher in:
     Julius Posener (ed.), *Schinkel zu
     Ehren*, Fröhlich und Kaufmann (no
     year), p. 24.

21   Hendrik Petrus Berlage, quoted after
     Werner Oechsl, in: *Eugène
     Emmanuel Viollet-le-Duc*, gta Verlag,
     Zurich, 2010, p. 11.

22   Gottfried Semper, *Eisenkonstruk-
     tionen* (1849) in: *Wissenschaft,
     Industrie und Kunst*, Florian
     Kupferberg Verlag Mainz, 1966,
     p. 22.

23   Gottfried Semper, *Wissenschaft,
     Industrie und Kunst—Vorschläge
     zur Anregung nationalen Kunst-
     gefühls* (1851) in: *Wissenschaft,
     Industrie und Kunst*, Florian
     Kupferberg Verlag Mainz, 1966,
     p. 68.

24   In: ARCH+159/160, *Formfindungen*,
     May 2002, p. 27.

25   Richard Lucae nach Sokratis
     Georgiadis, Nachwort zu Sigfried
     Giedion, *Bauen in Frankreich …*,
     Gebrüder Mann Verlag, Berlin, 2000,
     p. 10.

26   Sokratis Georgiadis, Nachwort zu
     Sigfried Giedion, *Bauen in
     Frankreich …*, Gebrüder Mann Verlag,
     Berlin, 2000, p. 2.

27   Le Corbusier, "Ausblick auf eine
     Architektur (1922)," in:
     Bauwelt Fundamente 2, Vieweg,
     Braunschweig/Wiesbaden,
     4th edition, 1982, p. 31.

28   Sigfried Giedion, *Bauen in
     Frankreich—Bauen in Eisen—
     Bauen in Eisenbeton*, Klinkhardt &
     Biermann, Leipzig/Berlin, 1928,
     p. 120.

29   See also: Alison & Peter Smithson:
     *Heroic Period of Modern
     Architecture*, Thames & Hudson,
     London, 1981.

30   Curt Siegel, *Strukturformen der
     modernen Architektur*, Callwey
     Verlag, Munich, 1960, p. 189.

31   Ibid.

32   Konrad Wachsmann, *Wendepunkt
     im Bauen*, Krausskopf-Verlag,
     Wiesbaden, 1959, pp. 230f.

33   Slavoj Žižek, *Was ist ein Ereignis?*,
     S. Fischer, Frankfurt a. M., 2014,
     pp. 11f.

34   Reyner Banham, Hiroyuki Suzuki:
     Modernes Bauen in Japan, Stuttgart
     (DVA) 1987, pp. 6f. See also: Martino
     Peña Fernández-Serrano,
     "El seminaro de Wachsmann en
     Japón," *rita_08*, Noviembre 2017,
     pp. 86f. at: https://www.academia.
     edu/36075613/The_Wachsmann_s_
     Seminar._Sharing_influences,
     accessed on February 5, 2019.

35   Rem Koolhaas, Hans Ulrich Obrist,
     Project Japan, Taschen Verlag,
     Cologne, 2011, p. 20.

36   Ibid.

37   Hans Hollein, in: *S+M*, François
     Burkhard, Paulus Manker (eds.),
     University of Applied Arts Vienna,
     2002, pp. 53f.

Science and technique render new possibilities requiring objective recognition and studies before creative concepts can be formulated

THE MACHINE IS THE TOOL OF OUR TIME, and cause of those effects which characterize the accepted order of our society

Possibilities of new materials, methods, processes, principles of flow of stresses, sociological valuations, and resulting planning tasks, must be accepted.

Following the conditions of industrialization, by multiplication of cell and element, the structure shall find its form.

Modular coordination systems, scientific methods of testing, rules of automation, and new definitions of precision should influence creative thinking.

These complex problems require closest and anonymous cooperation in working-teams, incorporating sciences, specialists, and industry.

Applications of contemporary knowledge and abilities will give new impulses to functions and the meaning of humanity and aesthetics of building in our time

Building in Our Time

Konrad Wachsmann,
Lecture AA London, 1957

(Unedited transcription
of the lecture)

In these theses, I try to point out the necessity of a new interpretation of the detail.

If I am so exclusively interested in the analysis of inventions and methods, based on industrialization, I certainly do not do so as a mean in itself, or even to be concerned as a perpetual inventor. I recognized that I had no tools to express myself as a contemporary designer according to the standard of our knowledge and our capabilities. I certainly wish I could spend all my life's time in building, as I have done before already. But since I recognize that greater potentialities are embodied in the present and not yet released for a general purpose, I cannot anticipate the effects to causes and retire into research.

Science and technique render new possibilities. This does not mean that we are confronted with problems which we have to accept, no matter if they are good or not. With the word "render" I try to explain that new discoveries are hard gained advantages opening doors into a new possible world which is not controlled by preconceived ideas.

The machine as the tool of our time does not seem to be an enlarged hand-tool. In the machine I see a new approach to the concept of the original. While any object, made by a skilled man, represents an original creation of an individual person—how often he might repeat these identical objects—the machine-made products are only copies. The true originals are those parts of the machine, such as dies, forms, knives, jig-tables, etc., which shape the final product. We have to distinguish the meaning of the negative and positive in creative work. Therefore, to-day not incidentally, the toolmaker is the qualified craftsman on the highest level. Now I wish the exact place of the contemporary comprehensive designer as a creative cooperator could be recognized in the line of this team in which he belongs: Scientists who formulate the fundamental principles, engineers who use these findings and apply them to actual tasks, economists estimating commercial view-points, technicians providing blueprints and other information to the toolmaker who creates the final originals, the tools.

If we know that brick and mortar joint, nail, rivet or welded seam, are fundamental causes which determine the concept of a structure, then we have to analyse exactly the new cells, joints, and elements and their relation to each other before we can conceive an idea of contemporary structures.

Accepting a system of order does not mean limiting our creative thinking. On the contrary, the applications of modular coordination systems will increase our sense for small differences and neutralize personal intuitions to expressions of general importance. Scientific methods of testing shall be a creative instrument with which the designer transforms the idea to reality. Rules of automation are further means of understanding of function, quantity, time, and distance, in regard to the creation of the smallest parts which will now become decisively important to the whole. But above all, the new thought of precision emerges. It is hard to imagine that the use of the yardstick should still represent an equivalent tool of measurement in modern times.

Confronted with these and many more problems of the same magnitude, I believe the work of a designer will move out of the hands of the individual, intuitive designer into the strong activity of the anonymous working-teams which by knowledge and imagination, prepared for the risk of the experiment, not being influence by prejudices, will find objective solutions in which the image of the whole merely becomes a by-product of all efforts.

Such thinking, knowing, and acting will give us new impulses which might develop the concept of the present and the future. Man will recognize that this is his real environment in harmony with his knowledge, and therefore in harmony with his feelings. His ideas about beauty, his aesthetic imaginations, developed from rational necessities, and transferred into the abstract idea of the symbol, will form a new environment for him.

Where will all this lead to? Is it possible to make any predictions? Is not a prediction already a prejudice again? I still would like to indicate to make myself clearer how I imagine a possible evolution of building.

Preparations will be more complicated, but the ideas of the designer will be much simpler than they are today. I do not remember that I have ever seen a building which was too simple in its general concept. I only saw buildings which by far have not been simple enough. But whenever I saw a real simple building, it always appeared to me as a very beautiful one. I hesitate to make any distinction between simple and naïve. Naivety is a virtue. And I somehow feel, truly modern buildings in future times on their highest level may be less clever than they are to-day, but more naïve.

The use of beams will more and more disappear. They will be replaced by horizontal slabs. People may look at columns quite differently than they do today. Columns will almost disappear so that they finally will not be noticed anymore even if they are there. Also the image of what we experience as walls, windows, or doors will change considerably. I could imagine that in times to come, there will be only surfaces: opaque, transparent, and flexible. And openings will be there and dynamic space, and the mechanical equipment will be extended to incredibly complicated systems, mainly in horizontal surfaces. But these surfaces will also carry the major stresses, one man may try to subdue what today is so often emphasized in the vertical.

Concerning structure, there might be a general tendency to follow relaxed stresses. It also could lead to systems of distribution of stresses in points in space. More and more, matter will be dissolved in smallest parts. They will meet in joints, thus creating the concept of points in space, connected with imaginary lines, around which material might be distributed, which by virtue of its own curvature and in itself punctured, reduced to the limit, will again produce greater strength. Curved and compound surfaces, slabs and cantilevers, may replace the still existing acceptance of the meaning of frames, columns, or beams. As much as we all agree already that the language of classical architecture would not be proper to be applied to contemporary creative tasks, it is as much impossible to think that any modern concept of building could exist which is built by conventional or rather classical methods of construction. This also may be the one reason why today we are generally inclined to accept as truly contemporary and excitingly modern the great structures of engineering and the dynamic mechanical machines.

Surfaces will diminish to zero which means an entirely smooth flat surface may prevail. A period may come in which men again will recognize the meaning and importance of lines, the play of lines, conditioned by joints and surfaces. These surfaces of small weight may dominate future structures. More than ever, lightness may prevail, strength and power might be subdued. The clear separation and distinction of object and function, as well in detail as in the whole, may also be one of the major concepts in buildings.

I will not talk about the way how people will live together in times to come, nor about city or regional planning, or traffic problems. But I know, there will be a continuous order, based on modular principles of the repetition of the nucleus, the structural cell of joints, an order which will create joints, surfaces, structures, space, buildings, streets, squares, and parks, thus creating city-scapes and finally the whole landscape of the civilized world.

And at this point, for the first time I hope that the new artist may emerge who by his genius and his vision is able to transfer facts and functions into the abstract language of art: the history of architecture would start again.

But under the circumstances under which we live somehow as pioneers, preparing the landscape of the future, we shall at present restrict ourselves to follow functions, and to be impersonally objective and modest.

Effect follows cause, "form follows function." As long as man has to integrate new insights and scientific discoveries, being occupied with the study and the analysis of practical experiences, as long this dynamic condition will exist which justifies this well known statement.

But if man recognizes the limitations, based on his ability of understanding, and is therefore able to master all comprehensive factors not only in the technical sense but also with regard to social reflections and their symbolic values and wishful expressions, then we can foresee the final ideal condition in which function may follow form, and causes may be subordinated to effects.

I cannot think of any higher goal for which mankind may strive.

Konrad Wachsmann's work is inseparably linked to one of central ideas of modern architecture: the belief that the complete industrialization of the building process would finally solve all the economic, social and technical problems of the infrastructure as well as those presented by mass housing for society. A part of this belief was that the use of standardized housing construction to meet everyone's essential housing needs would enable people to lead their lives in an individual and meaningful way.

Today, one hundred years after this vision was formulated, we know that it proved impossible to implement it in either a capitalist or socialist system in any comprehensive sense that would have shaped society. The areas of 20th century building in which industrial production processes were most widely used—panel housing construction in eastern Europe, the largely prefabricated private homes in the USA, housing developments in western Europe, technical and military applications and, in part, the construction of high-rise buildings—were either limited to certain periods or restricted to specific fields. A comprehensive mechanization (today: digitalization) of all building processes in all fields—from the definition of needs to planning to production—is, even in the early digital age, not yet in sight: throughout the world most buildings by far are still intuitively planned and produced by handcraft—adapted to suit local resources, mentalities and building regulations.[1]

In postwar Europe of the 1950s the chances for a profound rationalization of construction were still viewed optimistically. Postwar reconstruction and the incipient economic boom produced enormous demand. Many young architects—like their predecessors in the first postwar period of the 1920s—saw extremely widespread mechanization, standardization and industrialization as the future of the building industry, which was still largely based on manual labor to which there was no alternative. In Austria this return to the ideals of heroic modernism was also motivated by the wish of the young generation of those born around 1930 to distance themselves from their teachers, who had survived the age of dictatorships with the help of a "moderate" modernity that incurred no suspicion, and, naturally, also to create a distance to the continued impact of Nazi architecture through a number of its representatives, who were still working in the 1950s.[2] Konrad Wachsmann represented the opposite: from his exile in the USA, where, as a German Jew, he had been forced by the Nazi regime to flee, he undertook his consequential lecture tours in Europe in 1954 as an avant-garde hero of modernism and an exemplary representative of modernism's euphoric reception of industrialization.

First of All, the Balance: A Stimulator of European Postwar Architecture

In 1956, having been recommended by Egon Eiermann[3] as

A New Anonymity of Building on a Technical Basis

Konrad Wachsmann, modernism's vision of rationalization and its consequences in Austria

Matthias Boeckl; Fig.: 62–78

successor to the Zurich architect Hans Hofmann, Wachsmann took over the architecture course at the International Summer Academy in Salzburg, which had been co-founded by Oskar Kokoschka. Given the situation in Austria during the reconstruction period— at the time of the first Wachsmann course the postwar occupation of Austria by the Allies had ended only a year earlier—the course attracted a remarkably international range of students. Alongside the Austrian participants those who attended included people from Switzerland, Germany, the USA, Finland, Italy and other countries. Most of them were young architects who were eager to use their postgraduate period to acquire information about the state of indus-trialization in the building industry. Wachsmann's seminar, however, also functioned as a real initiation experience for a group of around 20 young Austrian architects around Friedrich Achleitner, Erich Boltenstern junior, Hermann Czech, Roland Ertl, Johann Georg Gsteu, Hans Hollein, Franz Kiener, Friedrich Kurrent, Bernhard Leitner, Otto Leitner, Wolfgang Mistelbauer, Gustav Peichl, Johan-nes Spalt, Ottokar Uhl, Michael Untertrifaller senior and Gunther Wawrik.[4] Here for the first time they were able to discover an old ideal of the modern movement in an authentic context, from one of its most important representatives. The Austrian modernism, in the spirit of which these hopeful architects had been educated by Clemens Holzmeister, Lois Welzenbacher, Erich Boltenstern senior, Oswald Haerdtl and other protagonists of the interwar and, in part, of the Nazi era, had—in contrast to the German avant-garde— essentially never questioned the traditional artisan approach to building. Even the highly progressive, social reform-oriented Viennese group around Josef Frank tended to entrust the social production of meaning to collectively practiced handcraft.[5]

But was Wachsmann really concerned only with the technical aspect of rationalization, i.e. the mere mechanization of construction that was generally associated with the term "industrialization"?[6] The recollections of his students convey a far broader picture of Wachsmann's message, which often was received, much abbreviated, on the formal level only, above all in the form of tube and node constructions.[7] In the long-term only a few of the Austrian architects among Wachsmann students were able to develop the experiences they acquired during the course into a consistently practiced plan-ning method, one example being the participation movement: at the Summer Academy planning in a (specialist) collective was trained, which Ottokar Uhl later expanded consistently by including the users. Both camps of the Wachsmann reception in Austria are exhaustively described further below.

Looking Back: Avant-garde and Industrial Building Production

How did this impact on postwar European architecture with all its consequences come about? Together with Walter Gropius, Hannes

Meyer, Martin Wagner, Ernst May, Georg Muche and others Wachsmann is numbered among the pioneers of a comprehensively understood rationalization of building, which, ultimately, was also intended
to lead to a new aesthetic.[8] This ideology contrasts sharply with modernism's pragmatic tradition which envisaged introducing industrial production into the existing construction industry only where
it could be integrated without technical difficulties and in line with
market conditions.[9]

The (mostly) industrial production of building using very different kinds of technologies for the prefabrication of elements (which
were later put together by hand on the building site) had already
existed for a long time before its "discovery" by the avant-garde
of the 20th century. For example: not even the *Crystal Palace* in
London, which Wachsmann always presented as the start of building
industrialization in 1851, was regarded as "architecture" at the time
it was erected.[10] As regards timber building the prefabrication of
timber elements for large-scale colonization projects had begun
decades earlier. From 1820 onwards the London firm of Manning
supplied systems of this kind for 5000 English settlers in the Cape
Province of South Africa and in the 1830s also for Australia.[11] The
rapid settlement of the West of the USA—a hundred years before
the activities of Wachsmann's *General Panel Corporation*—was
also, to a considerable extent, made possible by the use of prefabricated timber and iron panel systems. In the literature it is predom-
inantly English and American examples of the early industrialization of building before 1900—confined generally to settlements
—which are mentioned. A few systems dating from this era—such
as those produced by the English firm of *Calway & Co.*, owned by
the Liverpool engineer J. A. Brodie and the New York architect
Grosvenor Atterbury—were already based on concrete panels,
while the north German business *Christoph & Unmack*—in which
the then 25-year-old Konrad Wachsmann began his career in 1926
after having studied architecture under Heinrich Tessenow in
Dresden, had been producing timber elements for the barracks of
the Prussian military since 1882.[12]

The avant-garde discovered these systems for itself only shortly
before the First World War. In the 1920s it developed this euphoria
into the dogmatic term "industrial building," which was certainly
intended as the expression of a specific world view and which represented an ideological system analogous to the political systems of
the time, which were also conceived as absolutes that recognized no
alternatives. "We accept the machine as the tool of our time. This
means that we recognize a social order that has fully adapted its
basic structure to the consequences of industrialization."[13]

In the context of a free market economy this understanding of
building, which was based largely on ideas about reforming life—in

contrast to pragmatic concepts that were confined to new building methods that could be easily integrated—was doomed to failure, as it did not recognize the fundamental human need to draw distinctions. It was only in the special situation of a dictatorship or of the US war economy that such a concept could be implemented through state-subsidized projects in certain strictly defined areas.

Konrad Wachsmann's later partner Walter Gropius was the pioneer of that particular "philosophical world view" on industrialization. Paradoxically, however, this developed precisely under *artistic* auspices: when working for Peter Behrens Gropius, together with the former, wrote a "Programm zur Gründung einer allgemeinen Hausbaugesellschaft auf künstlerisch einheitlicher Grundlage m.b.H." ("Program for the Founding of a General House Construction Company on an Artistically Uniform Basis Ltd.") in 1909/10. Addressed to the management of the AEG company this manifesto was based on Behrens' experience with developing housing estates for this firm. However, it hardly lived up to the grandiloquent name, as, according to Winfried Nerdinger, "apart from suggestions on the standardization of building elements it (contains) hardly any ideas about manufacture and production—and in any case standardized prefabrication systems had already been developed in the USA, England and Germany much earlier."[14] The overall goal, the production of useful objects on an "artistically uniform basis," was derived from the *Gesamtkunstwerk* ideals of Art Nouveau and the Arts-and-Crafts movements around 1900 and their critical attitude to industry. It is also found in the program of the Deutscher Werkbund, which was founded in 1907 by Peter Behrens, Josef Hoffmann, Joseph Maria Olbrich, Paul Schultze-Naumburg and others.

An inherent contradiction, and one which was to accompany the history of the various Werkbund organizations, lies in the apparently paradoxical combination of the adjectives "uniform" and "artistic": can individuality (of the users) really be achieved through standardization (of the objects they use)? By means of an "artistic directorship" of the economy Gropius apparently wanted to bring about something "unartistic": standardized building production which with its radical standardization of the product—and possibly also of the ways in which the product is used—definitively demands an emancipatory effort from the consumer who wishes to realize a self-fulfilling way of life, an effort that not everyone can or is willing to make. Seen from such a perspective this was very much an elitist concept.

European Prototypes of the 1920s and 1930s: Gropius and Wachsmann

Initially the avant-garde's obsession with rationalization also produced a number of irrational planning results. A first example of such conflicts between technical standardizations and real user needs was offered by the housing development in Dessau-Törten 1926–28, where, on account of the production method chosen, Gropius had to orientate identical houses arranged in two parallel rows in *different* directions, in order just to demonstrate "rational conveyor belt production": here he consciously sacrificed an important functional requirement to a "higher goal."[15]

Due to the new technology involved and the limited number of units produced the construction costs of practically all similar early "industrialization" projects were higher than they would have been using established manual building techniques, which no longer caused any development costs. The enormous initial investment costs of the new production technology could only have been recovered in the distant future through far higher sales figures. Ever since that time the classic problem of financing the higher development costs of a new industrial method of production has accompanied all similar construction concepts. In the building industry—in contrast to the exemplary automobile industry—it never proved possible to solve this problem entirely, as prefabricated dwelling houses of a competitive quality hardly ever achieved the sales figures required to amortize the initial investment.[16]

A second case in which Gropius' ambitions to achieve a breakthrough to the mass market were frustrated was his contribution to the Werkbund exhibition of model houses in Stuttgart in 1927. House no. 17, which stands in the shadow (literally) of the houses by Le Corbusier, was constructed using a steel frame, with 8 cm thick Expansit cork panels and asbestos slate panels as infill. Winfried Nerdinger draws up a sobering balance for this prototype, too. "It was not the critics alone who referred to a barracks like quality to the buildings, Bauhaus students were also disappointed by their Director and thought that something like Le Corbusier's buildings should have come out of Dessau. In her diary Ise Gropius noted that Gropius criticized the buildings by Le Corbusier as backward, because the future, he said, lay in mechanizing the production of buildings."[17]

A third episode is the project for a "house building factory," which the founder of the Bauhaus wanted to erect in 1928 together with the Berlin building contractor Adolf Sommerfeld. With this goal in mind Gropius undertook an extended study trip to the USA and after his return, together with László Moholy-Nagy, he presented an exhibition that propagated the "American" building system. "But the house building factory," Nerdinger summarizes, "came to nothing and the much-invoked American building industry remained a nebulous term generally used only in statistics."[18]

Around this time metal constructions began to establish a position as the preferred technology for erecting houses in series, both on the market and in the form of prototypes conceived by architects:

as early as 1924 Friedrich Förster had developed an innovative wall element system that used timber frames with copper panels (improved in 1930 with Robert Krafft for the Hirsch Kupfer- und Messingwerke in Eberswalde): "There were no constructional models for this concept on the German house building market and indeed not even among the early, much admired British models."[19] After presentations of traditionally styled prototypes at building exhibitions Walter Gropius analyzed the *Hirsch System* in 1931 for the periodical *Bauwelt* and subsequently began to advise the company about experimental systematic improvement on the basis of model buildings. Ultimately however—despite negotiations about production in series with many developers in Europe, America and the Soviet Union—only a few dozen of these houses were produced, generally as prototypes, while a small number was also made for private end customers.

Around 1930 Austrian architects and businesses, too, made several attempts at producing prefabricated metal houses in series. The steel producer *Böhler*—the family that owned this company was closely connected with Viennese pioneers of modernism in Josef Hoffmann's circle[20]—developed a wall system with a steel frame, steel panels and internal Heraklith insulation. Prototypes of this system, several of them architect-designed, were also presented at building exhibitions in Germany. However, the concept failed to establish itself on the market—and the same applies to the steel house that Josef Hoffmann had designed for the Styrian producer *Vogel & Noot*.[21] At around the same time in the USA Richard Buckminster Fuller developed his *Dymaxion* concept for an industrially produced prefabricated aluminum house, which was produced between 1928 and 1930 only as two prototypes. His geodesic domes, made from industrially manufactured lightweight elements, followed from 1948. One of the main reasons for the success of this system was its easy adaptability for a wide range of different contexts and functions—with the major exception of housing.

Konrad Wachsmann, who worked with Gropius from 1941 when they were both in exile in the USA, had acquired his experience of rational production technologies in the area of timber building. After training as a carpenter and cabinet maker and attending the Kunstgewerbeschule in Berlin, he studied at the Dresden Akademie under Heinrich Tessenow in 1923, and in 1924 at the Berliner Kunstakademie with Hans Poelzig. In 1926 Wachsmann joined the timber and steel construction firm of *Christoph & Unmack* in Niesky, a town in eastern Germany. In 1929 he opened an architecture practice in Berlin which became known almost overnight through the timber holiday house Wachsmann designed for Albert Einstein in Caputh, near Potsdam. In 1930 he published a specialist book about timber building.[22] From the National Socialists' "assumption of power" in 1933 until his emigration to the USA in 1941 (made possible by Einstein) Wachsmann lived and worked in Italy, Spain and France. Even in these troubled times he maintained intensive contacts with the most important personalities of the German and European avant-garde from Tessenow to Poelzig, Gropius and Le Corbusier.[23] But while working on the Einstein project he had already recognized his mission in life: "having Einstein as a client brought me an amazing reputation. Although it was, in fact, crazy, I gave up my job as head architect (author's note: with *Christoph & Unmack*) in order to work in my own practice. My future was far from certain. I had discovered only one universal anonymous task: industrialization."[24]

The projects which Wachsmann developed between his arrival in America in 1941 and starting work as a lecturer at US universities in 1949 as well as the years from 1954 onwards spent traveling as a lecturer directly and indirectly commissioned by the US government have been the subject of numerous publications[25] and are also documented in this volume. The most important studies on the construction of large shed structures were a *Mobilar Structure* for the *Atlas Aircraft Corporation* and hangar projects for the US Air Force. Only the research costs were paid for. Neither of these two systems ever became marketable or ready to be produced in series.

The General Panel Corporation: The Success Criteria of Industrial Housing Construction

Nevertheless, together with Walter Gropius and the *General Panel Corporation* Wachsmann was able to achieve a short-lived market presence, precisely in the area of house building in the USA which, unlike in Europe, is extremely market-driven. Ultimately, however, the failure of this business, which was founded in 1941 and went into liquidation in 1951, put an end to many of the hopes of the avant-garde for a systematic, rational kind of housing construction which would provide the basis for the complete industrialization of building and for the social and aesthetic change that this was expected to bring about. The most profound analysis of this failure was made by Gilbert Herbert.[26] He identified a dramatic economic discrepancy as the reason for the lack of success: on the one hand to develop perfected serial production the company required enormous amounts of time and capital, while on the other, market conditions had changed radically since the end of the war in 1945— without the military as a major client and lacking goverment subsidies—as compared to the founding year 1941, leading to the development of a civilian consumers market. As a result, development costs increased, while market chances declined rapidly. An immediate consequence was low output: in the ten years of its existence the *General Panel Corporation* sold and delivered barely 200 houses. This was preceded by a capital investment (partly in the form of a state subsidy) of six million dollars, which was used almost entirely for technical development and the erection of a new factory building in California, rather than for the actual production. Further reasons for the decline were Wachsmann's perfectionism and his constant drive to improve things, which continuously delayed the final serial production of large numbers of houses. In addition, there was an almost total lack of marketing and the houses were not really competitive as they were not significantly cheaper than conventionally built houses but still bore the "stain" of a ready-made product. Other factors were the lack of financing models for prospective purchasers and considerable differences between the building regulations in various regions of the country, which made the complete, supra-regional standardization of dwelling houses far more difficult. In contrast the more flexible traditional building industry was easily able to meet the great demand on the market through economical, more individualized, easily financeable and technically convention-al solutions.

A short time later dwelllings that that were entirely industrially produced were successfully implemented in a very different context —namely in the form of the new type, the *mobile home*, which grew more and more attractive in the context of an increasingly mobile consumer society. Without incurring any substantial development costs this production method could be developed effortlessly from the existing automobile industry. Even though they constantly lauded the "Taylorism" of the car industry as exemplary[27] the members of the European avant-garde, partly because of their idealistic socialization, could hardly have anticipated this move towards a technically advanced free market economy.

For the idea of industrially produced, fixed dwelling houses a typical market, which is still relevant today along with the suitable technology developed in a niche area of the postwar economy: the *conventional* prefabricated house industry without the lofty techno-logical aspirations of the *General Panel Corporation*. Far removed from all ideological visions and at the price of dispensing with the goals of social reform, radical technical innovations or an "aesthetic change," a pragmatic understanding of industrial prefabrication was able to establish itself: in markets in threshold countries and in the less demanding market segments in industrialized countries this strategy, which makes use of existing prefabrication technologies and develops them further and is driven by sizable capital reserves, was and still is highly successful.

This is proven not only by the state subsidized concepts for *Plattenbauten* (prefabricated panel buildings) in the socialist Eastern Bloc and in social-democratic Western Europe, there are also several examples from the USA, of which Nelson Rockefeller's *International Basic Economy Corporation* (*IBEC*), was especially successful. This company built prefabricated houses in Puerto Rico on a large scale. The first designs, which were based on prefabricated concrete elements, were developed by Austrian exile architect Simon Schmiderer in collaboration with engineer Armando Vivoni. A second phase saw the introduction of in situ concrete houses, which were cast entirely in a single, re-usable formwork.[28] As these methods involved hardly any development costs and, as the building developer also offered customers extremely favorable financing models and the houses were erected only to order for a hungry market, the project was an economic success: in contrast to the *General Panel Corporation* IBEC was able to succeed thanks to a good knowledge of the market, tried and trusted financing instruments and the use of pragmatic technologies.

The Late Wachsmann: Idealistic Theory instead of Sobering Practice

When it became clear that the *General Panel Corporation* was destined to fail, what consequences did Wachsmann draw? His immediate reaction was to withdraw to academic life. As early as 1949, that is two years before the final liquidation of the business, Wachsmann accepted a call to Chicago to the *Institute of Design* at *Illinois Institute of Technology* (IIT). In the same year this design institute, which had been founded five years earlier by Bauhaus member László Moholy-Nagy, was incorporated in the IIT, where the former Bauhaus Director Ludwig Mies van der Rohe had been teaching since 1938 and had designed a new campus with several new buildings. Other exile artists such as the painter and sculptor Hugo Weber who had come from Paris, taught at IIT. And so, 16 years after his flight from Germany, Wachsmann returned to the familiar ambiance of the former European avant-garde. However, the Cold War introduced a geopolitical development in which new, strategically important tasks arose for the leading figures of German modernism who had emigrated to the USA in the 1930s. Alongside its military presence in Western Europe, the US administration supported reconstruction work in war-damaged countries through the Marshall Plan, also providing numerous *America Houses* as well as scholarships for European students at US universities, thus launching a wide-ranging educational program (through Fulbright Scholarships among others), which was intended to soundly anchor Western values among the European elite of the future.[29] A part of this strategy was the support of studies, exhibitions, research and lecture tours by American artists and academics throughout Europe.

In these programs those artists and architects who, having fled from National Socialism had been generously received in the USA and successfully integrated in cultural life there, naturally played a special role. As credible and convincing ambassadors for an American way of life, the fact that they had been socialized in

Europe enabled them to establish perfect communication with young European artists, scientists and politicians. This was shown not only by flagship projects such as the *Nationalgalerie* in Berlin by Mies van der Rohe (1962–68) or the *Gropiussiedlung* (Großsiedlung Britz-Buckow-Rudow, 1960–73), but also by Konrad Wachsmann's great impact in Austria from 1956 onwards. From 1954 until his death in 1980 he traveled tirelessly to lectures, seminars, and exhibitions, mostly in Germany, Italy and Austria. In 1954 Wachsmann taught as a lecturer at Egon Eiermann's chair in Karlsruhe, in 1955–56 he undertook a lecture tour to Japan, Israel, Germany and Austria for the US administration, which led to his appointment to the Salzburg Summer Academy, in 1959 he held a seminar in Lausanne, in 1962–64 he drew up plans for the city of Genoa, in 1969 he visited the Bauakademie in East Berlin and the Bauhausarchiv in West Berlin, in 1970 he was in the Soviet Union, in 1971 he sent a traveling exhibition about his work on tour, in 1973 he traveled through the GDR and Poland, in 1978 and 1979 through East Germany again. Parallel to this he held professorships and received numerous awards in the USA.

Wachsmann in Vienna

In the course of the global tour referred to above Wachsmann also came to Austria. Here he attended an "interdisciplinary manager seminar" at Semmering[30] and gave a lecture in Vienna under the title *Erziehung—Planung—Industrialisierung* (Education—Planning—Industrialization) that was to have a major impact. On 24 April 1956 the *Zentralvereinigung der Architekten (ZVA)* under President Erich Boltenstern, in collaboration with the *United States Information Agency (USIA)*, sent invitations to this momentous presentation that was given in the lecture theatre of MAK.[31] For established Viennese architects this meant a further confrontation with the technology-friendly branch of the avant-garde, which, despite a number of individual attempts by some architects and industrial companies in the period around 1930, had no tradition in Austria, but which now, through US exile, seemed to have achieved worldwide influence. Therefore, a serious attempt was made to examine this strategy. Roland Rainer, whose Stadthalle in Vienna was under construction at the time, and ZVA head Erich Boltenstern discussed their impressions of Wachsmann's lecture in the association's periodical *Der Bau*.[32] Rainer commented on Wachsmann's obsession with the most important construction detail of industrial building systems—the junction, a fixation that was more academic than suitable for the market: "Wachsmann has developed the detail, worked out with precision and thoroughness—not some detail or other but *the* characteristic detail of the ideal assembly of elements—into the "art of the joint," which for him is the starting point of the entire construction and, above and beyond this, the starting point of a venture into a new, unresearched area of design." As regards the discussion on the education of architects Rainer remarked that the idea of "elementary classes to develop an understanding of material and a feeling for construction" had certainly been cultivated in the Bauhaus but "it is also said to have existed in Vienna, e.g. under Strnad,—but that's a long time ago. Precisely in this area Wachsmann's observations could provide a direct stimulus for the further development of our own modern tradition."

Erich Boltenstern, who from 1929 to 1934 worked at what was then known as the Kunstgewerbeschule as assistant to Oskar Strnad (mentioned above by Rainer), could look at Wachsmann's ideas from the perspective of his (Boltenstern's) socialization in Viennese modernism—and even qualify them: "they apply first and foremost to America where, in terms of construction and technology, things are far more geared to the machine than is the case in Europe, but it seems likely that, here too, developments will increasingly take this direction." After describing Wachsmann's collectivist seminar system for the education of architects in teams, each with an uneven number of participants, Boltenstern also makes a comparison, without differentiating more closely, with Viennese modernism: "I remember only one teacher, Strnad, who from the deepest awareness of the basis of our lives and the world of forms that springs from this, followed a similar path to Wachsmann."

However, the impact of Wachsmann's lecture on the younger generation of architects, who had been trained according to far more traditional models and who thirsted for alternatives to the building industry of the reconstruction era that offered little in the way of innovation, was like a kind of enlightenment: "It made an incredible impression on us. Wachsmann seemed to offer much of what we had been looking for in Vienna in vain," Friedrich Kurrent recalls.[33]

Wachsmann's Rational Planning Method in Salzburg: "The Result Developed Logically of Its Own Accord"

The five summer seminars which Konrad Wachsmann held in Salzburg between 1956 and 1960 are described in detail in specialist literature.[34] Only two years after the start of the courses the first results of the work were documented and presented in Galerie Würthle in Vienna in the form of an exhibition and a catalog.[35] In 1960, the last year of the courses, an article appeared which presented the results of the "team work" of the first four years.[36] Wachsmann himself, 18 years after the last course, drew up a concluding balance of his involvement in Salzburg.[37]

Generally speaking, the memories of the fascinated course participants center on Wachsmann's innovative methods of work, and less on the concrete building designs that resulted from them. Compared to the familiar background of the traditional master classes in art schools and the technical universities of the Austrian system for

training architects, the open atmosphere of discussion, the formation of teams and the systematic course, followed by the studies
which were planned in the group, seemed entirely new. Although
the outcome initially remained open, the work was ultimately
steered towards certain goals, as Friedrich Achleitner, who took part
in the first two seminars in 1956 and 1957, recalls: "Anyone who
experienced the Wachsmann seminars, which were 'conducted' in a
masterly fashion, could even then have gained the impression that
Wachsmann himself, whether consciously or unconsciously, either
in a calculated or an instinctive way, aimed at a specific goal, at a
concrete idea of form, even though, until the very last minute, he
maintained the illusion that the procedure was entirely open." [38]

The collectivist teaching method was aimed at excluding individual "handwriting" and viewpoints as far as possible and at producing objectivity. The entire lengthy early history of the avant-
garde understanding of industrialized building, which, it was
believed, would replace "architecture" in an ideal future, had always
aimed at replacing individual, artistic planning of buildings by
rational collective methods—ultimately the full replacement of
artistic subjectivity by "objective" planning methods. "Industrialization" was only the expression of the total rationalization aimed at,
the machine was its tool, not its purpose.

At the first seminar in 1956 Wachsmann split up the 21 participants into seven groups of three. In the first two years the students'
eight-week practical work was done in the *Dombögen*, a suite of
rooms above the arcades that frame the late Renaissance ensemble on the Domplatz in Salzburg and connect the Residenz of the
Prince Bishops with the cathedral. [39] Friedrich Kurrent and Johannes
Spalt supported Wachsmann as assistants and had prepared themselves for this work by visiting the master at the *Hochschule für
Gestaltung* in Ulm. [40] Initially, concrete design tasks were avoided,
since first of all, the teams were to carry out general research work.
"The themes addressed were material/production, construction, elements, module, services planning and terms" [41] but also "joining and
connecting," Kurrent recalls. "The goal was always, on the basis of
these initial studies, to finally work on a joint project, of which a
model was also built." [42] The jointly designed building project in 1958
was a multi-functional events hall, which had been preceded in 1956
and 1957 by variable hall projects as examples of the application of a
modular technique that had been worked out earlier. [43]

On the way to the final joint project Wachsmann not only
ensured exchange of content through lectures by experts and above
all through the planned internal communication within the group,
but also saw to it that the individual design ideas remained anonymous: "As planning was done in weekly units (6 days) and a summa-
rizing discussion was envisaged for each weekend, the 'material'

had also to be divided into six parts. At the end of each day the teams exchanged information about the work they had done on the theme, i.e. they passed this information on, as at the end of the week each participant in the seminar had to be completely informed about all aspects of all the various problems. This procedure continued over several weeks and led to such a huge amount of written records and intermediate results that we could not imagine what the final results would look like. Wachsmann created this—from us—in a concluding and rhetorically brilliantly developed synopsis. For us the result was unique and also highly surprising, as it appeared to have developed entirely logically, as if of its own accord."[44]

The magic with which Wachsmann by the end of the seminar had drawn a concrete building plan from his amazed students and the bewildering wealth of material contradicts to a certain extent the rationalist aspirations of his method. He described this in a kind of manifesto in the 1958 exhibition catalog: "the existence of the machines determines the way we build in our time. The machine does not allow any arbitrary, individual decision about any theme. In contrast to something made manually, the industrially produced piece is part of a comprehensive order." And contemporary architectural training must, he said, orient itself on this fact: "The study plan is based on direct collaboration between all involved and on active work on analyzing the problems set. The results achieved do not depend on aptitudes and talents or on adapting the individual signature of a master but speak the objective language of what is today technically and organizationally possible, with the goal of shaping the image of our environment on the basis of present-day circumstances, while avoiding preconceived opinions." A fundamental reform of the training of planners would, he said, ultimately require the abolition of architectural design as a central subject: "during studies the various tasks set and the method used for working on a problem should be formulated as *the replacement of design theory*, in close collaboration with science, technology, industry, business and politics."[45]

In the 1958 exhibition catalog a number of key notions *On the Industrialization of Building*, which posed socio-political questions, were also printed: "The machine is the tool of our time. It is the cause of those effects through which the social order is manifested." Here, however, Wachsmann still interprets the possibilities of industry, which was already aware of consumer-oriented customization strategies, in a strictly mechanistic way: "in accordance with the circumstances of industrialization, through the multiplication of cell and element, the building should develop indirectly."

The catalog contribution written in Paris in 1957 by Swiss painter and sculptor Hugo Weber, who had worked together with Wachsmann at the Institute of Design at *IIT* in Chicago, follows the

same line. Weber was an author and filmmaker who, while an immi-
grant in the USA, had taught with Moholy-Nagy in the *New Bauhaus
Chicago*, he was a close friend of Mies van der Rohe, and in 1961
modeled a portrait bust of the famous architect. He made a striking
summary of Wachsmann's efforts to de-individualize building:
"building is burdened by habits, prejudices, and professional interests
like hardly any other area of our civilization. Securing for building
the best possibilities that machine-based techniques can offer
requires a more principle-based way of thinking and a more radical
approach. The works of Konrad Wachsmann can be discussed as an
alternative to an architectural movement that is expressed by a sculptural game: cube, space, façade, decoration. Fashion is contrasted
with the constants of a structural essence. A new anonymity of building on a technical basis is the goal, the expectation and the hope."[46]

Impact in Austria: New Planning Methods, New Professional Images

The almost one hundred male and two female participants in the
Salzburg summer courses, which several architects attended twice
and two enthusiasts [47] even three times, absorbed Wachsmann's
message, which was conveyed over the course of two short months,
in very different ways. Given the reality of the building industry in
Austria the "radical approach" mentioned above had to remain a
dream, as did the establishment of a research institute for industrial
building, which a number of the approximately 20 Austrian Wachsmann students unsuccessfully strove for.[48] Since the exhibition in
Vienna, the 1958 catalog and the appearance of his programmatic
text "Wendepunkt im Bauen" ("A Turning Point in Building") in
1959[49], Wachsmann made a clearly perceptible, more general impact
in Austria in the areas of architecture theory and planning methods.

It was Ottokar Uhl, who attended the Wachsmann course in
1957, who most consistently implemented the idea that all the processes involved in building could be planned. Therefore, of the Austrian architects it was Uhl who came closest to the avant-garde
ideal of the Wachsmann generation—rational planning as an instrument for social change. For Uhl, too, "technology" did not stop
short of social processes and should be made to serve them—rather
than the other way around. Shaped by and active in a Catholic
milieu, he saw human needs not as ballast for "overall" technoid
planning ideas but as the basis for socially oriented building. For
him any functions of building other than those that are communally
oriented—from the church to social housing—were inconceivable.
In making the connection between material and immaterial categories he defined the social field as a suitable area of action for
"technology" in general and for rational planning in particular: user
requirements, just like the technical and industrial preconditions
for building, were to be defined as parameters and integrated in

planning. This was how Uhl's participation models, which integrated individual user wishes in a rational planning *and* construction system, developed. Using largely industrialized building methods which could, however, be adapted in a modular way, he established a solid social basis for Wachsmann's ideas about "process-oriented planning"[50] for the first time. Uhl implemented this combination of participatory planning and industrialized construction methods in many housing projects. In the area of sacred building with his *Montagekirche* (literally: assembled church) system from 1962 he used the fundamental principles of Wachsmann's constructions of tubes and nodes in a more consistent way than most other Austrian architects.[51]

In the highly diverse work of Hans Hollein, who had taken part in the very first course in Salzburg, the inspiration he may have found is presented in a richly facetted way, as Wachsmann "approached things at a higher level than that of a universally applicable modernism."[52] Even before the first summer academy course, in his graduation thesis project in 1956 Hollein showed a World Fair pavilion with a space frame roof made from spatially organized tubes, demonstrating his awareness of advanced contemporary constructions. Shortly after taking part in the summer academy he studied between 1958 and 1959 at the *Illinois Institute of Technology*, where Wachsmann had taught from 1949 to 1954 and Ludwig Mies von der Rohe was about to retire. But even in 1959–60, while attending the *University of California in Berkeley*, Hollein used an organic archaicizing method of expression that was clearly also influenced by late Surrealism and early Pop Art. The individualization strategies of postmodern consumer society ultimately inspired him to develop systematic *design research*, which, in the broadest sense, could also be understood as a further development of Wachsmann's research-based planning strategies. This way of working was given visible expression in the exhibition *MAN transFORMS*, which Hollein conceived jointly with Lisa Taylor for the opening of the *Cooper Hewitt Museum of Design* in New York in 1976.

As an assistant at Hollein's *Institut für Design* at the University of Applied Arts in Vienna, Hermann Czech also worked on this exhibition. He had attended the summer academy courses in 1958 and 1959 and during his second year worked there as an assistant. Like Ottokar Uhl and Hans Hollein Czech also interpreted Wachsmann's theory at a more fundamental than formal level. It consisted, he said, "of the belief that design decisions could not be based on 'inspiration' but must be worked out methodically, partly because it must be possible to reproduce each of these ideas at the scale of industrial production in an unlimited way. Wachsmann's theory was borne by his belief in the technology of prefabrication, but behind this lay the intellectual aspects of planning responsibility and architectural quality. From the modular problems of prefabrication Wachsmann could open eyes to the structure of a Gothic hall or to the way the corner is solved in a Renaissance palace. In this world of ideas the formal concept does not stand at the beginning but rather at the end of the design process."[53] As early as 1959 Czech had searched in the Salzburg course for ways of inventively interpreting modular building principles with the greatest of freedom and proposed "equating the two central terms of modular addition—*element* and *connection*—viewing the connection as an element, thus being able to leave the orthogonal grid."[54]

Modular and Serial Building Methods in Austria since 1956

In modular methods of construction using industrially prefabricated elements Wachsmann's ideas were widely employed in Austria in numerous projects by his summer academy students Gerhard Garstenauer, Johann Georg Gsteu, Franz Kiener, Friedrich Kurrent, Johannes Spalt and Gunther Wawrik: in the 1960s steel constructions made of tubes and nodes, prefabricated concrete elements in the form of columns and beams, wall systems of steel and plastic panels, and a fundamental modular organization of the designs—fed from diverse sources[55]—had essentially become the mainstream of international modernism. Consequently, in Austria it was not only Wachsmann's students—to whom our presentation must be confined—who built a construction-based, light and modular modernism—reference should be made here to the pioneering work of Traude and Wolfgang Windbrechtinger, as representatives, and to the projects by Josef Lackner. In the miraculous years of apparently unlimited economic growth these building methods represented an undiluted belief in progress, like almost no other cultural practice. In addition—like contemporary paintings by abstract expressionists, which could be encountered in many of these buildings—they also clearly stood for the Western orientation of Austrian society in the Cold War. With Wachsmann at the forefront, constructive modernism was able to point to roots in the USA. By contrast, the other roots stemming from the 1920s German avant-garde were ideally suited to the early welfare state, which increasingly acquired a social democratic stamp.

The range of Wachsmann's reception in Austria extended across several areas of building, among which public commissions were dominant, in particular those from the Catholic church. At that time the Church followed a remarkable course marked by growth and a process of opening up, which led to numerous innovative sacred and community buildings. In Austria during this era it was almost only the Church which had the will and the potential to realize advanced contemporary architecture on a large scale. To what extent modular and prefabricated construction methods were employed in that area is exemplified by *Kolleg St. Josef* in Salzburg-Aigen, which the

Wachsmann students Friedrich Kurrent and Johannes Spalt, together with Wilhelm Holzbauer following his return from America, built in 1961–64 under the name Arbeitsgruppe 4: the residential and sacred building measuring 40 × 40 m was erected on the basis of a 2.5 × 2.5 m grid, with a centrally positioned arena chapel as a modular structured steel building with V-shaped roof beams which were exposed and therefore determined the nature of the interior. For his former students Wachsmann's visit to this building after his teaching work in Salzburg represented the master's recognition of their design achievement.[56]

The Arbeitsgruppe 4 had followed similar concepts between 1958 and 1961, together with Johann Georg Gsteu in the project for the *Seelsorgezentrum Steyr-Ennsleiten*. Here Wachsmann's idea of developing modular constructions out of as few prefabricated elements as possible was implemented in the form of X-shaped concrete columns which—stacked and connected with large concrete frames—could be combined in different ways to make building volumes of different sizes and proportions for the various functions of the church, the community center and the bell tower. In his *Seelsorgezentrum Baumgartner Spitz* in Vienna in 1960–65 Gsteu realized a similar radical modular construction made of concrete on a grid of 1.80 m, which through the use of cantilevering roof ribs created an impressive, column-free interior in the crystalline proportions of 1:1:1.

With his projects for Bad Gastein from 1968 onwards Gerhard Garstenauer demonstrated how Wachsmann's principle could be used in the area of tourism. In the *Kongresshaus* and in the *Felsenbad* he carried out large modular concrete skeleton frame constructions using prefabricated elements. The roof of the *Kongresshaus* was given four large light domes in geodesic construction made of steel tubes and nodes. A number of these lightweight constructions were flown by helicopter to the local skiing area where they were used as lift stations.[57]

In the same year Franz Kiener, who had attended the first Wachsmann course in 1956, demonstrated with the design of his own remarkable house in Salzburg-Gneis the possibilities of realizing buildings at a small, private scale that were conceived on a modular basis and made of prefabricated elements.[58] Gunther Wawrik had also attended the first course in 1956 and together with his partner Hans Puchhammer from 1961 carried out the *Markart House* in Perchtoldsdorf, the *Grothusen Office Building* in Vienna and the *Landesmuseum Eisenstadt*, a series of exemplary, strictly construction-based designs that used modular concepts and prefabricated elements.

Although this selection makes no claim to be complete, the participants in the Salzburg courses mentioned above and the projects referred to illustrate the relatively wide reception of Wachsmann in Austria in the 1960s. The fundamental and systemic nature of Wachsmann's theory, which had already been widely published,[59] ensured that a number of its elements can be encountered in almost all innovative architecture theories from this time (in some cases developed further by other thinkers)—whether in the form of conviction about the fundamentally modular, additive structure of building (as opposed to a more sculptural understanding), in the rationalization ideals of modernism, or in the shape of a general doubt about the relevance of intuitive, individual design strategies in the industrial era.

Perspectives: Do Architects Abolish Themselves?

This *rationalist* tendency of late modernism can be seen as a kind of revival of the idealistic, social reform ideologies of classic modernism. For this reason alone, it was anything but rational in all its aspects, for instance as regards the efficiency of means used —the performance of certain Wachsmann constructions could be matched or even surpassed by "conventional" building methods in less time and with less expenditure. This also applied to the most important criterion of consumer society, which during the Wachsmann revival in the 1960s was advancing at full steam in the West —that is the individualization and distinguishing of the consumer at all levels. These individual constructions of identity could be realized through a constantly differentiated mix of industrial and manual, "modern" and traditional readymade offers from the exploding building and decorating, consumer and user goods industries with a considerably lower expenditure of material and thought than would have ever been possible using the elements of a building kit: thanks to standardization it is possible to produce elements of the system building method inexpensively, but their concrete use always involves time-consuming recombination. Seen from this perspective the reintroduction of Wachsmann's reflections on basic standardizations which had, in fact, already been established during the early industrialization period, came decades too late, did not go far enough, and was completely out of touch with the technical and economic reality of consumer society.

The happy, naive and, quite literally, oblivious phase of postwar reconstruction consumer society was, however, only short-lived. The first resources crisis at the beginning of the 1970s clearly revealed its limits. Now (architectural) history repeated itself yet again: like in the early 19th century industrialization era the scientific, technical sector reacted far more quickly to the new situation than the aesthetic-creative sector. The basic motor forces of industrialization are the permanent increase in productivity, along with the improved quality that it makes possible. They now focused on consumer society's exploding need for the processing of information. In order to process it more efficiently using computing technology, the growing flood of data had to be coded more simply than was possible with language or images in the non-electronic communication of the human nature—and so recourse was made to binary data coding, which Claude Shannon had invented in the 1930s. As electrical circuits these data could be processed extremely quickly in calculating machines (processors) which, with the invention of transistors and integrated circuits, were developed into increasingly efficient computers from the 1960s onwards.

The analogy between industrialization and digitalization postulated by Nerdinger and others[60] would deliver sobering results as regards the situation that has developed since then: as with the *Crystal Palace* in London in 1851, when this revolutionary building made of prefabricated iron and glass elements was not recognized by a single expert as "architecture" and the construction industry continued to use historic materials and forms for a further half a century, at around the same time as the emergence of digitalization postmodern architecture's most intensive heyday began, as a more or less conscious counter-reaction. And so, just as industrial production had already achieved an advanced level of sophistication by around 1920 when the architectural avant-garde, having finally noticed its potential, used the dogma of standardization to interpret it in a romanticized and archaicized way that fell short of the mark, in much the same manner the creative branch is today using digitalization often in an uncritical, backward-looking and aestheticizing way.

Wachsmann failed to recognize the pragmatic nature of industry, which, far from striving for technical perfection, in fact only aims for productivity in the sense of efficiently meeting demand—with whatever means are needed. Through his aestheticizing drive towards perfection Wachsmann made excessive demands on industry, while by exaggerating standardization he did not demand enough in term of adaptability—both failings are illustrated in an exemplary fashion by the *General Panel Corporation*. Today Mario Carpo, in his analysis of current digital planning practices, confirms the existence of something similar: on account of current designers' naivety and their fundamental lack of understanding of the nature of *artificial intelligence* (AI), which is ultimately based on a "new, post-scientific logic," Carpo says: "we are likely to make a terrible mess of it, and of what remains of our own scientific logic at the same time."[61]

Just as Wachsmann and the avant-garde of his time reduced the complex system "industry" to "standardization" and the "machine," ignoring the reference system "market" that lies at the base of it, according to Carpo we are today using the rigid *trial and error* methods of AI in an irrational, artisan-like, even pre-industrial way:

"today's computational tools work like artisans, not like engineers."
Just as the avant-garde once believed in the social healing power of
the aesthetically standardized and constructively beautiful, today,
like in the Middle Ages, we again believe in magic, the magic of
digital robotics: "... the magical virtue of computational trial and
error. Making is a matter of feeling, not thinking: *just do it*. Does it
break? Try again ... and again ... and again. Or even better, let the
computer try them all (optimize). The idiotic stupor (literally) and
ecstatic silence that are often the primary pedagogical tools in many
of today's advanced computational studios rightly apprehend the
incantatory appeal of the whole process: whether something works,
or not, no one can or cares to tell why."[62]

Alongside this new anti-rationality, which is borne by AI and is
described by Carpo as a danger to civilization ("Why waste time to
argue? Ask the crowds. Why waste time on a theory? Just try it and
see if it works."), today on the practical level, too, the current AI
euphoria in the planning branch is confronted by numerous critical
questions. In different forms these questions have always accompanied the history of modernism. They include an aestheticism that is
detached from the world as well as avant-garde concepts that are far
removed from the reality of the market or the marginalization of
the architect—possibly partly caused by these phenomena. They
are all based on the general specialization process of evolution.
Since the start of modern times it advanced the development of a
concept of art which increasingly specialized in pure aesthetics and
viewed new social and technical developments exclusively from
this perspective. There are legitimate reasons for this: as, throughout
human history, ordered formal structures have always proven to be
indications of positive functionality, they were interpreted as beautiful.[63] And so artistic aestheticism, as the idealization of what is
made by man, the human(istic), developed a long, socially effective
tradition which extends from the beautiful cathedral to the perfect
Renaissance city plan to the meaningful, handcrafted beauty of the
Arts and Crafts movements. But in the course of this development
the potency of the beautiful was eroded: from an overall competence
in every aspect of environmental design, which, as a gift of God, it
still possessed in the Middle Ages, today, through specialization, it
has become just one of many sales arguments.

The logical reaction to this would be a de-specialization of the
architects who must emancipate themselves from the mere robotic
production of beauty (in form, construction and production) and
turn to the ultimately political questions about the distribution of
resources. The lack of pragmatism that caused Wachsmann's constructive technoid aestheticism to fail, today threatens the further
existence of the architect's social role. The world's problems in the
area of building are not of a technical or beauty-related nature but

are mainly political and economic. Practical, efficient and sustainable hybrid technologies for the basal infrastructure in developing countries and, in developed countries, for the adaptation of buildings to meet climate change have been available for a long time. Using them at a large scale basically needs *AI* just as little as, in the 1960s, the perfect industrially produced node was needed to create large amounts of reasonably priced and acceptable housing. If architects reject this social responsibility and prefer instead to invest their creativity in virtual technologies, then the architectural profession will be at stake. Architects themselves could be replaced by *IT* experts who, after all, are the real trained specialists for the development of digital tools.

1   On the analogy of the industrialization and digitalization of building cf. Winfried Nerdinger, Rainer Barthel, Richard Junge, Roland Krippner und Frank Petzold (eds.), *Wendepunkt/e im Bauen. Von der seriellen zur digitalen Architektur*, Munich (Detail, Institut für internationale Architektur-Dokumentation), 2010.

2   Established Nazi architects such as Friedrich Tamms, Wilhelm Kreis and Herbert Rimpl also left their stamp on the reconstruction of German cities that had been destroyed in the war.

3   Friedrich Kurrent says that, in response to a suggestion by Spalt and Kurrent the Salzburg art dealer and co-founder of the Summer Academy, Friedrich Welz, contacted the German postwar reconstruction pioneer Egon Eiermann as a possible successor to Hans Hofmann. Eiermann in turn suggested

Wachsmann, as he said that at the Technische Hochschule in Karlsruhe Wachsmann "is only ruining my students." Kurrent and Spalt supported this proposal, as only a short time earlier they had been greatly impressed by Wachsmann's theories on planning and training as outlined in the lecture he gave in Vienna on 24.4.1956 (conversation with the author, 2.12.2017).—My thanks to Friedrich Kurrent for providing much helpful information and correcting various perspectives.

4   Around one quarter of the roughly 100 architects who took part in the five Summer Academy courses between 1956 and 1960 came from Austria. The published lists of participants (Barbara Wally, *Die Ära Kokoschka. Internationale Sommerakademie für bildende Kunst Salzburg 1953–63*, Salzburg, 1993, pp. 191–198) are, however,

incomplete. Wachsmann did not choose his students according to their qualifications but strictly according to the order in which they registered—the first 21 candidates of a year were allowed to take part (information provided by Hermann Czech, 18.4.2018).— My thanks to Hermann Czech for providing much valuable information and correcting various perspectives.

5   Gerhard Garstenauer's reminiscences show that the different orientations of German and Austrian modernism were clear to the young architects of the 1950s: "At that time the Germans expressed their special relationship to industry, while the Austrians proved their 'feeling for handcraft'"(cf. Max Eisler in the volume Österreichische Werkkultur, 1916)—Gerhard Garstenauer, "Begegnung mit Konrad Wachsmann," in: Ina Stegen (ed.),

Das schönster Atelier der Welt.
25 Jahre Internationale Sommer-
akademie für bildende Kunst,
Salzburg, 1978, p. 54.

6   On the creation of this term cf.
Sigfried Giedion, *Mechanization*
Takes Command. A Contribution to
Anonymous History, New York,
1948, as well as Carlo Testa, *Die*
Industrialisierung des Bauens, Zurich
(Artemis) 1972—On the "philoso-
phy" of Wachsmann see Barbara
Dafft, *Autopoiesis. Die Genese des*
"Grape Vine Project" (1953) von
Konrad Wachsmann, master degree
thesis, ETH, Zurich 2009—On
the parallels in Concrete Art see
Richard Paul Lohse, *Normung*
als Strukturprinzip, in: werk/oeuvre
3/1974, pp. 348–354.

7   As an example of a superficial understanding of Wachsmann, Hermann
Czech mentions the former Casino
and Café Winkler on the Mönchsberg
in Salzburg by Cziharz Lenk-Meixner,
erected in 1974 and replaced between 2002–2004 by the new building for the Museum der Moderne by
Friedrich-Hoff-Zwink (discussion
with the author, 18.4.2018).

8   On the convergence of aesthetic
and political concepts see Boris
Groys, *Gesamtkunstwerk Stalin,*
Munich 1988.—Wachsmann student
Ottokar Uhl also deals with the
aesthetic consequences of rationalization and participation, "Thesen
zu einer Aneignung einer eigenen
Gestaltungskultur (Ästhetik) für
Betroffene," in: ibid., *Gegen-Sätze.*
Architektur als Dialog. Ausgewählte
Texte aus vier Jahrzehnten, Picus,
Vienna, 2003, pp. 180–181—As
far as I am aware no examinations of
the aesthetic dimension of the
industrialization ideal in general and
of the work of Wachsmann in
particular have as yet been made.

9   Gilbert Herbert, *The Dream of the*
Factory-Made House, Walter Gropius
and Konrad Wachsmann, The MIT
Press, Cambridge, 1984, pp. 67f.

10   Not even after his on-site analysis
of the 1851 Great Exhibition in
London and his experience of the
Crystal Palace did Gottfried
Semper, the leading German architecture theorist of the 19th
century, include the iron and glass
construction in his fundamental
categories of material in building.

11   Herbert (see note 9), p. 12.
12   Ibid, pp. 13, 89.
13   Konrad Wachsmann, Einführung,
manuscript for an exhibition
catalog, Konrad-Wachsmann-Archiv,
AdK, Berlin—On the "system
character" of modernism's vision
of industrialization see Herbert
(see note 9), pp. 7f., as well as
Steeve Sabatto, "Totipotenz und
Automation bei Konrad Wachsmann,"
in: Laurent Stalder and Georg
Vrachliotis, *Fritz Haller. Architekt*
und Forscher, gta Verlag, Zurich,
2015.

14   Winfried Nerdinger, *Walter Gropius,*
exhibition catalog, Gebrüder Mann,
Berlin, 1985, p. 12.
15   Nerdinger (see note 14), pp. 82–89.
16   Herbert (see note 9).
17   Nerdinger (see note 14), p. 19.
18   Ibid, p. 22.
19   Herbert (see note 9), p. 106.
20   Josef Hoffmann adapted houses for
Heinrich Böhler and recommended
Heinrich Tessenow to design Böhler's
villa in St. Moritz, Hans Böhler was
an important Expressionist painter
of the Secession movement and the
Neukunstgruppe.
21   Eduard F. Sekler, *Josef Hoffmann.*
Das Werk des Architekten,
Residenz, Salzburg, 1982, p. 412;
Standardhäuser—Die Häuslbauer,
exhibition catalog, Architektur-
zentrum Vienna, 1997.
22   Konrad Wachsmann, *Holzhausbau—*
Technik und Gestaltung, Wasmuth,
Berlin, 1930.
23   Overview of Wachsmann's personal
network in Michael Grüning,
Der Architekt Konrad Wachsmann,
Erinnerungen und Selbstauskünfte,
Löcker, Vienna, 1986 (= *Der*
Wachsmann-Report, Verlag der
Nation, Berlin, 1986).
24   Ibid, p. 223.
25   Dietmar Strauch und Bärbel Högner,
Konrad Wachsmann. Stationen
eines Architekten, Progris, Berlin,
2013—Claudia Klinkenbusch,
Das Konrad Wachsmann-Haus in
Niesky. Ein Holzbau der Moderne,
Lusatia, Bautzen, 2014—Steeve
Sabatto, *Innovation technique et*
programmation technologique dans
le contexte nord-américain de
l'après seconde guerre mondiale et
de la Guerre Froide. L'œuvre
architecturale de Konrad Wachs-
mann (1942–72) comme étude de

cas, Dissertation, EHESS Centre
Alexandre Koyré, Paris 2017—
Marianne Burkhalter and Christian
Sumi (eds.), *Konrad Wachsmann*
and the Grapevine Structure, Park
Books, Zurich, 2018.
26   Herbert (see note 9), pp. 299f.
27   "After having produced so many
canons, aircraft, and train carriages
in factories, one asks oneself:
couldn't houses be made in the
factory, too?"– Le Corbusier,
Kommende Baukunst, DVA, Berlin
and Leipzig, 1962, p. 197.
28   Matthias Boeckl, "Villen in Los
Angeles—Siedlungen in Puerto
Rico," in: ibid., *Visionäre &*
Vertriebene. Österreichische Spuren
in der modernen amerikanischen
Architektur, Ernst & Sohn, Berlin,
1995, pp. 320f.
29   It was scholarships of this kind
that enabled Hans Hollein and
Wilhelm Holzbauer, who were later
to become pioneers of postmodern
architecture, to study in the USA.
30   Grüning (see note 23), pp. 549f.
As Friedrich Kurrent recalls it may
well have been at this seminar
that contact was established with
Karl Schwanzer, and consequently,
with the Zentralvereinigung der
Architekten, which ultimately
brought Wachsmann to Vienna.
31   Expenses report from 27.4.1956,
Zl. 337–56, MAK, Vienna.
32   Konrad Wachsmann, "Planung und
Erziehung," in: *Der Bau* 5–6/1956,
pp. 120–121.
33   Kurrent (see note 3)
34   Among others in: Gerhard
Garstenauer, *Begegnung mit Konrad*
Wachsmann, in: Ina Stegen (see
note 5), p. 52–55.—Friedrich
Kurrent, "Konrad Wachsmann," in:
ibid., *Texte zur Architektur,* Müry,
Salzburg, 2006, pp. 194–199
—Bernhard Steger, "Das utopische
Potential des Bauens. Konrad
Wachsmann und die österreichische
Nachkriegsavantgarde," in: Elisabeth
Großegger und Sabine Müller (eds.),
Teststrecke Kunst. Wiener
Avantgarden nach 1945, Sonderzahl,
Vienna, 2012, pp. 250–259.
—Marko Pogacnik, "Konrad Wachs-
mann and The Teamwork Concept
in Salzburg. A Conversation with
Friedrich Kurrent and Hermann
Czech," in: Burkhalter and Sumi (see
note 25), pp. 134–139.

35   Konrad Wachsmann, *Bauen in
      unserer Zeit*, catalog for the exhibi-
      tion organized by the International
      Summer Academy for Visual Art
      Salzburg and the Zentralvereinigung
      der Architekten, Galerie Würthle,
      Vienna, 20.1.–22.2.1958.

36   "Teamarbeit an der Salzburger
      Sommerakademie," in: *Bauen +
      Wohnen* 10/1960, pp. 368–381.

37   Konrad Wachsmann, "Teamarbeit im
      Seminar," in: Ina Stegen (see note
      5), pp. 48–51.—His recollections
      also in Grüning (see note 23),
      pp. 549–51.

38   Friedrich Achleitner, Vorbemerkung,
      in: Grüning (see note 23), p. 6.

39   Kurrent (see note 3).

40   Pogacnik (see note 34), p. 134.

41   Steger (see note 34), p. 253.

42   Kurrent (see note 3).

43   Teamarbeit (see note 36).

44   Garstenauer (see note 34), p. 53.

45   Wachsmann 1958 (see note 35),
      pp. 18–20, emphasis Matthias
      Boeckl.

46   Hugo Weber, "Bau und Maschine," in:
      Wachsmann 1958 (see note 35), p. 9.

47   Andrew Rothe and Peter Schmid.

48   Kurrent (see note 3).

49   The first edition of this work
      appeared in Krausskopf-Verlag,
      Wiesbaden.

50   Ottokar Uhl, Prozesshaftes Planen
      (1993–), in: Bernhard Steger,
      *Vom Bauen. Zu Leben und Werk von
      Ottokar Uhl*, Dissertation,
      Technische Universität Wien, 2005,
      pp. 185f.

51   Uhl was also a pioneer in dissemi-
      nating the participatory SAR planning
      method, which came from Holland,
      in the area of industrialized building.
      This was then taken up by younger
      architects like Georg Reinberg who
      today still practice their planning
      strategies for social and building
      technology processes in this way, cf.
      Georg W. Reinberg, Matthias Boeckl
      (ed.), *Reinberg. Ökologische Archi-
      tektur. Entwurf-Planung-Ausführung*,
      Springer, Vienna-New York, 2008,
      pp. 10–16.

52   Quoted from Bernhard Steger, see
      note 34, p. 255.

53   Hermann Czech, *Über Konrad
      Wachsmann, Karl Kraus und Adolf
      Loos*, contribution to the exhi-
      bition *ex libris*, Architekturforum
      Tirol (aut), Innsbruck 2002—
      As regards Wachsmann's interest in

      architectural history Czech refers to
      the former's documentation of old
      buildings in an album of his own
      photographs: Konrad Wachsmann,
      Aspekte, Krausskopf, Wiesbaden,
      1961.

54   Hermann Czech, "Architektur, von
      der Produktion her gedacht," in:
      Hintergrund, no. 41, Architekturzen-
      trum Wien 2009, p. 25.

55   These also included Frei Otto, who
      —for his part shaped by Mies van
      der Rohe and the US engineering
      tradition—had been realising light-
      weight shell structures and modular
      construction systems since the
      1950s.

56   Kurrent (see note 3).

57   Gerhard Garstenauer, *Interven-
      tionen*, Pustet, Salzburg, 2002.

58   Ingrid Holzschuh (ed.), *Franz Kiener.
      Eine Ordnung als Anfang*, Park
      Books, Zurich, 2016, pp. 48–49.

59   Wachsmann's bestseller *Wendepunkt
      im Bauen* had appeared in 1959.

60   Nerdinger, see note 1.

61   Mario Carpo, *The Second Digital
      Turn. Design Beyond Intelligence*,
      The MIT Press, London-Cambridge,
      2017, p. 162.

62   Ibid, p. 164.

63   On the evolutionary function of
      the beautiful, see Wolfgang Welsch,
      *Blickwechsel. Neue Wege der
      Ästhetik*, Reclam, Stuttgart, 2012.

WF   My dear Eckhard, I'm delighted as always to be visiting you here in Bregenz! As we've discussed on the phone, our task today is to speak about Konrad Wachsmann, the man and his work, and your personal connection to him. How did you meet him, what fascinated you and what drew you to him?

ES-F   I learned about Wachsmann from the first German-language publication on the Hangar in *Baukunst* und *Werkform*.[1]

WF   When was this publication released?

ES-F   I don't remember the exact date, but it must have been in the mid-fifties. At the time Wachsmann had also come to Aachen for several days to attend a symposium. I was then working with my partners Altenstadt and Rudloff on plans for the Landeshaus in Cologne[2]—a project that stood in the tradition of Mies. Shortly after it was completed our team broke apart, and that gave me the opportunity to focus more on structural issues. This new orientation ultimately brought me to the *Space City*.

WF   When did you begin working on the *Space City*?

ES-F   I'd say as early as 1958. I couldn't share my ideas on spatial structures with the team. I had the feeling it was just my own business.

WF   What happened after the team broke apart?

ES-F   I'd say I had become used to working with spatial structures and did a lot of theoretical work, which of course did not translate into money (*laughs*). Fortunately, we didn't have any financial slack with the construction of the Landhaus.

WF   Were there any role models that were important to you at the time?

ES-F   The first figure that interested me, and whom I engaged with, was Mies van der Rohe. Very much like with Wachsmann, I had become aware of him, too, through a publication, more specifically, the master plan based on a rigid grid surface for the IIT campus in Chicago.

WF   How does Mies relate to Wachsmann in terms of your own work with spatial structures?

ES-F   Well, Wachsmann's Hangar hit like a bomb. Wachsmann then also worked for a long time in Austria, at the Summer Academy in Salzburg.[3]

WF   What appealed to you about the Hangar?

ES-F   This exemplary prefabrication, which has a claim to universality, even if I still believe today that the Hangar didn't quite do justice to it. I can remember exactly how I first measured the floor height of the Hangar on the basis of the model photographs, the floor being about three meters high. I thought to myself: you can pack almost anything into it!

WF   I take it you were not only intrigued by the structure and

Eckhard Schulze-Fielitz in Conversation with Wolfgang Fiel

Bregenz, March 13, 2018

Eckhard Schulze-Fielitz, Wolfgang Fiel; Fig.: 79–83

its claim to universal prefabrication, but also by the question of how to fill it?

ES-F   Precisely. That was and still is a central issue for me!

WF   We can assume that Wachsmann didn't ask himself this question. The support frame was supposed to cover as big a space as possible without load-bearing elements, as elegantly and as efficiently as possible.

ES-F   That's also what I reproached him for, in spite of all my respect, that he left all potential spaces unused that could have been used. There would have been other options, tires or what have you.

WF   Can you elaborate a bit on the aspect of the useful spaces in relation to the structure?

ES-F   At the time, I, like Yona[4], was interested in structure as a space-generating framework, which we had detached from existing urban development. We thus created useful spaces that could, in a certain sense, be placed over the existing topography as an additional layer. Yona generally interpreted this topography in an urban sense, which was not necessarily the case for me. What Wachsmann proposed with the Hangar was, as you've already said, to create a space as free as possible of load-bearing elements below the structure, which, in his case, assumed the function of a roof.

WF   Why do you think that he conceived the Hangar as an exemplary development of a space frame?

ES-F   Well, there was a project commissioned by the US Air Force. I don't know how he got it. Shortly before his book was published[5] he came back from a trip around the world which had been covered by the Air Force and on which he had given talks all over the world. He was a terrific storyteller, very good with words. His lectures were full of great photographs that he had taken on his journeys. And he made scathing remarks about his competitors. I remember, for instance, him saying that he didn't understand the world anymore with reference to Le Corbusier's Ronchamp.

WF   That's all the more amazing given that Wachsmann himself worked for a short time in Le Corbusier's office and basically saw in him an ally in propagating industrial building. Do you also remember colleagues being named whom he saw as a role model? Buckminster Fuller is someone who immediately comes to mind.

ES-F   He had a rather egomaniac disposition (*laughs*) even though he developed a prefab house together with Walter Gropius. This, however, didn't leave any lasting impression on me.[6] For me the connections to the Space City were more important, they were perfectly obvious.

WF   Did you discuss these connections with Friedman, did he engage with Wachsmann?

ES-F   I can't remember Friedman referring to Wachsmann or dealing with his work. At the time it wasn't like everything that emerged in the United States was immediately disseminated and taken up in Europe.

WF   Did you ever have the urge to talk with Wachsmann in person or to meet him?

ES-F   Well, it just simply happened! At the end of the fifties the city of Essen planned the so-called *German Building Exhibition*[7] where a congress was also supposed to take place. Since I already had a certain renown because of the Landhaus, the *Space City* and the church in Eller that was in the process of being built, they asked me whom they should invite. My list did not include heroes such as Mies or Le Corbusier but largely young names that were not so well-known at the time in Germany such as Frei Otto, Buckminster Fuller, Yona Friedman who wasn't known at all then, Kenzo Tange or Konrad Wachsmann.[8] Friedman later wrote at some point that the city of Essen had written to these people and they all came. In my view it was an outstanding congress.

WF   And as the one who compiled the list did you get to know all of them?

ES-F   In any case they all came to Essen. It was very interesting to experience and rub shoulders with all the great figures appearing on the horizon at the time!

WF   You also erected your own pavilion at this *DEUBAU* event, which the participants of the congress also got to see, I assume. Did you get any immediate responses to it?

ES-F   They must have seen it. It stood there smack in the center of the grounds.[9] It made a bigger impression on people than on me myself. I didn't have the feeling the visitors noticed that it was actually an expandable and thus unfinished building. That there was also an exhibition inside of it was only secondary for me at the time.

WF   Did you talk about your Space City with Wachsmann?

ES-F   Yes, after the congress. We drank several cups of coffee together and his reaction to the *Space City* was basically positive. I think also because my first thoughts on it were still more influenced by structural issues and less by its possible use.

WF   Your later development was mainly marked by your work on urban issues.

ES-F   Exactly. This interest didn't figure so much for Wachsmann as I see it.

WF   Which for him was perhaps one of the reasons why he didn't consider the possibility of filling it with something.

ES-F   Yes, I also reproached him for this, that he didn't take that small step further.

WF   Did he develop the technical and engineering-related solutions by himself or did he work with a team of experts on this?

ES-F   I know he had brilliant Japanese draftsmen in his office.

Moreover, his teaching activities at UCLA certainly reaped invaluable contacts with colleagues and talented students. What always fascinated me about Wachsmann was the suggestive power of his drawings. Also the fact that he solved the whole thing by cutting one single knot is very impressive! I didn't feel any guilt towards him.

WF   What do you mean by that Eckhard? Did he want to turn you into his accomplice and you said no?

ES-F   Since I began developing my *Space City* in the late fifties there was the real risk of it taking on the smack of plagiarism. However, there were major differences between our approaches. My model of the *Space City* was designed so that the spatial grid could be rotated in four different positions that I named alpha-, beta-, gamma- and delta-position. According to my definition the Hangar was to be classified as in alpha on the basis of a square prism, that is, a tetrahedron-octahedron package[10], which is why I always saw it as a potential *Space City*.

WF   Is this perspective related to the fact that unlike the first model of the *Space City* the later concrete application examples focused more on the question of implementation?

ES-F   Certainly, although I was in this sense, too, extremely taken by the unbelievably intricate elaboration of the Wachsmann designs, which at the time gave me the feeling that even architecture could be a manifestation of technological progress. Despite the fact that Wachsmann didn't build a whole lot there was never any doubt that the implementation or realization of his projects was very important to him. Since I, too, did not succeed in implementing my own *Space City* I have always seen Wachsmann as a kindred spirit in this respect, as someone who never gave up propagating technological advances in building and linking them to high formal standards.

WF   I think this is a wonderful final word and also an incentive for the coming generation. My dear Eckhard, I thank you warmly for this informative conversation!

ES-F   My pleasure (*laughs*).

1   Hangar for the us Air Force, pub-
     lished in *baukunst und werkform*,
     1954. See also "Hans Ulrich Obrist
     and Wolfgang Fiel in conversation
     with Eckhard Schulze-Fielitz" in:
     Wolfgang Fiel (ed.), *Eckhard
     Schulze-Fielitz, Metasprache des
     Raums/Metalanguage of Space*,
     Springer, Vienna/New York, 2010,
     p. 408.
2   Landeshaus Cologne (1955–59),
     Eckhard Schulze-Fielitz with Ulrich
     von Altenstadt and Ernst von Rudloff.
3   Wachsmann Master Class from
     1956 to 1969.
4   Ever since they met for the first
     time in 1959 Yona Friedman and
     Eckhard Schulze-Fielitz were bound
     by a close friendship, which also
     found architectural expression
     in a joint design for a bridge city
     over the English Channel (1963).
     Paying tribute to this special
     connection the Kunsthaus Bregenz
     in 2011 showed a dialogic pre-
     sentation of their works curated by
     Wolfgang Fiel and Eva Birkenstock.
5   *Wendepunkt im Bauen*, 1959.
6   "General Panel Corporation. A house
     to be built just with a hammer—
     1943," in: Konrad Wachsmann,
     "Timebridge, Konrad Wachsmann:
     An Autobiography," AdK, Konrad-
     Wachsmann-Archiv, Wachsmann
     2128, pp. 160, 184.
7   DEUBAU 62, German Building
     Exposition in Essen. The general
     themes of the congress were
     "Architecture and Urban Develop-
     ment. Siting and Goals" as well
     as "Design and Technology of
     Modern Space Structures." More-
     over, the main shows addressed
     urban planning, housing construc-
     tion, space structures, and school
     construction.
8   Apart from Eckhard Schulze-Fielitz,
     lectures were given by Felix Candela,
     Yona Friedman, Richard Buckminster
     Fuller, Zygmunt Stanislaw Makowski,
     Ernst May, Frei Otto, Hans Bernhard
     Reichow, Kenzo Tange and Konrad
     Wachsmann.
9   "DEUBAU Pavillon Essen," in:
     Wolfgang Fiel (ed.), *Eckhard
     Schulze-Fielitz, Metasprache des
     Raums/Metalanguage of Space*,
     Springer, Vienna/New York, 2010,
     pp. 110–111.
10   "Metaeder," in: Wolfgang Fiel (ed.),
     Metasprache des Raums / Meta-
     language of Space, Springer, Vienna/
     New York, 2010, pp. 358–395.

"During my stay in Los Angeles in the spring of 1963, I conveyed my idea of a building institute to the president of USC and to all people concerned. They accepted and promised to support such an institution and offered me the Armory Building across the campus, right above the Space Museum.

A year later the administration of USC and the Faculty of Architecture approved the creation of a building institute which was to start in the fall of 1964."[1]

Such was the version of events that Wachsmann offered in his unpublished autobiography, "Timebridge 1901–2001," which he wrote intermittently from the mid-1970s until his death in 1980. As is often the case, the reality of the situation was far more complicated.

Wachsmann was preceded in his move to Los Angeles by his former colleague from Chicago, Crombie Taylor, who had become associate dean of the USC School of Architecture in 1962. Taylor, who served as the acting director of the Institute of Design in the years from 1951–54, following the resignation of Serge Chermayeff, arrived at USC with a mandate to expand the school's graduate education programs.[2] One of Taylor's first acts as associate dean was to arrange for Wachsmann's appointment to the faculty as professor and director of the "Division of Building Research"; by the fall of 1964, the German architect was teaching at USC.

But contrary to the architect's recollection, no "building institute" existed at USC until May 1968, when Wachsmann's proposal for the "Building Institute at USC" was accepted by Sam T. Hurst, the dean of architecture, and by Dr. Milton Kloetzel, who was then the university's vice president for academic affairs.[3] Rather, Wachsmann had been first placed in charge of the school's "Building Research Division" in 1964, a departmental predecessor to the Building Institute, but nevertheless, an organization wholly different in kind. Indeed, before he ever arrived on campus, Wachsmann had already begun to make plans for something altogether more ambitious than just a graduate division in the architecture school.

Planning for what would become the Building Institute began in Italy in 1963, when Wachsmann was invited by Crombie Taylor to join the faculty at USC.[4] The two men had met several years prior in Chicago, where each had served at the faculty of the Institute of Design—what had been briefly called the "New Bauhaus." When they met, Wachsmann was working on his famous hangars for the US Air Force. Now, a decade later, Wachsmann was an aging, Bauhaus-era architect working in Genoa on what would ultimately be an ill-fated project to redevelop the city's port. He went to Los Angeles without hesitation.[5]

At USC, Taylor handed down a directive to reconceive the school's graduate programs, and accordingly, Wachsmann undertook a year-long study of the potential curriculum. This preliminary

Building Science: Konrad Wachsmann's Building Institute at the University of Southern California (USC), 1964–74

Phillip Denny; Fig.: 84–92

work was funded by the Graham Foundation, and took the form of a series of diagrams published in 1964. Wachsmann's proposed answer was the Building Institute, a research center that would allow graduate students to work collaboratively on funded research under the direction of faculty, in pursuit of a Master of Building Science.[6]

In some ways, the Institute replicated a model for conducting sponsored research that Wachsmann had developed at the Institute of Design a decade earlier. In Chicago, a government contract to produce a prefabricated building system for aircraft hangars had allowed Wachsmann and several students to develop tubular steel space frame structures over the course of five years. This first foray into sponsored research in the academic context, though it produced some of Wachsmann's best-known work, was not without difficulties.

Not long after Wachsmann's appointment to the faculty of the Institute of Design in January 1950—he was placed in charge of a "division for advanced building research and design,"—a clash erupted with the Institute's director Serge Chermayeff. After receiving the US Air Force research contract, Wachsmann proposed to enlist graduate students from the Institute of Design to assist the work in exchange for both pay and academic credits. Chermayeff refused the proposal, arguing that it represented unfair professional competition. In a letter to the dean of the Illinois Institute of Technology, Chermayeff cited his concern in setting "a very dangerous precedent for a school to undertake work which might be interpreted as an individual instructor's development of a private project cheaply with student labor."[7]

Simultaneously, a series of letters were circulated between Chermayeff and Bauhaus founder Walter Gropius, an ardent supporter of the so-called "New Bauhaus" in Chicago. Gropius did not mince words in his description of Wachsmann, a close friend and former collaborator in the General Panel Corporation: "Wachsmann, with all his charm, I know is so egocentric a man that I believe he should not be a teacher; his egoistic ambitions will always act like dynamite within a community with others. ... I have written directly to Wachsmann and have urged him to resign."[8] Wachsmann heeded his famous mentor's advice, relinquishing his position on May 15, 1951. Yet this was not to be the end for Wachsmann, but for Chermayeff, who resigned only a few weeks later.[9] Soon after, Wachsmann was back at the faculty, given a temporary, renewable contract under the acting dean of the Institute of Design, Crombie Taylor. Wachsmann's position in Chicago was contingent upon access to research funding, principally, the US Air Force contract, which lasted until 1955. He received his termination letter on March 31, 1955.[10]

The Building Institute at USC would also be premised on sponsored research, but finding sponsors proved to be a problem at first.

Although Wachsmann had been appointed in 1964, it wasn't until three years later, in 1967, that the Institute received its first sponsored research grant. In the meantime, the Institute pursued technical research in the context of Wachsmann's architecture practice, which was then engaged in the design of a city hall for California City. Although this project supported the Institute and its investigators, it represented only one small facet of the organization's stated mission as a "center of study, research, development, and information related to all aspects of industrialization and its impact upon planning and architecture."[11]

The founder of the Building Institute imagined it would be the nucleus of a continuously expanding network of allied disciplines spanning the sciences and the arts. In a memo to the university's president, Wachsmann outlined six basic components of the program: basic research, applied research, student training, teacher training, a doctoral program in building science, and an information center. The Institute would act as a medium for gathering the combined expertise of the university toward the transformation of the built environment. The scope and shape of the organization's mission had been defined in the series of diagrams that Wachsmann drafted soon after arriving in California, but it was the design of the Institute's space that would be tasked with translating these concepts into physical space.

As campus protests against the Vietnam War reached a boiling point at the end of the 1960s, Wachsmann, who had worked for the US military during and after World War II, established the Institute on the edge of the USC campus, in what was formerly the armory of the 160th Infantry Regiment. The building was well-suited to the Institute's needs: the vast drill hall at the center of the building gave researchers ample space to stage prototypes and exhibitions, and wings of offices on either side of the hall were renovated to accommodate the Institute's vision of an "interdisciplinary research organism." Successive drafts of the Institute's floorplan incrementally adapted the building to the structural clarity of the institutional diagram. Each space was developed in light of the essential activities of the Institute. For instance, the "laboratory" would be a machine shop for producing research prototypes, and the "information center" would provide a hard-wired connection to USC's mainframe computer and "include every possible medium of communication," according to its creator.

But the conference room was the heart of the Institute. Following the seminar protocols that Wachsmann had developed in the 1950s, structured discussions would be recorded and entered into the Institute's database for future reference. The ability to capture information as soon as it was broadcast allowed the Institute to close its own feedback loop back upon itself, recapturing information as an asset to future research. The social functioning of the room was strictly planned in Wachsmann's curriculum charts, which included a seating plan for optimum discussion between teams. Like the Building Institute's other spaces, the conference room was designed to facilitate the production and transmission of information. Whether taking the form of models, drawings, lectures, photographs, films, or prototypes, the Institute was essentially preoccupied with circulating information.

Maximizing the number of productive nodes enmeshed in the Institute's network was one strategy for raising the status of research. Bauhaus founder Walter Gropius and design theorist Horst Rittel both paid visits to the Institute, and Buckminster Fuller frequently stopped by on visits to Los Angeles during development of the "World Game" in the late 60s. Ludwig Mies van der Rohe also visited once, and in Wachsmann's recollection, the ailing master had to be lifted upstairs to the Institute by means of a forklift in the armory hall.[12] Fritz Haller, too, was a collaborator of the Institute from 1966–71, developing grid structures that anticipated his later commercial designs for building systems.

But the only project known to have been fully realized by the Institute was the Location Orientation Manipulator, "L.O.M.," a robotic arm designed by two doctoral students, John Bollinger and Xavier Mendoza. The purpose of the device was to study the "kinematics of prefabricated building," that is, the manipulation of objects in space. It was funded by a three-year grant from the Weyerhaeuser lumber corporation, and marked the Institute's definitive move into "basic research." That approach to work, which was defined by Vannevar Bush in 1945 as an experiment "performed without considering the practical ends," would produce "general knowledge and an understanding of nature and its laws,"[13] rather than any solutions. Whereas the study of structural systems for the California City City Hall was developed in the context of an architectural project, the L.O.M. device had no such immediate applications. Rather, the creation of this instrument for studying the problems of building assembly *was itself* the research agenda.

Indeed, outside of the Institute, the L.O.M. had no useful purpose. The device was not sophisticated enough to be taken up by the building industry, and thus its sponsors could not exploit it for production. Eventually, the impressive device was disassembled, boxed up, and lost. But between 1967–71, the L.O.M. proved immeasurably useful to the Institute's protagonists. For Wachsmann, the device was the Institute's *raison d'être*, a high-profile project that justified his organization's continued existence. For the sponsors, it was an opportunity to ally their corporation with cutting-edge building science research at a prestigious university. For the graduate students Bollinger and Mendoza, the device was an expedient to their doctoral degrees. Common to all of these purposes, however, was the device's ability to yield alluring images.

Whether appearing in photographs in Weyerhaeuser's publicity materials, in Bollinger and Mendoza's joint dissertation, or in Wachsmann's slide lectures, the L.O.M. was an object of distinct aesthetic presence that rather resembled László Moholy-Nagy's "Light-Space Modulator" than an experimental apparatus. As an object of considerable aesthetic quality but little value to either further research or applied use, the L.O.M. can be said to embody the Building Institute's central paradox: as Wachsmann's research agenda became more theoretically speculative, the value of his research to sponsors, whether government or corporate, diminished in kind.

After completion of the L.O.M. project in 1971, the Institute would constantly struggle to justify its existence as a venue for experimental work on building science and technology. The Institute had placed itself at odds with the prevailing dynamics of the Cold War research economy. First, by avoiding applied research, the Institute could not offer compelling arguments that would entice corporations to sponsor new projects. Second, in view of his "hypothesis-free" ethos, Wachsmann distanced himself from scientific research funded by public sources. In response to questions about what could be gained by undertaking projects like the L.O.M., Wachsmann replied, "... my answer always was, that I did not know. But this was the same answer I would always give when I worked on any task. If I would know the solution or the purpose, I would not start at all."[14]

The Building Institute was shut down for lack of funding in 1974, but not before Wachsmann had developed a teaching system that sought to standardize the production of knowledge and built a school to implement it. In the context of the architect's lifelong engagement with industrialization, the Institute represents his most sophisticated proposal for architecture's alignment with science and industry. That this confluence would take place on the grounds of a school resonated both with the program of the Bauhaus, as well as the emerging neoliberal transformation of the university, what President Eisenhower called in 1961 the "military-industrial-academic complex."

The case of the Building Institute is exceptional with respect to other organizations for building science in its time. It is unusual in that it was simultaneously unable to accede to the demands of research economy, and yet it nevertheless fashioned itself after the model of scientific research laboratories at university. Rather, the Institute sought to establish a pedagogical system whose parallel functions as a didactic environment and as an experimental laboratory would be coproductive. Whether in the conference room or in the laboratory, new information would be produced, captured, and capitalized upon as the product of sponsored research. Students would train to become participants in this circular production of valuable knowledge, and in the process, their academic labor would become the Institute's product.

But Wachsmann's unerring faith in the value of design did not match the evaluative calculus of his would-be sponsors. Still, the architect's systematic transformation of pedagogical activity into an economically productive process pointed in the direction that building science laboratories, and academic science in general, would take after the 1970s. As was true in the case of the Building Institute and other university laboratories, physical space organized the resources of the university—material and personnel—for the purpose of producing saleable research. In this respect, the Institute was established exactly at a critical point in history which marked the transition from industrial forms of production to the post-industrial knowledge economy. Whereas Wachsmann's early-career efforts to develop prefabricated building systems sought to subsume architecture within industry, the Building Institute thus attempted to reconstitute *architecture itself* as a technological product of scientific work.

1   Konrad Wachsmann, "Timebridge, Konrad Wachsmann: An Autobiography," AdK, Konrad-Wachsmann-Archiv, Wachsmann 2128, p. 260.

2   Taylor is credited with raising the profile of the school during his tenure 1962–85, James Lytle, "Crombie Taylor, Architect-Historian, 85," in: USC News August 30, 1999.

3   "Memo to Dr. Milton C. Kloetzel, Proposal to Authorize the Creation of a Building Institute, May 22, 1968," in: Crombie Taylor Papers, Ryerson and Burnham Libraries of the Art Institute of Chicago, Box 5, Series 19, Memos, Wachsmann USC.

4   The first sketch of the "Department of Building Research" floor-plan is signed "KW" and dated from "Genova," Italy; AdK, Konrad-Wachsmann-Archiv, Wachsmann 350.

5   In general, biographical details of Wachsmann's life have been assembled from the architect's unpublished autobiography, "Timebridge 1901–2001," held in the Konrad-Wachsmann-Archiv, AdK. In most cases, biographical details and dates have been verified by the author by interpolation with other materials and published scholarship. For example, letters between Crombie Taylor and

Konrad Wachsmann in 1963 confirm this telling of Wachsmann's move to Los Angeles.

6   A "Doctor of Building Science" degree was added later, after the first students fulfilled the Master's curriculum but elected to stay on in Wachsmann's research institute. The first doctoral committees were formed in 1967 on an ad hoc basis, and the first degree granted in 1969. See "Memo, Subject: Doctoral Program," in: Crombie Taylor Papers, Ryerson and Burnham Libraries of the Art Institute of Chicago, Box 5, Series 19, Memos Wachsmann.

7   Serge Chermayeff, "Letter to Dean William A. Lewis, Illinois Institute of Technology," May 15, 1951, Illinois Institute of Technology Archives, Institute of Design Records, Box 5, Institute of Design—General (1949–70).

8   See Walter Gropius, "Letter to Serge Chermayeff, Director of the Institute of Design, May 21, 1951, Confidential," Illinois Institute of Technology Archives, Institute of Design Records, Box 5, Institute of Design—General (1949–70).

9   Chermayeff had been under pressure to correct the Institute's financial straits since his appointment in 1946; he was unsuccessful. Serge Chermayeff, "Letter to Walter P. Paepcke," June 5, 1951, Illinois Institute of Technology Archives, Institute of Design Records, Box 5, Institute of Design—General (1949–70).

10   John T. Rettaliata, "Letter to Professor Konrad Wachsmann, Institute of Design," March 31, 1955, Illinois Institute of Technology Archives, Institute of Design Records, Box 5, Institute of Design—General (1949–70).

11   Wachsmann, "Memo to Dr. Milton C. Kloetzel," see note 3.

12   Interview with John Bollinger, Building Institute alumnus and recipient of the Doctor of Building Science Degree, July 1, 2018.

13   Vannevar Bush was director of the US Office of Scientific Research and Development during World War II. Vannevar Bush, "Science, the Endless Frontier" (1945).

14   Konrad Wachsmann, "The Future is Everything," in unpublished autobiography manuscript, "Timebridge, Konrad Wachsmann: An Autobiography," AdK, Konrad-Wachsmann-Archiv, Wachsmann 2128, p. 341.

A contribution to Huxley's *Brave New World*[1], *Wendepunkt im Bauen*[2].

Konrad Wachsmann's efforts to develop new building methods that would reflect modern technology should not be underestimated. These were, for the most part, wide-spanning constructions. The public was always adequately informed about the progress of these works when, finally, the book *Wendepunkt im Bauen* appeared, making it clear, even to those who had not experienced a seminar in Salzburg, Karlsruhe, Oslo or Tokyo, that it was about a kind of building "religion," which, incidentally, had already become palpable after the publications. We encounter not only dogmatic statements but also the prophecy (which, despite all assertions to the contrary, means a "preconceived opinion"), that the path proposed and followed is the sole correct one.

This dogmatic aspect with all its characteristics must not necessarily be assessed negatively, attention should merely be drawn to the dangers that can arise through the presentation of a theory by means of a number of exaggerated formulations and erroneous conclusions.

The statement that "empirical knowledge was replaced by exact science" seems exaggerated. As mathematics are used in building, the term "exact" is here, naturally, to be understood in the mathematical sense. But the mathematics applied are approximative. Only idealized model cases can be grasped using them. In making calculations arbitrarily defined values are used. If we are to continue to attach importance to this sentence, it should, at best, be put as follows: "Empirical knowledge was replaced by empirical science."

1. Five layers of reinforced concrete slabs without downstand beams, which were produced in stacked layers on the ground using the Youltz Lift Slab System, are raised simultaneously and the story-height columns are mounted in position.

2. Bridge over the River Severn, (1775–79), 30-meter span.
Design and execution: Abraham Darby

This replacement apparently happened when "... circumstances that have nothing more to do with the causes of earlier changes in appearance led to a turning point in building." As Fred Hochstrasser, Ulm and Winterthur, also confirms in Bauwelt 16/1960, the year 1850 in which Paxton built his Crystal Palace is to be regarded as this turning point. Without wishing in any way to belittle Paxton's achievements it should be noted that by the end of the 18th century cast iron bridges had already been built in England.[3] The constructions by J. B. Papworth (1821) and Rouhault (1833) and the first cable suspension bridge by Marc Seguin across the Rhône near Toulouse (1824) should also be mentioned. Evidently, one can neither speak here of a turning point nor of constructing node

Two Reviews
—
Construction Examples

Stefan Polónyi

Review *Wendepunkt im Bauen* from *Bauwelt* issue 29/1961

points as a central problem. All that one can talk of is a development period.

After the announcement of a "general summary of the current problems in building" as an introductory work, "following which, perhaps, complex problems can be dealt with individually in further publications by those competent to do so," the examples are interesting but one-sided. The development of reinforced concrete construction is almost entirely ignored, despite the material's far from negligible role in building over the past century.[4]

The illustrations of the wonderful Youtz Lift Slab System offer little consolation, as they are followed on the next pages by carpentry-like constructions by Felix Samuely made of reinforced concrete. These are accompanied by a reference to the fact that the design is not entirely suited to the nature of the material, but then why use this example in the first place?

Until assembly Wachsmann's constructions are adapted to a completely automatic production, but conditions must be provided that are generally only required for military and display purposes, namely:

1. Possibility of combination

2. Possibility to demount and use again in a different combination

3. Elements should be exchangeable within certain boundaries
In addition, there is the fact that Wachsmann always searches first of all for a skeleton frame and deals with the structure separately from the space-defining surfaces. By contrast, Buckminster Fuller integrates the surface areas in the structural function of his lightweight dome construction using standard aluminum elements. The result is that he has to resort to small basic elements, that the number of connections, (nodes) increases enormously, and that, for the most part, modern aids cannot be used for the assembly.

Therefore, compared to Paxton's work Wachsmann's constructions appear to be a backward step: in London in 1850 cranes were used for the assembly work, in the case of Wachsmann people run around with tubes under their arms, carrying connectors in a bag. Apparently, the difference between assembly on the building site and assembly on a conveyor belt was not noticed. Clearly, Wachsmann's prerequisites also led to constructions that waste material. The connectors restrict the selection of tubes that can be used. Possible variations are confined largely to the wall thickness and number of tubes. In the case of the compression tubes buckling also plays a role. Placing unconnected tubes beside each other does not reduce the buckling coefficient.

Example of calculation:

A   compressive force of 50 t is to be handled with a rod length
of 3.00 meters. Material: St 55.29, calculated according to DIN[5].
Required: 1 tube
Outer diameter: 191 mm
Wall thickness: 5.25 mm
Weight: 24 kg/m

B   Outer diameter determined
as   89 mm
Required: 4 tubes
Wall thickness of each: 8 mm
Weight: 64 kg/m

In example B the amount of material required is 2.67 times that
in example A, which was calculated normally.

The weld seams arranged in a cross-section at the nodal points
result in a loss of material. To avoid this, a special welding process
is required or all seams must be checked. In the case of tubes this is
difficult to carry out, especially in the construction for the US Air-
force, where welding must be done on the building site. The existing
"*dynamic structure*" was developed uninformed by knowledge of
statics. To avoid a node at which numerous elements meet and to
reduce the frame to just one or two basic elements the connections
are not at the head of the column but in the field or at the middle of
the column. This creates a triangular boomerang arrangement that
has to deal with considerable bending moments, in particular if the
position of the columns is staggered from floor to floor. In the case
of the sketched five-story building a calculation would produce a
shocking result. Part of the connections would have to be made rigid.
All these complicated node problems could be avoided if, instead of
looking for a skeleton frame, the problem was formulated differently:
areas are to be created that separate or define the rooms and meet
certain structural and other requirements. The question should
therefore be: How should these surfaces be designed or how should
they be equipped in order to meet these requirements? In this way
one arrives at shell or plate structures in which the connections are
not concentrated in single points but are distributed along lines.

The material for the "dynamic structure" is to be determined
later. Deciding on the construction in advance hinders the kind of
design that is appropriate to the material used.

Furthermore, Wachsmann and his team typically use the same
constructions or construction parts for fundamentally different
functions and stresses.

This false constructivist formalism will, by means of addition, create wide-spanning constructions "of a previously inconceivable kind," developing "not only (...) beauty, but also a new ethic of looking at art as a symbol of a new epoch."

The constructions are developed through teamwork, as it is "not the intention of the training team to develop talent," it is clear that Beta type[1] people work in the team, the machines are made by Gammas[1], and the assembly is carried out by Deltas[1].

1   Aldous Huxley: *Brave New World*,
     1932 and 1949, German edition:
     Schöne Neue Welt, Fischer Verlag,
     Frankfurt a. M., 1953.
2   Konrad Wachsmann: *Wendepunkt
     im Bauen*, Krausskopf-Verlag,
     Wiesbaden, 1959.
3   Eric de Maré: *The Bridges of Britain*,
     B. T. Batsford LTD, London, 1954.

4   Sigfried Giedion: *Space, Time and
     Architecture*, Oxford University
     Press, London, 1952, 9th edition.
5   Verein deutscher Eisenhüttenleute
     (ed.): *Stahl im Hochbau*, Verlag
     Stahleisen mbH, Düsseldorf, 1959,
     12th edition.

Preface

In 2009 I endeavored to study the work of Konrad Wachsmann, supported by a generous grant from the Advancing Scholarship in the Humanities and Social Sciences initiative at the University of Southern California. The work culminated in August 2010 in an exhibition entitled, *Connection Points: Konrad Wachsmann Reconsidered* at the Los Angeles Forum for Architecture and Urban Design, and included analytical drawings, 3D printed models, and animations. The research focused on three of Wachsmann's projects, the General Panel House (1941–49), the USAF-Hangar (1951), and the Study of a Dynamic Structure (1953). The following text is from the research work done during that time, particularly the Study of a Dynamic Structure.

Connection Points: Konrad Wachsmann Reconsidered

John A. Enright; Fig.: 93–97

Study of a Dynamic Structure, 1953 [→93–95]

The Study of a Dynamic Structure, also known as The Grapevine Structure, while unresolved to the level of Wachsmann's previous work, is the first where Wachsmann explored the notion of a continuous single building element or in his words, "... the problem was to design a single, universal structural element which ... could be used in building construction for every conceivable purpose."[1] This quest for the "universal" use of building components would consume most of his career, yet with The Study of a Dynamic Structure project, we see a different take on this problem. It does not recognize the joint or connection in the same manner. The joint is actually negated in such a way that the place where one would assume the connection of elements to be located is actually a void. This theoretical structure then is manifest as a series of line paths that never touch each other. While Wachsmann shows drawings of an encasement system that would presumably create workable floor plates and ceilings, and encapsulate the vertical columns, this project in its conceptual form represented a new direction in his research. For an architect who spent the better part of a career attempting to solve the joinery of material and building components, it is quite fascinating that he would propose a theoretical structure that in fact negates the joint altogether. In doing so, however, Wachsmann began to explore how a repetitive system of construction could create "dynamic" form, albeit one which would transform "... determined by stress conditions."[2]

The basic building block of the system is based on a twelve-foot module in the form of a cube. Wachsmann diagramed the geometric principles in a series of drawings that begin with a doubled cross in plan, followed by rotational operations that formed a pin-wheel. The pinwheel generated eight beam-like members that connected to the center of the module by a smaller cube, rotated by 45 degrees, at the center. The central cube formed four vertical column-like members that twist in plan from the forty-five degree angle to an orthogonal relationship at the top. This central rotated cube was further broken down into sixteen squares on each side and was where the system mediated between the sixteen beams of the pin-wheel to the eight columns four up and four down. Critical to the geometric play here is the diagonal slicing of the central cube, based on the rotational geometry that created the void. Here is the most curious element of the geometry, the actual node of intersection is denied and instead replaced with material and vectors that sur-round, yet never meet the center. The resulting "element" is then a unit which contained two horizontal beam-like members that form a "V" and connected to the base of the twisting vertical element, named "the wishbone." The completed piece then was eight wish-bones mediating between horizontal and vertical and floating in space, never touching each other. Wachsmann imagined this system as comprising a 24-foot by 24-foot structural grid module for a generic building type. This required the connecting of the "V" wish-bone elements with one other repetitive structural beam, paired and mediating between the upper and lower elements, presumably between and below the floor structure.[→96, 97]

Our modeling of the system required some level of interpre-tation given the fact the two-dimensional diagrams created were at some level not accurate enough, or distorted in the planimetric and sectional dimensions. Further, we assumed that the resulting twisted surfaces were to be "developable" in that they could con-ceivably be understood as flat planes which could be curved to the desired geometry. This required much trial and error and constant referencing back to the original diagrams. Our printed physical models show both the primary double mushroom structure, a "tree" of the primary load trace of one arm of the system, and a larger sys-tem model of the structure. It should be noted that since the traced lines of force and the elements themselves in reality do not connect as designed by Wachsmann, it was necessary to add small inserts, or "welds" in the 3D print models in order to display the system for demonstration purposes.

Wachsmann's drawings also modified the basic unit and pro-posed an offset relationship for the structure. Using the same exact elements, the continuous verticality of the columns is denied and instead creates an alternating shifted path of vertical elements. This demonstrates that Wachsmann began to explore variation within the system, one that could specifically create an adaptable relation-ship of shifting vertical elements. This theoretical structure, more of a spatial diagram than a seriously worked out structural solution, freed from the more pragmatic constraints of his other research, enabled Wachsmann to envision a much more plastic and dynamic expression of space.

Perhaps this new avenue was a response to criticism that the repetitive nature of structurally based solutions negated the more poetic aspects of architecture. As Itohan Osayimwese has pointed out, the critic Serge Chimayeff [sic!] charged Wachsmann "... with a 'panaceatic myopia that focuses only on a mythical universal joint.'"[3] Wachsmann himself in his description of the project emoted an almost defensive stance;

"Only a superficial appraisal could support the opinion that the technical-scientific approach, the consistent application of automatically controlled, industrial production processes and the systematic modular coordination of all building elements, parts and products, leads inevitably to monotony or, as I am continually hearing with astonishment, the total destruction of every spiritual and emotional impulse. A glimpse of the future such methods may really make possible is afforded by the following structural study, one among many."[4]

Wachmann's reference to the future is apropos given the contemporary aspects of the geometric complexity of the system. Our development of the digital models demonstrates the geometric accuracy and richness of his study drawings. Brought from two dimensions to three, the project exposes itself as an even more interesting construct as we are able to dynamically navigate the project. One can see this project as a fitting end to Wachsmann's research of the joint and connection, in the sense that the system depends on continuity, lines of force, and inevitably represents itself as negating "the connector" altogether. On the other hand, it can also be seen as a beginning point to another manner of approaching complex structures. In this sense, Wachsmann was perhaps ahead of his time, as today architects and engineers, empowered by new digital tools, look towards ever more complex systems.

Postscript

In June of 2018 I had the opportunity to visit the Biennale Architettura in Venice, Italy and see the work of Marianne Burkhalter and Christian Sumi and their related publication, *Konrad Wachsmann and The Grapevine Structure*. While any new interpretation of Wachsmann's work is to be welcomed, there exist a few differences in approach in our understandings of "The Study of a Dynamic Structure" which are important to point out. Burkhalter and Sumi, in both the drawings and the large-scale wooden sculpture, oversimplify the base geometry of the structure to straight lines, and created intersecting members where Wachsmann clearly did not originally intend. While this is perhaps a natural impulse to rationalize the structure, in my opinion it misses the point of what Wachsmann was heading towards. I believe that the structure as envisioned by Wachsmann was in fact a critique of the tyranny of the tectonic problem of the joint. The negating of the connection itself was both the point of, and the result of, the investigation. Further, as our research has shown, the structure is able to be rationalized as developable curved planes, so the structure could in fact be fabricated in steel plates and bent to form the planar surfaces of each member, without the need to crudely intersect the wishbone members. In the end, perhaps "The Study of a Dynamic Structure's" appeal for all of us is inherently contained in the wholly enigmatic nature of what it proposes. In this way it is beautifully unresolved.

1   Konrad Wachsmann, *The Turning Point of Building: Structure and Design*, translated by Thomas E. Burton, Reinhold Pub. Corp., New York, 1961, p. 194.
2   Ibid.
3   Itohan Osayimwese, "Konrad Wachsmann: Prefab Pioneer," in: *Dwell Magazine*, February 2009, p. 100.
4   Konrad Wachsmann, *The Turning Point of Building: Structure and Design*, translated by Thomas E. Burton, Reinhold Pub. Corp., New York, 1961, p. 194.

In the first part of his book *Wendepunkt im Bauen*[1] Konrad Wachsmann states: "Fundamentally different principles than those which were prevalent hitherto necessitate a complete revision of all complex problems which encompass not only single instances or parts but the whole field of construction." In his times it was the industrialization of the building process that gave rise to new possibilities and thus necessitated new approaches to structural design.

Serial production made it possible to produce large amounts of identical parts at low marginal costs. The problem to be solved now consisted in conceiving structures and building parts in such a way that the design intent could be expressed with a limited number of different types of structural elements. An example for this can be seen in fig. 1b[→99] which shows one of the models of the USF hangar. The structure utilizes one type of structural node, one beam length and one constructive system in rhythmic repetition within a three-dimensional modular hierarchy[2]. The new quality of Wachsmann's structures derives from quantity. In stark contrast, pre-industrial structures were rooted in tradition, craftsmanship and intuition. As an example, Fig. 1a[→98] shows the Old Walton Bridge. It features many differently sized load-bearing elements not amenable to serial fabrication but geared towards piecewise manual production and assembly. The inherent complexity of its construction principle results in a varied appearance but limits the possible building scale to what can be handled by a team of skilled carpenters.

Today the building industry is confronted with a similar paradigm shift as in the days of Konrad Wachsmann. Digital methods in planning and fabrication have fundamentally changed the approach to building construction. In existence since the 1970s, computer aided design (CAD) started as a replacement for drawing boards. Although the methodology initially was very similar to drawing by hand, CAD gradually supplanted ink and paper due to its accuracy and flexibility when it comes to duplicating or changing an existing drawing. Yet for CAD to be a game-changer in the realm of digital design an additional step was necessary: the advent of parametric geometry tools. These tools enable users to generate geometry via algorithms. By means of visual geometry scripting environments like Generative Components[3] or Grasshopper[4] users can formulate an arbitrary geometry by connecting functional building blocks (see fig. 2[→100]) which execute operations on a stream of data. This elevates the level of communication between user and computer from point and click methods—as embodied in the traditional CAD approach —to that of a language. As an example, fig. 2[→100] shows a curved surface which results from a visual script shown below the shape: input-sliders on the left side define the control points of the surface. The gray blocks represent one operation at a time to transform the

Parametric Structural Design as an Inspirational Tool for Revisiting Konrad Wachsmann's USAF-Hangar

Clemens Preisinger,
Andrei Gheorghe,
Moritz Heimrath,
Adam Orlinski; Fig.: 98–138

input on the left to the final shape which results on the right-hand side of the definition.

The effect of scripting on geometry production is like that of serial production: creating the parametric setup for a specific type of geometry or geometric idea is often time-consuming and tricky. Once done, however, a definition can be reused many times at nearly no cost.

Currently the visual scripting environment Grasshopper (GH)[5] which is based on the CAD program Rhinoceros enjoys wide-spread popularity in the geometry scripting community. Part of this success comes from its open program design which allows third-party developers to create plug-ins that enhance the capabilities of GH.

One of these plug-ins is Karamba3D[6]. It adds structural analysis functionality to GH and was one of the tools which the students of the 2017 course "Advanced Structures" at the University of Applied Arts Vienna used in their pursuit of a contemporary reinterpretation of the work of Konrad Wachsmann. Fig. 3a[→101] shows a Grasshopper definition which takes the image of a leaf as a starting point to define the thickness of a shell structure (see fig. 3b[→102]). Karamba3D seamlessly integrates into GH and provides objects like loads, supports, finite elements, cross sections, solution methods which make up a structural model analysis.

One feature which sets Karamba3D apart from traditional structural calculation programs is its interactivity: changes in the geometry immediately lead to an updated structural response. At first glance this seems like a minor thing but it has a major impact on the user's understanding of cause and effect in terms of structure. Instead of having only one result at a time like in traditional Finite Element programs, the user can flip through a variety of alternative geometries, thereby generating a film sequence of result images. Karamba3D features components for automatic cross-section design and topology optimization, which frees the user from routine work. Being part of the eco-system of Grasshopper plug-ins, Karamba3D can be combined with other tools like optimization engines which can be hooked to any parametric definition in order to drive a geometry towards arbitrary performance criteria.

In the course of the 2016 advanced structures seminar at the University of Applied Arts four groups of students were assigned with the task of analyzing and re-envisioning Konrad Wachsmann's USAF-Hangar design.

After an intense literature study of Konrad Wachsmann's work the students used the geometry of the USAF-Hangar as a starting point for their journey into the field of parametric geometries. Some of them started to experiment with cross-section optimization algorithms: Based on the flow of forces caused by external loads, each beam cross section gets reduced to the bare minimum. Fig. 4[→103] shows how such an algorithm results in structural patterns which react to force concentrations at the supports.

All student groups experimented with different parametrization strategies in combination with Finite Element analysis. This often resulted in highly irregular structures like in fig. 5[→104]. Here a topology optimization procedure based on Evolutionary Structural Optimization[7] was utilized to weed out structurally inefficient members of an initially overly dense geometry.

Although structure plays an important role in the Advanced Structural Design Class it is experimentation and a holistic view of building design which form the focus. In this respect parametric design lends itself particularly well to adapting structural geometries to different usage scenarios and contexts. Fig. 6[→105] and fig. 7[→106] show how a parametric definition supports a specific usage program by having two main support regions in the center and the roof touching the ground at opposing corners.

Over the years the Advanced Structural Design Class has proved to be a successful format which gives students the opportunity to reflect on examples of classic modern architecture, using them as starting points for their own imaginative designs. The gradual introduction of parametric tools like Grasshopper and Karamba3D opened new possibilities in this respect. Especially for a field like structural design, which architectural students sometimes view as dry and abstract, it is important to provide a motivating and playful approach to the subject. In this context parametric tools can play an important role in the curriculum of architectural schools.

1   Konrad Wachsmann, *Wendepunkt im Bauen*, Deutsche Verlags-Anstalt, Stuttgart, 1959.
2   Ibid.
3   Robert Aish, "SmartGeometry Workshop," ACADIA, 2004.
4   David Rutten, "Galapagos: On the Logic and Limitations of Generic Solvers," in: *Architectural Design— Special issue: Computation Works:*

The Building of Algorithmic Thought, 83(2), 2013, pp. 132–135.
5   Konrad Wachsmann, *Wendepunkt im Bauen*, Deutsche Verlags-Anstalt, Stuttgart, 1959.
6   Clemens Preisinger, Moritz Heimrath, "Karamba3D—A Toolkit for Parametric Structural Design," in: *Structural Engineering International*, vol. 24, 2014, pp. 217–221.

7   Yi Min Xie, Grant Prentice Steven, "A simple evolutionary procedure for structural optimization," in: *Computers & Structures*, vol. 49, 1993, pp. 885–896.

Biographies

GERALD BAST

Gerald Bast, born 1955, has been rector of the University of Applied Arts Vienna, Austria since 2000. After his studies in law and economics at Johannes Kepler University Linz, where he earned a Doctorate in Law, he worked at the Federal Ministry of Higher Education and at Ludwig Boltzmann Research Society. He is member of the European Academy of Arts and Sciences, and editor-in-chief of the book series "Edition Angewandte" and "Art, Research, Innovation and Society."

As university rector Gerald Bast initiated various new programs focusing on transdisciplinarity and the interrelations between the arts and society. He founded the "Angewandte Innovation Lab," accentuating the role of the arts in innovation processes by facilitating intercommunication between art, science & technology, economics and politics.

Gerald Bast has published in the fields of university law, university management as well as educational and cultural policy and held various invited lectures on the role of art, creativity, innovation and higher education, among them at Johns Hopkins University Washington D.C., Columbia University New York, Tsing Hua University Beijing, Tong Ji University Shanghai, City University Hong Kong, University of Auckland, Lalit Kala Akademi New Delhi, University of Porto, NTU Singapore, European Forum Alpbach and the European Culture Forum Brussels.

KLAUS BOLLINGER

Klaus Bollinger studied Civil Engineering at the Technical University Darmstadt and taught at Dortmund University, Germany. Since 1994, he has been Professor for Structural Engineering at the Institute of Architecture at the University of Applied Arts in Vienna and Dean of the institute since 1999.

In 1983, Klaus Bollinger and Manfred Grohmann established Bollinger + Grohmann Ingenieure. Today, the company is active in 10 cities and 7 countries with around 200 employees providing a complete range of structural and façade engineering, geometry, building physics and fire protection services for clients and projects worldwide.

FLORIAN MEDICUS

Florian Medicus studied architecture at the University of Applied Arts Vienna under the guidance of Wilhelm Holzbauer, Zvi Hecker and Zaha Hadid, and—in 2002—was a member of the Berlage-Institute-Masterclass with Rem Koolhaas in Rotterdam. Medicus obtained his diploma under the professorship of Wolf D. Prix in 2005 at the Angewandte. The same year, he started teaching the subject of "Structural Design" together with Klaus Bollinger at the University of Applied Arts Vienna. Further teaching engagements include his lecturing on the subject of Architectural Theory, together with Bart Lootsma at the Academy of Fine Arts, Vienna and at the Leopold-Franzens-University of Innsbruck, and his assistance of Itsuko Hasegawa at the Salzburg International Summer Academy of Fine Arts. Medicus publishes frequently within the fields of architecture, urban design and fine arts and curated the exhibition *New Frontiers* on "young experimental architecture" and "drawing" which toured Bratislava, Berlin, Krems, Paris and Vienna. He co-edited *Unbuildable Tatlin?!* (Springer, 2012) and *Endless Kiesler* (Birkhäuser, 2015). He lives and works in Salzburg, Vienna and Munich.

EVA-MARIA BARKHOFEN

Eva-Maria Barkhofen, born 1956 in Essen. State certified professional equestrian. Studied art history, classical archaeology and European ethnology at the Westfälische Wilhelms-Universität in Münster, Germany. 1990 PhD. 1990–91 volunteer at the Staatliche Museen zu Berlin Preussischer Kulturbesitz; 1991–94 scientific staff, department of inventarization, Brandenburgisches Landesamt / Brandenburg State Office for the Preservation of Historic Monuments; 1994–2006 head of the architectural collection, Berlinische Galerie, Landesmuseum / Provincial Museum of Modern Art, Photography and Architecture,

Berlin; 2006–2020 head of the Architecture Archives, Akademie der Künste, Berlin; 1998–2019 spokeswoman of the Federation of German Architecture Archives; since 2014 public appointed and sworn expert in architectural art and archive objects, nominated by the Chamber of Industry and Trade.

PARSA KHALILI

Parsa Khalili is an architect and founder of WAZEONE, a Brooklyn-based studio for architecture. He taught at Greg Lynn's studio at the University for Applied Arts, Vienna and is currently a Visiting Lecturer at the Princeton School of Architecture. He has previously collaborated with Elizabeth Diller, Richard Meier, Peter Eisenman, and Coop Himmelb(l)au. He studied at the ENSA-V in Versailles, the University of Illinois at Urbana-Champaign, and the Yale School of Architecture. Khalili has received numerous awards for his design and research work as well as published widely. His interests pertain to issues of design criticism, non-western forms of Modernism, visual and diagrammatic representations, and new digital media.

MARK WIGLEY

Mark Wigley is Professor of Architecture at Columbia University. As an historian and theorist, he explores the intersection of architecture, art, philosophy, culture, and technology. His books include: *Derrida's Haunt: The Architecture of Deconstruction; White Walls, Designer Dresses: The Fashioning of Modern Architecture; Constant's New Babylon: The Hyper-Architecture of Desire; Buckminster Fuller Inc.—Architecture in the Age of Radio; Are We Human? Notes on an Archaeology of Design* (co-authored with Beatriz Colomina); and *Cutting Matta-Clark: The Anarchitecture Investigation*. His most recent exhibition and book is *Passing Through Architecture: The 10 Years of Gordon Matta-Clark* (Shanghai: Power Station of Art, 2019).

ANGELA LAMMERT

Angela Lammert is head of inter-disciplinary special projects at the

Akademie der Künste, Berlin and PD at the Institute for Art and Picture History at the Humboldt-Universität zu Berlin. She has authored numerous publications and curated exhibitions on art from the 19th to the 21st century, including *Filme ausstellen*, in: *Display und Dispositiv. Ästhetische Ordnungen* (Munich 2018), *Bildung und Bildlichkeit von Notation. Von der frühen Wissenschaftsfotografie zu den Künsten des 20. Jahrhunderts* (Munich 2016), *Gordon Matta Clark. Moment to Moment. Space*. Eds. Hubertus von Ameluxen and Philip Ursprung (Nuremberg 2012)

MATTHIAS BOECKL

Matthias Boeckl, born 1962 in Vienna, Austria. Studies in art history, PhD at University of Vienna 1988, Professor of Architectural History at the University of Applied Arts Vienna. Editor-in-chief, *architektur. aktuell* magazine. Author and curator of numerous essays, books and exhibitions on modern and contemporary art and architecture.

WOLFGANG FIEL

Wolfgang Fiel is Senior Lecturer at the University of Applied Arts Vienna, Austria, and continues to work in various capacities and organizational settings as an architect, artist, designer, curator, researcher, and writer.

He is founding Director of the Vienna-based Institute for cultural policy, founding member of the collaborative artistic practice *tat ort*, consultant for the United Nations Industrial Development Organization, active member of the Arts and Culture Advisory Board in the Federal Chancellery of Austria, and member of the advisory board in Political Theory at Cambridge Scholars Publishing, UK.

He has published and written extensively. His most recent titles include the *Getting Things Done* series published by Birkhäuser and *Emancipating the Many: A Practice Led Investigation into Emergent Paradigms of Immediate Political Action* published by Cambridge Scholars Publishing.

PHILLIP DENNY

Phillip Denny is doing a PhD in architecture history and theory at Harvard University. His work focuses on interaction between design, media, and technology in the 20th century. His writing has appeared in the *New York Times*, *Volume*, *Metropolis*, and *Harvard Design Magazine*, among other publications. He is currently working on the first English-language translation of cybernetic artist Nicolas Schöffer's urban manifesto *La ville cybernétique* (*The Cybernetic City*). He holds master's degrees in architecture and architectural history from Princeton and Harvard.

STEFAN POLÓNYI

Stefan Polónyi (born in 1930 in Gyula, Hungary) is one of Germany's most distinguished civil engineers and professors. After receiving his diploma in Budapest (1952), Polónyi worked as a consultant engineer in Cologne from 1957 on. In 1965, he was appointed Professor of Structural Engineering at Technische Universität Berlin, where he remained until 1972. From 1973 to 1995, Stefan Polónyi held the Chair of Structures and Structural Design at Technische Universität Dortmund where he co-founded the Department of Civil Engineering.

Besides working on many outstanding projects together with architects such as Kurt Ackermann, Norman Foster, Frei Otto, Gustav Peichl and Oswald Mathias Ungers, Polónyi has published numerous groundbreaking books and articles towards a better understanding of architecture and structural design. His most recent publication is *Wie man die Architektur zum Tragen bringt*, Klartext Verlag, Essen, 2016.

JOHN A. ENRIGHT

John A. Enright, FAIA is Vice Director / Chief Academic Officer at SCI-Arc and a founding principal of Los Angeles, CA based Griffin Enright Architects, along with Margaret Griffin, FAIA. Their work has been extensively published; locally, nationally and internationally, and has received over forty awards for design excellence including, local, state and national AIA Awards and The American Architecture Award from the Chicago Athenaeum. Enright has taught design studios and technology seminars at SCI-Arc, Syracuse University, University of Houston, and the University of Southern California. His academic research focuses on design and building technology, including new digital paradigms as applied to fabrication and construction.

CLEMENS PREISINGER

Clemens Preisinger is a structural engineer and researcher. He started his career as a researcher at the Institute for Structural Concrete at the Technical University Vienna. Since 2008, Clemens has worked for the structural engineering company Bollinger + Grohmann Ingenieure, at the same time contributing to several research projects at University of Applied Arts Vienna. There, he is currently head of the "Digital Simulation" department which investigates possibilities to bring computational modeling techniques into early stage architectural design. Since 2010, Clemens has developed the parametric, interactive Finite Element program Karamba3D as a freelancer. He holds a PhD in Structural Engineering from the Technical University Vienna.

ANDREI GHEORGHE

Andrei Gheorghe is a licensed architect teaching as Assistant Professor at the University of Applied Arts Vienna. He studied at the Academy of Fine Arts Vienna and after receiving the Fulbright Scholarship, he went on to Harvard University where he graduated with distinction. Andrei Gheorghe has taught at the Academy of Fine Arts Vienna, SCI-Arc Los Angeles and Harvard Graduate School of Design (Career Discovery Program). Previously, he worked as an architect for Jakob + MacFarlane, dECOi Paris and Foreign Office Architects (FOA) London. His research focus lies at the interface of design & technology in architecture, structures and digital media, a topic for which he was awarded the Harvard Digital Design Award in 2009 and the international

AZ Award in 2015. Andrei Gheorghe completed his dissertation at the University of Applied Arts Vienna under the supervision of Hani Rashid and Klaus Bollinger.

MORITZ HEIMRATH

Moritz Heimrath studied at the Academy of Fine Arts in Stuttgart and finished his studies at the University of Applied Arts Vienna in 2010. He is currently Partner at Bollinger + Grohmann Ingenieure and part of the developer team of Karamba3D, an interactive parametric finite-element plugin for Grasshopper. His research focuses on the relationship between structure, computational strategies and aesthetic architectural concepts. He is specialized in parametric design methods and uses digital tools for evaluation, generative computation and optimization in his daily office practice. Moritz Heimrath is teaching the implementation of digital design strategies at the Institute of Technology GSO in Nuremberg, Germany and digital analysis and simulation at the Academy of Fine Arts, Vienna. In 2012 he received the MAK Schindler Scholarship from the Ministry of Arts, Culture and Education of Austria.

ADAM ORLINSKI

Adam Orlinski studied architecture at the University of Applied Arts Vienna, where he received his degree with the Honorary Prize of the Austrian Ministry of Science and Research for outstanding achievements. He is currently working at Bollinger + Grohmann Ingenieure in Vienna, and is part of the developer team of Karamba3D—an interactive parametric finite-element plugin for Grasshopper. He is an expert in parametric design tools such as Rhino 3D + Grasshopper, Karamba3D and Kangaroo2, and is frequently invited to host workshops on the topic of computational design strategies at various European universities. He co-authored the art based research project »n.formations« and »fluid bodies« (FWF-PEEK) that investigated the complex aesthetic potential behind advanced structural algorithms.

ACKNOWLEDGMENTS

This publication would not have been possible without the generous support of the University of Applied Arts Vienna and the yielding collaboration with the Baukunstarchiv at Akademie der Künste in Berlin.

The editors would like to personally thank Roswitha Janowski-Fritsch for her tireless efforts and Paulus M. Dreibholz for his endurance and sensitive graphic design.

Many thanks to all of our contributors: Gerald Bast, Eva-Maria Barkhofen, Parsa Khalili, Mark Wigley, Angela Lammert, Matthias Boeckl, Wolfgang Fiel, Eckhard Schulze-Fielitz, Phillip Denny, John A. Enright, Stefan Polónyi, Clemens Preisinger, Andrei Gheorghe, Moritz Heimrath and Adam Orlinski, the students of 2012 and 2016, and artists Andreas Zybach, Tomás Saraceno, Han Koning, Gego, Antony Gormley, Lilah Fowler, Tae Eun Ahn, Peter Smithson, Peter Jellitsch, Olafur Eliasson, Michal Bartosik, Mark Hagen and Jürgen Mayer H..

We also thank Ray Wachsmann, Eva-Maria Barkhofen and Tanja Morgenstern as well as Raffael Strasser, Camilla Nielsen, Roderick O'Donovan, Irina Pálffy-Daun-Seiler and Marina Brandtner for their valuable help.

After this long and sometimes quite arduous enterprise, we are now able to pay a truly fitting tribute to the life and great work of Konrad Wachsmann.

So once again: thank you all!

Klaus Bollinger, Florian Medicus

Stressing Wachsmann

Plates

1   THE FUTURE WAS EVERYTHING—KONRAD
WACHSMANN'S USAF-HANGAR
→ EN 9 / DE 8

Louis Blériot beats the world speed record at the
Champagne Meeting in Reims, August 28, 1909

2   the future was everything—konrad wachsmann's usaf-hangar → en 10 / de 8
Eugène Freyssinet, Hangar Orly Airport, Paris 1923. Credit: Association Eugène Freyssinet

3   the future was everything—konrad wachsmann's usaf-hangar → en 10 / de 8
Navy hangar 1, early construction showing framework of "Orange Peel" door. Hangar One Construction, 1932, source: NASA Image and Video Library

4   the future was everything—konrad wachsmann's usaf-hangar → en 10 / de 8
Aircraft hangars at Orvieto Airport by Pier Luigi Nervi 1935–1938; © Pier Luigi Nervi Project, Brussels

THE MUSEUM OF MODERN ART
11 WEST 53RD STREET, NEW YORK 19, N. Y.
TELEPHONE: CIRCLE 5-8900

FOR IMMEDIATE RELEASE

MUSEUM OF MODERN ART SHOWS REVOLUTIONARY NEW TYPE OF

STEEL CONSTRUCTION

What may at first glance appear to be a giant plaything put together from
a child's toy building set, the visitor to the Museum of Modern Art will find on
drawing nearer to be a remarkable half-inch scale model of an airplane hangar of
revolutionary construction. The great truss roof, which would actually measure
140 by 200 feet, is boldly cantilevered out from four supports of incredible
lightness. The floor area is almost entirely unobstructed, and removable external
walls allow maximum freedom of circulation.

Konrad Wachsmann, designer and architect of international reputation, has
based his new type of construction on two original inventions: first, a "mobilar"
tube joint which makes possible the assembly of tubular members without riveting
or hand-welding and which permits shop or field erection, easy extension or
modification, and 100% salvage; and, second, a mobile wall unit which for the
first time offers completely removable doors, uncomplicated by hinges or tracks.
Banks of these wall units are self-supporting and can be rolled away from the
building in which they function, since they in no way affect the building's
structural load. Paul Weidlinger, civil engineer, worked out all the difficult
calculations on stresses and functions which made this whole type of construction
possible.

The shadow of the model as thrown upon one wall of the Museum gallery
creates an illusion of actuality. On another wall is a dramatic montage, combin-
ing scale models of the removable doors with a drawing of a bridge which could be
constructed by Mr. Wachsmann's system of steel pipes and standardized connectors.
Also included in the exhibition is a group of drawings explaining the details of
the structural system, photographic enlargements of the model and an appreciative
preface written by the famous French architect Le Corbusier.

"Mobilar" construction is adaptable not only to airplane hangars, but to
railroad stations, public halls, storage houses, or any type of structure where
large unobstructed areas are essential. The model and other material in the
exhibition have been lent the Museum by the licensee, Atlas Aircraft Products Corp.
of 405 East 42 Street, New York. The exhibition will be on view in the first
floor architecture gallery of the Museum from February 6 through March 3.

"Exhibit Revolutionary New Type Of Steel Construction." Press release for the exhibition
"Architecture in Steel: An Experiment in Standardization by Konrad Wachsmann,"
MoMA, New York. Published February 4, 1946. New York, Museum of Modern Art
6   (MoMA). © 2019. The Museum of Modern Art, New York/Scala, Florence

Konrad Wachsmann teaching at the ɪɪᴛ in Chicago, ca. 1952, photographer unknown; Akademie der
Künste, Berlin, Konrad-Wachsmann-Archiv 0125_022

7   THE FUTURE WAS EVERYTHING—KONRAD WACHSMANN'S USAF-HANGAR   →   EN 12 / DE 10
Konrad Wachsmann, *The basic straps enclosing the standard joint*, ca. 1954, photographer unknown;
Akademie der Künste, Berlin, Konrad-Wachsmann-Archiv 0120_002

8   THE FUTURE WAS EVERYTHING—
     KONRAD WACHSMANN'S USAF-HANGAR
     →   EN 12 / DE 11
Cover of *Arts & Architecture*, John Entenza
(ed.), November 1947, Los Angeles,
with an article "House in Industry—Konrad
Wachsmann and Walter Gropius"

9   THE FUTURE WAS EVERYTHING—KONRAD
     WACHSMANN'S USAF-HANGAR
     →   EN 13 / DE 12
Cover of *L'Architecture d'Aujourd'hui*, N. 11,
November 1936, Paris, on "Architecture Industrielle"

the ERWIN-NEWMAN
Suspended Cantilever HANGAR

UNOBSTRUCTED CLEAR SPAN SPACE!
EXPANDABLE . . .
IN HEIGHT • IN LENGTH • IN DEPTH

ERWIN-NEWMAN hangars are built with an expandable future in mind. The length can be enlarged and still have clear span space up to several hundred or several thousand feet. Vertical clearance can be increased, in the future, by adding tail gates at any number of points across the front.

Our years of experience in design and construction make it imperative you consult with us when you plan a hangar of any size (no obligation of course).

Erwin
Newman Co.®

DESIGNERS AND CONSTRUCTORS
U. S. Patent No. 2,687,102

P. O. BOX 1308   HOUSTON, TEXAS

Due to certain patent infringements it is necessary to publish this
IMPORTANT PATENT NOTICE
The Erwin-Newman Suspended Cantilever Hangars are covered by United States Patent No. 2,687,102, and similar foreign patents issued to us and under which we hold exclusive rights. The Erwin-Newman Company must, and will, protect its rights under these patents against infringements.

1960 FORECAST
continued from page 131

year's vigorous upturn in motel building which is expected to continue through next year.

Houses. Although one- and two-family house building is not one of FORUM's primary concerns, this big branch of the building industry is of great importance to the economy in general. The outlook is bearish but by no means bleak. The number of privately financed one- and two-family starts will probably drop 11 per cent from 1,112,000 in 1959 to 990,000 in 1960. Expenditures in 1960 ($13.5 billion) will fall off somewhat less (about 6 per cent) because of the big carry-over of work begun in 1959 and because of the trend toward larger, higher quality, more expensive houses in keeping with the expected increase in family income.

Publicly financed housing of the one- and two-family size—most of it built on military posts—dropped sharply in 1959 to 10,000 units from 42,600 in 1958. It will probably drop to about 8,000 next year accounting for roughly $125 million of construction, including some carry-over from the current year.

Altogether, private and public expenditures for new one- and two-family homes in 1960 should be in the neighborhood of $13.5 billion, down 7 per cent from 1959.*

Other construction

Public utility construction is another big segment of private construction, but comprising mainly power, telephone, and telegraph lines. Only 5 to 10 per cent of it involves actual buildings such as power plants, telephone exchanges, substations, laboratories, maintenance shops, etc. Public utility construction this year expanded about 3 per cent. Next year an 8 per cent increase is forecast raising the total to $5.8 billion.

continued on page 236

*When this forecast was prepared important legislation, affecting particularly housing and highway building, was still pending in Congress, and the credit outlook contained many elements of uncertainty. However, it is possible that the resolution of these uncertainties will strengthen, rather than weaken, the prospects for building as they may now be seen. FORUM will take another look at the figures and publish such forecast revisions as may be indicated soon after the beginning of the year.

New annex to Indian
Architect: D. A. Bohle
and Fowler, Me

---

10   THE FUTURE WAS EVERYTHING—KONRAD WACHSMANN'S USAF-HANGAR   →   EN 13 / DE 12

Advertisement for "The Erwin-Newman Suspended Cantilever Hangar" on page 232 in *Architectural Forum*
9   (vol. 111, no. 4; TIME Inc., New York), October 1959

Konrad Wachsmann with the final USAF-Hangar model, ca. 1953, photographer unknown; Akademie der Künste, Berlin, Konrad-Wachsmann-Archiv 0126_050

11

     →   EN 15 / DE 15

Konrad Wachsmann with Elsa and Albert Einstein at their summerhouse in Caputh near Potsdam, ca. 1930, photographer unknown; Akademie der Künste, Berlin, Konrad-Wachsmann-Archiv 0152_14

Konrad Wachsmann in an exhibition on his work, ca. 1979,
photographer: Foto-Joppen; Akademie der Künste, Berlin,
Konrad-Wachsmann-Archiv 0205_145

Konrad Wachsmann in an exhibition on his work, ca. 1979, photographer unknown; Akademie der Künste, Berlin,
Konrad-Wachsmann-Archiv 0205_094

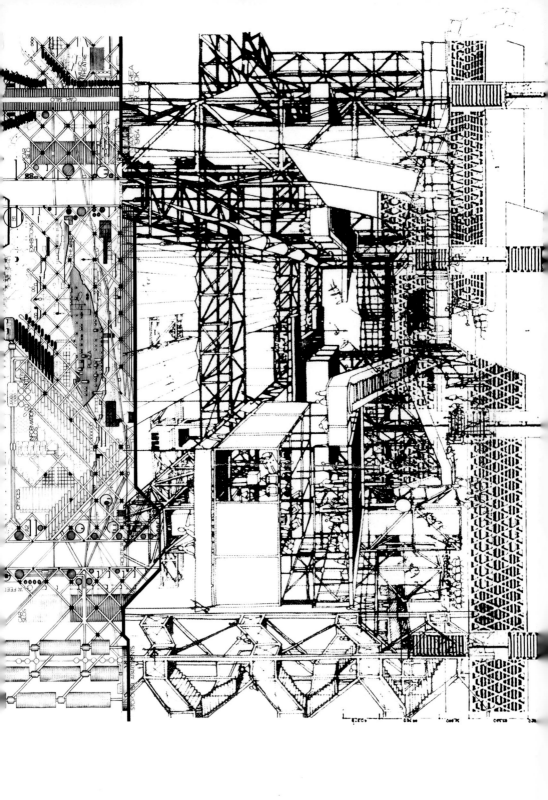

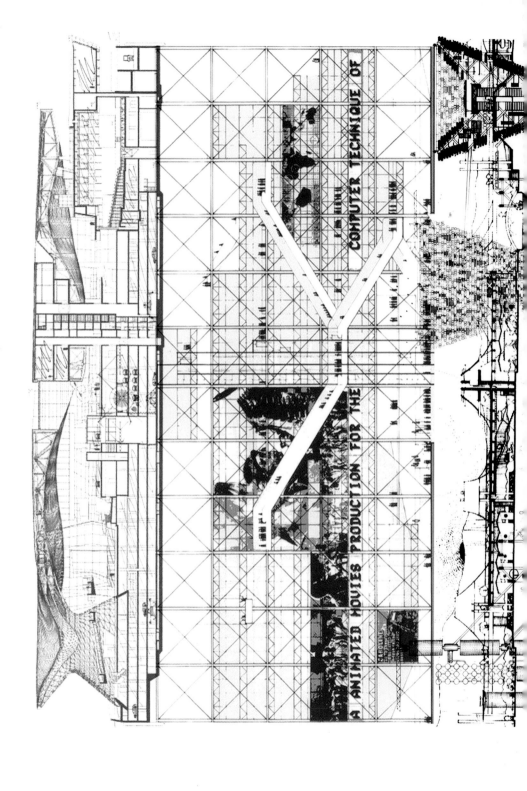

COMPUTER TECHNIQUE OF A ANIMATED MOVIES PRODUCTION FOR THE

Heydar Aliyev Cultural Centre, Zaha Hadid Architects; © Helene Binet; Courtesy Zaha Hadid Architects

From Demo(cracy) to Pluto(cracy), collage by Parsa Khalili, 2018

Konrad Wachsmann as a young carpenter,
ca. 1917, photographer unknown;
Akademie der Künste, Berlin, Konrad-
Wachsmann-Archiv 0210_12

Letter from Konrad Wachsmann to his mother, April 1924; Akademie der Künste, Berlin, Konrad-Wachsmann-
Archiv 1980_032_001

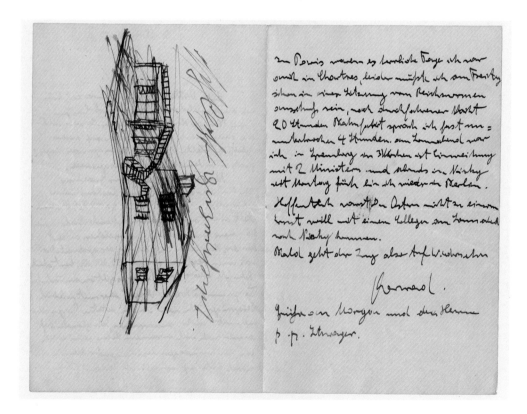

19   BIOGRAPHICAL NOTES
     → EN 21 / DE 23
Konrad Wachsmann in October 1921,
photographer unknown; Akademie
der Künste, Berlin, Konrad-Wachsmann-
Archiv 0210_034a

20   BIOGRAPHICAL NOTES
     → EN 21 / DE 23
Konrad Wachsmann with his mother,
ca. 1925, photographer unknown;
Akademie der Künste, Berlin, Konrad-
Wachsmann-Archiv 0210_009

21   BIOGRAPHICAL NOTES   →   EN 21 / DE 23
Letter from Konrad Wachsmann to his mother (with a sketch of Einstein's summerhouse in Caputh),
Konrad-Wachsmann-Archiv 1980_032_002

Monsieur,

je déclare avec plaisir que je connais personnellement M. Konrad WACHSMANN qui est un architecte bien doué. Sa spécialité est la construction en bois, et il a bâti autrefois pour mois une maison de campagne admirée par bien des gens. Je serais bien aise si cet homme habile pouviat être utile pour la France.

A. Einstein.

Professeur Albert Einstein

Octobre 2, 1939

September 9, 1940

The Commissioner of Immigration
  and Naturalization Service
Washington, D. C.

Dear Sir:

This is to draw your attention to the well known
German architect, Konrad Wachsmann, whom I have
known closely since 1933 and who left Germany when
the Nazi Government was established. He went first
to Italy. When the political changes came about
there, he went to France and, soon after the war
started, he was interned there. Just before the first
of August, 1940, he managed to get out of the concen-
tration camp. I helped him by writing to the Ambassa-
dor in Rome (M. Poncet) who wrote to the Government
in his behalf. Wachsmann is a most distinguished man
of very high standards and he would be very useful in
this country. He has published many articles and a
well-known book about building in wood, in which he
is a particularly advanced practitioner. He is in
his early thirties, very able, and a most reliable
character. I have heard that the Government has recently made arrangements whereby well-known personalities in science and the arts who are in distress
in France can be brought over here on a visitor's
visa. I recommend Mr. Konrad Wachsmann as being most
worthy of inclusion under this new plan. If I can be
of any further help, may I ask you to let me know.

Hoping that you will be able to give this case your
support, I am

                              Very truly yours,

                              Walter Gropius,
                              Chairman of the Department
                                 of Architecture

WG/SR

Letter of recommendation by Walter Gropius, September 1940; Akademie der Künste, Berlin, Konrad-Wachsmann-
19   Archiv 2526_1

Wachsmann with Walter Gropius at the construction site of a General Panel House, undated,
photographer: William F. Karsten; Akademie der Künste, Berlin, Konrad-Wachsmann-Archiv 0113_1

BIOGRAPHICAL NOTES
→ EN 21 / DE 23
Konrad Wachsmann teaching (USAF-
Hangar), undated, photographer unknown;
Akademie der Künste, Berlin,
Konrad-Wachsmann-Archiv 0129_2

26 BIOGRAPHICAL NOTES → EN 21 / DE 23
Konrad Wachsmann in Tokyo, 1955, photographer unknown; Akademie der Künste, Berlin,
Konrad-Wachsmann-Archiv 0209_87

27   BIOGRAPHICAL NOTES   →   EN 21 / DE 23
Konrad Wachsmann with Ludwig Mies van der Rohe, ca. 1966, photographer unknown;
Akademie der Künste, Berlin, Konrad-Wachsmann-Archiv 0198_14

28   BIOGRAPHICAL NOTES   →   EN 21 / DE 23
Konrad Wachsmann with Richard Buckminster Fuller, undated, photographer unknown;
Akademie der Künste, Berlin, Konrad-Wachsmann-Archiv 0200_1

LE CORBUSIER

Paris, le 30 Janvier 1950

Monsieur Konrad WACHSMANN
Illinois Institute of Technology
Institute of Design
632 North Dearborn
CHICAGO   ill.

Mon cher Wachasmann,

J'ai appris avec grande satisfaction
que vous alliez professer à l'Institut Illinois de
Chicago, pour enseigner et rechercher des méthodes
modernes dans la construction des bâtiments. Vous êtes
tout à fait préparé pour une telle tache, où il faut
grouper l'amour du beau et les qualités de réalisme
nécessaires. Je vous félicite et je félicite l'institut
qui vous a engagé.

Je pars en Colombie et je serais
absent en Février et Mars. Ma collaboration vous est
toute assurée, puisque ces problèmes m'occupent depuis
30 ans.

Croyez, mon cher Wachsmann, à mes
meilleurs sentiments.

LE CORBUSIER

35, RUE DE SÈVRES — PARIS (6·)
TÉL. LITTRÉ 99-62

Letter from Le Corbusier to Konrad Wachsmann, January 1950; Akademie der Künste, Berlin, Konrad-Wachsmann-Archiv 0919_5

My dear Wachsmann,

It was with great satisfaction that I learned about your appointment to become professor at the Illinois Institute in Chicago where you will be teaching and researching on modern industrial building styles. You are well prepared to take on such a task—bringing together a love for beauty with the necessary realistic qualities. I congratulate you and the Institute that hired you.

I will be leaving for Columbia and will be gone in February and March. You can certainly count on my collaboration, since these are issues I myself have been working on for thirty years.

Sending you, dear Wachsmann, my best wishes; I remain

Le Corbusier

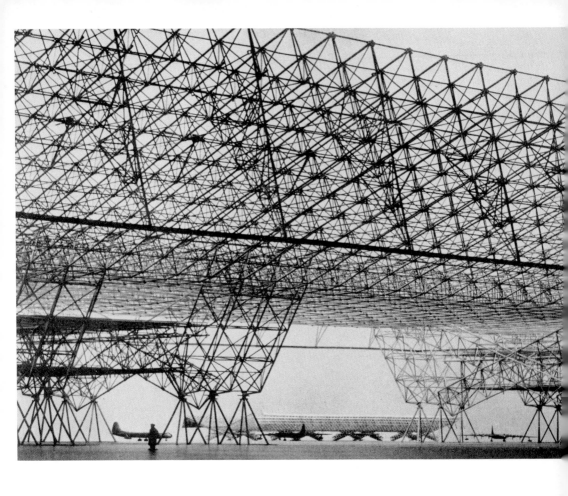

Model of the USAF-Hangar, ca. 1953, photographer unknown; Akademie der Künste, Berlin,
Konrad-Wachsmann-Archiv 0126_017

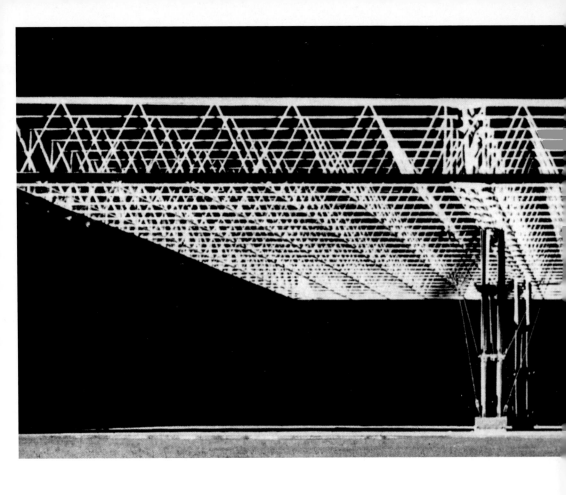

Model of a *Mobilar-Structure*, ca. 1945, taken from Wachsmann's book *Wendepunkt im Bauen*,
Krausskopf-Verlag 1959, p. 163

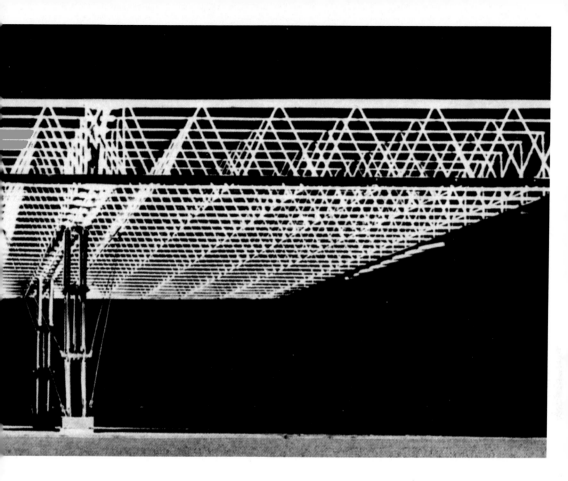

Structural model by six students at the Institute of Design Chicago, 1954–55, taken from Wachsmann's book *Wendepunkt im Bauen*, Krausskopf-Verlag 1959, p. 213

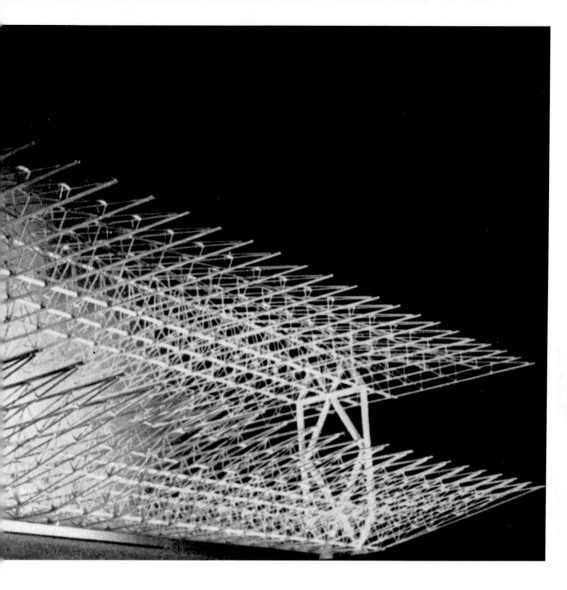

33   KONRAD WACHSMANN'S TELEVISION: POST-ARCHITECTURAL TRANSMISSIONS   →   EN 25 / DE 27
Student work (15 team members) for a "Concert Hall" at the Summer academy in Salzburg 1956, taken from Wachsmann's book
Wendepunkt im Bauen, Krausskopf-Verlag 1959, p. 217

34   KONRAD WACHSMANN'S TELEVISION: POST-ARCHITECTURAL TRANSMISSIONS   →   EN 25 / DE 27
Student work (24 team members) on a "Building System," at the Summer academy in Salzburg, 1958, taken from Wachsmann's book
Wendepunkt im Bauen, Krausskopf-Verlag 1959, p. 223

35   KONRAD WACHSMANN'S TELEVISION: POST-ARCHITECTURAL TRANSMISSIONS   →   EN 25 / DE 27
Student work (21 team members) on a "School-Pavilion," at the University of Tokyo, 1955, taken from Wachsmann's book

Wendepunkt im Bauen, Krausskopf-Verlag 1959, p. 216

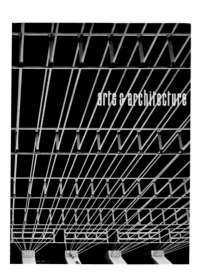

36 KONRAD WACHSMANN'S TELEVISION: POST-ARCHITECTURAL TRANSMISSIONS
    → EN 25 / DE 27
Konrad Wachsmann, Civic-Center-Project for California City, 1966–71, photographer unknown; Akademie der Künste, Berlin, Konrad-Wachsmann-Archiv 0140_003a

38 KONRAD WACHSMANN'S TELEVISION: POST-ARCHITECTURAL
    TRANSMISSIONS → EN 25 / DE 27
Konrad Wachsmann, Model view of the Civic-Center-Project for California City, 1966–71, photographer unknown; Akademie der Künste, Berlin, Konrad-Wachsmann-Archiv 0140_010a

37 KONRAD WACHSMANN'S TELEVISION:
    POST-ARCHITECTURAL TRANSMISSIONS
    → EN 25 / DE 27
Cover of Arts & Architecture, John Entenza (ed.) May 1967, Los Angeles, with a profound introduction to the work of Konrad Wachsmann

39 KONRAD WACHSMANN'S TELEVISION: POST-ARCHITECTURAL
    TRANSMISSIONS → EN 25 / DE 27
Konrad Wachsmann, Interior model view of the Civic-Center-Project for California City, 1966–71, photographer unknown; Akademie der Künste, Berlin, Konrad-Wachsmann-Archiv 0140_006a

Konrad Wachsmann, Model view of the Civic-Center-Project for California City, 1966–71, photographer unknown;
Akademie der Künste, Berlin, Konrad-Wachsmann-Archiv 0140_014_01

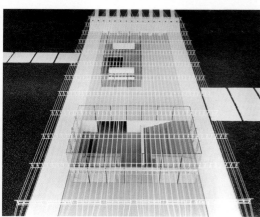

41   <small>KONRAD WACHSMANN'S TELEVISION: POST-ARCHITECTURAL TRANSMISSIONS</small> → <small>EN 25 / DE 27</small>
Konrad Wachsmann, Model view of the Civic-Center-Project for California City, 1966–71, photographer unknown;
Akademie der Künste, Berlin, Konrad-Wachsmann-Archiv 0146_060_a

42 <small>KONRAD WACHSMANN'S TELEVISION: POST-
ARCHITECTURAL TRANSMISSIONS</small>
→ <small>EN 25 / DE 27</small>
Konrad Wachsmann, Model view of the Civic-Center-
Project for California City, 1966–71, photographer
unknown; Akademie der Künste, Berlin, Konrad-
Wachsmann-Archiv 0141_019_a

43 KONRAD WACHSMANN'S CINEMATOGRAPHIC NOTATION → EN 39 / DE 43
Structural model for the USAF-Hangar, ca. 1952, photographer unknown; Akademie der Künste, Berlin,
Konrad-Wachsmann-Archiv 0125_025

44   KONRAD WACHSMANN'S CINEMATOGRAPHIC NOTATION   →   EN 39 / DE 43
Scale model for the USAF-Hangar, ca. 1954, photographer unknown; Akademie der Künste, Berlin,
Konrad-Wachsmann-Archiv 0130_18)

KONRAD WACHSMANN'S CINEMATOGRAPHIC NOTATION → EN 39 / DE 43
Scale model for the USAF-Hangar, ca. 1954, photographer unknown; Akademie der Künste, Berlin,
Konrad-Wachsmann-Archiv 0130_21

Konrad Wachsmann, *Grapevine Structure*—Study of a dynamic structure, development of a universal construction with students at the Chicago Institute of Design, 1953; Akademie der Künste, Berlin, Konrad-Wachsmann-Archiv 0318_12. Original drawing mirrored as shown in *Wendepunkt im Bauen*, pp. 200–201.

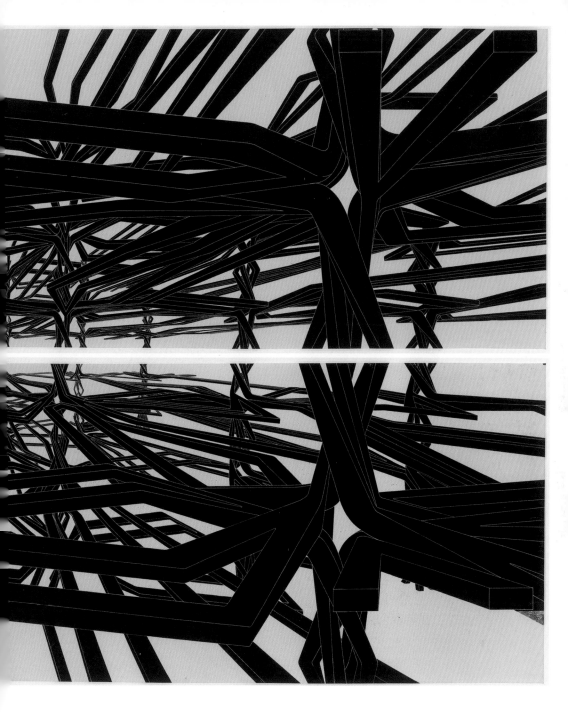

39

47   KONRAD WACHSMANN'S
     CINEMATOGRAPHIC NOTATION
     →   EN 40 / DE 44
Cover of Konrad Wachsmann's book
Aspekte, Otto-Krauskopf-Verlag,
Wiesbaden, 1961

48   KONRAD WACHSMANN'S CINEMATOGRAPHIC NOTATION
     →   EN 40 / DE 44
Pages 16/17 of Konrad Wachsmann's book *Aspekte*

49 ON TURNING POINTS → EN 46 / DE 52
Erratum in Sigfried Giedion's first publishing of *Bauen in Frankreich—Eisen —Eisenbeton*, Klinkhardt & Biermann Verlag, Leipzig/Berlin, 1928

50 ON TURNING POINTS → EN 47 / DE 53
Photomontage of the *Wolkenbügel* by El Lissitzky, 1925

51 ON TURNING POINTS → EN 48 / DE 54
Karl Friedrich Schinkel, *The Suspension Bridge across the Menai Strait near Bangor in Wales*, 1826; drawing, 14.4 × 35.1 cm; collection: Kupferstichkabinett; © photo: bpk / Kupferstichkabinett der Staatlichen Museen zu Berlin—Preußischer Kulturbesitz / Wolfram Büttner

13 Durchblick durch die aus einem gefalteten verglasten Rippen-
system bestehende Tonnenkonstruktion der Mittel- und Querschiffe
des Kristallpalastes

14 Paxton sagt, daß ihn in seiner Jugendzeit, in der er sich hauptsächlich als Gärtner betätigte, das Studium eines Blattes der
Victoria regia zu seinen Konstruktionskonzeptionen angeregt habe

15 Im Jahre 1837 begann er in Chatsworth den Bau des damals
größten Treibhauses der Welt für die Victoria regia, von der hier
der strukturelle Aufbau des Blattes gezeigt wird

16 Dachansicht mit Blick gegen das Querschiff des Kristallpalastes
in London, erbaut im Jahre 1851 von Sir Joseph Paxton. Links
unterhalb des Glasgewölbes sieht man die durchlaufenden, aus
verformten Blechen konstruierten Ventilationsklappen. Die ursprünglich völlig standardisierten, sägeförmigen Glasdächer wurden
teilweise durch spätere Umbauten verändert ▸

20

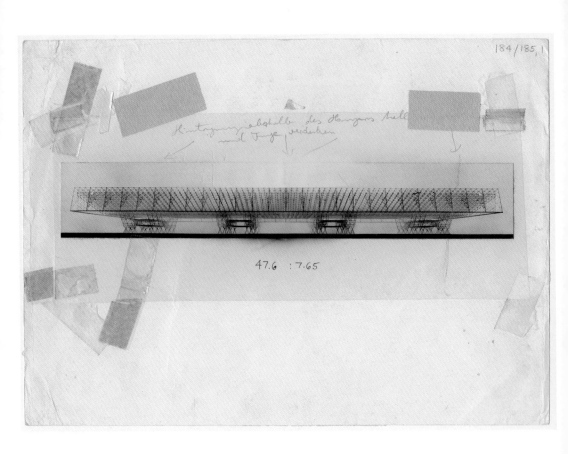

Konrad Wachsmann (IIT), *Model of the USAF-Hangar*, ca. 1953, photographer unknown; Akademie der Künste, Berlin,

   Konrad-Wachsmann-Archiv 0126_070a

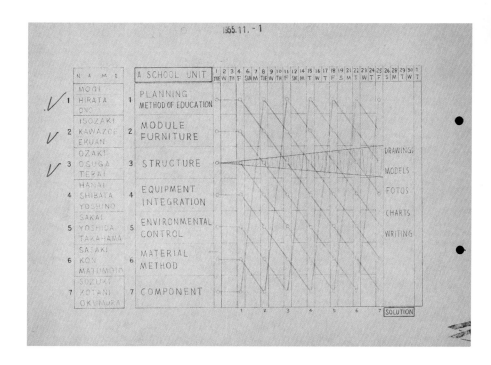

54   ON TURNING POINTS   →   EN 51 / DE 57
Konrad Wachsmann (IIT), *Model of the USAF-Hangar*, ca. 1953, photographer unknown; Akademie der Künste, Berlin,
Konrad-Wachsmann-Archiv 0126_073a

55   ON TURNING POINTS   →   EN 51 / DE 58
Konrad Wachsmann, Timeframe / Structure for Tokyo-Seminar, 1955; Akademie der Künste, Berlin,
Konrad-Wachsmann-Archiv 1094_114

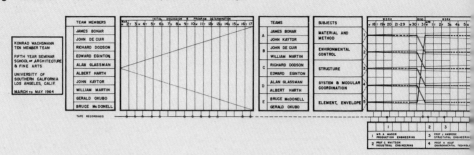

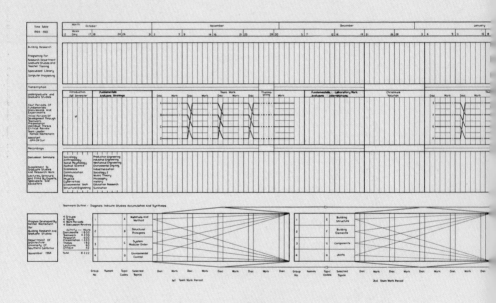

Konrad Wachsmann, building research program and timetable, University of Southern California, Los Angeles, 1964;
Akademie der Künste, Berlin, Konrad-Wachsmann-Archiv 0353_039

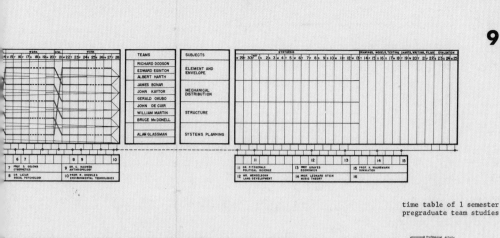

time table of 1 semester
pregraduate team studies

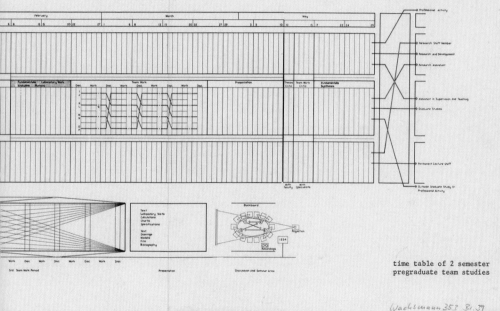

time table of 2 semester
pregraduate team studies

Wachsmann 353 B. 59

47

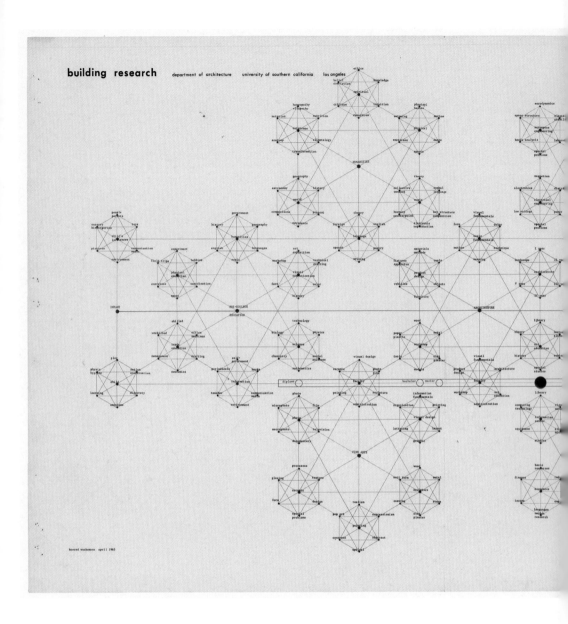

Konrad Wachsmann, building research Coordination of Educational Information, University of Southern California, Los Angeles, 1965; Akademie der Künste, Berlin, Konrad-Wachsmann-Archiv 0353_034

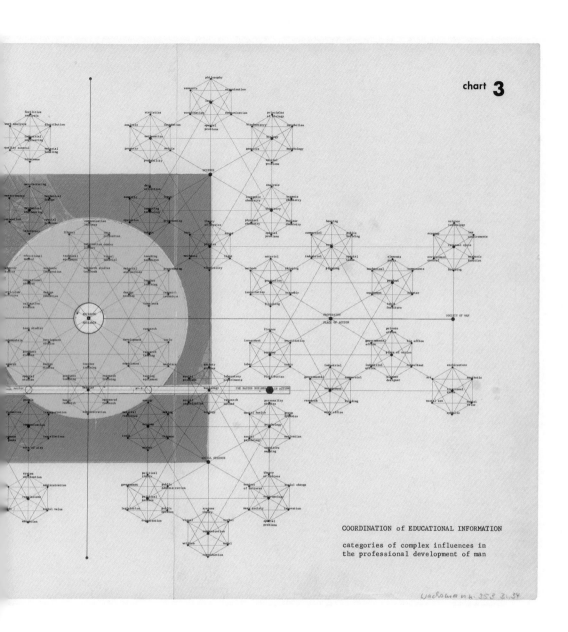

chart **3**

COORDINATION of EDUCATIONAL INFORMATION

categories of complex influences in
the professional development of man

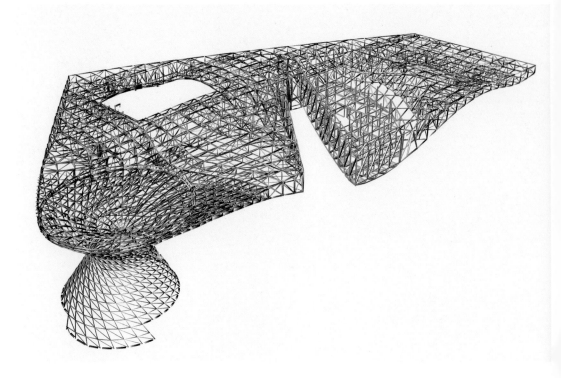

58   ON TURNING POINTS   →   EN 52 / DE 58
Cover of K. G. Pontus Hultén, *The Machine*, Museum
of Modern Art, New York, 1968

59   ON TURNING POINTS   →   EN 52 / DE 58
Cover of *JA* 113 (*The Japan Architect*),
reprint Edition Expo 70, Spring 2019

60   ON TURNING POINTS   →   EN 19, 52 / DE 20, 58
Coop Himmelb(l)au, Structure of BMW-Welt, Munich 2001–07; © Coop Himmelb(l)au

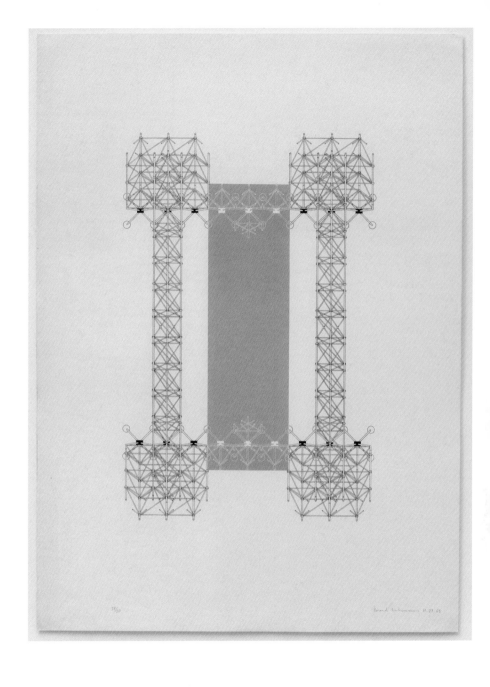

Konrad Wachsmann, *Tetradedons and Pyramids*, color lithograph, 1963, photographer: Edward Cella Art &
Architecture, Los Angeles

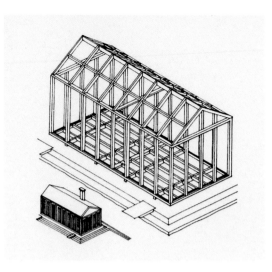

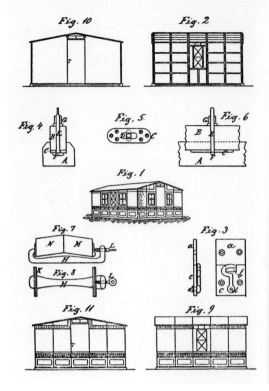

62　A NEW ANONYMITY OF BUILDING ON A TECHNICAL BASIS
　　→　EN 59 / DE 67
Manning Cottage, prefabricated building type in wood for the
British Colonies, 1820s; taken from Gilbert Herbert, *The Dream
of the Factory-Made House*, MIT press, Cambridge, 1984

63　A NEW ANONYMITY OF BUILDING ON A TECHNICAL BASIS
　　→　EN 59 / DE 67
Christoph & Unmack, Patent for a military tent, 1884; taken
from Gilbert Herbert, *The Dream of the Factory-Made House*,
MIT press, Cambridge, 1984

64　A NEW ANONYMITY OF BUILDING ON A TECHNICAL
　　BASIS　→　EN 59 / DE 67
Josef Hoffmann, Steelhouse-Prototype for Vogel &
Noot, 1928; taken from *Moderne Bauformen* XXVII,
1928

65　A NEW ANONYMITY OF BUILDING ON A TECHNICAL BASIS
　　→　EN 59 / DE 67
General Panel Corporation, Packaged House, ca. 1949,
photographer unknown; Akademie der Künste, Berlin,
Konrad-Wachsmann-Archiv 0102_005

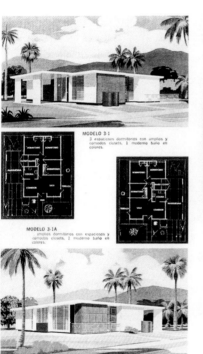

66   A NEW ANONYMITY OF BUILDING ON A TECHNICAL BASIS
         →   EN 59 / DE 67
Konrad Wachsmann, (Summer-)house for Albert Einstein, 1929, Caputh near
Potsdam; © WikiCommons, Cornelsen Kulturstiftung

67   A NEW ANONYMITY OF BUILDING ON A TECHNICAL BASIS   →   EN 59 / DE 67
Simon Schmiderer & Armando Vivoni, Housing Types for the International Basic Economy Corporation (IBEC),
Puerto Rico, ca. 1964; © IBEC / Archive M. Boeckl

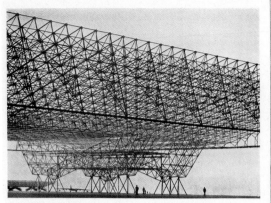

137 Konrad Wachsmann, Konstruktions-gerippe für einen Flugzeughangar

Konstruktion auf einem einzigen Knotenpunkt beruht. Wir haben bisher nirgends so schonungslose Klarheit und Folgerichtigkeit des Denkens an so viel schöpferischer Freiheit vereint gesehen — und damit einen fesselnden Blick in die geistigen Möglichkeiten unserer Zeit getan. Zweifellos hat Wachsmanns Vortrag zum Wesentlichsten gehört, was seit langer Zeit zu hören war. Besonders lehrreich war Wachsmanns Erläuterung seiner Erziehungsmethode, die nicht auf die Ansammlung von Wissen und Kenntnissen, sondern auf die Entwicklung von Fähigkeiten und die Entdeckung von Möglichkeiten abzielt. Elementarklassen zur Entfaltung von Materialverständnis und Konstruktionsgefühl, wie sie seit dem Bauhaus Dessau in immer zahlreicheren ausländischen Hochschulen geführt werden, soll es auch in Wien, z. B. unter Strnad, gegeben haben — das ist allerdings lange her. Gerade diesbezüglich könnten Wachsmanns Ausführungen unmittelbar Anregung für die Weiterführung unserer eigenen modernen Tradition geben.

Roland Rainer

Architekt Prof. Konrad Wachsmann (Chicago) sprach in einem Vortrag, der von der Zentralvereinigung der Architekten gemeinsam mit dem US-Informationsdienst veranstaltet war, und anschließend bei einer Tagung über die Erziehung zum Architekten.

Seine Lehre ist eine Kampfansage allen erstarrten und veralteten Lehrmethoden gegenüber, seine Ideen sind weit vorausschauend und aus einer autäen Erkenntnis unserer Lebensgrundlagen heraus entstanden. Sie gelten in erster Linie für Amerika, wo die Verhältnisse in konstruktiver und technischer Hinsicht noch weit mehr auf die Maschine abgestellt sind als in Europa, aber wahrscheinlich wird diese Entwicklung auch hier immer mehr diese Richtung nehmen.

Das Wesentliche, Allgemeingültige seiner Ansichten über die Erziehungsmethoden ist wohl die Forderung, daß die Studierenden nicht kritiklos Wissen anhäufen sollen, sondern durch eigenes Denken, durch selbständiges Erfinden, durch Probieren an der Maschine, durch Handhabung aller Art von Werkzeugen, durch Arbeiten mit verschiedenen Materialien ihren Weg selber finden sollen. Alle Mittel der heutigen Technik sollen hierfür zur Verfügung stehen. Werkstätten mit modernsten Maschinen und Behelfen sollen klarmachen, welche Präzision und Feinarbeit heute mit ihrer Hilfe erreicht werden kann. Alle modernen Behelfe der Photographie, des Films und des Tonbandes stehen den Studierenden zur Verfügung. In einem Grundkurs, der zwei oder drei Semester dauert, soll der Schüler aus eigener Erfahrung zu Erkenntnissen kommen. Beispielsweise wird ihm als Aufgabe gestellt, aus Strohhalmen ein Gerüst zu bauen, das einen Ziegelstein tragen kann. Erst nach langem Probieren wird ihm das gelingen, er wird das Gefühl für das Verbinden von Teilen, für Abstellungsmöglichkeiten, für Knickfestigkeit usw. aus eigener Erfahrung bekommen und er wird die Kräfte, wie sie in einem Bauwerk vorkommen, verstehen lernen.

Im Bauen gibt es nur drei Vorgänge: Hinzufügen, Wegnehmen und Formen. Die Vielgestalt der Erscheinungen läßt sich auf diese drei Grundvorgänge zurückführen, und alles ist dann leichter zu erfassen.

Die Tradition ist zu achten, aber sie darf nie mißverstanden werden. Jede Änderung in Gestalten braucht Zeit, geht allmählich vor sich und muß vom Leben diktiert sein. Nie kann aus der bloßen Nachahmung des Alten Brauchbares entstehen.

Gerade beim Bauen können solche Änderungen, die den Lebensnotwendigkeiten entsprechen, nur durch unermüdliche Forschungsarbeit erreicht werden. Wenn man bedenkt, wieviel Studien und Versuche nötig sind, um eine neue Maschine, ein neues Auto oder ein Flugzeug zu konstruieren, so ist es naheliegend, daß bei einem so umfassenden Problem, wie es das Bauen bedeutet, in erhöhtem Maße Forschungsarbeit nötig ist, eine Forschungsarbeit, die der Zukunft dient und sich auch erst in Zukunft auswirken wird.

In der Schule beginnt das Planen erst nach Absolvierung des früher geschilderten Grundkurses. Jede Aufgabe, sei es ein Wohnhaus, eine Schule, ein Krankenhaus oder eine Flugzeughalle, wird bis ins kleinste Detail durch mehrere Arbeitsgruppen studiert. Jede Arbeitsgruppe hat eine ungerade Anzahl von Mitgliedern (am besten drei oder fünf) und jede Aufgabe wird nach mehreren Richtungen untersucht. Die Erfahrungen werden im Beisein des Lehrers, aber ohne dessen Kritik, ausgetauscht, die Aufgabe wird gemeinsam bis zu ihrer Lösung weitergeführt. Erst dann setzt die Kritik des Lehrers ein, der alles genau verfolgt hat und an Hand aller gesammelten Zeichnungen und Unterlagen, deren Richtigkeit oder Unrichtigkeit er im einzelnen feststellt, folgt ein Gesamturteil über Erfolg oder Mißerfolg der Arbeit. Die Ausführungszeichnungen müssen von größter Exaktheit sein, zeichnerische Effekte dürfen nicht angewendet, Zeitschriften dürfen nicht benützt werden. Alles muß aus eigener Erkenntnis und aus dem gegenseitigen Gedankenaustausch kommen, nur so kann auch im Leben Brauchbares entstehen. Von allen Projekten und auch von Details werden Modelle gemacht. Ergänzende Vorträge aus wissenschaftlichen Fächern begleiten den Unterricht.

Das Ideal Wachsmanns ist es, in seiner Schule vorwiegend Lehrer zu erziehen, die ihre Erkenntnisse an anderen Schulen weiterverbreiten und so eine entsprechend breite Basis für eine allgemeine Beeinflussung des Bauens schaffen.

Wachsmann befindet sich auf einer Weltreise im Auftrage seiner Regierung. Er hat für Architekturstudenten ein zweimonatiges Seminar in Japan abgehalten und will jetzt das gleiche in Ulm tun. Schade ist, daß ein solches Seminar nicht auch in Österreich stattfinden kann.

Es ist selbstverständlich, daß alle jene, die ihren Lehrberuf ernst nehmen, innerhalb der Gedanken beschäftigen, wie man die Erziehung des Architekturstudenten zu selbständigen Gestalten führen soll und gerade bei uns sind schon viele wertvolle Beiträge hiezu gegeben worden. Ich erinnere nur an einen Lehrer, wie an Strnad, der aus tiefster Erkenntnis der Grundlagen unseres Lebens und der daraus entspringenden Formenwelt schon ähnliche Wege wie Wachsmann gegangen ist. Unsere Aufgabe ist es, unseren Verhältnissen heraus und unserer Zeit entsprechend, solche Ideen weiter zu entwickeln. Wachsmann aber sind wir dankbar, daß er uns von seinem Wissen und seinen Erkenntnissen soviel mitgeteilt hat. Er hat uns dadurch angeregt, die Probleme weiter zu verfolgen und uns zu sehen und hat uns vieles nähergerückt und klargemacht, was an Ähnlichem in der Welt vorgeht.

Erich Boltenstern

121

KONRAD WACHSMANN – PLANUNG UND ERZIEHUNG

Professor Konrad Wachsmann, der bekannte, jetzt in USA lebende deutsche Architekt, machte auf einer Vortragsreise um die Welt auch in Wien halt, sprach am 24. April 1956 über „Erziehung – Planung – Industrialisierung" und hielt kurz darauf am Semmering ein dreitägiges Seminar für Architekten und Fachleute aus den Behörden und einigen Lichtbildern das Wesentliche jener Probleme zur Sprache, die das Bauen in der Welt grundlegend zu verändern beginnen und vielleicht ganz verändert werden — auch wenn wir hier davon noch wenig bemerken sollten.

Ausgehend von der grundsätzlichen Bejahung industrieller Serienproduktion als des maßgebenden, formbildenden Faktors unserer Zeit, kam Wachsmann bald zu jenen besonderen Problemen, durch deren Lösung er auch als Mitarbeiter von Gropius bei den Fertighäusern der Pancel-Corporation bekannt ist: nämlich die bis ins letzte durchdachte Lösung der charakteristischen konstruktiven Punkte. Das mit der Gründlichkeit und Präzision eines Uhrmachers durchdachte Detail — nicht irgendeines, sondern das Eine, charakteristische Detail der besten Zusammenfügung der Elemente — hat Wachsmann zu jener „Kunst der Fuge" entwickelt, das ihm Ausgangspunkt für die gesamte Konstruktion, ja darüber hinaus Ausgangspunkt in unerforschtes Neuland der Gestaltung ist; was sein großartiges Hangarprojekt aus Stahlrohr am deutlichsten zeigt, dessen phantastische

120

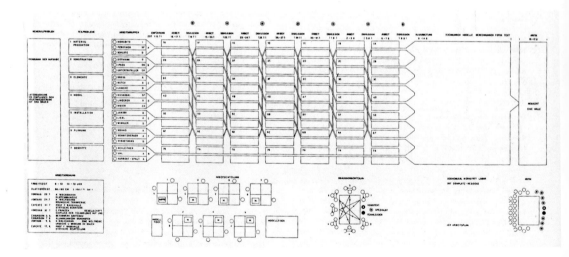

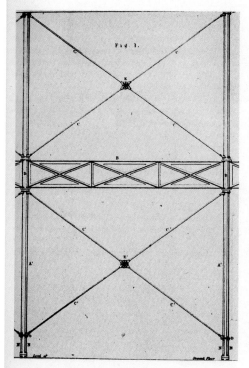

1 Konstruktionssystem eines Binderfeldes des Kristallpalastes in London, 1851. Achsenabstand der Stützen 24 Fuß

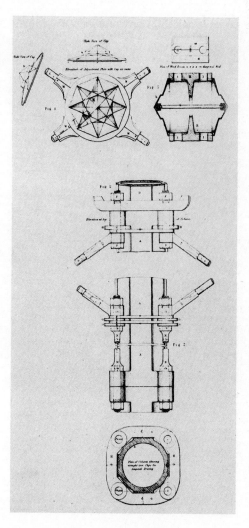

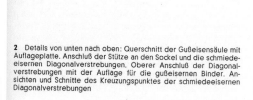

2 Details von unten nach oben: Querschnitt der Gußeisensäule mit Auflageplatte. Anschluß der Stütze an den Sockel und die schmiedeeisernen Diagonalverstrebungen. Oberer Anschluß der Diagonalverstrebungen mit der Auflage für die gußeisernen Binder. Ansichten und Schnitte des Kreuzungspunktes der schmiedeeisernen Diagonalverstrebungen

Details of Construction (joints) at Joseph Paxton's Crystal Palace (1851) as published by Konrad Wachsmann in
Wendepunkte im Bauen (p. 13), Krausskopf-Verlag, Wiesbaden 1959

Hermann Czech's presentation in the Salzburg Wachsmann course of 1959, photographer: Wolfgang Mistelbauer

Free developed roof construction, Wachsmann course 1957; taken from Konrad Wachsmann *Bauen in unserer Zeit*,

exhibition catalog, Munich, 1958

A NEW ANONYMITY OF BUILDING ON A TECHNICAL BASIS → EN 59 / DE 67
Ottokar Uhl, Demountable church in Vienna (Siemensstraße), 1960–64, interior, photographer:
Gernot Schlegel © Architekturzentrum Wien, collection, NL Uhl

74   A NEW ANONYMITY OF BUILDING ON A TECHNICAL BASIS   →   EN 59 / DE 67
Franz Kiener, Kiener House, Salzburg, 1956–59; © Atelier Kiener Vienna

75   A NEW ANONYMITY OF BUILDING ON A TECHNICAL BASIS   →   EN 59 / DE 67
Gerhard Garstenauer, Bad Gastein Congress, 1968–74; © WikiCommons, Gerd Fahrenhorst

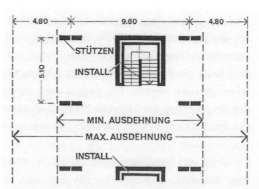

Wohnanlage „Wohnen morgen" Hollabrunn I, NÖ,
1971–76, Primärstruktur mit Festlegung der minimalen
und maximalen Ausdehnung

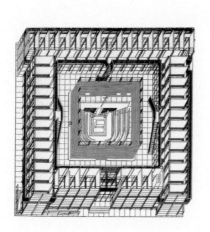

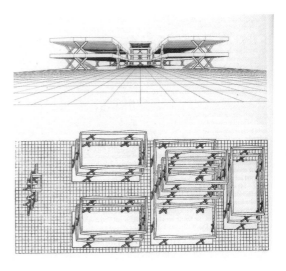

76   A NEW ANONYMITY OF BUILDING ON A TECHNICAL BASIS
     →   EN 59 / DE 67
Ottokar Uhl, Housing complex "Wohnen morgen," Hollabrunn,
1971–76, diagram of primary structure in relation to extension;
taken from: Ottokar Uhl, Pustet Verlag, Salzburg-Wien, 2005

77   A NEW ANONYMITY OF BUILDING ON A TECHNICAL
     BASIS   →   EN 59 / DE 67
Arbeitsgruppe 4, *Kolleg St. Josef*, Salzburg-Aigen,
1960–64, axonometric view; © Arbeitsgruppe 4
(Holzbauer/Kurrent/Spalt)

78   A NEW ANONYMITY OF BUILDING ON A TECHNICAL BASIS
     →   EN 59 / DE 67
Arbeitsgruppe 4 with Johann Georg Gsteu, *Seelsorgezentrum
Steyr-Ennsleiten*, 1958–61, perspective and axonometric view;
© Arbeitsgruppe 4 (Holzbauer/Kurrent/Spalt)

Eckhard Schulze-Fielitz, *The organization of three-dimensional space*, 1959; preliminary studies for the *Space City* © Eckhard Schulze-Fielitz

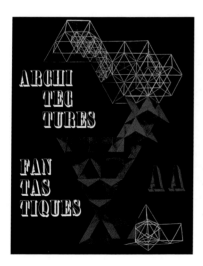

81   ECKHARD SCHULZE-FIELITZ IN CONVERSATION WITH WOLFGANG FIEL   →   EN 83 / DE 91
Eckhard Schulze-Fielitz, *Space City*, 1960, model view; © Eckhard Schulze-Fielitz

82   ECKHARD SCHULZE-FIELITZ IN
CONVERSATION WITH WOLFGANG FIEL
→   EN 83 / DE 91
Cover of *L'Architecture d'Aujourd'hui*,
Architectures fantastiques, June–July (102)
1962; © Archive Eckhard Schulze-Fielitz

83   ECKHARD SCHULZE-FIELITZ IN CONVERSATION WITH WOLFGANG
FIEL   →   EN 83 / DE 91
Eckhard Schulze-Fielitz with Yona Friedman, Manche, Bridge City over
the English Channel, 1963, model photo; © Archive Eckhard Schulze-
Fielitz

84   BUILDING SCIENCE: KONRAD WACHSMANN'S BUILDING INSTITUTE AT THE UNIVERSITY OF SOUTHERN CALIFORNIA (USC), 1964–74
     →   EN 89 / DE 97
Main workspace at the Building Institute at the University of Southern California, circa 1970. Source: courtesy of John Bollinger

85   BUILDING SCIENCE: KONRAD WACHSMANN'S BUILDING
     INSTITUTE AT THE UNIVERSITY OF SOUTHERN CALIFORNIA
     (USC), 1964–74   →   EN 89 / DE 97
The L.O.M. project was completed in 1971, when doctoral students
John Bollinger and Xavier Mendoza defended their joint disserta-
tion. Source: courtesy of John Bollinger

BUILDING SCIENCE: KONRAD WACHSMANN'S BUILDING INSTITUTE AT THE UNIVERSITY OF SOUTHERN CALIFORNIA (USC), 1964–74 → EN 89 / DE 97

Drawings of L.O.M. components on a drawing board in the Building Institute's workspace circa 1970. A partial prototype of the device can be seen near the corridor. Source: courtesy of John Bollinger

BUILDING SCIENCE: KONRAD WACHSMANN'S BUILDING INSTITUTE AT THE UNIVERSITY OF SOUTHERN
CALIFORNIA (USC), 1964–74 → EN 89 / DE 97
Buckminster Fuller and Konrad Wachsmann in conversation in front of an image of the California City project.
Taken at the opening of the exhibition "Konrad Wachsmann: 50 Years of Life and Work Toward Industrialization
of Building," at the USC Fisher Gallery in 1971. Source: courtesy of John Bollinger

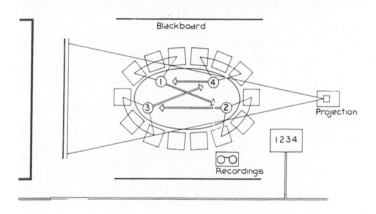

88   BUILDING SCIENCE: KONRAD WACHSMANN'S BUILDING INSTITUTE AT THE UNIVERSITY
     OF SOUTHERN CALIFORNIA (USC), 1964–74   →   EN 89 / DE 97
Conference room of the Building Institute at the University of Southern California, out-
fitted with ashtrays, panoramic slide projection wall at rear, telephone and audio
recording equipment at right; a microphone hangs at center, above the table. Source:
Akademie der Künste, Berlin, Konrad-Wachsmann-Archiv 180_004

89   BUILDING SCIENCE: KONRAD WACHSMANN'S BUILDING INSTITUTE AT THE UNIVERSITY
     OF SOUTHERN CALIFORNIA (USC), 1964–74   →   EN 89 / DE 97
Drawing of an ideal conference room set-up and seating arrangement for a "superteam"
of four, three-person groups working collaboratively on a task. Each group would cycle
through smaller tasks throughout the course of a larger project, thus ensuring that
each problem is addressed by the complete range of expertise and creative viewpoints
in any given team. Source: Akademie der Künste, Berlin, Konrad-Wachsmann-Archiv
detail from 353_39

90   BUILDING SCIENCE: KONRAD WACHSMANN'S BUILDING INSTITUTE AT THE UNIVERSITY OF SOUTHERN
       CALIFORNIA (USC), 1964–74 → EN 89 / DE 97
The General Panel Corporation raised capital for development by selling stock in the company. The first stocks
were sold in 1942, including 12 shares issued to historian Sigfried Giedion at a value of $3000. Source:
collection of the author

91   BUILDING SCIENCE: KONRAD WACHSMANN'S BUILDING INSTITUTE AT THE UNIVERSITY OF SOUTHERN
       CALIFORNIA (USC), 1964–74 → EN 89 / DE 97
The Building Institute's first sponsored research funds were received on August 21, 1967, in the form of a check
for $40,000. The contribution represented the first of three years of support that the Institute would receive
from Weyerhaeuser. Source: "Memos, Wachsmann" in Crombie Taylor Papers, Ryerson & Burnham Archives, Art
Institute of Chicago

COPY

WALTER GROPIUS
Architect A.I.A., A.S.P.A.
96 Mount Auburn Street
Cambridge 38, Massachusetts
Telephone University 4-9491

May 21, 1951

Mr. Serge Chermayeff, Director
Institute of Design
632 North Dearborn Street
Chicago 10, Illinois

Dear Serge:

I am much distressed about your letter telling me of your rift
with Konrad Wachsmann. I am particularly sorry about it because
several people coming from Chicago told me about their strong and
favorable impression of the achievements of the Institute. In
short intervals I talked with William Wurster, Pietro Belluschi
and Vernon De Mars. All were full of praise. We must succeed in
straightening out things. As I know you and Wachsmann both so well,
I should like to state here that there cannot be the slightest doubt
that I shall back you up to the hilt. Wachsmann, with all his charm,
I know is so egocentric a man that I believe he should not be a
teacher; his egoistic ambitions will always act like dynamite within
a community with others. He sees that clearly himself in enlightened
moments. A few weeks ago, he wrote me a very frank letter analyzing
himself and telling me that he feels he is no teacher; that he is
much more interested in the work itself than in the person who exe-
cutes it. I was hoping that this was a beginning of a maturing
process, but I am afraid that he has permanent character qualities,
which make him act in an irresponsible and inconsiderate manner,
besides his indubitably great talents as an inventor and an artist.

How can I help? The Institute must not be damaged by this clash.
It is much too important. I have written directly to Wachsmann and
have urged him to resign. And, of course, I will be glad to write
to President Heald and to give him my opinion if you want me to do so.

Meanwhile, I hope you will not be too depressed on account of the
deadlock which has arisen; I have gone through similar tensions
myself, and I know that this happens to leaders who have courage
to engage men with independent ideas, for these independent men are
always more difficult to go along with than run-of-the-mill men who
easily comply. But in the end, it was worthwhile even if dilemmas
arise as the present one in the Institute. Good luck, and I hope
to hear from you again.

Yours,

Walter Gropius

WG:sw

Walter Gropius writes to Serge Chermayeff in support of Konrad Wachsmann's resignation from the Institute of Design.
Source: Walter Gropius, "Letter to Serge Chermayeff, Director of the Institute of Design, May 21, 1951, Confidential,"
Illinois Institute of Technology Archives, Institute of Design Records, Box 5, Institute of Design – General (1949–1970)

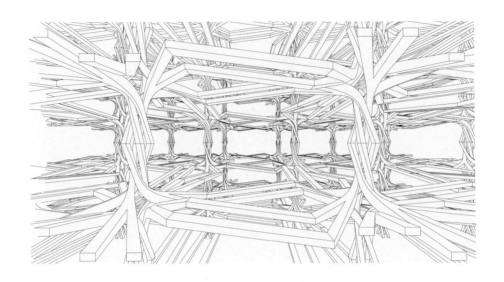

John A. Enright, *After Wachsmann*, 2010; perspective study of the structure taken at the corresponding point to

70   Wachsmann's original rendering and alternate views of the structure. © by the author

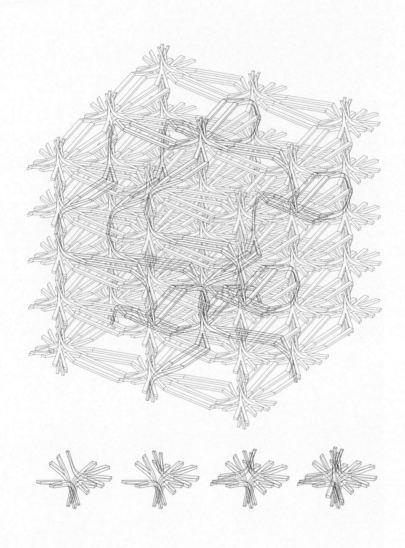

John A. Enright, *After Wachsmann*, 2010: overall axonometric diagram of the completed structure showing the four continuous paths of structural elements comprising the basic unit. © by the author

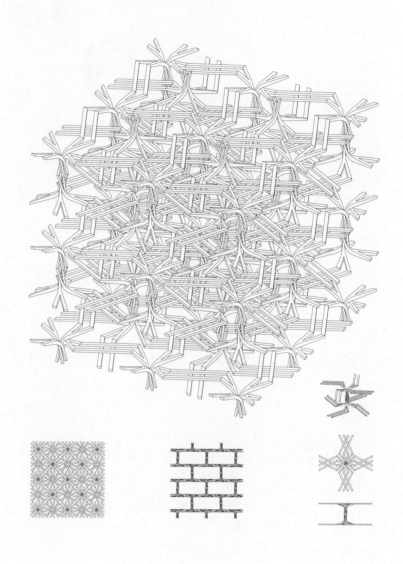

John A. Enright, *After Wachsmann*, 2010; overall axonometric diagram of the completed structure measuring sixty feet in cube form, including the "offset" relationship of shifted vertical supports in alternating layers. © by the author

98   PARAMETRIC STRUCTURAL DESIGN AS AN INSPIRATIONAL TOOL FOR REVISITING KONRAD WACHSMANN'S
        USAF-HANGAR
        →   EN 105 / DE 113
Canaletto (Giovanni Antonio Canal), *A View of Walton Bridge*, 1754; oil on canvas, 48.7 × 76.4 cm;
DPG600, Dulwich Picture Gallery, London

99   PARAMETRIC STRUCTURAL DESIGN AS AN INSPIRATIONAL TOOL FOR REVISITING KONRAD WACHSMANN'S
        USAF-HANGAR   →   EN 105 / DE 113
Image taken from Konrad Wachsmann's book *Wendepunkt im Bauen* (1959), reprint Verlag der Kunst
Dresden, 1989
        "Dissolution of the mass into its smallest parts in a geometrical order and bundling them on the
12 support points of each group of tubular truss columns."

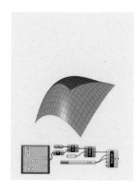

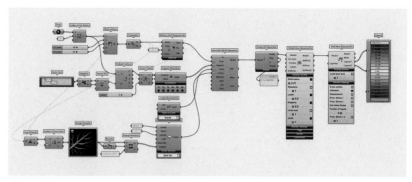

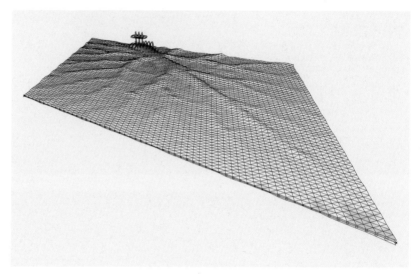

100 PARAMETRIC STRUCTURAL
DESIGN AS AN INSPIRA-
TIONAL TOOL FOR REVISIT-
ING KONRAD WACHS-
MANN'S USAF-HANGAR
→ EN 105 / DE 114
Parametric geometry generation
using Grasshopper

101 PARAMETRIC STRUCTURAL DESIGN AS AN INSPIRATIONAL TOOL FOR REVISITING KONRAD
WACHSMANN'S USAF-HANGAR → EN 106 / DE 114
Parametric configuration of a structural calculation using the Grasshopper plug-in based on the
reproduction of a leaf. Reprint courtesy of Moritz Heimrath

102 PARAMETRIC STRUCTURAL DESIGN AS AN INSPIRATIONAL TOOL FOR REVISITING KONRAD
WACHSMANN'S USAF-HANGAR
→ EN 106 / DE 114
Stress plot of a leaf-like structure under dead load. Green arrows and purple circles symbolize
translatory and rotatory support conditions. Reprint courtesy of Moritz Heimrath

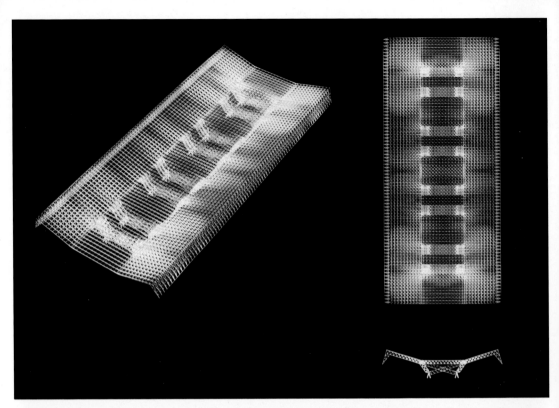

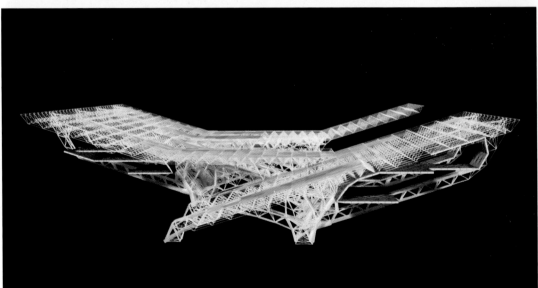

103 PARAMETRIC STRUCTURAL DESIGN AS AN INSPIRATIONAL TOOL FOR REVISITING KONRAD WACHSMANN'S USAF-HANGAR
→ EN 106 / DE 115
C showing cross-sections according to flow of forces; Students G. Goepel, J. Kim, A. Moisi, B. Schickermüller in their project for "Advanced Structural Design," at the University of Applied Arts Vienna, 2016

104 PARAMETRIC STRUCTURAL DESIGN AS AN INSPIRATIONAL TOOL FOR REVISITING KONRAD WACHSMANN'S USAF-HANGAR
→ EN 107 / DE 115
Stress analysis of a space framework based on Wachsmann's USAF-Hangar; Students A. Striezenec, A. Yonchev, C. Suter, J. Matarij in their project for "Advanced Structural Design," at the University of Applied Arts Vienna, 2016

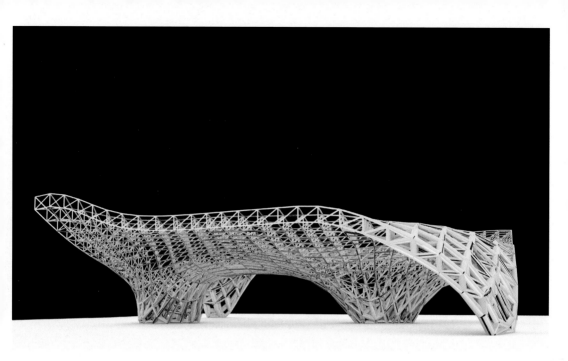

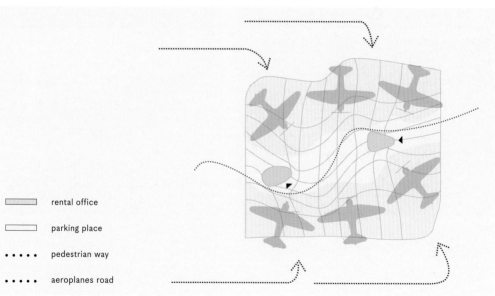

rental office

parking place

• • • • • pedestrian way

• • • • • aeroplanes road

105, 106   PARAMETRIC STRUCTURAL DESIGN AS AN INSPIRATIONAL TOOL FOR REVISITING KONRAD WACHSMANN'S
USAF-HANGAR → EN 107 / DE 115

77 Geometry of the hangar's structure resulting from the integration of application scenarios and structural examination

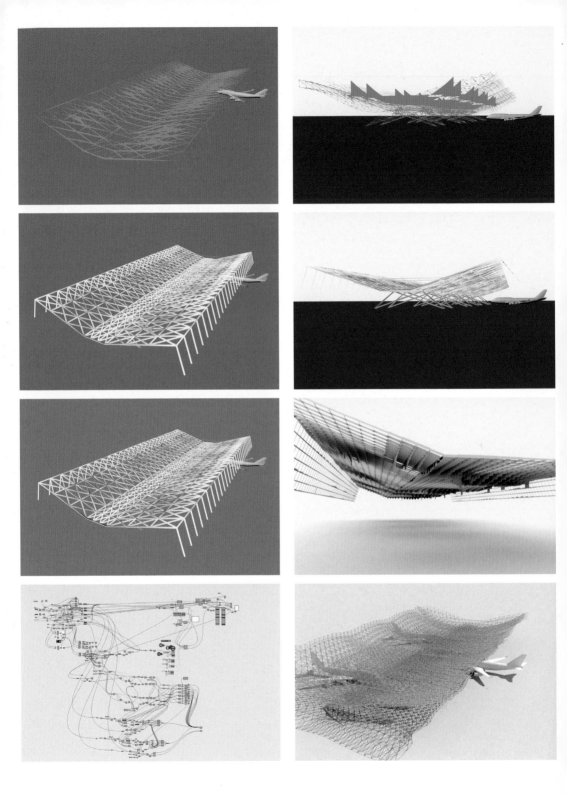

107–122   PARAMETRIC STRUCTURAL DESIGN AS AN INSPIRATIONAL TOOL FOR REVISITING KONRAD WACHSMANN'S USAF-HANGAR
→   EN 105 / DE 113
Varied images from the course "Advanced Structural Design," instructed by Klaus Bollinger, Andrei Gheorghe and Florian
Medicus, Summer term 2012

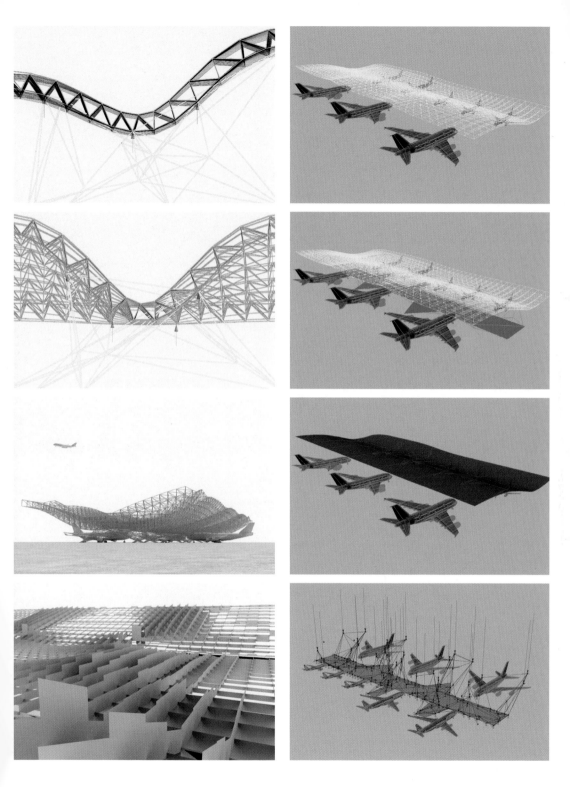

JOSIP BAJCER, DANIEL BOLOJAN, MELINA GIRARDI, MELANIE KOTZ, ARMIN SENONER, CHRISTOPH WUNDERLICH, LEA DIETIKER, LARISSA KONDINA, ELENA KRASTEVA, ALEKSANDRA MNICH, MARTA PIASECZYNSKA, MATTHIAS URSCHLER, EWA LENART, VIKI SÁNDOR, KLEMENS SITZMANN, STEPHAN TOMASI, SIEGFRIED BAUMGARTNER, PHILIPP REINSBERG, HAIG SERAYDARIAN, EMANUEL TORNQUIST, MARIE DRESCHER, ANNAMARIA DOBAI, KATHARINA KOHLROSER, MARIE LICHTENWAGNER, MING YIN

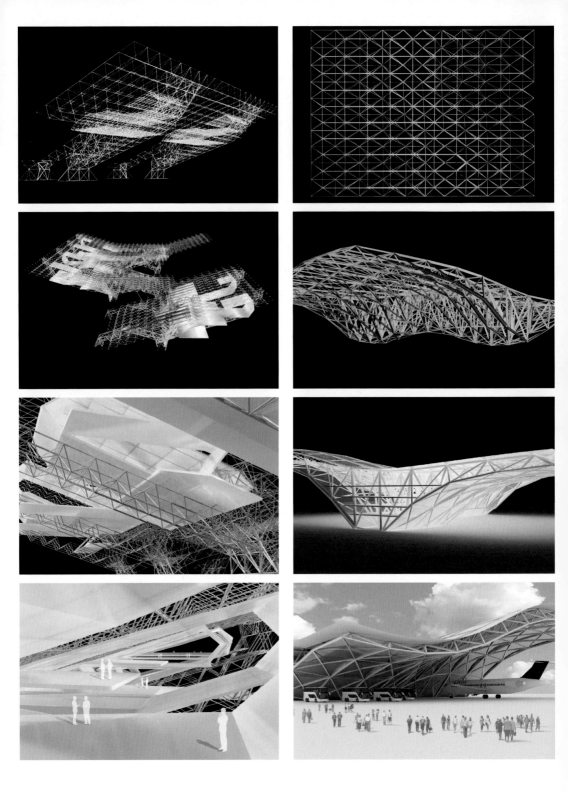

123–138   PARAMETRIC STRUCTURAL DESIGN AS AN INSPIRATIONAL TOOL FOR REVISITING KONRAD WACHSMANN'S USAF-HANGAR
        →   EN 105 / DE 113
        Varied images from the course "Advanced Structural Design," instructed by Klaus Bollinger, Andrei Gheorghe and Florian

Medicus, Summer term 2016

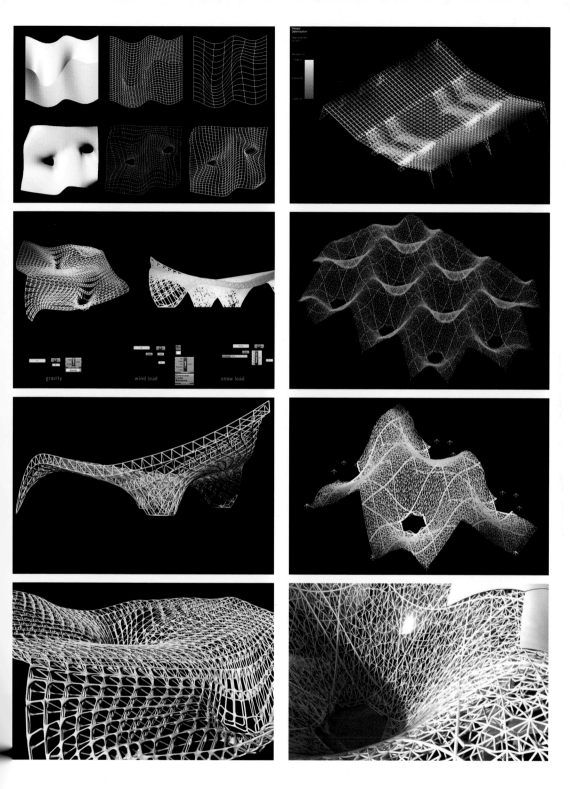

GARVIN GOEPEL, ALEXANDRA MOISI, BARBARA SCHICKERMÜLLER, JONGHOON KIM, JALAL MATRAJI, ANGEL YONCHEV, ANDREJ STRIEZENEC, COLBY SUTTER, ZARINA BELOUSOVA, OLIVIA JOIKITS, JIANG YI, JOHAN WIJESINGHE, ADRIAN WONG, JONATHAN PALJOR

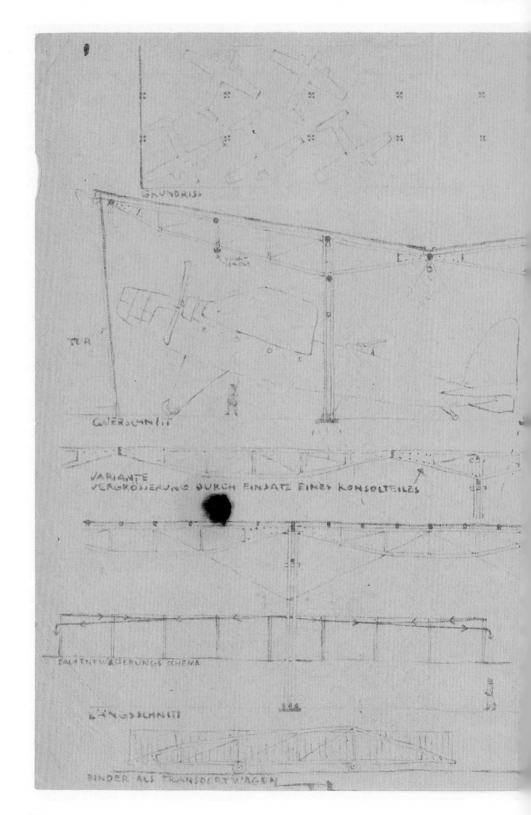

139 KONRAD WACHSMANN, *A NEW METHOD OF CONSTRUCTION* AND THE *USAF-HANGAR* FROM THE ARCHIVE AT AKADEMIE DER
     KÜNSTE, BERLIN
     Konrad Wachsmann, *Project for a demountable Airplane-Hangar*, concept drawing, 1939; Akademie der Künste, Berlin,
     Konrad-Wachsmann-Archiv 0300_001

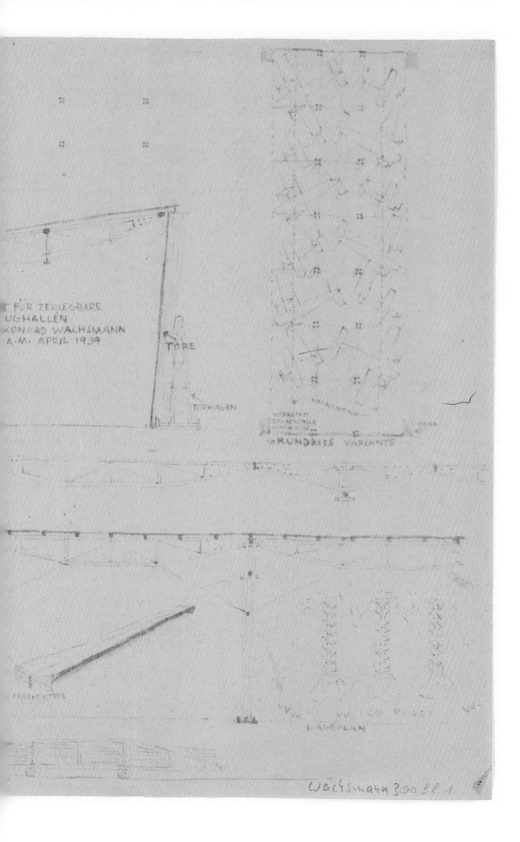

T FÜR ZERLEGBARE
UGHALLEN
KONRAD WACHSMANN
A·M· APRIL 1934

TORE

TORWAGEN

GRUNDRISS VARIANTE

PERSPEKTIVE

LAGEPLAN

Wachsmann 300 Bl. 1

83

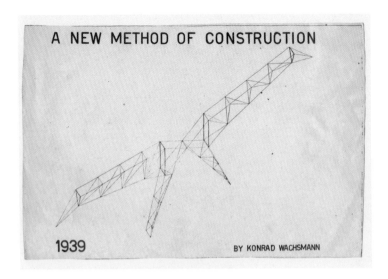

A NEW METHOD OF CONSTRUCTION

1939

BY KONRAD WACHSMANN

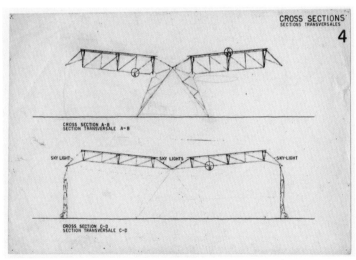

CROSS SECTIONS
SECTIONS TRANSVERSALES

4

CROSS SECTION A-B
SECTION TRANSVERSALE A-B

SKY LIGHT   SKY LIGHTS   SKY-LIGHT

CROSS SECTION C-D
SECTION TRANSVERSALE C-D

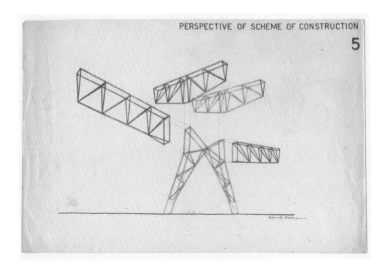

PERSPECTIVE OF SCHEME OF CONSTRUCTION

5

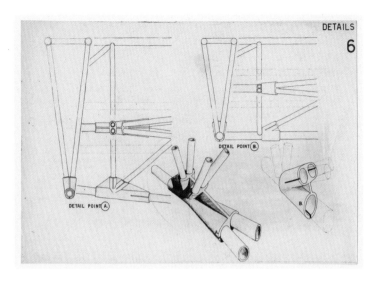

DETAILS

6

DETAIL POINT A.

DETAIL POINT B.

B

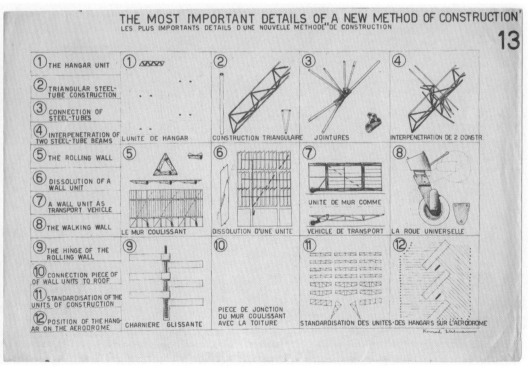

THE MOST IMPORTANT DETAILS OF A NEW METHOD OF CONSTRUCTION
LES PLUS IMPORTANTS DETAILS D'UNE NOUVELLE METHODE "DE CONSTRUCTION

13

① THE HANGAR UNIT

② TRIANGULAR STEEL-TUBE CONSTRUCTION

③ CONNECTION OF STEEL-TUBES

④ INTERPENETRATION OF TWO STEEL-TUBE BEAMS

⑤ THE ROLLING WALL

⑥ DISSOLUTION OF A WALL UNIT

⑦ A WALL UNIT AS TRANSPORT VEHICLE

⑧ THE WALKING WALL

⑨ THE HINGE OF THE ROLLING WALL

⑩ CONNECTION PIECE OF OF WALL UNITS TO ROOF

⑪ STANDARDISATION OF THE UNITS OF CONSTRUCTION

⑫ POSITION OF THE HANGAR ON THE AERODROME

① L'UNITE DE HANGAR

② CONSTRUCTION TRIANGULAIRE

③ JOINTURES

④ INTERPENETRATION DE 2 CONSTR.

⑤ LE MUR COULISSANT

⑥ DISSOLUTION D'UNE UNITE

⑦ UNITE DE MUR COMME VEHICLE DE TRANSPORT

⑧ LA ROUE UNIVERSELLE

⑨ CHARNIERE GLISSANTE

⑩ PIECE DE JONCTION DU MUR COULISSANT AVEC LA TOITURE

⑪ STANDARDISATION DES UNITES·DES HANGARS SUR L'AERODROME

Konrad Wachsmann

140–144   KONRAD WACHSMANN, *A NEW METHOD OF CONSTRUCTION* AND THE *USAF-HANGAR* FROM THE ARCHIVE AT AKADEMIE DER KÜNSTE, BERLIN

Konrad Wachsmann, *A new method of construction*, 1939, plates 1, 4, 5, 6 and 13; Akademie der Künste, Berlin, Konrad-Wachsmann-Archiv 0300_002, 0300_004, 0300_005, 0300_007, 0300_012

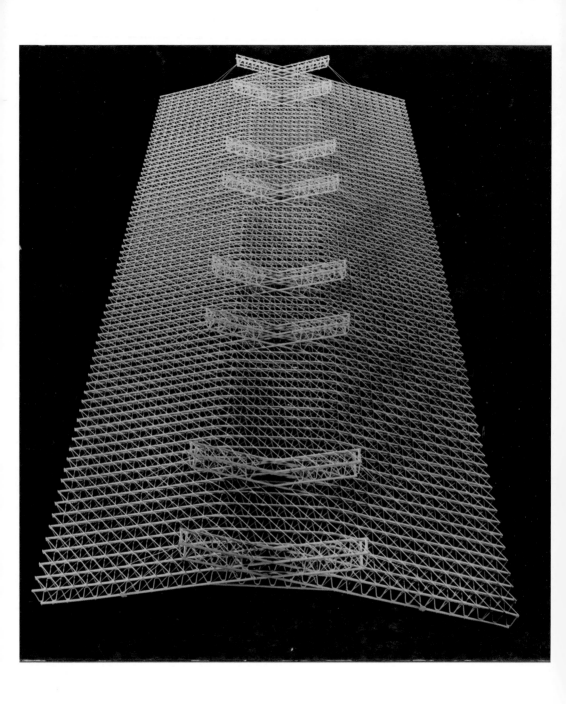

145 KONRAD WACHSMANN, *A NEW METHOD OF CONSTRUCTION* AND THE *USAF-HANGAR* FROM THE ARCHIVE AT AKADEMIE
  DER KÜNSTE, BERLIN
  Konrad Wachsmann (IIT), *Model-view of the USAF-Hangar,* first stage, ca. 1952; Akademie der Künste, Berlin, Konrad-
  Wachsmann-Archiv 0125_024

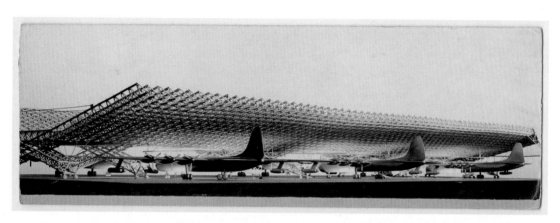

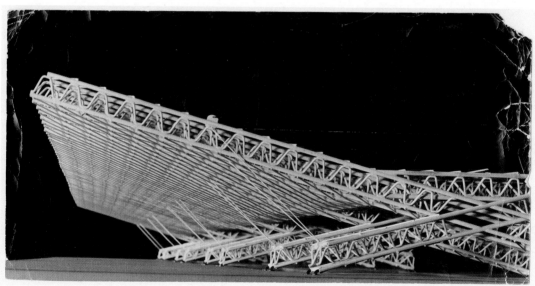

146, 147   KONRAD WACHSMANN, *A NEW METHOD OF CONSTRUCTION* AND THE *USAF-HANGAR* FROM THE ARCHIVE AT AKADEMIE
         DER KÜNSTE, BERLIN

Konrad Wachsmann (IIT), *Model-view of the USAF-Hangar*, first stage, ca. 1952; Akademie der Künste, Berlin, Konrad-
Wachsmann-Archiv 0125_028, 0125_030a

148 KONRAD WACHSMANN, *A NEW METHOD OF CONSTRUCTION* AND THE *USAF-HANGAR* FROM THE ARCHIVE AT AKADEMIE
DER KÜNSTE, BERLIN

Konrad Wachsmann (IIT), *Model-view of the USAF-Hangar*, second stage, interior ca. 1953; Akademie der Künste, Berlin,
Konrad-Wachsmann-Archiv 0126_027a

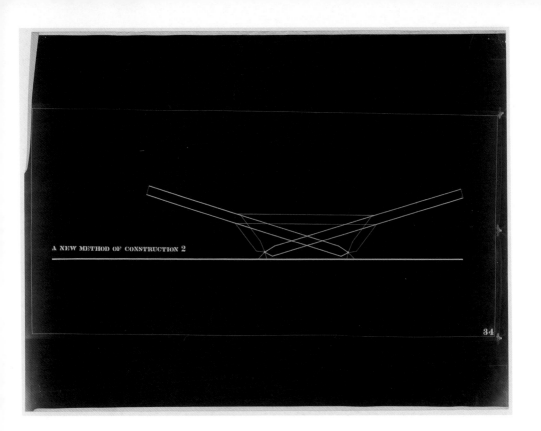

149–151   KONRAD WACHSMANN, *A NEW METHOD OF CONSTRUCTION* AND THE *USAF-HANGAR* FROM THE ARCHIVE AT AKADEMIE
           DER KÜNSTE, BERLIN

Konrad Wachsmann (IIT), Front page, *A new method of construction 2*, April 1952; Akademie der Künste, Berlin, Konrad-Wachsmann-Archiv 0322_015; plates 17 and 25; Akademie der Künste, Berlin, Konrad-Wachsmann-Archiv 0322_009, 0322_010

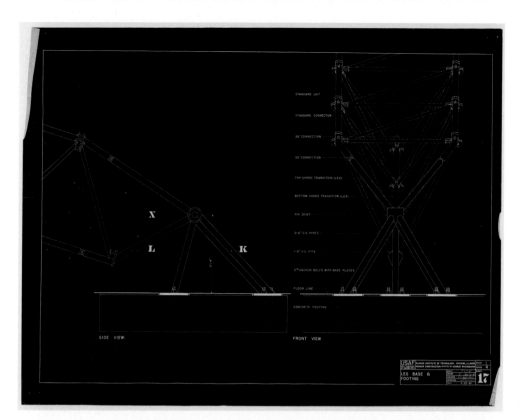

SIDE VIEW

FRONT VIEW

STANDARD UNIT

STANDARD CONNECTOR

30° CONNECTION

50° CONNECTION

TOP CHORD TRANSITION (LEG)

BOTTOM CHORD TRANSITION (LEG)

PIN JOINT

2-6" O.D. PIPES

1-6" O.D. PIPE

3"∅ ANCHOR BOLTS WITH BASE PLATES

FLOOR LINE

CONCRETE FOOTING

USAF ILLINOIS INSTITUTE OF TECHNOLOGY CHICAGO, ILLINOIS
HANGAR CONSTRUCTION ADAPTED BY KONRAD WACHSMANN

LEG BASE &
FOOTING

GROUP 1
SERIES 4

17

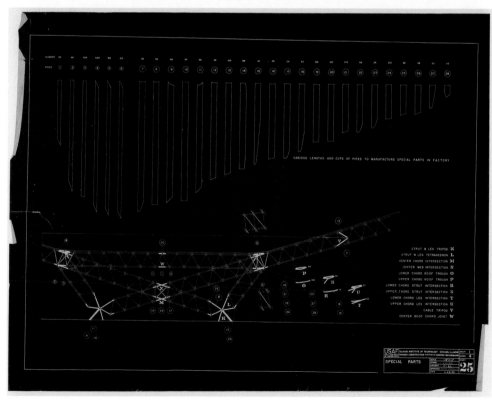

VARIOUS LENGTHS AND CUTS OF PIPES TO MANUFACTURE SPECIAL PARTS IN FACTORY

STRUT & LEG TRIPOD   K
STRUT & LEG TETRAHEDRON   L
CENTER CHORD INTERSECTION M
CENTER WEB INTERSECTION   N
LOWER CHORD ROOF TROUGH   O
UPPER CHORD ROOF TROUGH   P
LOWER CHORD STRUT INTERSECTION R
UPPER CHORD STRUT INTERSECTION S
LOWER CHORD LEG INTERSECTION   T
UPPER CHORD LEG INTERSECTION   U
CABLE TRIPOD   V
CENTER ROOF CHORD JOINT   W

USAF ILLINOIS INSTITUTE OF TECHNOLOGY CHICAGO, ILLINOIS
HANGAR CONSTRUCTION ADAPTED BY KONRAD WACHSMANN

SPECIAL PARTS

GROUP 1
SERIES 4

25

91

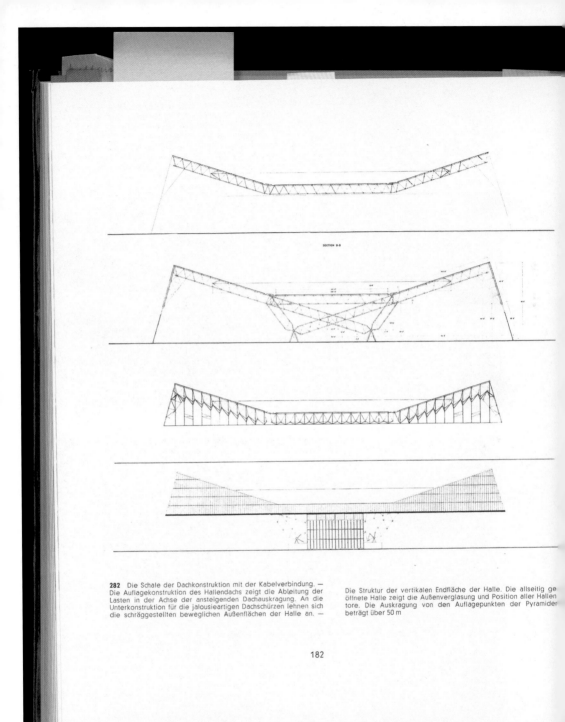

SECTION B-B

282 Die Schale der Dachkonstruktion mit der Kabelverbindung. — Die Auflagekonstruktion des Hallendachs zeigt die Ableitung der Lasten in der Achse der ansteigenden Dachauskragung. An die Unterkonstruktion für die jalousieartigen Dachschürzen lehnen sich die schräggestellten beweglichen Außenflächen der Halle an. —

Die Struktur der vertikalen Endfläche der Halle. Die allseitig geöffnete Halle zeigt die Außenverglasung und Position aller Hallentore. Die Auskragung von den Auflagepunkten der Pyramiden beträgt über 50 m

182

Pages 182/183 taken from Konrad Wachsmann's book *Wendepunkt im Bauen* (1959), reprint Verlag der Kunst

Dresden, 1989

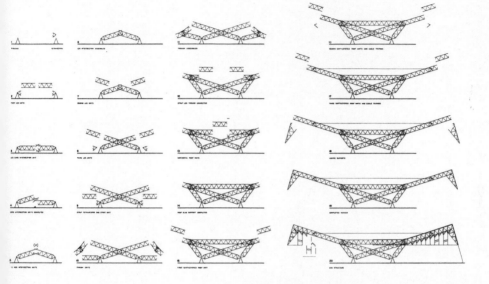

283 Die Sequenz des Aufbaus der Halle durch die Montage immer gleicher Standardteile ohne Baugerüste nur mit Hilfe von Kränen für eine maximale Belastung von 5 t

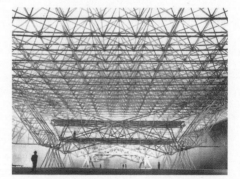

284 Innenansicht in die Längsrichtung der Halle

183

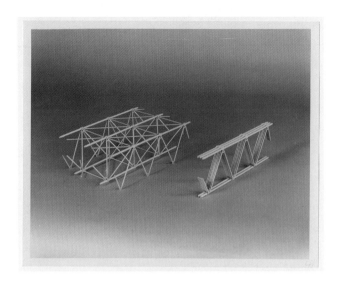

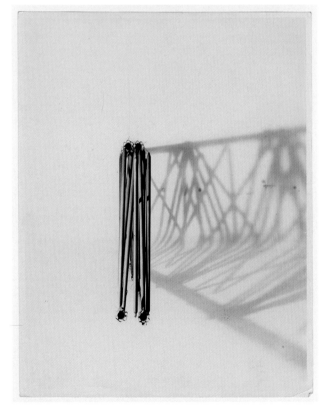

153, 154   KONRAD WACHSMANN, *A NEW METHOD OF CONSTRUCTION*
           AND THE *USAF-HANGAR* FROM THE ARCHIVE AT AKADEMIE
           DER KÜNSTE, BERLIN

Konrad Wachsmann (IIT), photographs of detailed structure-models,
ca. 1953; Akademie der Künste, Berlin, Konrad-Wachsmann-Archiv

0124_006_a, 0124_017_a

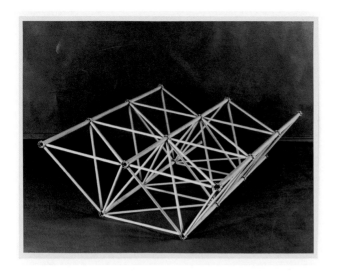

155, 156 KONRAD WACHSMANN, *A NEW METHOD OF CONSTRUCTION*
AND THE *USAF-HANGAR* FROM THE ARCHIVE AT AKADEMIE
DER KÜNSTE, BERLIN
Konrad Wachsmann (IIT), photographs of detailed structure-models,
ca. 1953; Akademie der Künste, Berlin, Konrad-Wachsmann-Archiv

0124_003_a, 0124_023_a

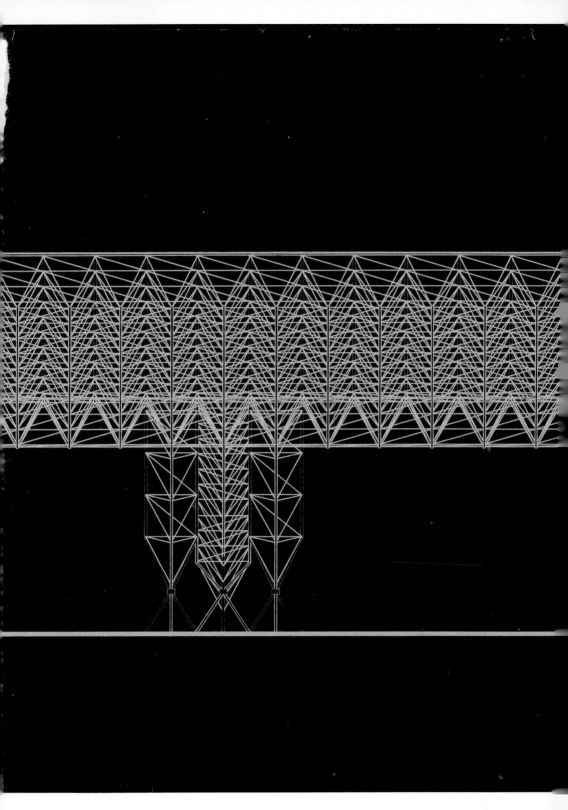

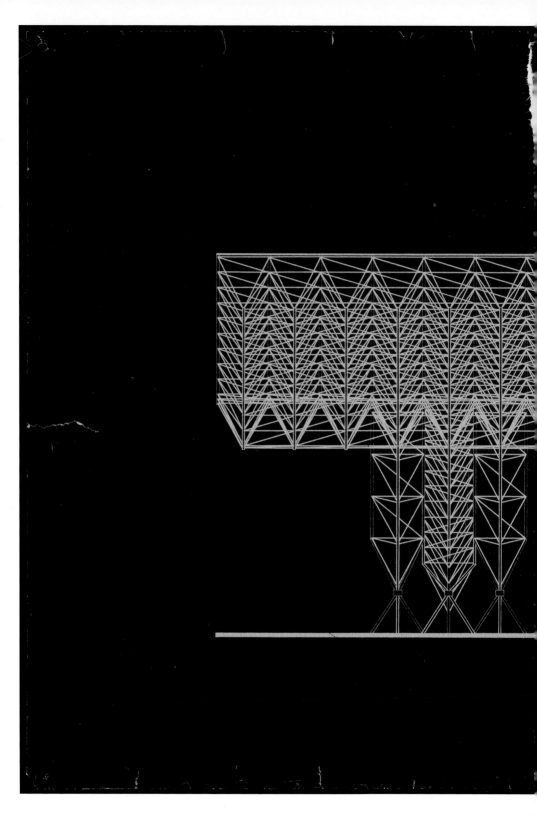

160 KONRAD WACHSMANN, *A NEW METHOD OF CONSTRUCTION* AND THE *USAF-HANGAR* FROM THE ARCHIVE
   AT AKADEMIE DER KÜNSTE, BERLIN

Konrad Wachsmann (IIT), *Structural elevation of the USAF-Hangar*, second stage, ca. 1953; Akademie der Künste,
Berlin, Konrad-Wachsmann-Archiv 0326_002

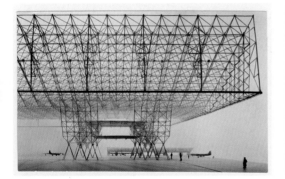

157–159   KONRAD WACHSMANN, *A NEW METHOD OF CONSTRUCTION* AND THE *USAF-HANGAR* FROM THE ARCHIVE
   AT AKADEMIE DER KÜNSTE, BERLIN

Konrad Wachsmann (IIT), *Model-views of the USAF-Hangar*, second stage, ca. 1953; Akademie der Künste, Berlin, Konrad-Wachsmann-Archiv 0126_021, 0126_ 003_a, 0126_ 002_a

161 KONRAD WACHSMANN, *A NEW METHOD OF CONSTRUCTION* AND THE *USAF-HANGAR* FROM THE ARCHIVE AT AKADEMIE DER
     KÜNSTE, BERLIN

Konrad Wachsmann (IIT), *Model-view of the USAF-Hangar*, second stage, ca. 1953; Akademie der Künste, Berlin, Konrad-
Wachsmann-Archiv 0126_008

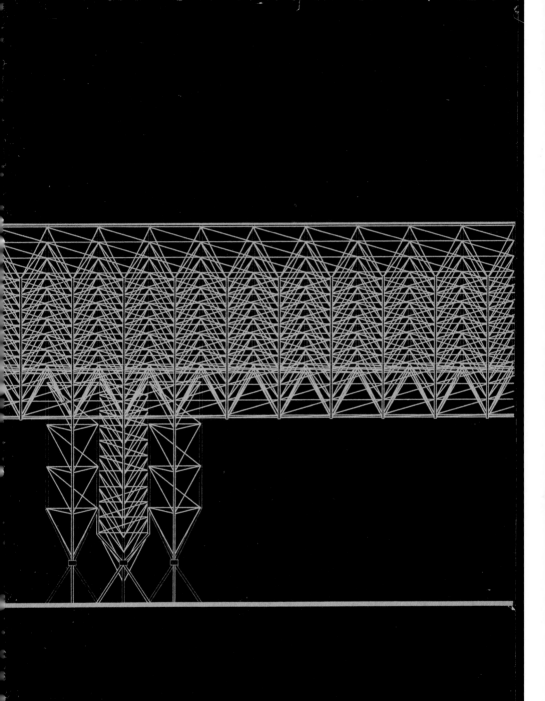

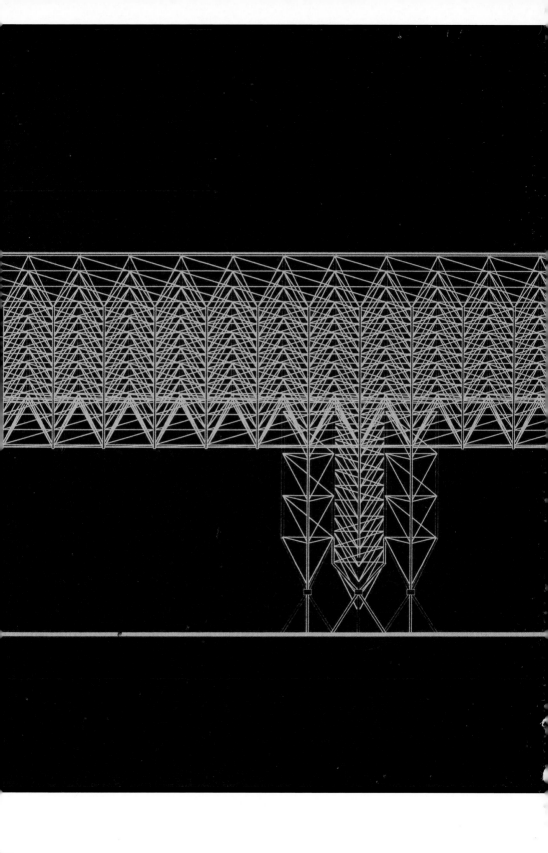

162 KONRAD WACHSMANN, *A NEW METHOD OF CONSTRUCTION* AND THE *USAF-HANGAR* FROM THE ARCHIVE AT AKADEMIE DER KÜNSTE,
     BERLIN
Konrad Wachsmann in a steel factory, ca. 1954, photographer unknown; Akademie der Künste, Berlin, Konrad-Wachsmann-Archiv
0127_040a

163 KONRAD WACHSMANN, *A NEW METHOD OF CONSTRUCTION*
     AND THE *USAF-HANGAR* FROM THE ARCHIVE AT AKADEMIE
     DER KÜNSTE, BERLIN
     The basic straps enclosing the standard joint, ca. 1954,
     photographer unknown; Akademie der Künste, Berlin, Konrad-
     Wachsmann-Archiv 0127_041

164 KONRAD WACHSMANN, *A NEW METHOD OF CONSTRUCTION* AND THE *USAF-HANGAR* FROM THE ARCHIVE AT AKADEMIE DER KÜNSTE, BERLIN
Clamps and Joint-Elements arrayed, ca. 1954, photographer unknown; Akademie der Künste, Berlin, Konrad-Wachsmann-Archiv 0120_017a

165 KONRAD WACHSMANN, *A NEW METHOD OF CONSTRUCTION* AND THE *USAF-HANGAR* FROM THE ARCHIVE AT AKADEMIE DER KÜNSTE, BERLIN
Basic Joint-Elements, ca. 1954, photographer unknown; Akademie der Künste, Berlin, Konrad-Wachsmann-Archiv 0120_015a

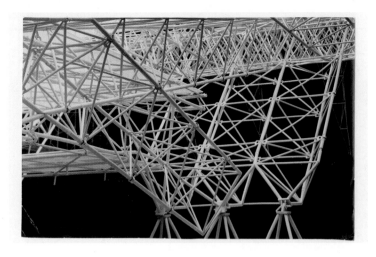

166–168   KONRAD WACHSMANN, *A NEW METHOD OF CONSTRUCTION* AND THE *USAF-HANGAR* FROM THE ARCHIVE
AT AKADEMIE DER KÜNSTE, BERLIN

Konrad Wachsmann (IIT), *Model-view of the USAF-Hangar*, final stage, ca. 1954; Akademie der Künste, Berlin,
Konrad-Wachsmann-Archiv 0126_036_a, 0126_038_a, 0126_015_a

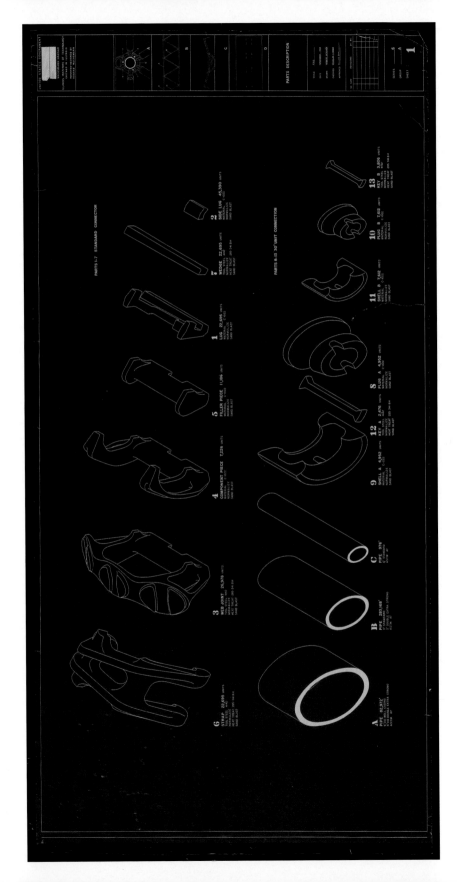

169 KONRAD WACHSMANN, A NEW METHOD OF CONSTRUCTION AND THE USAF-HANGAR FROM THE ARCHIVE AT AKADEMIE DER KÜNSTE, BERLIN
Konrad Wachsmann (IIT), Wachsmann Hangar for the USAF, 1954, plate 1; Akademie der Künste, Berlin, Konrad-Wachsmann-Archiv 0327_001

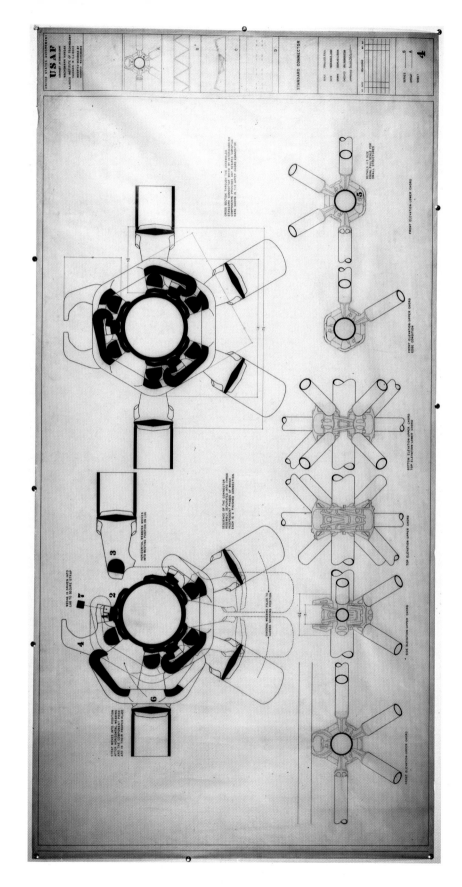

170 KONRAD WACHSMANN, A NEW METHOD OF CONSTRUCTION AND THE USAF-HANGAR FROM THE ARCHIVE AT AKADEMIE DER KÜNSTE, BERLIN
Konrad Wachsmann Hangar for the USAF, 1954, plate 4, Deutsches Architekturmuseum, Frankfurt am Main

171 KONRAD WACHSMANN, A NEW METHOD OF CONSTRUCTION AND THE USAF-HANGAR FROM THE ARCHIVE AT AKADEMIE DER KÜNSTE, BERLIN

Konrad Wachsmann Hangar for the USAF, 1954, plate 6, Deutsches Architekturmuseum, Frankfurt am Main

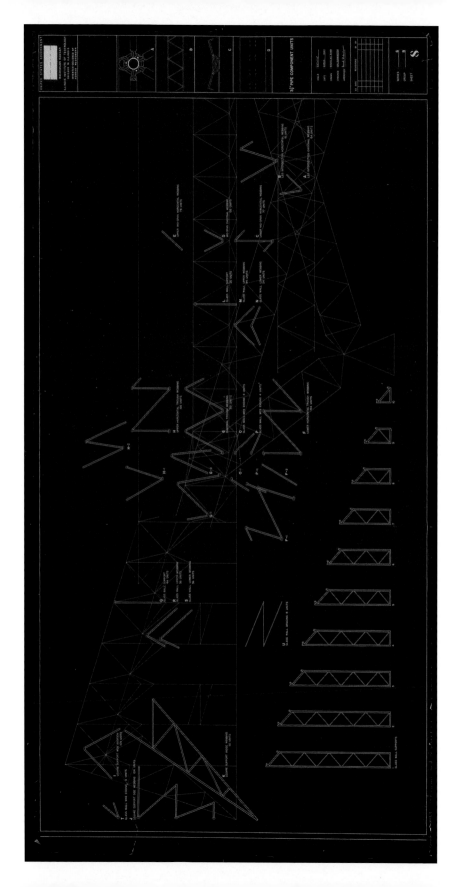

172　KONRAD WACHSMANN, A NEW METHOD OF CONSTRUCTION AND THE USAF-HANGAR FROM THE ARCHIVE AT AKADEMIE DER KÜNSTE, BERLIN
Konrad Wachsmann Hangar for the USAF, 1954, plate 8; Akademie der Künste, Berlin, Konrad-Wachsmann-Archiv 0327_007

173 KONRAD WACHSMANN, A NEW METHOD OF CONSTRUCTION AND THE USAF-HANGAR FROM THE ARCHIVE AT AKADEMIE DER KÜNSTE, BERLIN
Konrad Wachsmann (ILT), Wachsmann Hangar for the USAF, 1954, plate 10; Akademie der Künste, Berlin, Konrad-Wachsmann-Archiv 0327_008

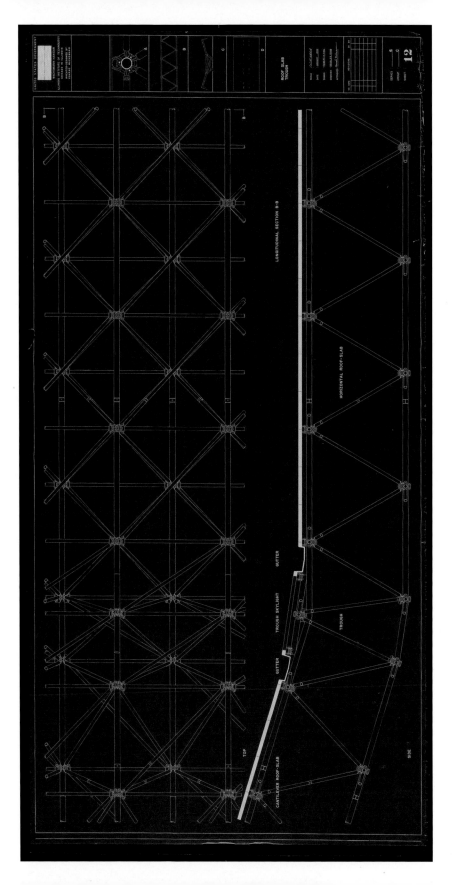

174 KONRAD WACHSMANN, *A NEW METHOD OF CONSTRUCTION AND THE USAF-HANGAR* FROM THE ARCHIVE AT AKADEMIE DER KÜNSTE, BERLIN
Konrad Wachsmann (IIT), *Wachsmann Hangar for the USAF*, 1954, plate 12; Akademie der Künste, Berlin, Konrad-Wachsmann-Archiv 0327_010

175   KONRAD WACHSMANN, A NEW METHOD OF CONSTRUCTION AND THE USAF-HANGAR FROM THE ARCHIVE AT AKADEMIE DER KÜNSTE, BERLIN
Konrad Wachsmann Hangar for the USAF, 1954, plate 13; Akademie der Künste, Berlin, Konrad-Wachsmann-Archiv 0327_011

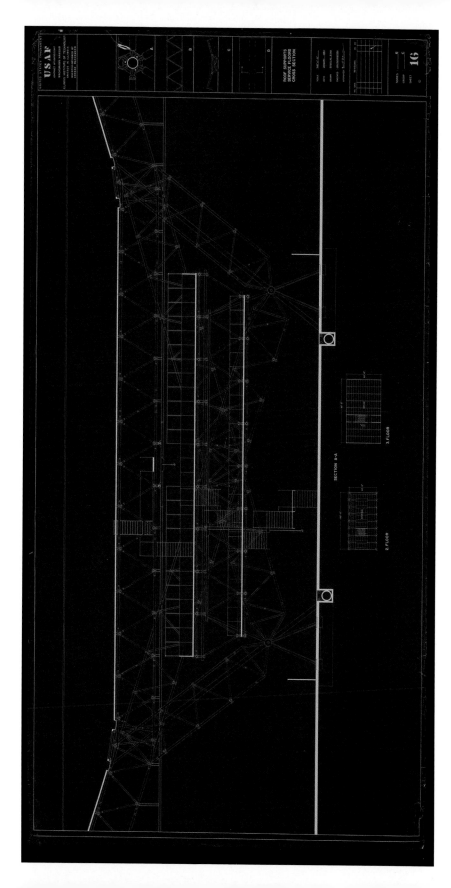

176 KONRAD WACHSMANN, A NEW METHOD OF CONSTRUCTION AND THE USAF-HANGAR FROM THE ARCHIVE AT AKADEMIE DER KÜNSTE, BERLIN
Konrad Wachsmann (IIT), *Wachsmann Hangar for the USAF*, 1954, plate 16; Akademie der Künste, Berlin, Konrad-Wachsmann-Archiv 0327_013

177 KONRAD WACHSMANN, A NEW METHOD OF CONSTRUCTION AND THE USAF-HANGAR FROM THE ARCHIVE AT AKADEMIE DER KÜNSTE, BERLIN
Konrad Wachsmann (IIT), *Wachsmann Hangar for the USAF*, 1954, plate 18; Akademie der Künste, Berlin, Konrad-Wachsmann-Archiv 0327_015

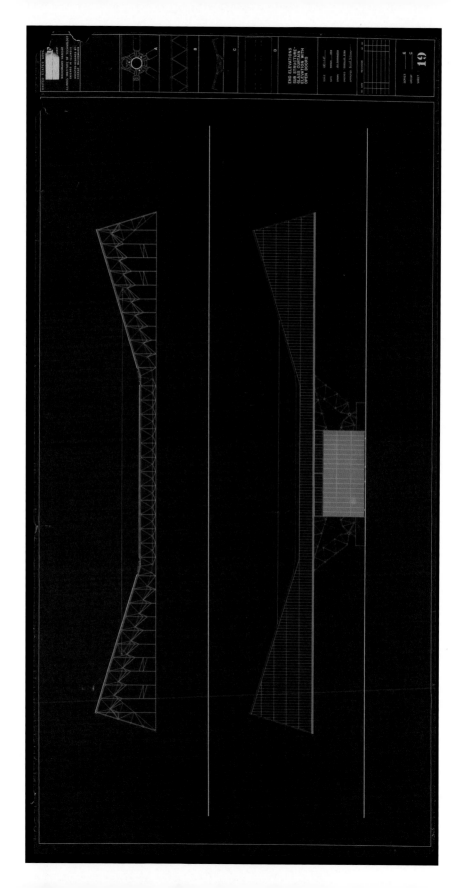

178 KONRAD WACHSMANN, *A NEW METHOD OF CONSTRUCTION* AND THE *USAF-HANGAR* FROM THE *ARCHIVE* AT AKADEMIE DER KÜNSTE, BERLIN
Konrad Wachsmann (IIT), *Wachsmann Hangar for the USAF*, 1954, plate 19; Akademie der Künste, Berlin, Konrad-Wachsmann-Archiv 0327_016

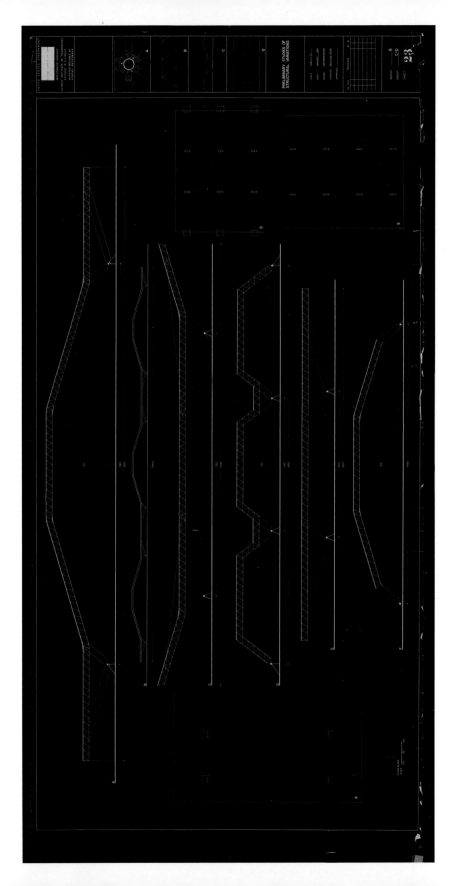

179 KONRAD WACHSMANN, A NEW METHOD OF CONSTRUCTION AND THE USAF-HANGAR FROM THE ARCHIVE AT AKADEMIE DER KÜNSTE, BERLIN
Konrad Wachsmann Hangar for the USAF, 1954, plate 23; Akademie der Künste, Berlin, Konrad-Wachsmann-Archiv 0327_019

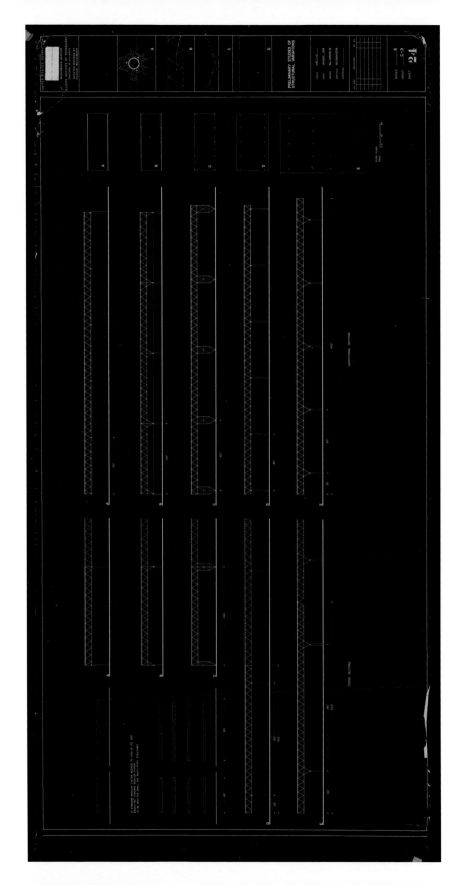

180　KONRAD WACHSMANN, *A NEW METHOD OF CONSTRUCTION* AND THE *USAF-HANGAR* FROM THE ARCHIVE AT AKADEMIE DER KÜNSTE, BERLIN
Konrad Wachsmann (IIT), *Wachsmann Hangar for the USAF*, 1954, plate 24; Akademie der Künste, Berlin, Konrad-Wachsmann-Archiv 0327_020

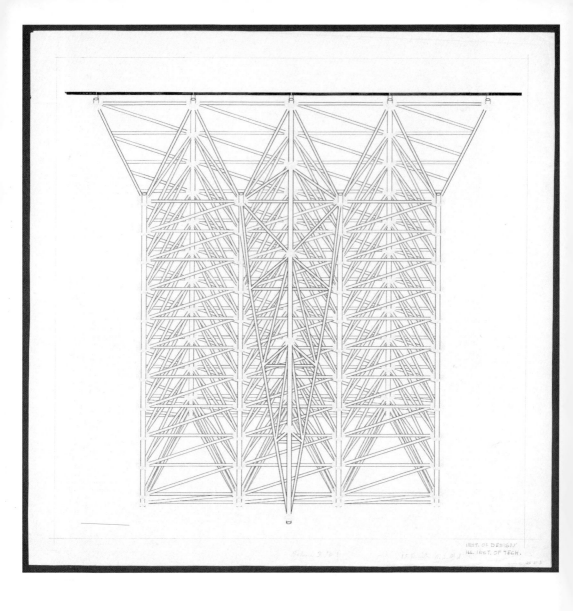

181 KONRAD WACHSMANN, *A NEW METHOD OF CONSTRUCTION* AND THE *USAF-HANGAR* FROM THE ARCHIVE AT AKADEMIE DER
     KÜNSTE, BERLIN

Konrad Wachsmann (IIT), Interior view of the (USAF-Hangar) structure, ink drawing, ca. 1953; Akademie der Künste, Berlin,

Konrad-Wachsmann-Archiv 326_003

182, 183   KONRAD WACHSMANN, *A NEW METHOD OF CONSTRUCTION* AND THE *USAF-HANGAR* FROM THE ARCHIVE
          AT AKADEMIE DER KÜNSTE, BERLIN
          Scale model for the USAF-Hangar, ca. 1954, photographer unknown; Akademie der Künste, Berlin,
Wachsmann-Archiv 0130_022, 0130_020

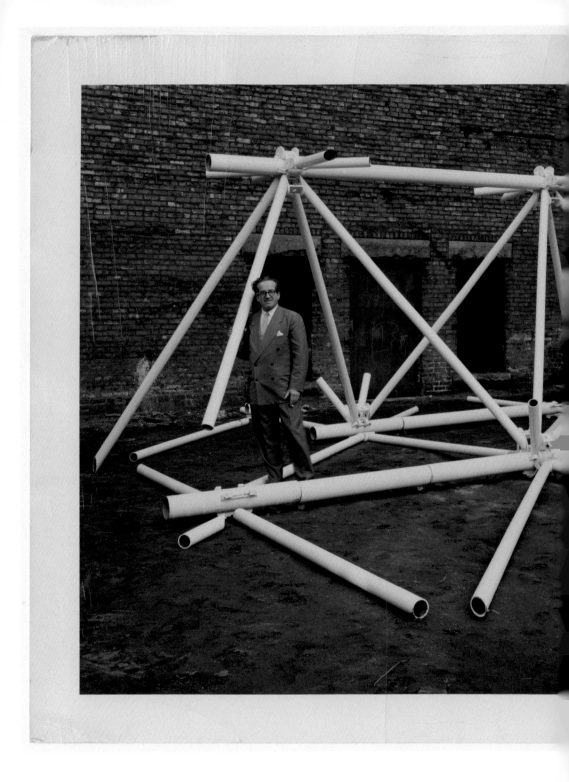

184 KONRAD WACHSMANN, *A NEW METHOD OF CONSTRUCTION* AND THE *USAF-HANGAR* FROM THE ARCHIVE AT AKADEMIE DER KÜNSTE, BERLIN
Konrad Wachsmann with his scale model for the USAF-Hangar, ca. 1954, photographer unknown; Akademie der Künste, Berlin, Konrad-Wachsmann-Archiv 0130_017

185 KONRAD WACHSMANN, *A NEW METHOD OF CONSTRUCTION
AND THE USAF-HANGAR* FROM THE ARCHIVE AT AKADEMIE DER
KÜNSTE, BERLIN
Scale model for the USAF-Hangar, joint and clamps ca. 1954,
photographer unknown; Akademie der Künste, Berlin, Konrad-
Wachsmann-Archiv 0130_024

168

186 KONRAD WACHSMANN, *A NEW METHOD OF CONSTRUCTION* AND THE *USAF-HANGAR* FROM THE ARCHIVE AT
AKADEMIE DER KÜNSTE, BERLIN

Pages 168 and 169 taken from Konrad Wachsmann's book *Wendepunkt im Bauen* (1959), reprint Verlag der
Kunst, Dresden, 1989

259 Blick in die Landschaft einer räumlichen Struktur

169

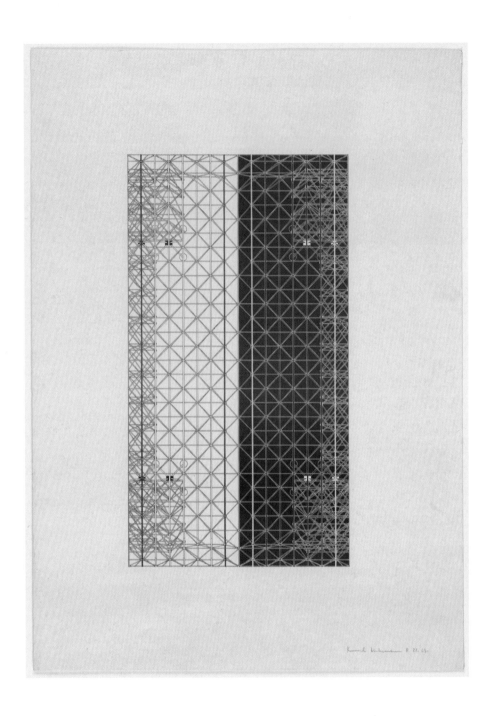

187 KONRAD WACHSMANN, *A NEW METHOD OF CONSTRUCTION* AND THE *USAF-HANGAR* FROM THE ARCHIVE AT
AKADEMIE DER KÜNSTE, BERLIN

Konrad Wachsmann, Airplane hangar, roof plan, 1963; New York, Museum of Modern Art (MoMA). Gift of Ivan
Chermayeff; acc. no.: 375.1969, 2019. The Museum of Modern Art; New York/Scala, Florence

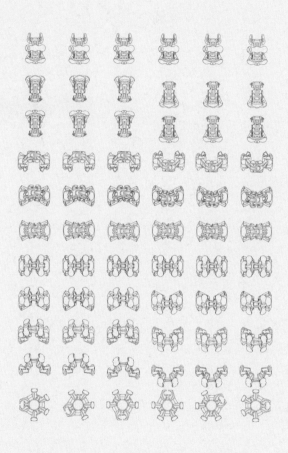

188 KONRAD WACHSMANN, *A NEW METHOD OF CONSTRUCTION* AND THE *USAF-HANGAR* FROM THE ARCHIVE AT
        AKADEMIE DER KÜNSTE, BERLIN

Konrad Wachsmann, Joints in Motion, 1963. Offset lithograph, composition: 43.5 × 29.4 cm; sheet:
69.7 × 49.8 cm. Publisher: Galleria del Deposito, Genoa, Italy. Edition: 50. Gertrud A. Mellon Fund. acc. no.
306.1964. New York, Museum of Modern Art (MoMA), 2019. The Museum of Modern Art, New York/Scala,
Florence

B 1520 E

189, 190   KONRAD WACHSMANN, *A NEW METHOD OF CONSTRUCTION* AND THE *USAF-HANGAR* FROM THE
           ARCHIVE AT AKADEMIE DER KÜNSTE, BERLIN

122   Cover and page 384 of *Bauen + Wohnen*, October 1960, Verlag Bauen und Wohnen GmbH, Munich

Teamarbeit an der Universität Tokio

1. November bis 15. Dezember 1955

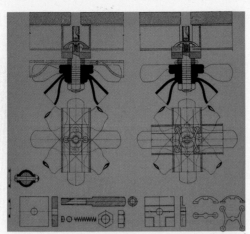

Je 3 Delegierte von 7 Universitäten bildeten das Team. In Japan, wo der Begriff der Triangulation in der Konstruktion nicht so selbstverständlich ist, war das Team daran interessiert, eine Methodik zur Entwicklung einer dreidimensionalen Tetraederstruktur zu studieren. Besondere Beachtung sollte dabei der Beziehung der Auflagepunkte der Stützen zum räumlichen Faltwerk geschenkt werden.

Im Verlauf der Arbeit entwickelte sich ein Konstruktionssystem, bei dem man lange Aluminiumrohre verwendete, die in Intervallen flachgedrückt, gebogen, gestanzt und mit einem speziell entwickelten Schraubenaggregat in Knotenpunkten festgehalten wurden. Ein Schulgebäude wurde geplant, das dank der Verwendung der in Japan üblichen Schiebewände jede Kombination zwischen dem vollkommen offenen und geschlossenen Raum gestatten sollte. Außerordentlich umfangreiche Studien und Untersuchungen über die Installationen, Klimakontrollen usw. begleiteten diese Arbeit.

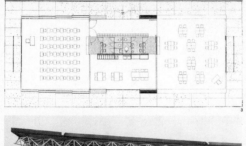

1
Schnitt und Aufsicht der Standardknotenpunkte und die Befestigung der Fußbodenplatten an der Konstruktion. Darunter die Details der Bolzenverschraubung und des Metallteils, das die Fußbodenplatte an der Konstruktion festhält.
Section et vue des points de croisement standard. Fixation des plaques de sol. En dessous détails de raccord à la construction.
Section and view on to the standard knot and the securing of floor tiles to the construction. Underneath the details of bolting and the metal part that holds a floor tile to the construction.

2
Die Struktur und die Verteilung der horizontalen Lasten auf flächige Stützenaggregate.
Structure et répartition des charges horizontales sur les éléments porteur.
The structure and the distribution of horizontal loads on level support units.

3 und 4
Zwei Grundrißkombinationen.
Deux possibilités de plan.
Two combinations of ground plans.

5
Teilansicht eines Schulpavillons.
Vue partielle d'un pavillon d'école.
Partial view of a school pavilion.

bouwen in onze tijd

konrad wachsmann

museum fodor   keizersgracht 609   amsterdam c

191 KONRAD WACHSMANN, *A NEW METHOD OF CON-*
    STRUCTION AND THE *USAF-HANGAR* FROM
    THE ARCHIVE AT AKADEMIE DER KÜNSTE, BERLIN
    Cover of Konrad Wachsmann's *Bauen in unserer Zeit*,
    exhibition catalog, Munich, 1958

192 KONRAD WACHSMANN, *A NEW METHOD OF CONSTRUCTION*
    AND THE *USAF-HANGAR* FROM THE ARCHIVE AT AKADEMIE DER
    KÜNSTE, BERLIN
    Cover of Konrad Wachsmann's *bouwen in onze tijd*, Museum
    Fodor, Amsterdam 1959

194, 195 ANDREAS ZYBACH

Arabidopsis seeds, water, nutrient solution, aluminum tubes, pump; 460 × 80 × 300 cm (2006)

Based on the example of the model plant *Arabidopsis Thaliana*, biological research investigates the principles of plant structures and how they function. It is theoretically possible for any plant to grow into endless dimensions. This idea of infinite expansion reappears in Konrad Wachsmann's draft of an airplane hangar. Commissioned by a research department of the us Air Force in 1951, he developed a modular construction system whose parts could be disassembled and reassembled at a different location as reusable architecture. His concept of a building that can be assembled and disassembled responds to the reproductive principle of plants that, after a period of growth, invest their energy in seed production in order to continue to grow in a different place later on. In the project "Arabidopsis Thaliana—Konrad Wachsmann," both systems are combined within the smallest possible space. Nutrient solution and *Arabidopsis* seeds circulate through the circulatory system of the elements of a scaled down fragment of the airplane hangar.

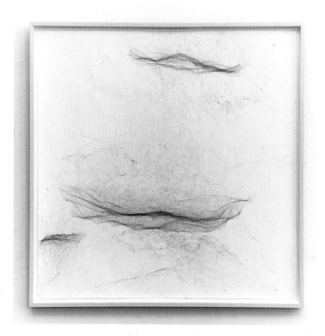

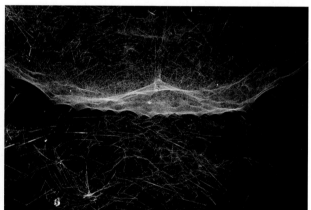

196 TOMÁS SARACENO

Solitary semi-social mapping of PKS 1101+384 by one Nephila clavipes –
one week and three Cyrtophora citricola *– three weeks,* 2016,
spidersilk, paper, glue, ink, 89 × 89 cm, courtesy of the artist; Andersen's,
Copenhagen: Ruth Benzacar, Buenos Aires; Tanya Bonakdar Gallery,
New York/Los Angeles; Pinksummer contemporary art, Genoa; Esther
Schipper, Berlin, © photography: Studio Tomás Saraceno, 2016

197 TOMÁS SARACENO

Omega Centauri, one Nephila kenianensis, four Cyrtophora
citricola, 2014, spidersilk, carbon fiber, light, tripod, installation
view from "Vanitas" exhibition at the Georg Kolbe Museum, 2014,
Courtesy of the artist; Andersen's, Copenhagen: Ruth Benzacar,
Buenos Aires; Tanya Bonakdar Gallery, New York/Los Angeles;
Pinksummer contemporary art, Genoa; Esther Schipper, Berlin,
© photography: Studio Tomás Saraceno, 2014

198 TOMÁS SARACENO

In Orbit, 2013, installation view at Kunstsammlung
Nordrhein-Westfalen, K21 Ständehaus, Düsseldorf,
Germany, curated by Marion Ackermann and Susanne
Meyer-Büser, engineered by Bollinger and Grohmann,
installed by Bernd Schliephake and Studio Tomás
Saraceno, courtesy of the artist; Andersen's,
Copenhagen: Ruth Benzacar, Buenos Aires; Tanya
Bonakdar Gallery, New York/Los Angeles; Pinksummer
contemporary art, Genoa; Esther Schipper, Berlin,
© photography: Studio Tomás Saraceno, 2013

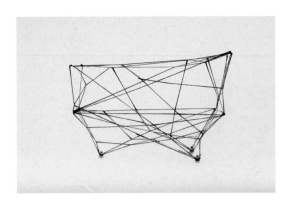

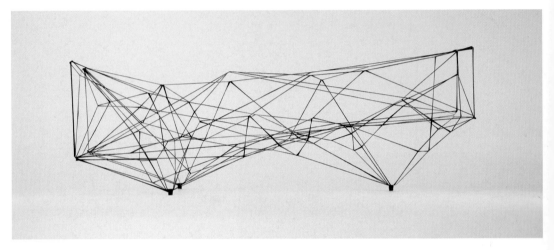

199–201 HAN KONING

SpaceFrame CarbonCopy is a carbon fiber object constructed in a framed space. Once released its now tight lines start a relation with their new habitat and act as a conversation piece in your home or office. *SpaceFrame cc* is available in three sizes and although all *CarbonCopies* are equally enticing, not two are identical. To make your *cc-s* or *m* stand out even more, you can add the construction frame and a sturdy wooden shipping crate to your order. *cc-l* comes in a shipping crate as standard; the construction frame is also an option here. *SpaceFrame cc-l* can be equipped with light fixtures of your choice to make it suitable as ambient or task lighting.

SpaceFrame SiteSpecific is a bespoke version of *SpaceFrame*. It's a firm gesture that draws out the connections between creative people and good ideas. Your *SpaceFrame ss* will be custom made on location using the finest yarns; the space it will be part of suggests its size and materialization. Quality lighting can be added to emphasize the structure and turn it into an equally wonderful experience at night.

202, 203 GEGO

Gego on installation of *Reticulárea*. Galería de Arte Nacional, Caracas, 1980. Credits: Christian Belpaire;

Fundación Gego Archives

Reticulárea (Environmental work), 1969. Museo de Bellas Artes, Caracas. Credits: Paolo Gasparini;
Fundación Gego Archives

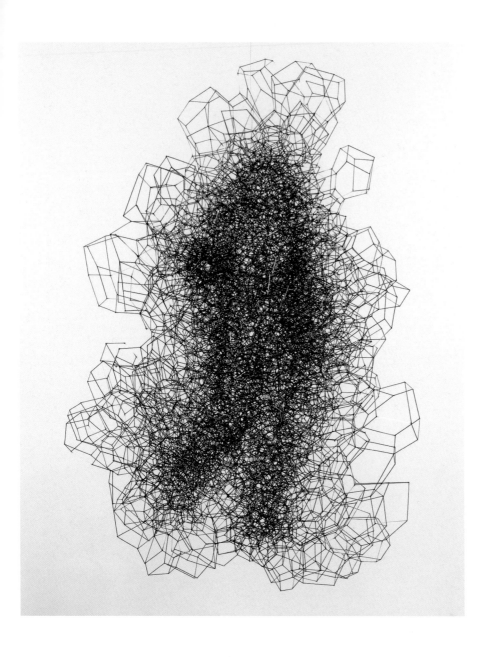

Ferment, 2007; 2 mm square section stainless steel bar; 283 × 177 × 192 cm, photographer: Stephen
White, London; © the artist

Drift, 2009; 12.7 mm square section stainless steel bar and 32 mm stainless steel ball bearings; 2300 × 3960 × 1460 cm;
Commissioned by Moshe Safdie on behalf of Marina Bay Sands; Permanent installation, Marina Bay Sands, Singapore,
photographer: Han, Singapore; © the artist

33

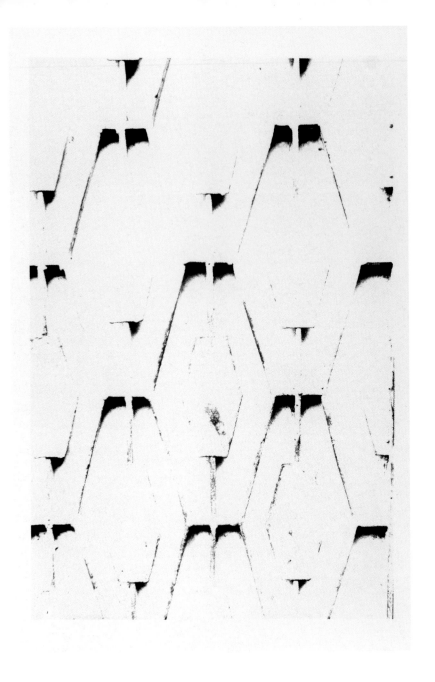

207 LILAH FOWLER
Grille #2, 2012, 55 × 38 cm, screenprint. Credits: image courtesy of the artist
134   and Galerie Gisela Clement

208 LILAH FOWLER
Untitled (light pink and turquoise space frame); with *Untitled* (yellow and turquoise space frame), 2009;
600 × 300 × 310 cm dimensions variable, steel. Credits: image courtesy of the artist and Galerie Gisela Clement,
photographer: Moritz Steigler

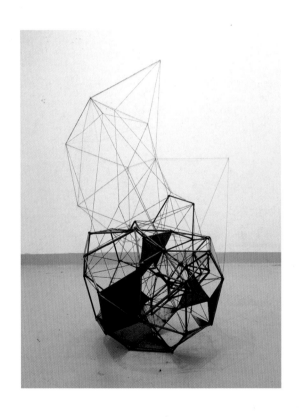

The Comet, still and string, dimension variable, 2012,
photographs by Tae Eun Ahn

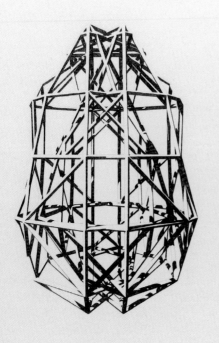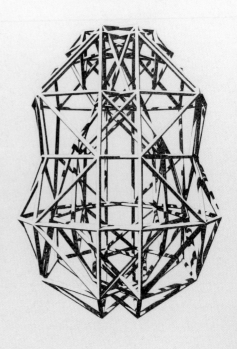

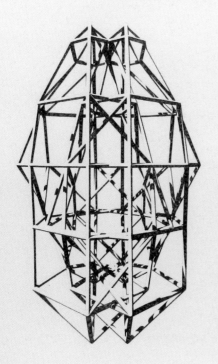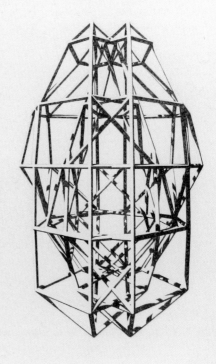

211 PETER JELLITSCH
Doppelgänger (Var.350 Var.351), crayon and pencil on paper, 65 × 95 cm, unique

212 PETER JELLITSCH
Doppelgänger (Var. 169 Var. 170), crayon and pencil on paper, 65 × 95 cm, unique

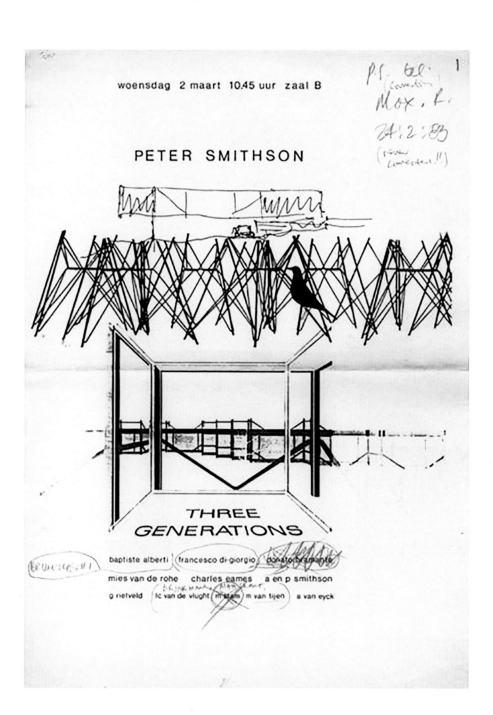

39   Alison and Peter Smithson Archive. Courtesy of the Frances Loeb Library, Harvard Graduate School of Design

214 OLAFUR ELIASSON

The structural evolution project, 2001; Zometool construction sets, wood; Installation view: Tate Modern, London, photographer: Anders Sune Berg; Hamburger Kunsthalle. On permanent loan from the Stiftung für die Hamburger Kunstsammlungen; © 2001 Olafur Eliasson

215 OLAFUR ELIASSON

Green light—An artistic workshop. In collaboration with Thyssen-Bornemisza Art Contemporary Wood (European ash), recycled yogurt cups (PLA), used plastic bags, recycled nylon, LED (green) 35 × 35 × 35 cm 57th International Art Exhibition of La Biennale di Venezia VN A ARTE VN A, 2017, photographer: Damir Zizic Courtesy of the artist and Thyssen-Bornemisza Art Contemporary;

© Olafur Eliasson

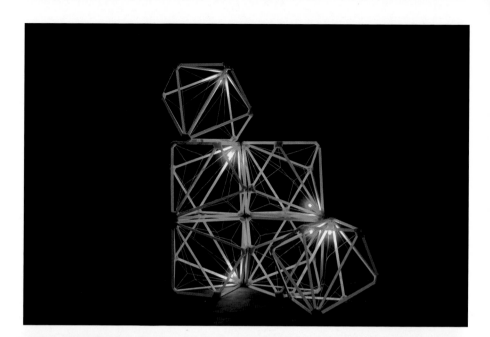

216, 217 OLAFUR ELIASSON
Green light, 2016, co-produced by Thyssen-Bornemisza Art Contemporary, photographer: Thilo Frank & David de Larrea
41   Remiro / Studio Olafur Eliasson, 2016

218 MICHAL BARTOSIK

The *Fluorescent Dome* investigates the corollary relationship between platonic form, structural systems, and the material with which gravitational forces are distributed.

The luminous geodesic structure, akin to the Icosahedron, actualizes its topological uniformity through off the shelf fluorescent lamps as its principle structural components. The inherent fragility of the glass lamp and electric current flux therein visually render and plot the momentless efficiency and movement logic of forces through the act of materializing visible light. The Tensegrity Lights, by extension, further eliminate these perceived redundancies between lamp and fixture. Whereby, the light source and its electrical wiring now work mutually in compression and in tension to yield a unified system of structural correlation, and produce a seemingly discontinuous field of light defined only by its tectonic form of lamp and lattice.

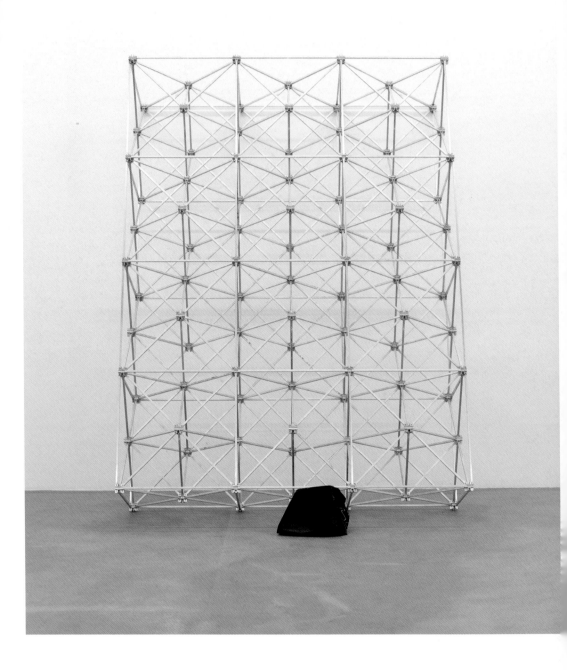

219 MARK HAGEN
Non-Sédentaires (Subtractive and Additive Sculpture), 2013, aluminum and stainless steel space frame, rainbow obsidian, space frame: 327.5 × 245.5 × 82 cm, stone: 45.5 × 35.5 × 35.5 cm (overall dimensions variable)

The Alhambra, 2013, aluminum and stainless steel space frame, 388.2 × 462 × 614.5 cm (overall dimensions variable). Credits: Robert Wedemeyer

221, 222 JÜRGEN MAYER H.
The *Schaustelle* was a temporary pavilion and platform for the four collections housed at the Pinakothek
der Moderne in Munich

Stressing Wachsmann
Strukturen für eine Zukunft

.

Texte

»Neue Materialien, Methoden, Prozesse, statische und dynamische Erkenntnisse, Planungen, soziologische Verhältnisse müssen akzeptiert werden«, schreibt Konrad Wachsmann in seinem Manifest *Vom Bauen in unserer Zeit.* »Humane und ästhetische Vorstellungen werden neue Impulse erhalten durch kompromisslose Anwendung zeitgenössischen Wissens und Könnens«, heißt es weiter.

Das Bauen in unserer Zeit muss sich am aktuellen Stand von Wissenschaft und Technik orientieren – so ließe sich dieser Text aus dem Jahr 1958 paraphrasieren. Wachsmann hat Zeit seines Lebens eine Architektur vertreten, die wissenschaftliche Versuchsmethoden und Automationsgesetze zu seinen Instrumenten machte. Er gilt als Pionier des industriellen Bauens. Architektur verstand er als massenhaft organisiertes Unterfangen, Teamarbeit als absolut notwendig. Er plädierte für eine umfassend gedachte Rationalisierung des Bauens, die letztlich auch Ausdruck in einer neuen Form finden sollte: Die Funktion soll der Form folgen statt »form follows function«.

Seine Ideen und Gedanken klingen gerade heute wieder besonders aktuell. Digitale Fertigungsverfahren sowie algorithmische Planungstechniken bestimmen den aktuellen Architekturdiskurs wesentlich mit. Überlegungen zu industriellem Bauen aus Wachsmanns Zeit überlappen inhaltlich mit zeitgenössischen Debatten zu algorithmischem Bauen. Es lohnt sich daher, ArchitektInnen und TheoretikerInnen wie Wachsmann neu zu betrachten, zu hinterfragen und von ihren Erkenntnissen, Errungenschaften, aber auch Irrtümern zu lernen.

Denn die Umbrüche unserer Zeit fordern uns auf, kritisch gegenüber Versprechungen zu sein und mit korrelativen und kreativen Denkansätzen dagegenzuhalten. Sie verlangen, neue Technologien kritisch zu hinterfragen, um sie progressiv und visionär einsetzen zu können. *Stressing Wachsmann* ist ein wichtiger Beitrag dazu und zeigt vor, wie Architekturgeschichte ein Schlüssel zu zeitgenössischen Architekturdebatten, aber auch aktuellen gesellschaftlichen Herausforderungen sein kann.

Vorwort

Gerald Bast

»Und dann, wer sollte mich beraten und wem sollte ich glauben in einer Umwelt, die noch ganz zu der nach-viktorianischen Zeit gehörte, während ich schon sehnsuchtsvoll nach dem Zeppelin schaute?«

Konrad Wachsmann über seine Kindheit[1]

Nach *Unbuildable Tatlin?!* (Springer Verlag, 2012) arbeiteten wir ab 2013 an einer weiteren Publikation zu unseren seminaristischen Untersuchungen ungebauter Architekturikonen des 20. Jahrhunderts: Friedrich Kieslers *Endless House.* Dieses Buch (*Endless Kiesler*, Birkhäuser Verlag), das in enger Zusammenarbeit mit der Wiener Kiesler-Stiftung entstand, konnte dann im September 2015 im New Yorker *MoMA* präsentiert werden. Bei diesem Anlass war es Mark Wigley, der uns fragte, wie wir diese schöne Reihe denn fortzusetzen gedenken? Wir hatten mit unseren Studierenden des Instituts für Architektur zwar etliche schöne Seminararbeiten gemacht (Lissitzky, Melnikov, Mies van der Rohe, Wachsmann, Price, Domenig/Huth u. a.), dass wir uns allerdings in diesem Ausmaß mit Konrad Wachsmann auseinandersetzen würden, ist nun einzig der Anregung von Mark Wigley zu danken. Er sagte damals, es sei doch eigenartig, dass der so vielfältig und international bedeutsame Wachsmann immer wieder nur am Rande auftaucht, in Summe aber doch grob unterschätzt würde.

Seit diesem warmen Abend in New York arbeiten wir und dankenswerterweise viele andere an diesem Buch, von dem wir nun hoffen dürfen, einen ebenso umfassenden wie angemessenen Beitrag zur Lückenfüllung und Neubewertung Konrad Wachsmanns, seines Werks und seiner Wirkung zu leisten.

Die Hangars

Konrad Wachsmanns USAF-Hangar, mit dem wir uns in zwei Seminaren (»Advanced Structural Design«, 2012 und 2016; einige ausgewählte Arbeiten finden sich in diesem Buch[→107–138]) beschäftigt haben, steht als historischer Typus am Ende einer tatsächlich aufregenden Reihe konstruktiver Experimente. Wo für Karl Marx noch die Lokomotive das Sinnbild der Moderne war (und sich daraus die ebenso großartigen wie zwiespältigen Infrastrukturbauten des 19. Jahrhunderts lesen lassen), so sehen wir grob ab 1910 doch die vorerst zivile Luftfahrt und ihre kühnen Protagonisten ebendieses Sinnbild übernehmen. Franz Kafka hat das in Brescia so schön beschrieben: »Nun aber kommt der Apparat, mit dem Blériot den Kanal überflogen hat; keiner hat es gesagt, alle wissen es. [...] Hingegeben sehen alle zu ihm auf, in keinem Herzen ist für einen anderen Platz. [...] Hier oben ist 20 m über der Erde ein Mensch in einem Holzgestell verfangen und wehrt sich gegen eine freiwillig übernommene unsichtbare Gefahr.«[2] Die Überwindung der Schwerkraft konnte nicht mehr nur durch mehr oder weniger statische »leichter-

Die Zukunft war alles
—
Konrad Wachsmanns USAF-Hangar

Klaus Bollinger, Florian Medicus; Abb.: 1–11

als-Luft-Ballone« erfolgen, sondern mit krachenden Motoren und
ihren neuen Geschwindigkeiten.[1] Es ist wohl kein Zufall, dass im
gleichen Jahr (1909) Marinetti in seinem »futuristischen Manifest«
die »Liebe zur Gefahr«, die »Schönheit der Schnelligkeit« und »den
gleitenden Flug der Aeroplane, deren Schraube knattert wie eine
im Winde wehende Flagge und die klatscht wie eine beifallstobende
Menge«[3], besingt. Ebenfalls 1909 erscheint Fritz Wicherts schöner
Text *Luftschifffahrt und Architektur*, in dem er durch den nunmehr
frontalen Wert der Dächer die monumentale »Schwerkraftarchi-
tektur« überwunden sieht. »Das Flugzeug«, wird Le Corbusier 1922
schreiben »hat Erfindungskraft, Intelligenz und Kühnheit mobili-
siert: *Phantasie* und *kühle Vernunft*«[4], wie sich auch Peter Sloterdijk
sicher ist: »Wer also vom Auftrieb nicht reden will, mag auch von
der Moderne schweigen.«[5]

Ab der Wende vom 19. zum 20. Jahrhundert entstehen, vorerst
unbeachtet, tatsächlich riesige, dabei aber meist leichte, raffinierte
Hallenkonstruktionen zum Bau und zur Wartung der Luftschiffe
als industrielle Zweckbauten und teils auch vollkommen bizarre
mechanische Strukturprojekte, deren Kühnheit auch heute noch
erstaunen. (In Rainer Graefes *Geschichte des Konstruierens* gibt es
dazu einen schönen Beitrag von Angelika Osswald und Berthold
Burkhardt.) Exemplarisch erwähnt seien an dieser Stelle aber die
klassischen *Luftschiffhallen in Orly* von Eugène Freyssinet (1922–24,
ausgefachte, parabolische Stahlbetonbögen), deren kolossale Ab-
messungen von 300 × 90 m und knapp 60 m Höhe Le Corbusier in
der zweiten Auflage von *Vers une architecture* 1924 mit zwei Bau-
stellenfotos dem Hauptschiff der Kathedrale Notre-Dame (12 m
breit, 35 m hoch) triumphal gegenüberstellt.[2] 1933 eröffnet dann im
kalifornischen Sunnyvale der vom deutschen Ingenieur Karl Arnstein geplante *Hangar One*, der mit seiner überbauten Fläche von
345 × 94 m und einer Höhe von 60 m (Bogenfachwerkträger aus
Stahl) noch immer eine der größten Hallenkonstruktionen weltweit
ist.[3] Und zwischen 1935–38 baut Pier Luigi Nervi in Orvieto einen
ebenfalls ikonenhaften Hangar: eine gedeckte Tonnenschale aus
sich diagonal kreuzenden Betonträgern mit den wunderbar zarten
Querschnitten von 110 × 15 cm und nur drei Stützen an der Tor-
seite.[4] Spannend hierbei ist sicherlich, dass Nervi, wie zeitgleich
Eduardo Torroja in Madrid, diese Konstruktionen mit Strukturmo-
dellen vorab testet und dass er aus diesen auch ein Patent für industrielle Fertigteilbauweisen (Patent-Nr. 377969, 1939: »Bausystem
für die Realisierung von tragenden Skeletten für Gewölbe, [sic]
[und] Kuppeln und allgemeinen statischen Systemen durch im
Werk gefertigter [sic] Elemente, die durch Stahlbetonfugen verbunden werden«) entwickelt.[6]

Während Freyssinet und Arnstein noch für die sogenannte
»Starrluftfahrt« der großen Zeppeline bauten, deren große Zeit

spätestens mit dem zweiten Weltkrieg zu Ende ging (Explosion der *Hindenburg*, 1937), beschäftigte sich Nervi ausschließlich mit Hallen für Flugzeuge, die er selbstbewusst nicht mehr als rein ingeniöse Zweckbauten sondern als vollwertige Architekturbeiträge im *Casabella* veröffentlicht.

USAF-Hangar

Konrad Wachsmann hatte 1939 noch in Frankreich eine »New method of construction for a [sic] Aeroplane Hangar (prefabricated, demontable, transportable)«[7] und Jahre später noch als »Präsident der *General Panel Corporation* of New York« und im Auftrag der *Atlas Aircraft Corporation* einen Flugzeughangar, seine *Mobilar Structure*[8], entwickelt, die im Frühjahr 1946 im *MoMA* ausgestellt wurde,[→5] ein wichtiges, und, wie sich zeigen würde, wegweisendes Projekt. Denn ein paar Jahre später, genauer gesagt Ende 1949, wurde Wachsmann von Serge Chermayeff nach Chicago gebeten, um dem nach Moholy-Nagys frühen Tod schwankenden *Institute of Design* (1937 als *New Bauhaus* gegründet und damit dem *Illinois Institute of Technology* zugehörig; Mies van der Rohe und Ludwig Hilberseimer waren schon dort) ein solides technisches Programm vorzustellen. »In die Chicagoer Zeit gehören auch zwei der sicher entscheidendsten Erkenntnisse meines Lebens«, wird Konrad Wachsmann später erzählen: »Ich entdeckte die Bedeutung der Teamarbeit und begriff zugleich, dass man den Persönlichkeitskult rigoros bekämpfen muss. [...] Und damit war ein Weg beschritten, der mich [mit] meinem Generalthema, der Industrialisierung des Bauens, an Universitäten und Architekturschulen fast aller Kontinente führte.«[9]

Im Frühjahr 1951 bekam Wachsmanns Institut, das *Department of Advanced Building Research* des *IIT* eher zufällig den folgenreichen Auftrag zur Entwicklung einer »new method of construction for Airplane Hangars based on a [sic] invention by Konrad Wachsmann« (eben der bereits erwähnten *Mobilar Structure*) und dazu die stattliche Summe von vorerst $80 000. Der Vertrag zwischen der *US Air Force* und dem »Advanced Building Research« beschreibt »the development of an airplane hangar designed of unusual dimensions and structural features in which the structure shall provide a new type of metallic construction which is suitable for any kind of structure, where speed of erection and dismounting, of uniform standard parts, flexibility of layouts, large unobstructed floor areas, and unlimited accessibilities are desired. [...] This contract further requests an extreme reduction of the variety of parts and the simplicity of connections such that any structure so designed can be readily erected by members of the Armed Forces.«[10/→6]

Wachsmann startet die Arbeiten im Frühsommer 1951 mit einer Gruppe älterer Studierender und Assistenten in den Räumen der

Armour Research Foundation. Dabei wurde allen Beteiligten schnell klar, ein »nicht gerade einfaches Problem angepackt zu haben. Der rechte Winkel war in Frage gestellt, es galt sich für eine neue Raumkonzeption zu entscheiden. Der Knotenpunkt und das räumliche Dreieck als Schlüssel zur Arbeit mit dreidimensionalen Strukturen eröffneten mir ganz neue Aspekte.«[11] »Sometimes we worked day and night, seven days a week. We had also finished a large model which played an important role in the whole research and the evolution of the design, more important than drafting, since it was extremely difficult to visualize every angle of this three-dimensional structure.«[12] Im April 1952, nach zweimaliger Verschiebung, kann Konrad Wachsmann einen ersten Report übermitteln: »In fulfillment of our Contract, we have in the foregoing submitted a project consisting of forty drawings, many models, numerous photographs, and a report consisting of weight figures, cost estimates, and stress analysis.«[13] Vor allem die vorgestellten Dimensionen (beidseitige Auskragung von 50 m auf unwahrscheinlich zarten Pyramiden-Stützen) und die narrative Qualität des Modells und seiner Fotografien begründeten den »inspirierenden Imagecharakter« im Sinne einer »Inkarnation konstruktivistischen Bauens«[14], wie es im Buch *Vision der Moderne – das Prinzip Konstruktion* später schmeichelhaft heißen wird.

In seiner Zusammenfassung von 1952 schrieb Wachsmann abschließend, dass der so aussichtsreichen Forschung nunmehr Zeit und Geld fehle und er gerne mit weiteren Untersuchungen fortfahren würde, wenn die *US Air Force* nur weitere Mittel zur Verfügung stellt. Was sie auch tat: über die nächsten drei Jahre sollte die Militärverwaltung insgesamt knapp $ 250 000 in Wachsmanns Forschungen investieren.[15] Ermöglicht wurden damit die detaillierten Untersuchungen der Verbindungsknoten[→7], der Bau von Prototypen und weitreichende Verfeinerungen, wenngleich auch die letzten Fragen nach Raumabschluss bzw. Eindeckung und Tormechanik schließlich unbeantwortet bleiben mussten. Die letzten großen Pläne[→169–180] und eine ausführliche Beschreibung beschließen das Projekt 1954. Wenig später (1955) entschied der Kongress der Vereinigten Staaten keine weiteren Grundlagenforschungen ohne genaue Anwendung als Projekt zu unterstützen und aus strategischen Gründen eher in unterirdische, atombombensichere Hangars zu investieren.[16]

Knoten

Reyner Banham war in aufgeregter Höchstform als er 1963 mit *The Dymaxicrat* eine Hymne auf Buckminster Fuller schrieb. In dem Maß, in dem er Fullers Zuversicht und visionäre Größe (sich nicht notwendigerweise mit lästigen Details abzugeben) preist, belächelt er Robert le Ricolais ebenso wie Konrad Wachsmann: »while Wachsmann has done little more than pursue certain problems of structural jointing with the same fiendish narrow ingenuity than other typical German genii have applied to clockwork mice and magnetic mines.«[17] Diesem Eindruck sollte man doch barsch entgegentreten, wobei Banham im Hinblick auf die Knotenproblematik nicht ganz Unrecht hat: Wachsmann scheint von Knotendetails, von Verbindungsstücken generell nahezu besessen gewesen zu sein.[18]

Nach den großartigen Experimenten Graham Bells entwickelte während des zweiten Weltkrieges der deutsche Ingenieur Max Mengeringhausen (auch so ein »typical German genius«) sein Mero-Raumfachwerk und den universellen Schraubknoten für bis zu 18 Stabanschlüsse; erste, wenn auch kleinere Einsätze als transportable Tragsysteme noch für die Luftwaffe folgten. Erst 1957 hatte er bzw. sein Mero-System mit der *Halle der Stadt von Morgen* auf der Berliner Interbau den großen Durchbruch. Wir dürfen annehmen, dass dieses einnehmend-einfache Detail auch Wachsmann vorab bekannt war. Vielleicht ebenso bekannt wie Robert le Ricolais' Schrift *Les Tôles Composées et leurs applications aux constructions métalliques légères* von 1935, in der der kommenden Baukunst die leichten, tragenden Außenbaukonstruktionen der fortschrittlichen Flugzeugtechnik nahegelegt werden. Natürlich: Wachsmann zeigt Bells Aussichtsturm mit vorfabrizierten Tetraedern von 1907 ebenso wie den Mero-Knoten im *Wendepunkt im Bauen* (Seite 133), ohne bei letzterem jedoch auf dessen volle Kapazitäten und mögliche Folgen näher einzugehen.

Es geht bei Raumfachwerken seltener um die Frage, aus welchen Stäben bzw. Elementen sie zusammengesetzt sind, als darum, wo und wie sie auflagern und wie die Knoten konstruiert werden. Der Mero-Knoten ist dabei so einfach wie klug, wenngleich geometrisch und damit formal limitiert. Wachsmanns Knoten wollte mehr: die tatsächlich universelle Lösung, die totale gestalterische Freiheit wenn er schreibt: »Das Ergebnis fast zweijähriger Entwicklungsarbeit war ein universeller Knotenpunkt, der sich ringartig um die Hauptrohre schließt, von dem die Nebenrohre nach allen Richtungen in jeder beliebigen Kombination und jedem Winkel ausstrahlen können. Dieser Knotenpunkt ist imstande, bis zu 20 Konstruktionsstäbe aufzunehmen. Das bedeutet eine fast unbegrenzte Anpassungsfähigkeit an jedes geometrische System, zumal entsprechend der verschiedenartigen Beanspruchungen der einzelnen Stäbe sich auch exzentrische Anschlüsse als erlaubbar erweisen.«[18] Dort allerdings, wo das entscheidende Moment in seiner totalen Rationalisierung gelegen hätte, war Wachsmanns mehrteilige Knotenmechanik zu kompliziert, die Typisierung der Stäbe und ihrer Querschnitte letztlich für eine universelle Struktur untauglich, war das Formwollen des Hangars über sich hinausgewachsen.

Denn es gab zeitgleich zu Wachsmann und auch zuvor gekonnt industrielle Architekturen (siehe z. B. *L'Architecture d'Aujourd'hui,*

Nov. 1936[→9]), bereits patentierte und gebaute Hangarstrukturen[→10], wie auch andere, nicht weniger taugliche Konstruktionsansätze. Die Art aber wie Konrad Wachsmann in der Lage war, vorhandene Ideen und Elemente mit eigenen Anliegen neu zusammenzusetzen und anzureichern hebt ihn noch heute deutlich heraus. Unter den gegebenen Umständen hätte, genau hundert Jahre nach Paxtons *Crystal Palace*, nämlich auch ein viel langweiligeres Objekt entstehen können, das dadurch natürlich weit weniger in der Lage gewesen wäre, die dynamischen Ambitionen der industriellen Gegenwart und Zukunft zu inspirieren. Der USAF-Hangar selbst, so einzigartig und gewollt ikonenhaft seine Form auch immer ist, war somit wohl eher narratives Vehikel zum Nachweis der unausweichlichen Folgerichtigkeit des industriellen Bauens und der ebenso unverzichtbaren Arbeit im und als Team. Ein streitbares Sinnbild seiner Zeit freilich (siehe dazu Stefan Polónyis kritische Rezension von 1961 auf Seite 105) aber war die konstruktive Potenz der Maschine, die offene Methodik und wie Wachsmann selbst doch ein erweiterter und ständig erweiterbarer Ausdruck der Zuversicht »vers une architecture«. Denn »plötzlich hieß es, ich hätte mit dem Hangar das Raumgefühl des 21. Jahrhunderts vorweggenommen. Zu meiner eigenen Verwunderung wurde ich dann auch von den schärfsten Kritikern als kühner Prophet der Zukunftskultur gefeiert«[19/→11], erzählte Konrad Wachsmann und amüsierte sich darüber.

1   Wulf Herzogenrath (Hg.): *Selbstdarstellung – Künstler über sich*, Düsseldorf (Droste Verlag) 1973, S. 225.

2   Franz Kafka: *Die Aeroplane in Brescia*, Fischer Bibliothek, Frankfurt a. M. (S. Fischer Verlag) 1977, S. 21 f.

3   F. T. Marinetti: *Manifest des Futurismus*, in: Norbert Nobis (Hg.): *Der Lärm der Straße*, Ausstellungskatalog, Sprengel Museum Hannover, 2001, S. 367.

4   Le Corbusier: *1922 – Ausblick auf eine Architektur*, Bauwelt Fundamente 2, Braunschweig/Wiesbaden (Vieweg) 1982, S. 89.

5   Peter Sloterdijk: *Sphären III – Schäume*, Frankfurt a. M. (Suhrkamp) 2004, S. 718.

6   Siehe dazu Claudio Greco: *Pier Luigi Nervi*, Luzern (Quart Verlag) 2008, S. 179 u. 285. Nervis Patent vom November 1939 sieht auch die Verwendung von Stahlrohr-Fachwerkträgern vor.

7   Akademie der Künste, Berlin [kurz: AdK], Konrad-Wachsmann-Archiv, Wachsmann 0300.

8   Siehe dazu: Heinrich Klotz (Hg.): *Vision der Moderne*, München (Prestel Verlag) 1986, S. 242 f.

9   Konrad Wachsmann in: Michael Grüning: *Der Wachsmann-Report*, Berlin (Verlag der Nation) 1986, S. 543.

10   AdK, Konrad-Wachsmann-Archiv, Wachsmann 0605 006.

11   Wachsmann in Grüning 1986 (zit. Anm. 9), S. 540.

12   Konrad Wachsmann: *Timebridge, Konrad Wachsmann: An Autobiography* (1981). Unveröffentlichte Autobiografie. AdK, Konrad-Wachsmann-Archiv, Wachsmann 2128, S. 199.

13   AdK, Konrad-Wachsmann-Archiv, Wachsmann 0605 051.

14   Klotz 1986 (zit. Anm. 8), S. 16 u. 236 f.

15   Siehe dazu N. M. Newmark: *Evaluation Of* [sic] *Aircraft Hangar Design*, Report to General Mr. Eric H. Wang, 31 May 1952, III. Recommendations, AdK, Konrad-Wachsmann-Archiv, Wachsmann 2090, S. 14 f. »From the preceding discussion and the earlier report, the following recommendations and suggestions appear to be reasonable: 1. The design of the structure can probably be made adequate to resist the applied loads by either selection of the material

or by increasing the size of some of the critical members. Therefore, it appears that the present design of the structure can serve as a basis for further development and may be a rational starting point for the final design. 2. The design of the connectors presents the biggest problem in the design of the structure. A great deal of development is required to be sure that the connectors can perform their function properly. […]«

16   Wachsmann 1981 (zit. Anm. 12), S. 200.

17   Reyner Banham: A Critic Writes, Berkeley and Los Angeles (University of California Press) 1996, S. 94.

18   Konrad Wachsmann: Wendepunkt im Bauen, Wiesbaden (Krausskopf-Verlag) 1959, S. 172. Interessant hierzu auch die rechnerischen Nachweise und physischen Belastungsversuche der Knotenpunkte von Frank J. Kornacker & Associates (Armour Research Foundation of Illinois Institute of Technology): Calculations on the Wachsmann Hangar, August to October, 1953, IV. Conclusions and Recommendations, AdK, Konrad-Wachsmann-Archiv, Wachsmann 600, S. 30 f. »[…] Thus, the web member joint can be considered slightly stronger; and with the two pieces acting together in an actual connecting assembly, it appears quite certain that the strap will fail first, especially in the view of the fact that the wedge stresses in the strap have been excluded in the Stresscoat tests. The Stresscoat results indicate, however, that some simple changes in the design can be made in the web member joint which can strengthen the part. […] It is recommended that these changes be made since they not only lead to simpler geometry, but they will not increase the weight of the part significantly.«

19   Wachsmann in Grüning 1986 (zit. Anm. 9), S. 541.

Das Konrad-Wachsmann-Archiv wurde am 14.4.1999 an das Baukunstarchiv der *Akademie der Künste*, Berlin, übergeben. Die *Akademie der Künste* erwarb es von dessen Witwe Judith Wachsmann aus der *Huntington Library* in San Marino (USA), wo es zuvor mehrere Jahre als Depositum aufbewahrt worden war. Mit dem Archiv kam eine detaillierte Liste, die bereits 1977, noch zu Lebzeiten Wachsmanns, von Robertson Ward an der *University of Southern California* (USC) erstellt worden war und vier Bereiche umfasste: »File 1«, 22 Boxen mit Schriftgut und Fotos; »File 2«, zwei Hängeregisterschränke mit Sachakten und Unterlagen aus Wachsmanns Tätigkeit als Professor der *USC*; »File 3«, 23 Boxen mit Schriftgut und Fotos. Und in der vierten Liste waren die Pläne und Zeichnungen zusammengefasst. Darüber hinaus wurden nicht in diesen Listen erfasste Materialien übergeben: Bücher, Zeitungen und Zeitschriften, Fotografien und Schriftgut sowie Tonbänder und Filme. Zum Archiv gehören diverse Modellteile der Verbindungsknoten etwa vom P*ackaged House System* und dem USAF-Hangar. Auch Fotografien und Pläne zu frühen Projekten aus der Zeit bei der Holzbaufirma *Christoph & Unmack* in Niesky (1926–29) und Material zu verschiedenen Projekten im Exil (1933–41) sind vorhanden. Am umfangreichsten sind die realisierten und nicht realisierten Projekte in den USA dokumentiert. Darunter sind vor allem das *Packaged House System*, das er zusammen mit Walter Gropius (1942–51) als *General Panel Corporation* vertrieb und für verschiedene Flugzeughangars (*Mobilar Structure*), die im Auftrag der *Atlas Aircraft Corporation* (1939–45) und der *United States Air Force* (1951–53) entstanden. Aber auch Manuskripte und Fotos für die Publikationen *Holzhausbau* (1930) und *Wendepunkt im Bauen* (1959) und Manuskripte und Fotos zu Vorlesungs- und Vortragsreisen durch Europa und Israel sowie Japan und Russland in den 1950er bis 1970er Jahren sind vorhanden. Das Archiv enthält neben privater Korrespondenz aus den 1920er und 1930er Jahren umfangreiche Briefwechsel mit international tätigen Architekten. Besonders aufschlussreich ist das Manuskript seiner unveröffentlichten Autobiografie *Timebridge 1901–2001*. Insgesamt zeugt das Archiv in Inhalt und Aufbau von der ungeheuren Akribie, mit der Wachsmann seine gesamten Arbeiten dokumentiert hat. Das lässt Schlüsse auf seine Arbeitsweise insgesamt zu.

Konrad Wachsmann ist Zeit seines Lebens ein Suchender und Experimentator geblieben, der niemals zu endgültigen Ergebnissen in seinen Bemühungen kam, das Bauen strukturell zu einem massenhaft organisierten Unterfangen zu machen und dabei gleichzeitig Ressourcen und Umwelt zu schonen. Am Ende seiner Biografie *Timebridge* prophezeite er euphorisch eine neue Zeit jenseits des Jahres 2001: »The year 2001 will inaugurate the new epoch, so fantastically exciting. No period in the history of civilization has ever

Konrad Wachsmann
—
der künstlerische Nachlass eines Experimentators in der Akademie der Künste, Berlin

Eva-Maria Barkhofen;
Abb.: 12–14

offered anything so promising, so humane, so effective, so intelligent and so meaningful.«

Der Zeitraum des Konrad-Wachsmann-Archivs beinhaltet Dokumente aus den Jahren 1920 bis 1980 und umfasst in Volumen gemessen: 30 Lfm. Akten, Fotografien und Schriftgut, ca. 2030 Pläne und Zeichnungen, 13 Modelle und diverse Modelleinzelteile sowie knapp 100 Tonbänder mit Originalmitschnitten seiner Reden, Vorlesungen und Diskussionen sowie Filme mit Dokumentationen experimenteller Projekte. Das Archiv ist heute weitgehend archivarisch erschlossen und kann im Baukunstarchiv der *Akademie der Künste* in Berlin eingesehen werden.

Von der Meditation zur Mediation: eine Wiederaneignung des Erbes von Konrad Wachsmann

Parsa Khalili; Abb.: 15, 16

1 – Eine wesentliche Erhaltung

Verborgen und quer durch die verzerrten Felder der architektonischen Repräsentation und Praxis ist man bis zum heutigen Tag Zeuge des Erbes von Konrad Wachsmann. Tatsächlich wissen wir nicht, dass wir ihm und seinem Streben nach einer Formalisierung und Bändigung des endlosen Raumes einiges verdanken. Er bot eine Alternative zu dem heroischen Beharren der Moderne auf den monolithischen Eigenschaften des Betons, aber auch zu den Beteuerungen der Moderne, die Probleme der Architektur und deren gesellschaftlichen Nutzen durch die Verquickung von Dogma und Ideologie mit der gebauten Form gelöst zu haben. Von den erhabenen Darstellungen von unmöglichen Bauvolumina, die in seinen Raumfachwerken untergebracht sind, zu den radikal autokratischen Diagrammen für seine modularen Bausysteme und Verbindungsstücke kannten seine Obsessionen in Ausmaß und Reichweite wohl keine Grenzen – zumindest dem Eindruck und der Legende zufolge. In einem nicht ganz klar bestimmbaren Terrain ist er, der etwas zwischen einem gescheiterten Technofuturisten[1] und einem präutopischen Stadtplaner[2] darstellte, untergegangen. Dass er der inhaltlichen Kritik oder der Berücksichtigung entgangen ist, erklärt sich aus dem willkürlichen Fokussieren der Architekturhistoriker auf das Scheitern des von ihm entwickelten *General Panel System*. Auch zeigte sich die Architektur nicht imstande, seine Relevanz über die üblichen Manifestationen des Gesamtscheiterns der Moderne hinaus zu begründen – einer Moderne, die der Architektur kein humanistisches Projekt sichern konnte, das nicht letztendlich durch entropische Unentschlossenheit in reinem Nutzen und Funktionalismus enden würde.

Zu den wesentlichen Ansatzpunkten für eine mögliche »Erlösung« von Wachsmanns Lebenswerk von dem weitgehend verzerrten Narrativ der Architektur selbst – was bekanntlich der Grund für Tafuris Abrechnung mit der operativen Kritik war – zählt neben der Repräsentation und der Konstruktion die Untersuchung mikrohistorischer Studien zu Themen der Industrialisierung und Architektur. Eine solche befreiende Neulektüre würde dann unweigerlich die Dekonstruktion der Prämisse erfordern, dass Wachsmanns Bedeutung für die Moderne auf irgendeiner Steigerung der Wirkungsmacht des *Crystal Palace* (1851) und dem impliziten Glauben beruht, dass sich über die Technik ein universelles Konstruktionssystem finden ließe, das in den Dienst der gesellschaftlichen Fortschrittsagenda oder eines neuen Utilitarismus der Moderne gestellt werden könnte. Paradoxerweise eröffnet die Befreiung von Wachsmanns Erbe von einer derartigen Ideologie ein Mittel zum Verständnis seiner Rolle sowohl in Bezug auf das Scheitern des utopischen Projekts der Moderne (eine Voreingenommenheit, die eine Überbetonung seiner persönlichen Misserfolge rechtfertigt), als auch

seiner Rolle als Humanist (niemals auf reinen Nutzen reduzierbar).
Entfernt man die seine Erfolge und Misserfolge definierende rein
utilitaristische Rhetorik, findet man den Schlüssel zur Rekonstruktion seines Erbes. Die Verbindung zwischen der von Wachsmann
geschaffenen Bildwelt und den geradezu explosiven Auswirkungen
seiner Bestrebungen auf eine neue Generation von Architekten der
Nachkriegszeit ist unübersehbar. Die technische Ausgereiftheit und
Komplexität der von ihm hergestellten Systeme befreite die Praxis
junger Architekten von den erdrückenden Dogmen beruflicher Ver-
pflichtungen der damaligen Zeit und bot ihnen die Werkzeuge und
die Sprache für einen radikalen Einsatz und die Vergegenwärtigung
neuer utopischer Ideale – wenn nicht in einer Art obskurer revolu-
tionärer Verblendung, so doch zumindest auf der Ebene der Bildwelt. Die Systeme, die ihm vorschwebten, die er aber nie ganz voll-
enden konnte, transzendierten sowohl kulturelle als auch geogra-
fische Grenzen, und dies hat sich auch in der zweiten Hälfte des
zwanzigsten Jahrhunderts iterativ und kontinuierlich fortgesetzt.
Vor dem Hintergrund soziokultureller Veränderungen hat sich sein
Projekt und Erbe bis zum heutigen Tag weiterentwickelt. Bekanntlich sind viele dieser Zeitperioden ihrerseits auch »futuristisch«,
und dieser Aspekt der humanistischen Vorstellung wird durch eine
zu genaue Betrachtung der angewandten Systeme außer Acht gelassen.

ii – Evolutionäre Mutation

Die unmittelbare Rezeption seiner Arbeit erfolgte in Form von
Projekten als *radikale Hyperbeln*. Mit *La Ville Spatiale* (1960) von
Yona Friedman, *Space City* (1959) von Eckhard Schulze-Fielitz und
New Babylon (1959) von Constant Nieuwenhuys wird jeweils über
die unmögliche Zukunft einer vor allem in ihrer Ausrichtung (und
der Wirkung der Schwerkraft gegenüber) befreiten Architektur
spekuliert. Die Leichtigkeit und endlose Reproduzierbarkeit des
Raumfachwerks bedeutete Omnidirektionalität und Wachstum,
Unbegrenztheit in Bezug auf Funktion und Zweck, die intellektuel-
len Grundlagen der Auswirkung einer vollständigen Loslösung vom
Boden selbst, vor allem jedoch eine symbolische Auslöschung der
Kontinuität der architektonischen Tradition in ihrer Gesamtheit.
Dieser »Neubeginn« befreite den utopischen Geist der Moderne
von der Ideologie der Moderne. Der entscheidende Punkt ist die
Gegenüberstellung von Überschwang und Fantasie mit dem nüch-
ternen technologischen Utilitarismus, der selbstverständlich in der
allgegenwärtigen, damals von jedermann verachteten (und Mies et
al. angelasteten) Moderne Mitte des 20. Jahrhunderts verankert ist.
An dieser Stelle sei darauf hingewiesen, dass die »antikapitalisti-
sche« Stadt *New Babylon* 1959 erstmals konzipiert wurde!

Auf diesen Urknall folgte eine kurze Pause in den wilden
Spekulationen, die eine nur mehr geringfügig ernüchterte zweite

Phase des *hyperbolischen Funktionalismus* einleitete, in der man auf ein Überdenken Wachsmanns in einem realistischeren Rahmen drängte. *Tokyo Bay* (1960) von Kenzo Tange, *Fun Palace* (1964) von Cedric Price, *Plug-In City* (1964) von Archigram und *Agriculture City* (1960) von Kisho Kurokawa fingen einige der Fantasien der vergangenen Jahrzehnte ein und brachten plausible, wenn auch noch extreme Anregungen für neue Modelle für Wohnungsbau, Erholung und Urbanität hervor. Diese Projekte schränkten das Raumfachwerk auf überschaubare System- und Programmnetzwerke ein, wobei die einzelnen Einsatzstücke oft zuerst erdacht und in einem zweiten Schritt nach oben, nach außen hin und darüber hinaus propagiert wurden; dieser Reifungsprozess spiegelt eine Entwicklung in Wachsmanns Ansatz wider – von einer Top-down-Hierarchie zu einer Bottom-up-Hierarchie.

In der dritten Phase der *funktionalen Sichtbarkeit* wurde das Raumfachwerk – im wörtlichen wie im übertragenen Sinn – zum Rahmen für die Würdigung sowohl der Weiterentwicklungen im Bereich der mechanischen Bausysteme als auch der Abhängigkeit von diesen und führte zu vollkommen neuen Systemen, die Struktur entweder ironisierten oder fetischisierten. Am deutlichsten zeigt sich dies am Beispiel von Renzo Piano, Richard Rogers und Gianfranco Franchini, die den Nutzen des Raumfachwerks in dem offenkundig pragmatischen Sinn für den alltäglichsten Gebrauch mit dem *Centre Pompidou* (1971) voranbrachten. Mit dem Sichtbarwerden des Schreckgespensts von Friedman und Price an den Rändern wird die Allgegenwart des Raumfachwerks mit den verschiedenen Bausystemen ausgefüllt (und werden diese gewürdigt), die für die Schaffung der ununterbrochenen und nicht verpflichteten Offenheit des Innenraums notwendig sind. Einzig und allein aufgrund dieses Innengerüstes war eine Befreiung des Raumes möglich – dies stand auf allen Ebenen in krassem Gegensatz zu den damaligen normativen Konstruktionsmitteln und -methoden. In vielerlei Hinsicht ist Wachsmanns »strukturelle Logik« ein offenes System; auf ihren postmodernen Abwegen kam sie mangels Alternative als Teil einer architektonischen Neuverquickung des modernen Funktionalismus/Utilitarismus und der Vermanschung der Großraumkonzepte zum Einsatz. Letzteres ermöglichte es der Avantgarde, sich diese anzueignen, und dank ersterem konnte diese Phase von der nächsten abgelöst werden.

In der aktuellsten Erscheinungsform, einer namenlosen *vierten Phasendrift*, die in etwa dem entspricht, was in der Kunstwelt als *Super Contemporary* bezeichnet wird[3], könnte man meinen, dass Wachsmanns Ethos seither hyperstilisiert, stark berechnet und als Serviceleistung für die verzerrte, verdrillte und verborgene strukturelle Logik der heute errichteten Bauten optimiert wurde. Ohne diese Neuformulierung wären die heroischen Projekte des

Digitalzeitalters entsetzlich unökonomisch, wenn nicht sogar unmöglich. Diese Drift lässt sich von Shoei Yohs *Prefectura Gymnasium*
(1991) über Coop Himmelb(l)aus *BMW Welt*[→60] (2001) bis hin zum
Hedar Aliyev Centre[→15] (2007) des Büros *Zaha Hadid Architects*
ausmachen bzw. rückverfolgen. Die implizite Ideologie dieser Verschiebung betrifft den Siegeszug der neuen Spektakelformen der
Architektur. Es bleibt unklar, ob Wachsmann auf der architektonischen Seite dieser kulturellen Verschiebung bewusst assimiliert
wurde oder über die Entwicklung der Instrumente zum Bau dessen,
was als spiegelbildlicher Zustand des Hyperkapitalismus tatsächlich »räumliche Drift« ist, lediglich daran beteiligt war.

In Verlegenheit gebracht durch das eigene Klischee und ver-
altete Bild von der Wirksamkeit des Industriezeitalters, megastruk-
turalistischer utopischer Innengerüste oder vergegenständlichter
Gebäudesystemtechnik, wurde Wachsmanns technisch-formalisti-
sche Ausdrucksweise zuletzt hinter die dünnschalige Aluminium-
verkleidung der gehaltlosen zeitgenössischen tektonischen Sprache
der Architektur gedrängt. Diese Sprache legt auch den Begriff der
Drift in Verbindung mit der Hyperkapitalisierung der Architektur
als Ultrarohstoff frei (konstruiert, um die kapitalistische Abdrift
selbst zu verkörpern).

III – Protohumanismus

Eine Rekonstruktion seines Erbes aus einer breiteren historischen Perspektive ergibt eine vom Ende der fünfziger Jahre bis ins
21. Jahrhundert hineinreichende Übertragungslinie von gebauten
und nicht gebauten Arbeiten, in denen Wachsmanns strukturelle
Innovationen assimiliert wurden, auch wenn die Arbeiten von seiner utopischen Agenda abweichen und schrittweise eine Umgrup-
pierung in spektakuläre Architektur erfahren, wobei sämtliche Beispiele auf der einen oder anderen Form des Überschwangs beruhen.
Aus diesem Grund lässt sich sagen, dass ein weiterer Aspekt Wachsmanns dabei über Bord geworfen wurde und nur ein Teil seines
Erbes erhalten geblieben ist. In vielerlei Hinsicht unterstützten
Architekturhistoriker durch die Darstellung Wachsmanns als un-
verbesserlichen Technologen daher die Übertragung seines Erbes
an das Bauingenieurwesen, während das, was sich hinter dem mo-
dernistischen Streben nach Industrieproduktion und Präzisions-
handwerk verbarg, fallen gelassen wurde.

Nach dem Scheitern seiner Experimente veröffentlichte Wachsmann seine *Sieben Thesen*[4] (1957) zur Kontextualisierung der Vorstellung von Materialprozessen innerhalb der Architektur (aber
nicht als Ersatz für die Architektur). Es versuchte als Manifest die
Fundamente seines breiteren ideologischen Projekts neu zu positionieren, und dennoch ist nur in einem Punkt die Abwesenheit auf
Tektonik oder Systeme bezogener Ausdrücke wie Wissenschaft,
Technologie, Maschine, Werkzeug, Werkstoffe, Prozesse, Industria-

lisierung, wissenschaftlich, Automation oder Industrie auffallend. In Abschnitt 7 wird schließlich Wachsmanns »Rosebud« erkennbar, ein subtiler Protohumanismus, der im direkten Gegensatz zu dem Technodeterminismus steht, der zumeist als sein Erbe bezeichnet wurde. Abschnitt 7 besagt: »Die humanen und ästhetischen Vorstellungen werden durch die kompromisslose Anwendung des zeitgenössischen Wissens und Könnens neue Impulse erhalten.«[5]

Über die in diesem Text skizzierten Perioden und die verschiedenen Arbeiten, die Wachsmanns (von den Architekturhistorikern allerdings verzerrte) Sprache sozusagen erneut verkörpern, ist das einst Radikale und Protohumanistische seither zur Parodie, wenn nicht zum Opfer einer vollkommenen Verzerrung geworden. Wachsmann vor beiden zu bewahren erfordert daher eine Lektüre *seines* Abschnitts 7 vor dem Hintergrund des – und parallel zu dem – von dem österreichischen Philosophen Ludwig Wittgenstein verfassten *Tractatus logico-philosophicus* (1922): »Wovon man nicht sprechen kann, darüber muss man schweigen.« (»What we cannot speak about we must pass over in silence«.[6]) Was wir nun wissen, ist technisch ableitbar, doch worauf es ankommt ist, wie wir damit umgehen.

1   Vgl. Reyner Banhams kompromiss-lose Kritik in: *I complessi della prefabbricazione*, Casabella, Sept. 1986, Bd. 50, Nr. 527.

2   Siehe Kenneth Framptons: *I tecnocrati della Pax Americana: Wachsmann & Fuller*, Casabella, Jan.–Feb. 1988, , Bd. 52, Nr. 542–543.

3   Dieser Begriff kam nach 2000 auf, ursprünglich als Bezeichnung des Medienspektakels, das zu der Zeit die Kunstwelt ergriff.

4   Siehe S. 61 in dieser Publikation.

5   Konrad Wachsmann: *Seven Theses*, in: Ulrich Conrads (Hg.): *Programs and manifestoes on 20th-century architecture*, Cambridge, MA (The MIT Press) 1970, S. 156.

6   Auf Seite 5 von Francesca Hughes Werk *The Architecture of Error: Matter, Measure, and the Misadventures of Precision* (The MIT Press, 2014) werden Wittgenstein und Wachsmann in unmittelbare Nähe gebracht. Hughes verbindet das logisch-positivistische Universum des frühen Wittgenstein mit der rationalistischen und wissenschaftlichen Neigung des späten Wachsmann. Hughes zufolge waren beide in diesem Fall bis zur *Irrationalität* von Genauigkeit besessen. Diese Kritik an Wachsmanns Zwanghaftigkeit wurde während eines Großteils seines beruflichen Werdegangs erhoben.

Konrad Wachsmann war ein unangepasster und geradezu besessen in die Zukunft planender Baumeister. Die Forschung befasst sich zumeist mit seinen visionären technischen Entwürfen, fast nie wird nach dem Menschen und dessen Herkunft gefragt. Doch ist sein Werk und Wirken ohne Kenntnis seiner frühen Biografie kaum begreifbar.

Konrad Wachsmann wurde am 16. Mai 1901 als drittes von vier Kindern des Apothekerehepaars Elsa und Adolf Wachsmann in Frankfurt an der Oder geboren. Die Apotheke befand sich in einem gotischen Stadthaus, direkt am Marktplatz, über der die Familie auch wohnte. Die starke Traditionsverhaftung und die Kaisertreue der Eltern haben den jungen Konrad offenbar zu einem Rebellen gegen alles pflichtgeprägte Gehorchen werden lassen. Der frühe Tod des Vaters 1908 muss die Opposition des Jungen nachhaltig gefördert haben. So kann man seinen späteren Aufzeichnungen entnehmen, dass er die Schule gehasst hat. Nachdem er zweimal sitzen geblieben war und das soziale Miteinander der städtischen Gesellschaft im Armenviertel Frankfurts suchte, musste er aus der Schule genommen werden. Seine Mutter brachte ihn ab April 1917 in einer Lehre bei der Tischlerei Münning in Frankfurt/Oder unter, wo er auflebte. Das Arbeiten mit Holz gab ihm die Gelegenheit, handwerkliche und technische Kenntnisse zu erwerben und befriedigte seinen Geist.[1] Die Hauptproduktion der Tischlerei lag während des Weltkriegs in der Produktion von Särgen. Er selbst gibt an, 1918 an jedem Arbeitstag einen Sarg gezimmert zu haben, morgens den unteren Teil und nachmittags den Deckel. Er erinnert sich, sich mittags zur Pause mit angezogenen Beinen in das fertige Unterteil gelegt zu haben, denn die Särge waren aufgrund von Sparmaßnahmen sehr kurz gebaut. Sonntags musste er die fünf Särge Wochenproduktion auf einem Handwagen zum Militärkrankenhaus bringen. Wachsmann legte nach dreijähriger Lehrzeit am 31. März 1920 die Gesellenprüfung ab und plante den lang gehegten Wunsch Architektur zu studieren endlich umzusetzen. Ihn zog es nach Weimar an das Bauhaus, doch der Mutter behagten die sozialistischen Ideen nicht, und sie schickte ihren Sohn im Alter von 20 Jahren nach Berlin an die Kunstgewerbeschule zu Bruno Paul. Dort empfand er sogleich seine altbekannte Ablehnung gegen den schulischen Zwang. Er verließ die Kunstgewerbeschule nach nur einem Jahr 1922.

Wie sehr er unter allem, was an ihn herangetragen wurde, litt und wogegen er rebellierte, belegt ein unveröffentlichter Brief des 19-Jährigen an seine Mutter. Allein die ersten Sätze sind von enormer Bedeutung für das Verständnis seines späteren Werks: »Liebes Muttel! Nur derjenige versteht richtig zu leben, der immer das will, was er muss, d. h., der sich immer in das Unvermeidliche zu fügen versteht und bei dem eben der Zwang immer gleich der Wille ist. Ich werde das wohl nie lernen.«[2] Dass er diese Qual über weitere drei

Biografische Notizen

»Nur derjenige versteht richtig zu leben, der immer das will, was er muss […]«
(Konrad Wachsmann)

Eva-Maria Barkhofen;
Abb.: 17–29

Briefseiten ausführt, macht nachdenklich. Sein Verhältnis zu Mutter und Schwester war nie ein herzliches. Nach Verlassen der Kunstgewerbeschule hielt er sich mit Gelegenheitsaufträgen über Wasser, die sich meist aus seinen täglichen Aufenthalten im Romanischen Café am Potsdamer Platz ergaben. Er diskutierte dort mit Bertolt Brecht, Else Lasker-Schüler, Erwin Piscator und anderen Künstlern. Eine Ahnung, wohin ihn sein Leben führen sollte, hatte er nicht. Direkt vom Kaffeehaustisch wurde er für den Bau von Filmkulissen angeheuert. Nur durch die Unterstützung einer wohlhabenden Berliner Tante konnte er überleben. Dass seine Familie seinen Lebenswandel nicht billigte, ist nicht schwer zu verstehen. Seine Mutter beschloss ihn aus dem schädlichen Einfluss herauszunehmen. Er wurde nach Dresden an die Kunstakademie zu Heinrich Tessenow geschickt, dessen Architektur ihn zunächst inspirierte. Doch wieder konnte er sich dem Lehrbetrieb nicht unterordnen und kehrte 1924 nach Berlin zurück. Er nahm eine Stelle als Zeichner bei Leo Nachtlicht an. Auch dort hielt es ihn nicht lange. Er suchte Kontakt zu Hans Poelzig, dessen Großes Schauspielhaus ihn faszinierte. Poelzig nahm ihn als Meisterschüler in sein Atelier auf. Doch nun drückte ihn der Goldene Käfig, in dem er bei Poelzig saß. Wachsmann wollte aus Deutschland heraus. 1926 reiste er nach Holland, um bei Pieter Oud zu arbeiten. Wegen fehlender Aufenthaltspapiere wurde er ausgewiesen. Er reiste nach Paris zu Le Corbusier, aber eine unbezahlte Stelle konnte er sich nicht leisten. Hätte ihm seine Schwester nicht die Rückfahrkarte nach Berlin bezahlt, wäre er – nach eigener Aussage – in den Straßen von Paris verloren gegangen. 1926 schließlich vermittelte ihn Hans Poelzig an die Holzbaufirma *Christoph & Unmack* in Niesky (Lausitz, Brandenburg), wo er zum ersten Mal ganz in seiner Aufgabe aufging. Diese Tätigkeit, die bis 1929 dauerte, sollte die Grundlage für alle späteren Projektideen zu vorfabrizierten Bauten und seinen Vorstellungen von der automatisierten Welt bilden.

Sein wichtigstes Projekt bei *Christoph & Unmack* war der Bau des Holzhauses für Albert Einstein in Caputh bei Potsdam, das 1929 realisiert wurde.

Die Wirren der Kriegszeit führten ihn als Flüchtling, er war Halbjude, an diverse Orte in Europa, aber – vermittelt durch Gropius und Einstein – erhielt er 1940 das Visum für die USA. Wachsmann sprach kein Wort Englisch außer einem Satz, den ihm ein englischer Maler in Rom beigebracht hatte: »a thunderstorm refreshes the atmosphere«.[3] Walter Gropius versuchte eine Arbeit für ihn zu finden, doch die mangelnden Sprachkenntnisse verhinderten die Lehre an der Universität. Gropius lud ihn zu sich nach Boston ein. Da Marcel Breuer sich gerade von Gropius als Büropartner getrennt hatte, konnte Wachsmann in laufende Arbeiten einsteigen. Er berichtete Gropius von seinem universalen Bausystem für Fertighäuser, das er

in Marseille entwickelt hatte, und zeigte ihm die 13 Skizzen, die er
retten konnte. Gropius war begeistert. Im Heizungskeller des Ap-
partements stellte Wachsmann drei Zeichenbretter auf, in die Mitte
einen Drehstuhl, so dass er gleichzeitig an allen arbeiten konnte. Im
Frühjahr 1942 war der Entwurf in 44 Zeichnungen baureif. Er hatte
oft Auseinandersetzungen mit Ise Gropius, da er seine Bleistifte
auch im Schlafzimmer auf dem weißen Teppich anspitzte. Sie mein-
te, so jemanden wie ihn sollte man in einen Vogelkäfig sperren, der
ein Gitter als Boden hätte, damit aller Dreck sofort aufgefangen
werden könnte.[4]

Zeichnungen Modelle, Beschreibungen und Patentanmeldun-
gen existierten nun für das *General Panel System*, aber woher sollte
das Geld für die Umsetzung kommen? Mögliche Investoren zweifel-
ten noch am Erfolg des Konzepts. Aber Wachsmann hatte schließlich
ein Schreiben eines Ingenieurs des MIT als Referenz bei sich und
ging im Juni 1942 auf Investorensuche. Ise Gropius soll zum Ab-
schied gesagt haben: »You can only come back WITH your shield or
ON your shield«[5], was hieß, entweder als Gewinner oder als toter
Verlierer wiederzukommen. Im September desselben Jahres kam er
als Gewinner zurück. Die offizielle Gründung der *General Panel
Corporation* wurde auf den 12. 9. 1942 gelegt als Erinnerung an die
Ankunft Wachsmanns in den USA am Tag genau ein Jahr zuvor. Vier
Monate später war ein Testhaus mit Hilfe deutschsprachiger Tisch-
ler fertig. Eine Zeit großen Erfolgs brach an.

Ab Ende 1949 begann Wachsmanns Karriere als Lehrender am
IIT *Institute of Design in Chicago*. Er, der stets alles Schulische gehasst hatte, tauchte in eine neue Welt ein und stellte fest, dass er
weder Ahnung von der Lehre noch vom Design hatte. Und dennoch
begann eine steile Karriere als Lehrer und Vortragender, der bis zu
seinem Tod am 26. 11. 1980 die Verbreitung seiner Ideen von flexi-
blen und vorfabrizierten Baustrukturen auf hunderten Vortragsreisen in die Welt trug.

Im letzten Satz der Autobiografie fasst Wachsmann sein Le-
bensmotto treffend in einem Satz zusammen: »My friends: The past
is the past, the present is only in passing, but the future is everything.«[6]

1   Diese und die folgenden Angaben
    sind der unpublizierten Autobio-
    grafie: Konrad Wachsmann: *Time-
    bridge, Konrad Wachsmann: An
    Autobiography* (1981), entnommen.
    AdK, Konrad-Wachsmann-Archiv,
    Wachsmann 2128.
2   Brief an seine Mutter vom 3. 6. 1920.
    AdK, Konrad-Wachsmann-Archiv,
    Wachsmann 1077.

3   Wachsmann 2128 (zit. Anm. 1),
    S. 153.
4   Ebd., S. 159 f.
5   Ebd., S. 164.
6   Ebd., S. 469.

Ende 1973 und Anfang 1974 arbeitete Konrad Wachsmann in Los Angeles an einer Reihe von hand- und maschinenschriftlichen Entwürfen eines maßgeblichen, aber letztendlich unveröffentlicht gebliebenen Textes mit dem Titel *Manifest for the Evolution of Assembling the Artificial Human Environment between Time and Space.*[2] Das von dem damals 75-jährigen Experten für Montagebau verfasste 49-seitige Manuskript löst die bloße Vorstellung eines Gebäudes endgültig auf. Es beginnt mit der folgenden Proklamation: »Bauen ist Energie und Bewegung in Zeit und Raum.« Demnach sei die Form von Strukturen, Umgebungen und Gesellschaften seit jeher durch die Verfügbarkeit von Energie bestimmt worden und der vor relativ kurzer Zeit erfolgte Einzug der elektrischen Energie habe durch die »Herbeiführung« des Maschinenzeitalters das gesamte physische, soziale und ökonomische Leben drastisch verändert. Unser als Raumschiff den Weltraum durchlaufender Planet sei bereits von einer »Energiedecke« umhüllt, »einer Decke elektrischer Energie, der keinerlei Grenzen gesetzt sind«, und Kernenergie beschleunige diese Aufhebung von Grenzen. Massivbauten würden unweigerlich diaphanen »Punktenetzen« im Weltall weichen, die von computergestützter, kybernetischer Rückkopplung geleitete temporäre Raumkonfigurationen unterstützten. Wände, Böden, Säulen, Türen und Fenster würden durch eine neue Bautechnologie ersetzt werden, »die noch nicht in Worte gefasst wurde«. Die durch die traditionellen Gebäude getragenen Illusionen der Dauerhaftigkeit würden sich letztendlich der »ununterbrochenen Anpassbarkeit« einer scheinbar masselosen Struktur beugen, deren »durchlässiger« Charakter durch die in ihrem Inneren als »Bewegungsebenen« verteilt aufgehängten temporären dünnen Horizontalflächen und den in noch stärkerem Ausmaß temporären Vertikalflächen als »glänzende Schirme« verstärkt werden würde. Diese Schirme ermöglichten den Aufbau eines Gefühls der Distanz zwischen den innerhalb dieser dichten urbanen Konfigurationen lebenden Menschen. Umgekehrt führten Fernsehbildschirme zu einer Verringerung der Distanz für die in isolierteren Milieus Lebenden. Die bebaute Umwelt werde zu einer Punktwolke, die unbegrenzt temporäre Konfigurationen beweglicher Schirme unterstütze, durch die der Distanzeffekt entweder erzeugt oder aufgelöst werde. Raum pulsiert. Die Architektur als solche tritt nicht in Erscheinung. Sie fehlt auch nicht.

Dieses Bild von der nahen Zukunft korrespondiert in hohem Maße mit den ausgedehnten über dem Boden schwebenden Spinnennetzen als Megastrukturen, die von Constant Nieuwenhuys, Cedric Price, Yona Friedman, Eckhard Schulze-Fielitz, den Metabolisten, Superstudio und vielen anderen von den späten 1950er bis zu den 1970er Jahren angeregt wurden.[3] Hervorzuheben ist jedoch Wachsmanns wesentlicher Einfluss auf sie alle und die Art, wie sein Projekt radikaler blieb.

Konrad Wachsmanns Television: postarchitektonische Übertragungen[1]

Mark Wigley; Abb.: 30–42

Von zentraler Bedeutung in Wachsmanns Schilderung ist der
Umstand, dass die Fähigkeit zur drahtlosen Übertragung und zum
Empfang von Informationen die bebaute Umwelt umgestalte. Information diene nicht nur als Basis für effizientere und reaktions-
fähigere Gestaltung. Sie sei ein eigenständiger Baustoff, ja der ulti-
mative Baustoff. Fernsehbildschirme würden nie einfach in einer
existierenden Umwelt aufgehängt werden, sondern konstruierten
vielmehr eine völlig neue Umwelt, wie das *Manifest* betont:

»Durch Energiewellen, die ihm Informationen übermitteln,
die er annehmen oder ablehnen kann, wie es der Fall des Fernseh-
bildschirms zeigt, wird er mit seiner Gemeinschaft und der Welt
stets untrennbar verbunden sein. Wie sehr sich dies auf den Begriff
der Bedeutung und Funktion des Hauses, der Straße, der Gemeinschaft, des urbanen oder regionalen Systems auswirkt, ist offensichtlich.«[4]

Diese Energiewellen lösen konventionelle Gebäude auf und
damit auch den Unterschied zwischen den Gebäuden, der Gesellschaft, der Wirtschaft und der Politik. Was als abgegrenztes Gebäude angesehen wurde, wird zu einem in eine immer größere Reihe
von verschachtelten Systemen eingebetteten System von Systemen.
Keine Abgrenzung zwischen Gebäude, Straße, Stadt, Gemeinschaft
und Gehirn bleibt übrig. Die bloße Vorstellung von dem Gestalter
und der Gestaltung wird von interdisziplinären Teams abgelöst und
die Trennung zwischen solchen Expertenteams und den Stadtbe-
wohnern wird letztendlich von einer breiteren Ökologie des Infor-
mationsaustauschs über Computer abgelöst werden. Die Sammlung,
Aktualisierung, Klassifizierng, Speicherung, Analyse und Zugäng-
lichkeit von Informationen erlangen entscheidende Bedeutung. Die
von Wachsmanns Teams erstellten Skizzen von Informationssys-
temen waren genauso detailliert wie jene von Gebäudesystemen.
Tatsächlich wurden Informationssysteme wie Gebäudesysteme behandelt. Gebäude, Institutionen, gesellschaftliche Gruppen und
Vorstellungen mussten auf die gleiche Weise gedacht werden.

In einer solchen Welt sei Architektur nach traditionellem Verständnis »fakultativ«. Dennoch betont Wachsmann, dass sich eine
weltweit gemeinsame Ästhetik als eine Art Zusammenarbeit her-
ausbilden würde. Das Vorhaben, die Architektur zum Verschwinden zu bringen, ist paradoxerweise ein ästhetisches Vorhaben. Das
Verschwinden selbst ist ein genau durchdachtes Ereignis. Er versucht, eine Architektur ohne Grenzen, d. h. eine Architektur ohne
Architektur, für »weit offene und freie Räume relativ unbegrenzter
Dimensionen und die Überlagerung von Räumen relativ unbegrenzter Ausmaße und die Überlagerung von Räumen relativ unbegrenzter Zahl« mit einer »unbegrenzten« Energie-»Versorgung« zu
visualisieren. Er vermutet sogar, dass die elektrische Energiedecke,
die den Planeten mit einem »Drahtgeflechts-Gurt« umwickelt, bald

durch ein Netzwerk umlaufender Satelliten ersetzt werden könnte, das die Sonnenenergie umwandeln und in konzentrierten »drahtlos übertragenen Energiewellen« an den Einsatzort ausstrahlen werde. Jegliche drahtlose Übertragung sei nicht nur eine Art die Umwelt formende Energiewelle. Vielmehr würde die Energie selbst als Rohstoff der bebauten Umwelt zu einer drahtlosen Übertragung werden. Ebenso wie sein enger Freund Buckminster Fuller war Wachsmann letztendlich ein drahtlos arbeitender Architekt.[5]

Wachsmanns Arbeit bestand in einer geradezu obsessiven Form der Systemforschung, die sich auf die Materialorganisation und -montage konzentrierte und daher tendenziell nicht unter ästhetischen, philosophischen, ethischen oder politischen Gesichtspunkten betrachtet wird. Aus seiner Sicht war sie mehr als alles andere mit diesen Bereichen befasst.[6] In seinem *Manifest* argumentierte er, dass die neue Verfügbarkeit drahtloser Energie, die keine räumlichen Grenzen kenne, beispielsweise bedeute, dass Krieg unnötig werde, während kontinuierliches politisches Engagement jedoch wesentlich sei, wie es ihm zufolge vom Fernsehbildschirm dargestellt wird, der Echtzeitinformationen und das Recht vergibt, darauf zu reagieren. Wachsmann hob die Notwendigkeit einer Änderung der Regierungsstruktur hervor – selbst in der Verantwortung des »großen Auftrags der Information«, mit einer möglichst breiten Öffentlichkeit über die Tatsache zu kommunizieren, dass das 20. Jahrhundert lediglich eine Vorbereitungsphase auf einen neuen Lebensstil und neue soziale Ordnungen darstelle, die bereits »durch die Verfügbarkeit neuer Informationsmedien wie beispielsweise des Fernsehens herbeigeführt« worden seien. Anders ausgedrückt muss das Fernsehen die eigene kontinuierliche Wirkung in einer gesellschaftlich transformativen Rückkopplungsschleife vermitteln. Es besteht eine enge Beziehung zwischen der Entgrenzung des Bauens, dem Zugriff auf Informationen und politischem Engagement.

Als Geflüchteter, dessen persönliches Leben von der Notwendigkeit, der Gewalt eines bestimmten, von den Nazis potenzierten Vorurteils zu entkommen, und nicht nur der Ermordung seiner Mutter, seiner Schwester und seines Neffen, sondern auch dem Mord an Millionen anderer Menschen bestimmt war, stellte sich Wachsmann in der nahen Zukunft eine Gesellschaft ohne Bezugnahme auf ethnische Herkunft, Geschlecht, Religion, Klasse oder Nation vor. Es ist, als sei der Gedanke, dass Elektrizität keine Grenzen kennt, die Grundlage für ein idealistisches Bild einer Gesellschaft geworden, die die Grenzen der Gewalt überschreitet, indem sie jede dauerhafte Trennlinie zurückweist, aber beständige Wachsamkeit gegenüber einzelnen Autoritätspersonen, Eliten und Mobs in einer Art Techno-Optimismus einfordert, der angesichts der heute so effizienten Begünstigung eben dieser Gewalt durch die Informationstechnologien und der vermeintlichen *Sharing Economy* sicherlich erschaudern würde.

Gegen Ende des *Manifests* skizziert Wachsmann diese zukünftige Welt in seinem USAF-Hangar-Projekt, einem mit Studierenden und Kollegen zwischen 1951 und 1954 entwickelten Gebäude »nahezu unbegrenzten Ausmaßes«, das auf die Megastruktur-Bewegung nach der zeitgleich erfolgten umfangreichen Publikation darüber in den bedeutendsten internationalen Zeitschriften im September 1954 massiv Einfluss genommen hat.[7] Diese paradoxerweise für die Unterbringung von Kriegsmaschinerie konzipierte, jedoch als für Strukturen jeder Art anwendbar präsentierte Architektur für eine neue Nachkriegskollektivität war buchstäblich ein »spinnennetzartiges« Gebilde von unzähligen miteinander verbundenen Metallröhren zusammen mit einer Reihe beweglicher Schirme, die stellvertretend für alle traditionellen Elemente der Dächer, Wände, Böden, Türen und Fenster wirkten. Die Struktur scheint durch dramatische Auskragungen auf beiden Seiten der Schwerkraft zu trotzen. Sie schwebt wie eine Wolke auf einer Reihe minimaler durchsichtiger Stützen, die so tief von ihren Kanten angesetzt ist, dass die polemischen Horizontalen Frank Lloyd Wrights und Mies von der Rohes als nicht ausreichend horizontal erscheinen.

Zeitschriftenherausgeber konnten der Versuchung nicht widerstehen, auf einigen über zwei Seiten veröffentlichten Bildern die Wirkung einer tief fliegenden, etwa 245 Meter langen Stahlwolke einzufangen, die auf jede beliebige Länge ausgedehnt werden konnte. Die Raumfachwerkstruktur des Netzwerks ist per Definition ein dreidimensionales Netz, und Wachsmann betrachtete seine Struktursysteme als omnidirektionale Strahlungsdiagramme. Den Höhepunkt des Projekts bildet jedoch ein massives horizontales Statement. Es ist, als sei das antihierarchische politische Projekt zwangsläufig horizontal, als spreche es buchstäblich jeden Nachbarn und hypothetisch alle Nachbarn an und erweitere das Gemeinschaftsgefühl, indem alle auf die gleiche Ebene gebracht werden. Das Raumfachwerk ist in erster Linie ein Angriff auf die Vertikale durch die Auflösung aller Säulen und Wände zur Entfernung jeder dauerhaften seitlichen Unterteilung.

Auf vielen der veröffentlichten Fotografien des polemisch komplexen, etwa 5 Meter langen Modells der Hälfte des Gebäudes sind einige wenige winzige menschliche Figuren am Boden unter dem gewaltigen horizontalen Netz ersichtlich, bei dem es sich sowohl um ein auf die Aufgabe der Unterbringung von Luftfahrzeugen abgestimmtes spezifisches technologisches Artefakt als auch um ein ästhetisches Bild von der neuen Netzwerklogik einer elektrischen und zunehmend drahtlosen Welt handelt.

In Wachsmanns *Manifest* wird der außerweltlich erscheinende USAF-Hangar als eine Fortsetzung der Erprobung des Montagebaus präsentiert, der mit dem von Paxton entworfenen *Crystal Palace* im Jahr 1851 eingeleitet worden war. Letzteres Gebäude wurde ebenso als ein System von werkseitigen standardisierten Metallelementen konzipiert, das ohne die traditionelle Beschäftigung mit der Form in jeder Kombination für jede gewünschte Funktion vor Ort montiert werden konnte. Paxtons 563 Meter lange Struktur hatte jeden traditionellen Bedeutungsgehalt von Wand und Dach bereits in eine Reihe von »Punkten im Raum« aufgelöst und war das erste riesige horizontale Spinnennetz aus Verbindungen, das Eintretende zwergenhaft erscheinen ließ. Schon durch die Strenge seines technischen und logischen Bekenntnisses zur Industrialisierung war der *Crystal Palace*, wie Wachsmann betont, ein Kunstwerk, eine visuelle Darstellung der neuen, noch ungesehenen Realität unserer vernetzten Welt.

Der Versuch der Entwicklung einer radikalen Horizontalität hatte bereits mit der *Mobilar Structure* begonnen, die Wachsmann zwischen 1944 und 1945 in New York entwickelt hat (nachdem er das Konzept zuvor nach seiner Freilassung aus einem Internierungslager 1939 in Grenoble skizziert hatte). Es handelte sich einfach um ein riesiges schwebendes horizontales Konstrukt, das aus Hunderten von miteinander verbundenen 2,5 Meter langen Stahlröhren bestand und mit einer Reihe von selbstragenden Faltwänden auf motorisierten Rädern ausgestattet war, die jede Konfiguration annehmen konnten. Alles in der Vertikalen war temporär. Selbst die innerhalb der Grenzen des horizontalen Netzes tief angesetzten vier Schenkel weisen eine eigene netzartige Beschaffenheit auf, so als wären sie nur temporäre Erweiterungen des horizontalen Geflechts, das immer dünner wurde, bevor sie den Boden leicht berührten und durch einige kaum sichtbare Kabel verstärkt wurden. Die Struktur wurde erneut als Hangar für zahlreiche Luftfahrzeuge konfiguriert (»Dutzende oder Hunderte großer Flugzeuge«) und bildete dann die Grundlage der ersten Gespräche mit der USAF im Herbst 1950 und des daraus resultierenden Auftrags im Frühjahr 1951, eine um ein Vielfaches größere Konstruktion zu entwickeln. Sie wurde aber auch für die Verwendung in jeder Art von Gebäude angeboten, wie in der Patentanmeldung von Mitte 1945 vorgebracht wurde.[8]

Ein sehr detailliertes, etwa 2,5 m langes Modell wurde Anfang 1946[9] im *Museum of Modern Art* in New York ausgestellt und zugleich erschienen auf dem Titelbild der Zeitschrift *Progressive Architecture* von Anna Wachsmann erstellte Fotografien davon, auf denen bereits eine winzige zwergenhafte menschliche Figur zu sehen war.[10] Mies van der Rohes Folgeprojekte für fließende Horizontalen mit kaum sichtbaren Stützen (*Museum for a Small City*, 1942; *Convention Center* für Chicago, 1953–54; *Bacardi*-Bürogebäude für Havanna, 1957; und *Nationalgalerie* Berlin, 1968) wurden so sehr

Teil des gängigen Kanons, dass die damalige Radikalität von Wachsmanns Projekt schwer zu begreifen ist – es fand sich nicht einmal eine Glaslinie zur Festlegung der äußeren Grenze. Die beiden Kollegen am IIT waren gut befreundet und verbrachten »unzählige Nächte« bei Speis und Trank miteinander. Studierenden erinnern sich daran, dass die erforderlichen Lehrveranstaltungen bei Wachsmann sogar wöchentlich als mit Gin aufgepeppte Seminare mit Mies in seiner Wohnung gehalten wurden, und die beiden unternahmen ausgedehnte Roadtrips zusammen. Im Jahre 1952 erstellte Wachsmann für *Arts & Architecture* eine 16-seitige Studie zu Mies' jüngstem Schaffen und gemeinsam mit Studierenden arbeiteten die beiden an einer großen tiefliegenden Raumfachwerkstruktur anhand des Struktursystems des USAF-Hangars. Daraus entstand das mit drei Studierenden mit einem ersten Hochschulabschluss angefertigte *Convention Center*.

Die Mies'schen Horizontalen – visuell offene aber hermetisch abgeschirmte verglaste Räume, in denen die Horizontalebene visuell unübersichtlicher war – hatten jedoch nicht die gleiche politische Ambition und vertraten eine neue Monumentalität, eine neue Beständigkeit anstelle von Vergänglichkeit. Schwebende dünne Oberflächen unterhalb der Horizontale waren ein integraler Bestandteil des Mies'schen Konzepts, wie die (erneut mit IIT Studierenden angefertigte und nicht durch Zufall auf einer Fotografie des Innenraums des von Albert Kahn im Jahre 1937 entworfenen riesigen Flugzeugmontagegebäudes überlagert angezeigte) *Concert Hall-Collage* von 1942 beispielhaft verdeutlicht. Typischerweise nehmen diese Abhängungen jedoch eine dauerhaft fixierte Position ein. Wachsmann stellt diese Flächen buchstäblich auf motorisierte Räder und ermöglicht über die Festlegung neuer Innenräume und Außengrenzen oder eine vollständige Entfernung eine Änderung der Konfiguration nach Belieben. Selbst die grundlegende Netzwerkstruktur ist für eine Zerlegung und neue Montage an einem anderen Ort oder in einer anderen Form ausgelegt.

Wachsmann realisierte eine Projektabfolge, deren Ziel in der Herstellung einer neuartigen extremen Horizontale mit optionalen beweglichen Vertikalelementen unterhalb, an der Kante oder außerhalb bestand (wie bei den im Rahmen von Seminaren für Studierende abgehaltenen Workshops in Chicago [1954], Tokio [1955], Salzburg [1956, 1957 und 1958] sowie Lausanne [1959] beispielhaft gezeigt), und die er als solche theoretisiert hat. Seine Tokio-Vorlesungen vom Oktober 1955 beschrieben beispielsweise das kompromisslos horizontale Projekt, in dem »der Mensch das zu unterwerfen versuchen mag, was heute so oft in der Vertikale in den Vordergrund gestellt wird«.[11] Sie prognostizierten, dass Säulen »ganz verschwinden« würden, sodass wir sie schließlich gar nicht wahrnehmen, auch wenn sie da sind, als wenn es »nur Flächen: opak und durchsichtig, keine davon mit einem Bezug zur Struktur gäbe«. Auch diese Flächen würden sich tendenziell »auf null reduzieren« und zu immer dünneren, leichteren, flacheren und glatteren Ebenen werden. Die Materie selbst würde sich in um »Punkte im Raum« verteilte kleinste Teile »auflösen«. In seiner Abfolge von Modellen und Zeichnungen von spitzenartigen horizontalen Netzen, die auf den minimalsten vertikalen Elementen schweben, versucht Wachsmann, diese unvermeidliche und wünschenswerte Auflösung des Bedeutungsgehalts von Masse in kaum greifbare Strahlungsdiagramme zu visualisieren.

Bei einem im März 1947 an der *Princeton University* abgehaltenen Symposium (*Building for Modern Man*) für die weltweit namhaftesten modernen Architekten hatte Wachsmann bereits die Vorstellung von einer durchlässigen, leichten rekonfigurierbaren modularen Struktur, die unzählige Kombinationen beweglicher modularer Flächen unterstützt, mit der Frage der Energie und Elektrizität in Verbindung gebracht.[12] In seinem Vortrag, den er 1948 sowohl an der *University of Southern California, Los Angeles* (UCLA) als auch am *Institute of Design* in Chicago (erste Begegnung mit Mies) gehalten hat, verwies er erneut auf die von der Elektrizität herbeigeführte Transformation des gesamten politischen Lebens von Gemeinschaften und des Staates und fügte zu Kühlschränken und Luftfahrzeugen auch Radios und Fernsehgeräte als Modelle des industrialisierten Bauens hinzu, die die Rückständigkeit der Gebäude hervorheben.[13] Im Laufe der nächsten drei Jahrzehnte entwickelte sich aus dem Aufruf zu einem horizontalen Punktenetzwerk und durch Elektrizität mit Energie versorgte Abhängungen eine Diskussion über Transistoren, Computer, Funk und Fernsehen. In seinem einflussreichsten Buch über Struktur – *Wendepunkt im Bauen* (*The Turning Point of Building*) aus dem Jahr 1959 – erhebt Wachsmann beispielsweise nicht nur die Forderung nach »freiem Raum« ohne sichtbare Stützen, in dem die die Umwelt definierenden Flächen vorübergehend »aufgehängt« sind, sondern thematisiert den Umstand, dass »jedes Signale, Wörter, Töne oder Bilder übertragende technische Gerät« inklusive Fernsehgeräte den Begriff des »universellen Raums« aktiviere, der jede Funktion erfüllen könne, und dass ein solcher Raum von seiner unmittelbaren Umwelt abgeschirmt werden könne, wobei ihn die gleiche Kommunikationseinrichtung jedoch »jederzeit in engste Verbindung mit der Außenwelt« brächte, »ohne dass er im physischen Sinne geöffnet« werde.[14] Die Art und Weise, wie Räume funktionieren und interagieren, werde von elektronischen Signalen vollkommen verändert. Die Struktur sei nicht mehr dieselbe.

Es ging nicht um den Einzug der neuen Medien in die Architektur, sondern mehr um die Notwendigkeit einer Auflockerung der Architektur, um in die bereits existierende Signal- und Elektronikwelt eintreten zu können. Wachsmann beharrte darauf, dass die materielle Welt bereits revolutioniert wurde und dass eine konzeptuelle Revolution folgen musste. Die neuen Energie-Informationsflüsse in Form von Radio, Telefon, Fernsehen, Flugzeugen und Maschinen hätten die Erdoberfläche vollkommen verändert.[15] Seine Worte beschworen keine futuristischen Science-Fiction-Szenarien oder Utopien herauf, sondern beschrieben eine Dringlichkeit der Gegenwart. Nur durch ein Aufholen des Rückstands gegenüber den sich bereits zugetragenen dramatischen Veränderungen konnte sich die Gestaltung für alles noch Bevorstehende positionieren.

In einer 1965 im Rahmen der internationalen Designkonferenz in Aspen gehaltenen Rede argumentierte Wachsmann, dass die von der Elektrizität ausgelöste radikale Transformation nur der Anfang sei, da »unsere Gebäude und unsere Welt« in einem drahtlosen Zeitalter, in dem Energie durch elektrische Wellen übertragen werde, ganz anders aussehen würden. Der Vortrag war im Grunde genommen eine Ankündigung, dass das neu gegründete Bauforschungsinstitut an der UCLA errichtet wurde, um sich den Herausforderungen dieser drahtlosen Übertragung zu stellen.[16] Nicht durch Zufall wurde Wachsmanns symbolträchtigstes Projekt der Umsetzung einer extremen Horizontalen für ein elektronisches Zeitalter, das letztlich nicht realisierte Verwaltungszentrum für California City (*Civic Center*), nur ein paar Monate später am Institut auf den Weg gebracht.

Das Projekt, das vom Team an der USC von Ende 1965 bis 1972 entwickelt wurde, ist mehr Mies als Mies. Es handelt sich lediglich um eine ohne sichtbare Stütze über dem Boden schwebende Horizontalebene. Eine leichtgewichtige 12,7 cm starke aus einem Schaumkern und Glasfaserdeckplatten bestehende Sandwichkonstruktion (ca. 24,38 × 54,86 m) ist auf einer Reihe von achtzig parallelen, ca. 3,18 cm dicken paarweise im horizontalen Abstand von 0,61 m und im vertikalen Abstand von 0,46 m verlegten Stahlkabeln aufgehängt. Die Kabel werden zwischen ca. 58,5 m voneinander entfernte und ca. 21 m tief im Boden verankerte abgewinkelte Strebepfeiler aus Stahl gesteckt und in massiver Spannung gehalten. Die sich daraus ergebende Struktur ist eine Mischform zwischen einer Brücke und einem Zelt. Wachsmann betonte, dass die ca. 4,9 m unter jedem Ende der Horizontalebene herausragenden Kabel nicht sichtbar sein würden, wodurch der Effekt eines fliegenden Teppichs entstünde, unter dem die Stadt im Zuge ihrer weiteren Entwicklung ihre Räume in »im Wesentlichen unbegrenzten Variationen« kontinuierlich reorganisieren könnte. Sogar der dünne Rand des Teppichs würde kaum sichtbar und erst dann erkennbar sein, wenn sich Besucher darunter befänden. Sie könnten jedenfalls direkt unten durchgehen, als würden sie in einem Garten spazieren. Die vollkommene Abwesenheit fixierter Vertikalelemente würde mit politischer Transparenz und Interaktivität assoziiert. Die Hauptkammer der Stadtverwaltung auf der untersten Ebene würde stets von oben belichtet und mehr einem versunkenen Landschaftselement als einem Raum gleichen. Sie könnte bequem betreten werden bzw. wäre über eine 34 m hohe Antenne als wesentlichen Bestandteil der baulichen Gestaltung, von den Wohnungen der Bürger bzw. dem Ort, an dem sich ihr Fernsehgerät befindet, aus leicht zu beobachten. Über ein Lokalprogramm mit geringer Sendeleistung würden sämtliche Aktivitäten der Verwaltung live übertragen werden und das Gebäude selbst wäre eine Art Galerie, in der Aktivitäten, Ausstellungen und Archive fortlaufend angezeigt würden. Die Struktur wäre in erster Linie eine Informationsmaschine.

Es war, als seien der scheinbar unbegrenzte Raum in der Mohave-Wüste, der Traum von einer neuartigen Stadt und Bürgerschaft, und das Industrialisierungsversprechen in einem einzigen Projekt verschmolzen. Die horizontale Ausdehnung der leerstehenden Wüste diente als Modell für freien Raum und die neue Stadt als Modell für eine selbstbewusste Gemeinschaft, die sich kybernetisch durch Rückkopplung anpasste. Wachsmann hatte den Standort der Stadt erstmals im Jahr 1960 mit deren Entwickler Nathan Mendelsohn vom Flugzeug aus besichtigt (der ihn zehn Jahre zuvor nach Kalifornien eingeladen hatte, um ihm zu helfen, die Baracken eines Feldlagers in Privatwohnungen umzuwandeln). Mendelsohn hatte im April jenes Jahres einen Vortrag Wachsmanns an der UCLA besucht und Wachsmann verspürte sofort eine besondere Neigung, sich an diesem Projekt zu beteiligen. Er hielt schriftlich fest, dass »die Vorstellung, dass sich hier eine kaum zu überschätzende Aufgabe stellt, fast von [ihm] Besitz ergriffen habe«.[17] Er regte einen massiven Einsatz an, wobei auf jeder Ebene überdacht werden sollte, was eine Stadt in ihrer Organisation, in ihrem Aufbau und in ihrer Entwicklung sein könne. Im Blick hatte er die Durchführung von regionalen Studien und Verteilungsplänen für den Verkehr, Erholungszonen, Schulen und Krankenhäuser, mitsamt Materialentwicklung, Konstruktionsverfahren, Umweltkontrolle und Wohnungstypologien, vor allem aber den Gedanken an »das neue Bild von einer neuen Stadt, einer Stadt unserer Zeit« im Sinne seines Vortrags.[18] Mendelsohn unterbreitete das Angebot eines »gesamten Gemeindekerns« für die Arbeit daran und Wachsmann erhielt eine monatliche Vorschusszahlung, um das ganze Jahr 1961 hindurch darüber nachzudenken, konnte jedoch scheinbar nichts sagen, während er sich auf die englische Ausgabe seines Hauptwerks *Wendepunkt im Bauen* konzentrierte.[19] Nach jahrelangen Unterbrechungen wurde aus dem Projekt für California City schließlich nur ein einzelnes Gebäude, auch wenn es das kollektive, administrative und repräsentative Zentrum der Stadt werden sollte.

Die Arbeiten am *Civic Center* begannen erst Ende 1965, das

Projekt kam jedoch rasch voran und nach dem bereits erstellten
Konzept des Schweißens eines scheinbar stützenlosen Dachs und
einer Fernsehantenne besuchten Mendelsohn und Vertreter der
Stadtverwaltung Wachsmann im Februar 1966 in seinem Büro an
der UCLA und führten bei einem Abendessen weitere Diskussionen
darüber. Einige Tage später beauftragte ihn der Bürgermeister offi-
ziell mit der Gestaltung des Gebäudes und brachte die einstimmige
Unterstützung von Wachsmanns Vorstellungen seitens der Verwaltung zum Ausdruck.[20] Die erste öffentliche Bekanntmachung erfolgte umgehend in der Märzausgabe der Zeitung *California City
Sun* unter Hervorhebung der zweifachen Innovation einer schwebenden Horizontalebene und der vertikalen Fernsehantenne. Die
Hochspannungskabel »wären« vermeintlich »mit bloßem Auge nicht
erkennbar, was den Effekt eines riesigen Schwebedaches erzeugt«,
das über einem versunkenen Garten aufgehängt ist, und »ein Fernsehturm für Anwendungen mit geschlossenem Fernsehkreis würde
über dem Dach in den Himmel emporragen [...]. Womit diese Berichterstattung weltweit erstmals für eine Bürgerschaft verfügbar
sein würde [...]. Wir würden über unsere Fernsehbildschirme daran
teilnehmen. [...] California City und die Berichterstattung der Stadtverwaltung würden vom einen Ende der Welt zum anderen Bekannt-
heit erlangen.«[21] Eine kaum sichtbare Struktur sollte die größte
Sichtbarkeit aufweisen. Im gleichen Monat teilte Wachsmann dem
Bürgermeister mit, dass er mit Ingenieuren die technischen Probleme des Fernsehens bespreche und hoffe, Ende April über ein
Modell und Skizzen zu verfügen.

Die letzte vor dem Hintergrund der umliegenden Landschaft
dargestellte Fotografie des Modells samt der Antenne wurde zum
Standardbild des Projekts. Verwendet wurde sie beispielswiese in
California City – a Success Story, einer 95-seitigen Broschüre, mit
der Menschen dafür gewonnen werden sollten, der Stadt beizu-
treten. Darin wurde Wachsmanns Projekt als »ultimativer Raum«
beschrieben, der als »Gral« der zeitgenössischen Architektur er-
träumt wurde.

»Der Zweck bestand in der Schaffung eines vollkommen offenen
Raumes, der innerhalb oder an der Außengrenze des Gebäudes von
keinerlei Säule oder Stütze unterbrochen oder durchdrungen wird;
gleichsam in der Schaffung eines ›ultimativen‹ Raumes. Unter der
schwebenden, zeltähnlichen Decke können mit dem Wachstum der
Stadt einhergehend bei Bedarf Räume geschaffen werden.«[22]

Im Rahmen einer ausführlichen Publikation des Projekts in
einem in der Zeitschrift *Arts & Architecture* vom Mai 1967 erschienenen Überblick über Wachsmanns Arbeiten wurden die gleiche Fotografie und der gleiche Text verwendet. Bezeichnenderweise bildet eine Fotografie der Hochspannungskabelstruktur des
Civic Center, die Wachsmanns Faszination für horizontale Netze

einfängt, den Umschlag der Zeitschrift.[23] Andere Fotografien in der Ausgabe zeigten den Raum inklusive oder exklusive der internen Elemente zur Hervorhebung der enormen Offenheit des Konzepts. Verstärkt wurde diese durch das Reflexionsbecken unter dem Dach, den Umstand, dass die vorübergehende Innenteilung das Dach nicht berührte und die Informationsanzeigetafeln für die Öffentlichkeit den Boden nicht berührten. Auf den Modellfotografien sind die Fernsehantenne und deren Stützdrähte zu sehen, und viele der unveröffentlichten Fotografien lenken den Blick durch die abstrakte, mit Beton ausgekleidete Senke in der Landschaft mit der ebenso abstrakten, phantomartig darüberliegenden weißen Horizontalebene und die Drähte der Antenne, auf deren Mastspitze sogar eine sehr detaillierte Übertragungsausrüstung vorgesehen war, einfach hindurch (wobei die Ausrüstung letztendlich jedoch vom Standardbild ausgeschnitten wurde, um die Oberseite des Hintergrundbildes von der umliegenden Landschaft zu verbergen).

Die exakt gezeichnete Antenne und deren Stützkabel in der Zeichnung des Hauptabschnitts bildeten die einzige Konstante in einem sonst undefinierten offenen System. Tatsächlich war die Offenheit der Horizontalen von der Antenne abhängig. Wie er sich später erinnerte, interessierten Wachsmann und Mies auf ihrem ausgedehnten zwanzigtätigen Roadtrip nach Kalifornien, den sie während ihrer Arbeit an der Entwicklung schwebender Raumfachwerke am Institut in Chicago unternahmen, letzten Endes nicht die Gebäude, sondern »jene Tausende von Fernsehantennen auf den Hausdächern«[24].

Wachsmann betrachtete das vom Fernsehen gebotene offensichtliche Fehlen von Grenzen als Antwort auf den ursprünglichen Auftrag, für »die fortschrittlichste und zukunftsweisendste Struktur unserer Zeit [...] ein auf das zwanzigste Jahrhundert weisendes Gebäude« für eine »skaliert perspektivisch nahezu unbegrenzte« Stadt zu entwickeln. Dies ging aus seinem Schreiben an den Bürgermeister am Vortag der öffentlichen Abstimmung im November 1967 über die Frage der Fortsetzung des Projekts hervor. Darin beschrieb Wachsmann die Struktur als Symbol alles Zukünftigen und dessen Gravitationszentrum:

»In der weiten offenen Umwelt sehe ich eine im Raum schwebende Schutzfläche, unter der sich die Menschen versammeln können ... einen unbegrenzten Raum ... einen Raum, der so offen ist wie die riesige Landschaft, so offen wie der gesamte Plan für die zukünftige Stadt, so offen wie die zukünftige Tragweite dieser Gemeinschaft.«[25]

Das Fernsehen war ein zentrales architektonisches Element für die Erweiterung dieser symbolischen und praktischen Offenheit. Weiter in dem Schreiben insistiert Wachsmann, dass »das Fernsehen inklusive des Sendemastes, der auch Fernsehkamera, Emp-

fangsantennen und Verstärkereinrichtungen aufnehmen soll, ein
integraler Bestandteil des Gestaltungskonzeptes für dieses Gebäude ist.« Ein demokratischer Glaube an gleiche Rechte für alle er-
fordere »ein Regierungssystem, dessen Feedbackfunktion nicht nur
innerhalb eines Gebäudes in einer vorgegebenen Form erfolgt, sondern jede Wohnung der gesamten Stadt einbezieht und beeinflusst«.
Diese »Lebensader der Kommunikation« ermögliche die Teilnahme
aller Bürger an »der zukünftigen Entwicklung der eigenen Umwelt«.
Laut Wachsmann ist politische Aktion per Definition Umweltak-
tion. Umgekehrt ist die Gestaltung der Umwelt per Definition
politisch. Dies verlange kontinuierliche »Informationsausstellun-
gen« im Gebäude. Telefonaufzeichnungen und Bänder sollten wie
»Sofortinformationsquellen« für den Austausch und die Entscheidungsfindung zwischen der Stadtverwaltung und den Bürgern behandelt werden. Das Gebäude selbst sei primär ein Informations-
system.

Wachsmann konnte an der öffentlichen Sitzung vor der Abstimmung nicht teilnehmen (wobei das Gebäude selbst dem demo-
kratischen Feedback unterlag, das es zu erleichtern beabsichtigte).
Doch ganz im Sinne des Projekts übermittelte er aber eine aufge-
zeichnete Mediennachricht, die besagte, dass es sich um ein Gebäude für das 21. Jahrhundert handle, in dem Kabel »eine Wirkung
des totalen Raums« erzeugen.[26] In den Zeitungen wurde der inte-
grierte Fernsehturm erneut in den Vordergrund gerückt[27] und einige
Tage später wurde der erfolgreiche Ausgang der Abstimmung bekannt gegeben. Allerdings wurde das gesamte Gebäude mit unzähligen Konstruktionsprüfungen an Vorführmodellen dann mehr als
viermal neu gestaltet. Ein endgültiger Zeichnungssatz wurde erst
im Dezember 1970 fertiggestellt und das Projekt wurde erneut zu
einer öffentlichen Abstimmung vorgelegt – dieses Mal zur Geneh-
migung der Ausgaben – und Wachsmann leitete eine Reihe weiterer
öffentlicher Sitzungen mit dem Modell. Diese führten zu einer posi-
tiven inoffiziellen Abstimmung im April 1971 und dann zur formel-
len Schlussabstimmung für die Fortführung im Mai.[28]

Der endgültige Zeichnungssatz vom Dezember 1971 (in dem die
gesamte architektonische, strukturelle und mechanische Ausstat-
tung und sämtliche Einbauten detailliert ausgeführt wurden) ge-
langte ohne Aufnahme der Antenne zur Ausschreibung, wobei
»FUTURE TV ANTENNA« am Stromlageplan gekennzeichnet wurde.[29]
In der Bekanntmachung (erschienen in der Ausgabe vom Dezember 1974 der Zeitschrift *Architectural Record*), dass die Freigabe für
den Baubeginn bevorstand und die Fertigstellung für Januar 1974
geplant war, wurde die übliche Modellfotografie herangezogen.
Dabei wurde die Antenne allerdings aus dem Bild retuschiert.[30]
Das ans Ende der Architektur und an den Anfang der Fernsehpo-
litik gesetzte Antigebäude blieb schließlich ganz auf der Stelle.

Wachsmann engagierte sich jedoch mehr denn je für die Fernseharchitektur. Tatsächlich hatte das Fernsehen die Macht übernommen.

Im Jahr 1973 sprach Wachsmann erneut von einer unmittelbar bevorstehenden drahtlosen Zukunft (Elektrizitätsübertragung durch Wellen; Einziehen von Drähten in die Wand nicht mehr notwendig, Transistorisierung und der letztendliche Ersatz der Gestaltungsteams durch Computer), während er jedoch erneut jegliche Unterscheidung zwischen physischen Strukturen und »eng mit sozialen Problemen verknüpften« politisch-ökonomischen Strukturen zurückwies.[31] Der »in das Korsett der Architektur eingezwängten« traditionellen Bauindustrie mitsamt deren Entwürfen müsse durch das gleichzeitige Einschalten der Regierung und der gesamten Gesellschaft Widerstand entgegengebracht werden: »Dies kann beispielsweise über den Fernsehbildschirm, ein nicht zu unterschätzendes Kommunikationsmedium, erfolgen.«[32] Im gleichen Jahr hoffte Wachsmann noch auf die Umsetzung seines Projekts von 1971 für ein neuartiges interdisziplinäres Zentrum, »ein« auf jede Dimension der Entscheidungsfindung und Produktion im Zeitalter der Industrialisierung ausgerichteter »vollkommen neuer Organismus«, der wie all seine Gebäude somit auf »die von elektrischer Energie geformte Multiplikation der Inkremente der Elemententeile«, ausgerichtet war, wie es im Katalog einer im Jahre 1971 gezeigten Retrospektive seines 30-jährigen Schaffens in den USA in der Einführung des Konzepts ausgedrückt wurde.[33] In seiner unveröffentlichten Autobiografie, die er in seinen letzten Lebensjahren verfasste, thematisierte er abschließend den Umstand, dass sein Modell für »die Notwendigkeit zeitgleicher Informationen an die und umgekehrt Rückmeldungen aus der Öffentlichkeit mittels des besten zur Verfügung stehenden Kommunikationsmediums« in diesem Konzept für das, was die gegenwärtige Universität letztendlich ersetzen werde – die Auflösung der Grenzen zwischen den Disziplinen und zwischen dem Zentrum und der Öffentlichkeit – das Fernsehen sei: »Das Fernsehen hat mich von Anfang an fasziniert; nicht so sehr als Unterhaltungsformat, sondern mehr als eine Möglichkeit der Aufklärung.«[34] Letztendlich wurde Wachsmann bewusst, dass das neue Zentrum nie zustandekommen würde. Schließlich fasste er jedoch ein Konzept für eine aus 13 Sendungen bestehende Fernsehserie ab. Anschließend erklärte er sich dazu bereit, ein Buch als Grundlage für eine Fernsehserie zu erstellen, die ausgestrahlt werden und dann in Form von Fernsehkassetten erhältlich sein sollte.

Im Epilog des Manuskripts der Autobiografie kehrt Wachsmann bezeichnenderweise zu dem für ihn seit den 1940er Jahren zentralen Argument zurück, dass »die Einführung elektrischer Energie unvorstellbare Konsequenzen nach sich zog«. Diese habe zu Transistoren, Computern, Kern- und Solarenergie geführt, die ihre eigenen, unvorhergesehenen Auswirkungen hätten und eine »völlige Umstrukturierung« der politischen, sozialen, ökonomischen, wissenschaftlichen, technischen und künstlerischen Ideen im 21. Jahrhundert erforderten. Dieser Abschluss griff eine frühere Stelle des Manuskripts, in dem er das 1929 entstandene Sommerhaus für Albert und Elsa Einstein beschreibt, auf, an der Wachsmann darauf verwies, die transformative Wirkung der elektrischen Energie auf Werkstofftechniken und somit auf die Gesellschaft erkannt zu haben. (Er entwarf für dieses Haus sämtliche Bauteile für die Vorfertigung in einer Fabrik, die dann vor Ort zusammengebaut wurden.) Im Gegensatz zu Einstein war der 28-jährige Gestalter überzeugt davon, dass dies die traditionelle Auffassung von Architektur irrelevant mache. Er wusste jedoch noch nicht, wodurch sie ersetzt werden würde.

Letztendlich war Wachsmann sich nie sicher. Zunehmend vom Fernsehen inspiriert, konzentrierten sich die nachfolgenden horizontalen schwebenden Netze schlichtweg auf die Auflösung der Architektur, wie wir sie kennen; ihre Zerlegung in immer kleinere Teile und letztendlich in Strahlungsdiagramme von Funksignalen. In einem bemerkenswerten im Zeichen der Anti-Architektur stehenden Lebensprojekt, das zu radikal war, um als solches anerkannt zu werden, wurden aus Gebäuden Übertragungen.

1   Dieser Aufsatz wurde dem demnächst erscheinenden Buch von Mark Wrigley: *Konrad Wachsmann's Tele-vision: Post-Architectural Transmissions*, Berlin (Sternberger Press) 2019, entnommen.

2   Konrad Wachsmann: *Manifest for the Evolution of Assembling the Artificial Human Environment between Time and Space*. Von 1974 datiertes unveröffentlichtes Manuskript, endgültige maschinenschriftliche Fassung. Akademie der Künste, Berlin [kurz: AdK], Konrad-Wachsmann-Archiv, Wachsmann 2323, S. 1.

3   Mark Wigley: *Network Fever*, in: Grey Room 04/2001, S. 82–122.

4   Wachsmann 1974 (zit. Anm. 2), S. 68.

5   Mark Wigley: *Buckminster Fuller Inc. Architecture in the Age of Radio*. Zurich (Lars Müller Publishers) 2016.

6   »Whereas design and planning are of secondary importance within the context of such work, aesthetics, philosophy and ethics play a vital and autonomous part.« Konrad Wachsmann: Einführung zu *Studium im Team*, in: Bauen + Wohnen 10/1960, S. 352 f.

7   Die Pressemitteilung zur Gestaltung des USAF-Hangars wurde vom

Illinois Institute of Technology im September 1954 veröffentlicht. In einem choreographierten Werbeblitz wurde das Projekt im gleichen Monat mit umfangreichen Modellfotografien in den Septemberausgaben von *L'Architecture d'Aujourd'hui, Baukunst und Werkform* und *Architectural Forum* sowie in der Oktoberausgabe von *Werk* präsentiert.

8   US-Patent 2,491,882 (eingereicht am 22. Juni 1945, patentiert am 20. Dezember 1949).

9   »Museum of Modern Art Shows Revolutionary New Type of

Steel Construction«, MoMA-Presse-mitteilung für die Ausstellung vom 5. Februar bis zum 6. März 1946.

10   *Mobilar Structure*, in: Progressive Architecture, März 1946, S. 87–99.

11   Konrad Wachsmann: *Building in Our Time. Toward Industrialization of Structure, The Training-Research Process and Contemporary Concepts.* Manuskript datiert 1955. AdK, Konrad-Wachsmann-Archiv, Wachsmann 460, S. 43.

12   In seinem nach Walter Gropius ge-haltenen Vortrag definierte Wachsmann die Grenzen und Mög-lichkeiten der Gestaltung in Bezug auf Energie, wobei die ma-schinell gesteuerte Elektrizität die neue Form von Energie ist, die die Gestaltung neu definiert, die Massenproduktion und Standardi-sierung fördert und neue Arten von Verbindungen herstellt, die immer leichtere Strukturen stützen, in denen die Vertikalflächen nur eine visuelle und akustische Rolle spielen und »unzählige Kombina-tionen von Flächenelementen die uns umgebende Welt schaffen«. Konrad Wachsmann: *Machine Energy: The Technique of Our Time*, in: Thomas H. Creighton (Hg.): *Building for Modern Man. A Symposium*, Princeton (Princeton University Press) 1949, S. 46–48.

13   Konrad Wachsmann: *The Means for Design*. Text einer im Rahmen des Society and Design Semi-nars am Illinois Institute of Techno-logy im Frühjahr 1948 gehaltenen Rede. In: *Serge Chermayeff Papers*, Avery Drawings and Archives, Avery Library, Columbia University.

14   Konrad Wachsmann: *Wendepunkt im Bauen*, Wiesbaden (Krausskopf-Verlag) 1959. Übersetzt von Thomas E. Burton unter dem 1961 erschienenen Titel *The Turning Point of Building. Structure and Design*. New York (Reinhold), S. 110.

15   »Through its advancing dynamic force and technology, electricity more than anything else is changing the direction of world progress. Mass communication and informa-tion, such as the radio, telephone, and television, airplanes, engines and all things run by electricity, have completely changed the appearance of the surface of the earth. New communication methods and new education have created a new base.« Konrad Wachsmann: *A High Level in Function is Indeed Beauty: Hiroshima Should be Made a Functional City*, 29. Oktober 1955, AdK, Konrad-Wachsmann-Archiv, Wachsmann 2271, S. 1.

16   Konrad Wachsmann: *To Build is Everything or Nothing is Built*. Manuskript der im Rahmen der 15. Internationalen Designkonferenz in Aspen gehaltenen Rede. AdK, Konrad-Wachsmann-Archiv, Wachsmann 1777.

17   Konrad Wachsmann: Vom 25. April 1960 datierter Brief an Nathan Mendelsohn. AdK, Konrad-Wachs-mann-Archiv, Wachsmann 0513.

18   Konrad Wachsmann: Vom 27. Juni 1960 datierter Brief an Nathan Mendelsohn. AdK, Konrad-Wachs-mann-Archiv, Wachsmann 0613.

19   Nathan Mendelsohn: Undatierter etwa auf Oktober 1960 zurückgehender Brief an Konrad Wachsmann. AdK, Konrad-Wachs-mann-Archiv, Wachsmann 0613.

20   Vom 28. Februar 1966 datierter Brief des Bürgermeisters Jim Riley an Konrad Wachsmann. AdK, Konrad-Wachsmann-Archiv, Wachsmann 1871.

21   *Eighth Wonder Here! Civic Center to Have »Floating Roof«*, California City Sun, März 1966, AdK, Konrad-Wachsmann-Archiv, Wachsmann 1890.

22   *California City – a Success Story*. Undatierte Werbebroschüre. AdK, Konrad-Wachsmann-Archiv, Wachsmann 1890.

23   *A New American City Hall*, in: Arts & Architecture, Mai 1967, S. 23–26.

24   Konrad Wachsmann: *Timebridge, Konrad Wachsmann: An Autobio-graphy* (1981). Unveröffentlichte Autobiografie. AdK, Konrad-Wachsmann-Archiv, Wachsmann 2065, S. 245.

25   Konrad Wachsmann: Vom 1. Novem-ber 1967 datierter Brief an Bürger-meister Jim Riley. AdK, Konrad-Wachsmann-Archiv, Wachsmann 1871.

26   »Even though I am unable to be with you in person, modern science and technology has made it possible for me to talk to you anyway…«. Konrad Wachsmann: Transkription einer aufgezeichneten Stellung-nahme für die öffentliche Sitzung vom November 1967. AdK, Konrad-Wachsmann-Archiv, Wachsmann 1871.

27   *Noted Architect Named to Design Civic Center*, in: The Bakersfield Californian, 23. November 1967, Wachsmann 1887.

28   Vor der Abstimmung zählte Wachs-mann die Gründe für den Bau eines Gebäudes auf, das tatsächlich einem »wide open space … undisturbed by any load-bearing wall or column … which in turn would be located in a wide open space« entsprechen würde und lieferte eine Chronologie aller unterschiedlichen Prüfungen und des für die Umsetzung benötig-ten Expertenwissens. Konrad Wachs-mann: Statement to City Council of California City. Datiert vom 15. März 1971. AdK, Konrad-Wachsmann-Archiv, Wachsmann 1872.

29   *California City Civic Center*. Im Dezember 1971 überarbeiteter endgültiger Zeichensatz. AdK, Konrad-Wachsmann-Archiv, Wachsmann 362.

30   *California City Civic Center*, in: Architectural Record, Dezember 1972, S. 41.

31   »Structures are not only physical phenomena but also ordering systems and resulting geometries. They are political and finance political systems which are tightly connected with social problems and capital invest-ment, amortization, wages, etc.« Konrad Wachsmann: *The Future between Space and Time*. Englisch- und deutschsprachiges Manuskript einer Vorlesung im Rahmen des Seminars über Industrialisierung des Bauens an der Technischen Univer-sität Hannover vom 12. Oktober 1973. Wachsmann 2065, S. 8.

32   Ebd., S. 9

33   Konrad Wachsmann: *Toward Industrialization of Building*. Katalogtext zu einer Ausstellung am Department of Architecture der University of Southern California und der Graham Foundation for Advanced Studies in the Fine Arts. Los Angeles: USC, 1971, S. 1.

34   Wachsmann 1981 (zit. Anm. 24), S. 468.

Für Konrad Wachsmann bestand das Wesen der seriellen Fertigung im Prozessualen. Es verwundert nicht, dass seine um 1953 entstandenen Perspektivzeichnungen der sogenannten Weinrebenkonstruktion (Grapevine) als Notation bezeichnet werden können – nämlich als Aufzeichnung eines Formbildungsprozesses.[1] Dieses Vorhaben von Wachsmann zeugt von der Suche nach einem einzigen universalen, industriell herstellbaren Verbindungselement.[2] Gedacht als Grundbaustein einer sich dynamisierenden Struktur sollte deren modularer Charakter die Errichtung eines gleichsam schwerelosen Gebäudes ermöglichen. Gegenwärtig fasziniert daran besonders, dass die Natur zum Modell wird, in diesem Fall die Weinrebe. Wachsmann redet von »dreiarmigen wünschelrutenähnlich gedrehten Standardelementen«[3]. Im Zusammenhang mit seinem wohl bekanntesten Projekt – dem Entwurf eines Flugzeughangars aus Stahlkonstruktionen (1951) – ist mit Blick auf eine dynamische Raumsyntax von »spinnenwebartiger Struktur« die Rede, wie eine handschriftliche Notiz verrät.[4] Wachsmann bedient sich in den Zeichnungen zoomartig herangerückter Ausschnitte einer sich überlagernden Modulstruktur. Das Teil – jedes Teil – steht für das Ganze. Dieses Prinzip wird im Folgenden als »kinematografische Notation« beschrieben. Es begegnet uns nicht nur in Konstruktionszeichnungen, sondern vor allem in der Abfolge von Architekturfotografie: in vielen seiner für Publikationen und Ausstellungen verwendeten Fotografien und in den von ihm selbst aufgenommenen. Pablo Picasso soll in einem Treffen mit Wachsmann geäußert haben: »Sie reden so, als wären sie selbst ein Fotograf!«[5] Walter Gropius, der Wachsmann in den 1930er Jahren in der Nähe von Split beim Fotografieren beobachtete (die beiden kannten sich zu diesem Zeitpunkt persönlich noch nicht), sah den Architekten im Fotografen – »because of the way you photograph«[6]. Für den Architekten, der sich etwas kokett eher als Hobbyfotograf gerierte, fungierten Fotografie und Film als ideales »Medium der Registrierung«[7]. Wachsmann gab – ein bisher in der Literatur kaum beachteter Aspekt seines Wirkens – mehrere Fotobücher heraus.[8] Umso beachtlicher ist es, dass dieses sequenzielle Prinzip in der 2010 in München gezeigten Retrospektive seines Werkes in München ein Echo fand – als Ausstellungsdispositiv.[9] Um den Kern seines Denkens – das Prozessuale – sichtbar zu machen, entschied man sich filmische Montagen auf Bildschirmen jedem ausgestellten Architekturmodell zuzuordnen. Man könne nur sehen, wie er gebaut und zusammengesetzt hat, wenn man bis zu dreißig Fotografien hintereinanderlege, heißt es in einem Werbefilm zur Ausstellung. Für diese kinematografische Montage wurden Zeichnungen und Fotografien aus seinem Werkprozess in gleicher Weise verwendet.[10] Das erscheint angesichts aktueller Überlegungen zur Bildlichkeit von Architektur von zentraler Bedeutung.[11]

Kinematografische Notation bei Konrad Wachsmann

Angela Lammert; Abb.: 43–48

Mitte der 1930er Jahre erschienen von Wachsmann drei Foto-
grafiebücher zu den Städten Prag, Salzburg und Berlin.[12] In seinen
späteren Schriften, Ausstellungen und Publikationen wird er immer wieder auf Grunderfahrungen dieser Zeit zurückgreifen: auf
die Vergleichbarkeit der Rippengewölbe des Hradschins in Prag
oder der gotischen Doppelwendeltreppe des Schlosses in Graz[13] mit
dynamischen Verbindungsstrukturen einer zukünftigen Architektur. 1961 erscheint ein weiteres Fotobuch. Dessen Titel – *Aspekte*[→47,48] – bezieht sich genau auf diese Erfahrungen. Dieses Fotobuch
beginnt mit einem herangezoomten Ausschnitt eines gepflasterten
Treppenaufgangs. Das Gebäude selbst ist weitgehend abgeschnitten
und nur im Sockelbereich aufgenommen. Die Textur der Linien-
führung des diagonal ins Bild gesetzten Geländers setzt sich in den
vertikalen Streben des angeschnittenen Rumpfs des Baukörpers
fort: ein abstraktes Spiel schwereloser linearer Ordnungssysteme.
Auf der folgenden Doppelseite erahnt man den Boden, auf dem die
durch vertikale Schatten strukturierten Bauten stehen – als isolier-
te Körper sind sie in ihren jeweiligen bis zum Bildrand im Ausschnitt
wiedergegebenen Formen nicht erkennbar. Diese serielle Fotografie-
abfolge mündet in zwei Dach- bzw. Turmkonstruktionen. Also eine
nur in der Bewegung sukzessiv wahrnehmbare visuelle Argumentation. Wachsmann schreibt auf diese Fotografieserie folgend: »Trans-
formierungen oder die Überwindung des Begriffs des Endlichen der
Wand erscheinen als immer existierende Herausforderung zum Zer-
legen, Gliedern, Auflösen.«[14] An anderer Stelle wird die schräg auf-
genommene Untersicht der Oberkirche des Kapitols in Rom mit
Blick auf ein rundes, mit Maßwerk strukturiertes Fenster mit einer
Fotografie kombiniert, bei der dasselbe Maßwerk formatfüllend
und frontal ins Bild gesetzt wird. Die filmische Aufeinanderfolge
von unterschiedlichen Aufnahmen eines Baukörpers verweist ebenso wie die Häufung fotografischer Ausschnitte auf die Komplexität
des Ganzen. Umgekehrt findet sich im Ganzen das Detail – ein
Prinzip, das in seiner späteren Suche nach dem Universalelement
wiederkehrt.

Wachsmann insistiert dabei auf subjektive Aufzeichnung – die
Notation jenseits des Indexikalischen. Die Kamera wird zum abstra-
hierenden, klärenden Übertragungsmittel. Eine gotische Kathedrale,
eine Struktur, ein Bauwerk, ein Platz oder eine ganze Landschaft
der Vergangenheit wünscht man nur unter den Aspekten zu sehen,
die in der Gegenwart angenehm sind, und nicht als das, was sie
wirklich bedeuteten. Wachsmann ging es mit der Fotografie darum
ein Mittel zu finden, um bestimmte Strukturen oder Details in diesem Sinne zu registrieren und den Gedanken, der die Dinge formte,
sichtbar zu machen und zu notieren. In seinen Worten: »Bedient
man sich der Fotografie, so wird auch hier das Ergebnis nicht eine
objektive Dokumentation sein, sondern die subjektive Transformie-

rung in eine beabsichtige Bildsprache. Selbst der unbeseelte Registriermechanismus einer Kamera wird einen Gegenstand nicht so wiedergeben, wie er ist, sondern nur so, wie ihn der, der sie bedient, zu sehen fähig ist oder zu sehen wünscht. [...] Ob dieses Medium der Registrierung auch in Zukunft gesteigerten Ansprüchen noch genügen wird, ist zweifelhaft, da der Film bessere Möglichkeiten anbietet. Durch ihn kann das Objekt in seiner räumlichen Beziehung umschritten oder in seiner eigenen Bewegung gezeigt werden.«[15] Er geht hier sogar soweit, sich dabei perspektivisch eine Einbeziehung des Tons vorzustellen. Um die Maschine als Werkzeug der neuen Zeit, als neue Annäherung an den Begriff des Originals zu charakterisieren, greift er ebenfalls auf das fotografische Negativ- und Positiv-Verfahren zurück.[16] In einem bisher unveröffentlichten Manuskript aus dem Nachlass findet sich ein Hinweis darauf, dass Wachsmann selbst einen ca. zehnminütigen Film drehen wollte.[17] Dieser Film hat sich im Zuge der Recherche zu diesem Text aufgefunden und bestätigt als solches die hier vorgetragene Argumentation.[18]

Das kinematografische Denken seiner Fotobücher findet sich auch als visuelle Strategie in seiner 1959 erschienenen wohl bekanntesten Publikation, dem *Wendepunkt im Bauen*. Seine Fotografien fungieren auch dort als »Momente, Details, Torsen, Reflexionen impulsiver Bewegungen oder Gedanken zur Verdeutlichung dynamischer Vorgänge«. Wachsmann war sich des Zusammenspiels in der Abfolge der Fotografien bewusst.

Der in der *Akademie der Künste* in Berlin befindliche Nachlass beinhaltet darüber hinaus mehrere nicht publizierte Fotografien. Sie haben mich schon während der Vorbereitung zur Ausstellung *Notation. Form und Kalkül in den Künsten*[19] (2007) begeistert. Mit Blick auf die neueren Forschungen zur Bildlichkeit von Architektur und mit Wachsmanns Fotografiebüchern zusammen gelesen erscheint es mir notwendig, sie in einem neuen Blickwinkel zu betrachten. Drei Aspekte seien darum skizziert.

Zoom

In den Fotografien von modularen Konstruktionen beeinträchtigen Bildausschnitte, Nahaufnahmen und Unschärfen die funktionale Lesbarkeit. Ihre filmische Wirkung des zunehmenden Heranrückens und Vergrößerns eines Fragments der modularen Stahlkonstruktion ist so radikal, dass sie sicherlich nicht zufällig zu den unveröffentlichten Fotografien zählen. Gerade aus diesem Grunde sind sie eine schöne Entdeckung. In ihrer sequenziellen Abfolge eines Wahrnehmungsprozesses von Architektur sind sie das Gegenteil von der in der Architekturfotografie weit verbreiteten ikonischen Einzelaufnahme.

Unterschiedliche Aufnahmen desselben Modells finden sich auch in seiner Publikation *Wendepunkt im Bauen*. Das sukzessive Wahrnehmen durch die Bewegung des Betrachters ist weniger offensichtlich. Ausschnitt und Zoom wiederholen sich jedoch an mehreren Stellen. So sind auf einer Doppelseite der frontal aufgenommenen fotografischen Aufnahme eines Architekturmodells zwei Detailaufnahmen des modularen Systems gegenübergestellt: zum einen eine Großaufnahme zur Visualisierung des Kräfteverlaufs am Auflagepunkt einer Stütze und zum anderen der Zoom einer Aufsicht auf die Dachkonstruktion zur Darstellung der Haupt- und Nebenbinder.[20] Beide Aufnahmen sind von seiner Frau Anna Wachsmann aufgenommen worden und können als intimer Ausdruck eines gemeinsamen gedanklichen Kosmos gelten. Diese Abfolge erfährt durch die Platzierung einer einzigen Fotografie auf einer Doppelseite eine Steigerung. Das Spiel und die schichtweise Überlagerung von Schatten, Licht und Struktur erscheint im Zoom des Kameraausschnittes eine Eigendynamik zu entwickeln. Bezeichnenderweise ist sie mit dem Titel *Blick in die Landschaft einer räumlichen Struktur* versehen. Sie stammt von Harry Callahan, mit dem Wachsmann zusammen in Chicago arbeitete und der wie Anna Wachsmann mit seinem Credo vertraut war.[21] Die sequenzielle Abfolge von Fotografien, die in der am Rand abfallenden Großaufnahme des Ausschnitts einer räumlicher Struktur mündet, entspricht dem filmischen Zoom.

Dynamische Struktur

Wachsmann setzt sein Konzept dynamischer Struktur neben der sequenziellen Abfolge von Fotografien auch mit der Anordnung mehrerer gleichartiger Module auf einem Bildformat für seine Publikationen um. Dafür überlässt er oftmals professionellen Objektfotografen die Aufnahmen von Verbindungselementen als Modul dynamischer Strukturen. Die Fotografien von Aaron Siskind (*IIT Institut of Design*, Chicago) fallen hier besonders ins Auge. Die ineinandergestapelten Elemente der Gliederkette eines Knotenpunktes[22] erinnern an die Ästhetik vergrößerter Pflanzenfragmente von Karl Blossfeldt aus den 1920er Jahren. Die Eigenästhetik dieser Fotografien gewinnt vom funktionalen Standpunkt aus dysfunktionale Züge, wie die Aufnahme von fünf Präzisions-Standardelementen im *Wendepunkt im Bauen* zeigt, deren fragmentarischer Ausschnitt aus der Struktur der Konstruktionssysteme nur drei davon in rhythmischer Wiederholung wiedergibt.[23]

Das Konzept dynamischer Strukturen führt gegenwärtig zur Praxis digitaler Animation im Entwurfsprozess und zur Rekonstruktion. Eine kürzlich von Christina Sumi vorgenommene »Bildwerdung von Architektur« der Grapevine-Struktur mit filmischen Mitteln scheint besonders dafür geeignet zu sein, die Darstellung des Zeichenhaften der Architektur mit der Animation körperlicher Wahrnehmung zu überlappen.[24] Es wird eine sich situativ entwickelnde Räumlichkeit suggeriert und simuliert. Filmische und virtuelle Architekturen haben veränderte Wahrnehmungsformen von

Bildlichkeit zur Folge und produzieren und strukturieren sie zugleich. Eine solche Herangehensweise hat nicht nur Potential zum Forschungsinstrument zu werden, sondern macht bisweilen die etablierte Trennung zwischen Bauentwurf und Bauausführung hinfällig.[25]

Team

Konrad Wachsmanns Forderung, dass die notwendige industrielle Fertigung nur in Teamarbeit zu entwickeln ist, zeigt sich auch in bisher unveröffentlichten Fotografien aus dem Nachlass der *Akademie der Künste.* Anders als in seinem Konzept, dass kleine Arbeitsgruppen parallel an verschiedenen Teilaufgaben arbeiten, ist in diesen Fotografien die gemeinsame Aktion eines Teams von Architekten zu sehen, das eine Dreieckskonstruktion aus Stangen trägt. Nicht der Prozess des Bauens, sondern das Potential einer schnellen Montage wird inszeniert. Geradezu utopisch mutet die Fotografie der Dreieckskonstruktion ohne die Akteure an: der Baukasten, den es leicht zu bedienen gilt. Überraschend ist dabei, dass auch hier mit Aufsicht und Frontalansicht operiert wird. Architekturfotografie ist hier nicht allein die Inszenierung des Gebauten oder des Modells, sondern die Notation von Prozess und dynamischer Struktur.

Für seine im *Wendepunkt im Bauen* eingesetzten Fotografien taucht bisweilen als Autor ein gesamtes Institut auf – so das IIT *Institute of Design* in Chicago. Nur der schon angeführte Harry Callahan, der als Professor in Chicago wirkte, und Aaron Siskind sind namentlich genannt. Dasselbe trifft auf seine Frau Anna Wachsmann zu. Insofern verwundert es nicht, dass das fotografische Konvolut in der *Akademie der Künste* ebenfalls weitgehend mit anonymer Autorschaft inventarisiert wurde. Das entspricht seinem Konzept von Teamarbeit – das er, wenn man ironisch anmerken darf – nur zu seinen Gunsten und im Zusammenhang mit seinen Fotografiebüchern aufhebt. Dies allerdings mit der Geste des Hobbyfotografen. Es würde sich jedoch lohnen, die Herkunft einzelner Fotografien und deren Funktion im Zusammenhang mit seinem architektonischen Konzept genauer unter die Lupe zunehmen. Eines scheint jedoch schon bei einer ersten Skizzierung dieses methodischen Zugriffs auszumachen zu sein: Notation im architektonischen Denken von Konrad Wachsmann kann fotografische bzw. kinematografische Registrierung des Formfindungsprozesses bedeuten.

Dies schließt an die derzeitige Diskussion zur Bildlichkeit von Architektur an, die um drei Schlüsselbegriffe kreist: semiotischer Bildbegriff, die Architektur als auf das Körperliche zielende Immersionskunst und die Bildwerdung von Architektur. Es geht dabei nicht allein um die Wirkkraft von Bildern oder um eine phänomenologische Herangehensweise. So haben Andreas Beyer, Matteo Burioni und Johannes Grave in ihrer 2011 erschienenen Publikation

Das Auge der Architektur die zeichenhafte Funktion von Architektur als eine Konzeption von Bildlichkeit beschrieben, die an die mediale Vermittlung durch Fotografien und Filme und einen semiotischen Bildbegriff gebunden und insofern zu kritisieren ist.[26] Georges Didi-Hubermans Polemik gegen die ikonografische kunsthistorische Methode, die er in seiner 1999 publizierten Schrift *Was wir sehen, blickt uns an*[27] entwickelt, wird dabei von den Autoren angesichts einer postmodernen Baupraxis auf die Architektur übertragen. Eine weitere hier nicht weiter auszuführende und weniger ausdrückliche Variante dieses Konzeptes liegt in der Analyse begrenzter flächiger Bauphänomene wie etwa dem Erscheinen von gerahmten Flächen. Ein semiotisches, auf die Flächigkeit bezogenes Konzept von Architektur – oftmals gebunden an eine ikonische Architekturfotografie – blendet die räumlichen und immersiven Eigenschaften von Architektur als Raumkunst bzw. als Produktion von Atmosphären aus. Sie vernachlässigt auch darum deren durch das Medium erzeugten Status. Die Opposition von Zwei- und Dreidimensionalität ist daher nur die andere Seite der Medaille.

Vor diesem Hintergrund verspricht der Fokus auf die kinematografische Notation bei Konrad Wachsmann für den Diskurs über die Bildlichkeit von Architektur ein bisher weniger beachtetes Potential zu bergen. Es gilt nicht nur, Wahrnehmungsprozesse von Bildern und damit von der Architektur als Bild in den Blick zu nehmen, sondern auch den Eigenwert visueller Denkformen, die von Architekten produzierten oder eingesetzten Bilder und damit die Grenzverwischung zwischen Entwurf und Werk zu befragen. Walter Benjamin sprach vom »Grenzfall« Architekturzeichnung.[28] »Eben der Grenzfall aber ist es, in dessen Durchforschung die Sachgehalte ihre Schlüsselpositionen am entschiedensten geltend machen.«[29]

1   Angela Lammert: *Bildung und Bildlichkeit von Notation. Von der frühen Wissenschaftsfotografie zu den Künsten des 20. Jahrhunderts*, München (Verlag Silke Schreiber) 2016, o. S.

2   Marianne Burkhalter, Christian Sumi (Hg.): *Konrad Wachsmann and the Grapevine Structure*, Zürich (Park Books) 2018, o. S.

3   Konrad Wachsmann in: *Auf dem Weg zur Industrialisierung des Bauens*, Katalog einer Ausstellung im »Octagon« der American Institute of Architects Foundation, Washington, D.C. März 1972 (Deutsche Ausgabe Juni 1972), o. S.

4   Konrad Wachsmann: *Hangar-Flugzeughallenkonstruktion*, in: Akademie der Künste, Berlin [kurz: AdK], Konrad-Wachsmann-Archiv, Wachsmann 410, S. 5.

5   Michael Grüning: *Der Wachsmann-Report. Auskünfte eines Architekten*, Berlin (Verlag der Nation) 1985, S. 322. Der Leiter der Villa Massimo in Rom, Herbert Gericke, stellte Wachsmann zur Dokumentation seiner »unkonventionellen Betrachtung« von Architektur seine Leica-Kleinbildkamera zur Verfügung. Wachsmann experimentierte im Labor mit Fotogrammen, die er als Kompositionselement in Architekturfotografien montierte. In: Ebd., S. 264–267. Er nutzte ein langes Teleobjektiv und einen speziellen Bildsucher. In: Konrad Wachsmann: *Timebridge, Konrad Wachsmann: An Autobiography* (1981). Unveröffentlichte Autobiografie. AdK, Konrad-Wachsmann-Archiv, Wachsmann 2128, S. 86.

6   Ebd., S. 87.

7   Konrad Wachsmann: *Aspekte*, Wiesbaden (Krausskopf-Verlag) 1961, o. S.

8   Ausnahme ist das zweite Kapitel der Publikation von Otto Maier: *Die räumliche Syntax. Konrad Wachsmanns Beitrag zum Bauen in unserer Zeit*, Dissertation, Universität Karlsruhe 1989. Allerdings liegt dabei der Schwerpunkt auf Wachsmanns Zeitverständnis und nicht auf seinen Fotografien.

9   Winfried Nerdinger in Zusammenarbeit mit Rainer Barthel, Richard Junge, Roland Krippner und Frank Petzold (Hg.): *Wendepunkt/e im Bauen. Von der seriellen zur digitalen Architektur*, München (Detail, Institut für internationale Architektur-Dokumentation) 2010, o. S.

10   Winfried Nerdinger 2010 in: https://www.youtube.com/watch?v=3rxEKZFL8zQ (Stand: 20.5.2018).

11   Andreas Beyer, Matteo Burioni, Johannes Grave: *Einleitung. Zum Erscheinen von Architektur als Bild*, in: Dies. (Hg.): *Das Auge der Architektur*, München 2011, S. 12. – Angela Lammert: *Bildlichkeit von Architektur als Prozess*, in: Ulrike Kuch (Hg.): *Das Diaphane. Architektur und ihre Bildlichkeit* (Reihe: ArchitekturDenken, hg. von Jörg Gleiter), Bielefeld (transcript) 2019, o. S.

12   Konrad Wachsmann: *Salzburg – Die Altstadt, Berlin – Unter den Linden, Prag*, Berlin (Grieben Verlag) 1934. Siehe: Otto Maier: *Die räumliche Syntax. Konrad Wachsmanns Beitrag zum Bauen in unserer Zeit*, Dissertation, Universität Karlsruhe 1989. Diese Reiseführer entstanden über die Vermittlung von Victor Goldsmith und waren für den damals arbeitslosen Wachsmann eine gute Einnahmequelle. In: Wachsmann 1981 (zit. Anm. 5), S. 82.

13   Konrad Wachsmann: *Wendepunkt im Bauen*, Dresden (Verlag der Kunst) 1989, S. 28 u. 195.

14   Wachsmann 1961 (zit. Anm. 7), S. 5. Es gibt diesem Prinzip entsprechend keinen Foto- oder Bildnachweis und damit keine Zuordnung der Architekturfotografien von Wachsmann.

15   Ebd., o. S.

16   Konrad Wachsmann: *Vom Bauen in unserer Zeit* (Vortrag Hochschule für Gestaltung Ulm, Dezember 1956), in: AdK, Konrad-Wachsmann-Archiv, Wachsmann 466, S. 3.

17   Konrad Wachsmann: *Die Zukunft aus Situationen zwischen Räumen und Zeiten* (Vortrag TU Hannover, 12.10.1973), in: AdK, Konrad-Wachsmann-Archiv, Wachsmann 2065, S. 16.

18   GTA Zürich, Fritz Haller Archiv.

19   Hubertus von Amelunxen, Dieter Appelt und Peter Weibel (Hg.) in Zusammenarbeit mit Angela Lammert: *Notation. Form und Kalkül in den Künsten der Nachkriegszeit*, Akademie der Künste, Berlin 2007, o. S.

20   Wachsmann 1989 (zit. Anm. 13), S. 162 f.

21   Andere von Callahan verwendeten Fotografien sind an den Seiten beschnitten, betonen mit Unschärfen das Schwebende der Konstruktion oder rücken an den rechten unteren Bildrand. In: Ebd., S. 186.

22   Ebd., S. 174.

23   Ebd., S. 177.

24   In: http://www.griffinenrightarchitects.com/projects/connection-points/ (Stand: 4.4.2018). Bei Computerspielen wird bekanntermaßen vom Effekt der Immersion gesprochen.

25   Bálint András Varga: *Gespräche mit Iannis Xenakis*, Zürich/Mainz (Atlantis Musikbuch-Verlag) 1995, S. 29.

26   Beyer, Burioni, Grave 2011 (zit. Anm. 11).

27   Georges Didi-Huberman: *Was wir sehen, blickt uns an*, München (Verlag Wilhelm Fink) 2005, o. S.

28   Benjamin bezeichnet in seiner ersten Fassung des Textes »Strenge Kunstwissenschaft« 1931 mit Blick auf Carl Linferts Publikation *Die Grundlagen der Architekturzeichnung* die Architekturzeichnung als einen »Grenzfall«.

29   Zitiert bei: Walter Benjamin: *Kritiken und Rezensionen. Gesammelte Schriften Band III*, Frankfurt a. M. (Suhrkamp Verlag) 1991, S. 367 f. Carl Linferts Publikation erschien 1931.

Der von mir hoch verehrte Justin Vernon (Bon Iver) sagte 2016 in einer Pressekonferenz, die besten Geschichten seien eben doch die, die versuchen allfällige Zweifel so weit als möglich aufzulösen (»suspend your disbeliefs as much as possible«)[1]. Das ist nun, wenig überraschend, auch das erklärte Ziel nicht nur dieses Textes, sondern des gesamten Buchs *Stressing Wachsmann*. Denn es gab und gibt ganz offenbar etliche, vorsichtig formuliert »Unsicherheiten« in Bezug auf Person, Werk und Wirkung Konrad Wachsmanns. Andernfalls wäre die Architekturgeschichte der letzten Jahrzehnte reicher an substanziellen Auseinandersetzungen mit diesem »Pionier der Architektur des 20. Jahrhunderts«, wie ihn Friedrich Achleitner nannte; nicht ohne gleich im Sinne Wachsmanns nachzusetzen und zu schreiben, er selbst hätte sich wohl lieber als »Pionier des Bauens« verstanden gewusst.[2] Es ist also eine weitere selektive Spurensuche, es kann gar nicht anders sein! Und so versuche ich an dieser Stelle, Wachsmann mit seinem dauerhaften Optimismus in vorhandene und kommende Industrien, seinem Faible für geometrische Strukturen im Allgemeinen und Wendepunkte im Speziellen aus der deutschsprachigen, mithin materialistischen Tradition heraus zu verstehen. Zumal, und hier lasse ich William Faulkner dem sonst so zukunftsfrohen Konrad Wachsmann[3] (vgl. dazu seinen Vortrag von 1956 ab Seite 61) gern widersprechen: »The past is never dead. It's not even past.«[4]

Wachsmanns zentrale Theorie und Interessensgeschichte war 1959 unter dem Titel *Wendepunkt im Bauen* veröffentlicht worden. Ein schönes Buch, das in seiner Erstauflage nach wie vor preiswert zu bekommen ist. Aber warum ein oder gar *der* »Wendepunkt«? Gibt es tatsächlich derart eindeutige, gemeint sind hier verbindliche Wendepunkte in der Geschichte? In der mathematischen Kurvendiskussion, ja: Da bezeichnet ein Wendepunkt eben genau den Punkt, an dem ein Funktionsgraph seine Richtung oder genauer gesagt sein Krümmungsverhalten ändert. Solche Wendepunkte wären, sofern übertragen auf Kulturgeschichtliches, meist an gewisse Daten, Personen, an erfolgreiche oder gescheiterte Vorhaben und Ereignisse gebunden. Aber sind es nicht selbst dann eher Überlagerungen, Steigerungen und Versetzungen als wirkliche Wendepunkte? War Paxtons *Kristallpalast* wirklich eine derart eindeutige und spürbare Zäsur, war es die *Bessemer-Birne*, und wenn ja, wann und für wen? In Peter Collins' *Changing Ideals in Modern Architecture* finden wir dazu den passenden Satz: »From 1750 onwards, architects were motivated by a number of notions which had previously played little or no part in the formation of their ideals, and these new notions did not simply succeed one another as an evolutionary sequence; they were to recur continually, in various combinations and with various expressions, during the whole of the following two centuries.«[5] Ganz ähnlich Manuel De Landa: »But the resulting

Über Wende-punkte

Florian Medicus; Abb.: 49–60

emergent structures simply add themselves to the mix of previously existing ones, interacting with them, but never leaving them behind as a prior stage of development (although, perhaps, creating the conditions for their disappearance.«[6] Ein historischer Wendepunkt ist also immer ein theoretisches Konstrukt, wie auch die kritische Reduktion der Geschichte auf nur einen linearen Graphen. Wobei das natürlich gut und griffig klingt: »Ein Wendepunkt«! Wachsmanns langjähriger Freund Klaus Mann (vierzehn namentliche Erwähnungen in Grünings *Der Wachsmann-Report*, zusätzlich die Abbildung von dessen Grab in Cannes[7]) hat den zweiten Teil seiner Autobiografie 1942 *The Turning Point* genannt, das allerdings vor dem Hintergrund seiner freiwilligen Meldung zur *US Army*.

Das bereits erwähnte Buch *Wendepunkt im Bauen* von 1959 schließt Konrad Wachsmann so: »Aber die objektive Frage, die über alle Handlungen letzten Endes dominiert, was man unter dem Begriff Baukunst verstehen wird, muss offenbleiben. Erst wenn der Mensch fähig ist, die Umwelt als die Seinige, die ihm Eigene zu erkennen und sich mit ihr völlig zu identifizieren, wird die Frage in ihrer ganzen Komplexität klar erkennbar sein. Die Antwort darauf wird sich von selbst ergeben.«[8] Er scheint sich in diesem Ausblick trotz aller Anstrengung und gebotener Zuversicht selbst nicht ganz sicher zu sein – weder im »Wendepunkt im Bauen« noch im Begriff der kommenden »Baukunst« – nicht »Architektur« wohlgemerkt! Dieser etwas eigentümliche Versuch einer formalen Abgrenzung erinnert auch stark an den wunderbaren, weil bezeichnenden Druckfehler in Sigfried Giedions (auch ein langjähriger Freund, 12 Erwähnungen bei Grüning) Buch *Bauen in Frankreich – Bauen in Eisen – Bauen in Eisenbeton* (1928). Hier hätte nach der fetten Überschrift »ARCHITEKTUR« eigentlich ein bedeutendes, ebenso fettes Fragezeichen stehen sollen.«[49] Zwischen den beiden Büchern liegen dreißig Jahre Weltgeschehen und trotzdem soll die entscheidende Frage nach der vollständigen Implementierung zeitgenössischer (industrieller) Strukturformen in das klassische Verständnis von Baukunst weiter »offen bleiben«, so wie Giedions Frage schon zuvor, »ob der beschränkte Begriff ›Architektur‹ überhaupt bestehen bleiben wird«[9]. Genau das hatte 1914 Antonio Sant'Elia (mit Marinettis Hilfe) auch schon überlegt: »Die Berechnung der Materialfestigkeit, die Verwendung von Eisenbeton und Eisen machen eine ›Architektur‹ im klassischen und herkömmlichen Sinn unmöglich. [...] Wir haben in der Tat den Sinn für das Monumentale, das Wuchtige und Statische verloren und unser Empfinden durch den Geschmack am Leichten, am Vergänglichen und Raschen bereichert.«[10] Dass sich das in den Manifesten oft und radikal Geforderte nicht unmittelbar materialisieren im Sinne von direkt umsetzen ließ (wobei Sant'Elias und auch Mario Chiattones Zeichnungen sonst bestimmt zum Allerfeinsten gehören!), dass es oft nicht schneller ging, ist sowieso für die gesamte Kulturgeschichte bedauerlich. Doch lustig liest sich heute Paul Scheerbarts *Glasarchitektur* von 1914; oder spannend auch El Lissitzky, der beschrieb zu seinen *Wolkenbügeln*[50] mit großer Selbstverständlichkeit Baumaterialien, die es so noch gar nicht gab: »Leichte und gut wärme- und schalldämmende Materialien sind für Decken und Trennwände vorgesehen. Desgleichen chemisch bearbeitetes Glas, das Lichtstrahlen hindurchlässt und Wärmestrahlen abschirmt.«[11]. Sehr gute Ideen, anno 1925! Wachsmanns Sprache aber ist nicht die der jungen Avantgarden – er war beim *Wendepunkt im Bauen* auch schon in seinen späten Fünfzigern – er will auf etwas anderes hinaus. Insofern ist das ganze Buch trotz aller Bestimmtheit abgeklärt und generell vorsichtiger, was meiner Meinung nach seinen Grund auch in der etwas überhitzten Geschichte um Stein und Eisen in Deutschland seit 1820 hat. Deshalb:

Stein und Eisen

Konrad Wachsmann hatte nach seiner Lehre als Bau- und Möbelschreiner zuerst bei Tessenow in Dresden und dann 1924–26 an der Kunstakademie Berlin studiert und bezeichnete sich später dabei als »Meisterschüler von Hans Poelzig«[12]. Und dieser Hans Poelzig hat 1931, also nur drei Jahre nach Giedions Frankreich-Buch in seinem Aufsatz »Der Architekt« unter anderem Folgendes geschrieben: »Worum handelt es sich bei der Architektur? Wohl um Form, und zwar um symbolische Form. Sind die technischen Formen symbolisch, können sie es jemals sein? [...] Der Ingenieur geht unbeirrt seinen Weg, aber seine Schöpfungen bleiben Natur, – sie werden nicht symbolhaft, sie werden nicht Stil. [...] Die technischen Formen [...] sind und bleiben errechnet, unsymbolisch, und selbst wenn eiserne Träger vergoldet werden, verlieren sie die Starrheit ihrer mathematischen Entstehung nicht.«[13] Das klingt nun etwas eigenartig, da wir doch, etwa mit Julius Posener[14] sehr von der Idee ausgehen wollen, dass es sich in der Architektur seit jeher um das Raumschaffen ganz im Sinne von symbolischen Formen handelt. Und genau das wird Wachsmann in gebotener Zuversicht schreiben: »Aus den Mitteln der Zeit wird sich nicht nur eine neue Ästhetik und eigene Sprache bisher unbekannter Schönheitsbegriffe entwickeln, sondern darüber hinaus eine neue Ethik der Kunstanschauung überhaupt als Symbol einer neuen Epoche.«[15] Beide aber, Poelzig wie Wachsmann, und etliche vor ihnen beziehen sich hier, bewusst oder unbewusst, auf einen deutschen Diskurs, der sich seit dem frühen 19. Jahrhundert mit eigenartiger Hartnäckigkeit aufrecht hielt.

Lesen wir, was Arthur Schopenhauer 1820 in Berlin, zeitgleich mit Hegel, zu unterrichten versuchte, nämlich u. a. in seiner *Metaphysik des Schönen*: »Diesem zweiten Zweck der schönen Baukunst, das Licht seinem Wesen nach zu offenbaren, kann der in unseren Tagen und hier in Berlin zuerst gemachte Versuch architektonischer Werke in Eisen, kein Genüge thun: weil die schwarze Farbe des

Eisens die Wirkung des Lichts aufhebt, das Licht verschluckt. [...]
Dem ersten ästhetischen Zweck der Baukunst, Schwere, Starrheit,
Kohäsion zur Anschaulichkeit zu bringen, entsprechen eiserne Gebäude sehr wohl: denn sie haben jene Eigenschaften in noch höhe-
rem Grade: aber eben weil in ihnen die Proportion beider Kräfte
zu einander eine verschiedene ist als beim Stein und weil die Tena-
cität des Eisens hinzukommt, so sind die Proportionen welche für
steinerne Gebäude und ihre Theile als die besten befunden worden,
nicht auf das Eisen sofort anwendbar: daher müßte man für die
schöne Baukunst aus Eisen andre Säulenordnungen und andre Regeln überhaupt erfinden. An dem Monument läßt sich das nicht
erläutern weil es leider Gothisch ist und die Gothische Baukunst
meiner ästhetischen Theorie nicht entspricht. (Suo loco.)«[16] Es
müssten also für Konstruktionen in Eisen »andre Regeln überhaupt
[erfunden]« werden, was ebenso nachvollziehbar wie machbar
scheint, aber nicht hundert Jahre hätte dauern dürfen; zumal gerade
diese Unentschlossenheit vor allem in Deutschland zu einer denk-
bar unproduktiven Pattsituation führte.

Nur ein paar Jahre nach Schopenhauers gescheitertem Lehrver-
such war Karl Friedrich Schinkel begeistert von Thomas Telfords
Menai-Strait-Hängebrücke und zeichnete vor Ort »die Situation,
um die Colossalität des Gegenstandes festzuhalten«[17/→51]. Schinkel
verwendete dann auch sehr unaufgeregt und elegant schlanke, guss-
eiserne Bauteile im Palais des Prinzen Albrecht (1829). Überhaupt
Schinkel – Wachsmann nannte dessen Verehrung den gemeinsamen Nenner zwischen ihm und Mies van der Rohe: »Obwohl Mies
dann auch von Berlage und Wright beeinflusst wurde, konnte er
sich aus dem Schwerkraftfeld Schinkels nie richtig befreien«[18] –
erkrankt aber und stirbt viel zu früh und so fiel es fünf Jahre nach
seinem Tod dem sonst etwas glück- und folgenlosen Architektur-
philosophen Carl Gottlieb Wilhelm Bötticher zu, in seiner wort-
reichen Festrede *Schinkel zu Ehren* die Zukunft der deutschen Baukunst in der Eisenarchitektur festzumachen: »In jeder Bauweise
handelt es sich daher zuerst um die Entwicklung einer statischen
Kraft aus der baulichen Materie, welche als wirkendes Prinzip in
das System der Deckung eingeführt wird. Drei statische Kräfte sind
es nur, welche baulich genutzt werden können und, wie es die technische Sprache bezeichnet, als absolute, relative und rückwirken-
de Festigkeit oder als Resistenz gegen Zerreißen, Zerbrechen und
Zerdrücken in der Materie eingeschlossen liegen.«[19] Bötticher beschreibt hier die drei statischen Beanspruchungen von Druck (Balken und Stütze bei den Hellenen), Schub (in Bögen und Gewölben,
besonders der Gotik) und Zug, dem allerdings noch zu wenig Beachtung geschenkt wurde, denn: »so kann man sagen: dass es in der
Tat das Eisen sei, welches auch die letzte bis dahin als Prinzip noch
ungenutzte der drei statischen Kräfte in die Baukunst einführe.«[20]

Arthur Schopenhauer wurde zeit seines Lebens kaum gehört und gelesen; ebenso dürfen wir annehmen, dass Boettichers bemühte Rede anno 1846 keinen tatsächlichen Skandal oder gar einen Wendepunkt provozierte. Es macht somit auf nationaler Ebene eben doch einen spürbaren Unterschied, ob der große Proponent der schönen und mithin modernen Baukunst pro oder contra Eisenkonstruktionen war: in Frankreich Eugène Emmanuel Viollet-le-Duc (von 1814 bis 1879), in Deutschland Gottfried Semper (von 1803 ebenfalls bis 1879); es sind auch diese beiden, die H. P. Berlage 1904 als die beiden großen Theoretiker des 19. Jahrhunderts und Vertreter einer »praktischen Ästhetik« gegenüberstellte. Berlage wendete sich dabei von Semper (und damit Schopenhauer) ab und dem »Gotiker« Viollet-le-Duc zu, »[...] denn er war einsichtig darin, dass die mittelalterliche Kunst prinzipiell für die moderne Zeit die richtige Grundlage angeben konnte; sie steht nämlich nicht nur auf rein konstruktiven Boden, sondern sie bildet gewissermaßen den Faden zwischen alt und neu, und wir müssen diesen Faden an der richtigen Stelle wieder aufnehmen.«[21]

Nahezu zeitgleich mit Viollet-le-Duc in Paris war Gottfried Semper fast dreißig Jahre nach Schopenhauer noch dessen Einschätzung gefolgt, denn: »so viel steht fest, dass das Eisen, und überhaupt jedes harte und zähe Metall, als konstruktiver Stoff seiner Natur entsprechend in schwachen Stäben und zum Teil in Drähten angewendet, sich wegen seiner geringen Oberfläche [...] dem Auge umso mehr entzieht, je vollkommener die Konstruktion ist, und dass daher die Baukunst, welche ihre Wirkungen auf das Gemüt durch das Organ des Gesichtes bewerkstelligt, mit diesem gleichsam unsichtbaren Stoffe sich nicht einlassen darf, wenn es sich um Massenwirkungen und nicht bloß um leichtes Beiwerk handelt.«[22]

Semper wird seine Meinung auch zwei Jahre später nicht ändern, als er im Herbst 1851 in Paxtons *Crystal Palace* steht, in dem er die seiner Theorie gegenläufige Tendenz zur Entmaterialisierung durch dieses »glasbedeckte Vakuum, das zu allem passt, was man hineinbringen will«[23]. ärgerlich bestätigt sieht, wie er in einem langen Aufsatz an den »deutschen Leser« schreibt. Gottfried Semper sieht darin aber keine faktische Zäsur, wie das Konrad Wachsmann etwa hundert Jahre später erwiesen sah: »Der Kristallpalast kann in der Tat als der nun sichtbar gewordene Wendepunkt angesehen werden, durch den die gesamte Entwicklung der Baugeschichte in eine andere Richtung einschlug. [...] Aus Vernunft und Logik, den Gedanken des technischen Zeitalters intuitiv erfassend, entstand eine neue Schönheit, wie sie nie vorher erkannt, gewertet und empfunden wurde. Der Kristallpalast war ein Kunstwerk.«[→52]

Der deutsche Diskurs sollte sich selbst über die Erfahrungen der großen Weltausstellungen, besonders natürlich 1889 in Paris, wo »die Galerie des Machines zeigte, wie ein neuer Werkstoff (Stahl) und ein neues Nachdenken über Statik neue Formen hervorgebracht haben«[24] (Jörg Schlaich), nicht zur Anerkennung oder gar normativen Eingliederung der Ingenieur-Ästhetik in die schöne Baukunst entschließen können. »Die Schönheit der Bausysteme«, hatte der Architekt des Frankfurter Opernhauses, Richard Lucae noch 1870 gesagt, »hat ihren Grund gerade im Überschuss an Masse über das zum Tragen notwendige Material«[25]. Und so sollte es auch bitte bleiben!

Anders Frankreich

Und obwohl sich etliche gute Köpfe zwischenzeitlich redlich um die Etablierung eines durch die »Ingenieur-Ästhetik« (s. etwa Joseph August Lux, 1910) erweiterten Begriffs der Baukunst bemühten, war das selbst Ende der 1920er Jahre noch die große Unsicherheit, gegen die Sigfried Giedion anschrieb. Die Französisierung, die offene Parteinahme für Le Corbusier, Garnier und Perret, wurde seinem Buch naturgemäß übelgenommen, wobei es eben jener Le Corbusier überhaupt war, der Giedion »auf die Quellen der heutigen Architektur lenkte: auf die Eisenarchitektur des 19. Jahrhunderts, auf die großen Weltausstellungen, wo sie am sichtbarsten auftrat«[26]. Und trotz – oder gerade wegen? – der Grabenkämpfe um die Stellung der klassischen *École des Beaux-Arts* und der immer mächtigeren Ingenieurschulen kann in der französischen Geschichte doch eine gewisse Kontinuität in der Sache festgestellt werden, die sich über den konstruktiven Rationalismus (die Boullée-Schüler J.-B. Rondelet und J.-N.-L. Durand), über Labrouste und Viollet-le-Duc, über Eiffel und Contamin (mit C. L. F. Dutert) hin zu Auguste Choisy, Tony Garnier, den Brüdern Perret (die sich, obwohl von der École kommend »constructeurs« und nicht »architectes« nannten) und natürlich Le Corbusier spannt. Sein Befund ist klar: »Auch die Ingenieure betreiben Architektur, denn sie üben die aus den Naturgesetzen abgeleitete Berechnung, und ihre Werke lassen uns Harmonie empfinden.«[27]

Frankreich war in Theorie und Praxis tendenziell offen für Neues. England dagegen scheint trotz der frühen Eisenbauten und Paxton weit vorsichtiger, auch heterogener (*Arts-and-Crafts*-Bewegung), und Deutschland leider nur in seiner Unentschlossenheit bedeutsam. Insofern war Giedions Frankreich-Buch zwar etwas einseitig im Fokus auf die industrielle Verwendung von Eisen und Beton, wichtig aber wegen seiner historisch-kohärenten Zusammenfassung und letztlich des optimistischen Ausblicks, dass »auch unsere Zeit ein neues Baumaterial finden wird, das ihren Forderungen homogen ist«[28]. Giedion meint damit allerdings weder Eisen noch Beton, das waren die bekannten, hinlänglich erprobten Stoffe des 19. und beginnenden 20. Jahrhunderts. In dem Maß, in dem Giedion hier etwas gänzlich Neues in den noch unbekannten Raum stellt, sieht er die erste Phase der modernen Baukunst, als die klassische Architektur sich noch von zeitgenössischer Konstruktion trennen ließ, als erfüllt und damit erledigt an.[29] Von dieser Basis aus sollte nunmehr etwas gänzlich Neues unternommen werden.

Wachsmann als Wendepunkt

Es sollte jedoch weitere dreißig Jahre dauern, bis sich diese Einschätzung, nämlich die eines historischen Abschlusses der ersten Moderne, greifbar und umfassend etablieren würde. Durch Sputnik 1 (1957) und später durch Yves Kleins *Sprung in die Leere* lösten sich die bekannten Raumgrenzen ebenso auf wie 1959 die *Congrès Internationaux d'Architecture Moderne*. Zeitgleich erschien eine große Zahl an sehr relevanten Büchern zum Thema: 1957 Eduardo Torrojas *Razón y ser de los tipos estructurales* (1961 auf Deutsch erschienen als *Logik der Form*) und Bruno Zevis *Architecture as Space* endlich in englischer Übersetzung; 1958 dann Henry-Russell Hitchcocks großer Überblick *Architecture: Nineteenth and Twentieth Centuries* und Jürgen Joedickes *Moderne Baukunst* (Curt Siegel gewidmet!). 1959 Konrad Wachsmanns *Wendepunkt im Bauen*. 1960 Leonardo Benevolos *Storia dell'architettura moderna*; Curt Siegels *Strukturformen der modernen Architektur*; Conrads' und Sperlichs *Phantastische Architektur*; Reyner Banhams *Theory and Design in the First Machine Age* (mit dem großen Aufsatz *Funktionalismus und Technologie*) und das Manifest des Metabolismus anlässlich der *World Design Conference* in Japan.

Konrad Wachsmann erfüllt bei all dem unfreiwillig eine Doppelrolle. Er ist sowohl Protagonist als auch unvollständig-historisches Objekt des versuchten Abschlusses einer Epoche. So wird Wachsmann etwa bei Benevolo nur in Zusammenhang mit Gropius und der *General Panel Corporation* und dabei als »reiner Forscher«[30] erwähnt, gleiches gilt übrigens – und sonderbar genug – für die 1964 erfolgte Überarbeitung von Giedions *Raum, Zeit, Architektur*; Hitchcock und Banham erwähnen Wachsmann gar nicht. Joedicke bleibt höflich neutral, druckt aber zumindest zwei Bilder vom USAF-Hangar. Ähnlich unleidenschaftlich Conrads und Sperlich. Curt Siegel bleibt immerhin skeptisch: »Inwieweit die Verwirklichung so kühner Projekte (USAF-Hangar, Anm.) in mobiler Bauart möglich ist, steht dahin.«[31/→53, 54]

Die Art und Weise, wie Konrad Wachsmann in diesen Jahren übergangen wurde (auch später noch!, etwa in Banhams *Megastructure* oder Dahindens *Stadtstrukturen für morgen*) hat etwas Seltsames. Ich nehme an, dass man ihn und sein zentrales Anliegen noch nicht zur Gänze wahrgenommen und verstanden hatte. Denn Wachsmann selbst bot sich als Wendepunkt an und sah dabei das neue Bauen losgelöst vom tatsächlichen (Bau-)Projekt als weit gefassten Begriff der Kommunikation. Er schrieb: »Vielleicht ist es nur der Gedanke, die Idee, in der sich diese Zeit vollkommen auszudrücken vermag, während das Werk selbst Akt des vorübergehenden

Zustandes ist und darum seine Bedeutung nicht in seiner Perma-
nenz haben kann. [...] Es sind andere Ziele, durch die sich die Kultur
der kommenden Epoche ausdrücken wird, mit anderen Mitteln zu
erreichen, die die Zivilisation mit ihren eigenen Kräften anstreben
muss.«[32] Das neue Baumaterial, von dem Giedion schrieb, zeigt sich
bei Wachsmann als größtmögliche Steigerung des Industriellen und
Mobilen: Kommunikation und Inspiration, als Vermittlung von Idee
und Ideal, die spielerische Entwicklung zeitgemäßer, interdisziplinärer und zukunftstauglicher Modelle, die jedoch nicht notwendigerweise in ein (an)greifbares Projekt oder einen klassischen Bau
führen.[→55, 56] Eine scheinbar rigide Struktur sich wiederholender,
verdichteter Wendepunkte führt in seinen Seminaren zur totalen
Auflösung des Bekannten und als prägendes Ereignis, nach Žižek,
zum »Auftreten von etwas Neuem, das jegliches stabile Schema
unterläuft« und »damit eine Veränderung des Rahmens bewirkt,
durch den wir die Welt wahrnehmen und uns in ihr bewegen«[33/→57].

Als Veränderer oder besser Erweiterer des Rahmens war Konrad Wachsmann erfolgreich wie sonst kaum jemand in diesen Jahren. Seine gut dokumentierten Seminare, seine Teamarbeiten, ob in
Chicago, Karlsruhe, Tokio oder Salzburg, zeigten unmittelbare Folgen in der Entwicklung visionärer Systeme und (Mega-)Strukturen.
Es ist demnach auch nicht weiter verwunderlich, dass Wachsmann
so den jungen Metabolisten geistig ebenso Pate stand wie Cedric
Price oder Archigram. Die Einladung nach Japan erfolgte 1955
durch Kenzo Tange; bei dem Seminar selbst trafen sich Noboru
Kawazoe, Kenji Ekuan, der aktuelle Pritzker-Preisträger Arata
Isozaki, Mamoru Kawaguchi, Hiroshi Sasaki, Kazuhide Takahama;[34]
»the ideas from this key meeting of East and West arguably filtered
down into Metabolism five years later«[35], schreibt Hans Ulrich
Obrist. Peter Cook hat später gesagt: »Konrad Wachsmann was
even more important to us than Bucky (Fuller).«[36] Ich vermute auch
über Anne Tyng einen gewissen Einfluss auf Louis Kahn, und dass
es ohne Wachsmann Kenzo Tanges *Big Roof*[→59] zumindest in dieser
Form nie gegeben hätte. Fritz Hallers (freier Mitarbeiter an
Wachsmanns Bauforschungsinstitut an der *University of Southern
California*) zeitlos elegante Bausysteme seien ebenso erwähnt wie
zeitgenössische Spuren etwa bei Coop Himmelb(l)aus wunderbar-
wahnwitziger *BMW-Welt* in München.[→60]

Wachsmanns Ideen und Idealbilder sprechen beharrlich von der
Überwindung gedanklicher und räumlicher Grenzen in Neufassun-
gen der Begrifflichkeiten Wechsel, Überspannung und Auskragung
durch zeitgemäße (Bau-)Methoden. Für die industriell-ästhetische
Erweiterung des Architekturbegriffs (ohne dabei je »Architektur«
zu sagen!) ist Konrad Wachsmann in dieser Hinsicht also ebenso zu
danken wie das Vorstellen einer gänzlich neuen, vollkommen egali-
tären interdisziplinären Teamarbeit. Es wäre demnach nur angemes-

sen, würde man die Wirkung und damit Bedeutung Wachsmanns
von den materiellen Nachweisen lösen und eher an der Vielzahl an
Neuordnungen messen, die ihn und seine Methodik unmittelbar re-
ferenzieren. Natürlich ist bei all dem auch Vorsicht und Kritik geboten, es ging ja auch vieles nicht wie gedacht und manches sogar
ziemlich daneben. Wobei in der größeren Zusammenschau doch der
Eindruck überwiegt, dass die Figur Konrad Wachsmann sich wunderbar sowohl als markanter End- als auch als Anfangspunkt eignet,
und damit alles vereint, was einem tatsächlichen historischen Wendepunkt zumindest nahekommt. Wachsmann war der Endpunkt in
der langen deutschen Geschichte von Stein und Eisen und gleich-
falls Beginn eines neugeborenen internationalen Optimismus. »Alle
sind Architekten. Alles ist Architektur.«[37] wird der Seminar-Teil-
nehmer Hans Hollein 1967 schreiben; wie letztlich Sigfried Giedions bereits erwähnter Überschrift auch nicht das Frage-, sondern
das Ausrufezeichen dahinter fehlte: ARCHITEKTUR! Zumal es ja bei
jeder guten Geschichte darum gehen sollte, allfällige Zweifel so weit
wie möglich aufzulösen.

Nachsatz

Ich hatte Glück, als ich im Herbst 2018 über die feine Galerie
von Edward Cella (Los Angeles) eine sehr schöne Druckgrafik von
Konrad Wachsmann relativ günstig ankaufen konnte. Sie zeigt einen Auflager-Ausschnitt der Konstruktion des USAF-Hangars und
wurde in einer Auflage von 50 Stück hergestellt. Es gibt aus dieser
Serie noch andere Blätter und Ausführungen, wobei man sich natürlich und sofort die Frage stellen könnte, warum der sonst so uneitle
Konstrukteur Wachsmann sich hier derart künstlerisch betätigt hat.
Wie auch immer: Neben der Signatur »Konrad Wachsmann« steht
auch das Datum: 22. November 1963[→61]; Wachsmann war da, glaube
ich, mit seiner jungen Familie noch in Genua. Dieser Freitag war
auch der 27. Geburtstag meines Vaters, Gottfried Medicus.

Nach dem Signieren der Druckbögen rauchte Wachsmann vermutlich ein paar Zigaretten unten am Hafen, während um 12:30
Ortszeit John F. Kennedy in Dallas erschossen wurde, was sich
in vielerlei Hinsicht als historischer Wendepunkt herausstellen
sollte.

1   Bon Iver: 22, A Million Press Conference, nachzusehen unter: https://www.youtube.com/watch?v=eNqCVfC4oj4 (Stand: 10.3.2019).

2   Friedrich Achleitner: Vorwort in Michael Grüning: Der Architekt Konrad Wachsmann, Wien (Löcker Verlag) 1986, S. 6.

3   Konrad Wachsmann: Timebridge, Konrad Wachsmann: An Autobiography (1981). Unveröffentlichte Autobiografie. Akademie der Künste, Berlin, Konrad-Wachsmann-Archiv, Wachsmann 2128, S. 340 f. »Industrialization, and with it the whole chemistry of the process, based on the principles of the available abundance of energy, are the supreme reasons why the ›second coming of futurism‹ can no longer be stopped. […] The year 2001 will inaugurate this new epoch, so fantastically exciting. No period in the history of civilization has ever offered anything so promising, so humane, so effective, so intelligent and so meaningful.«

4   William Faulkner: Requiem for a Nun (1950/51), London (Penguin Random House) 1996, S. 85.

5   Peter Collins: Changing Ideals of Modern Architecture (1965), Montreal (McGill Queen's University Press) 1998, 2. Aufl., S. 15.

6   Manuel De Landa: A thousand years of nonlinear history, New York (Swerve Editions) 2000, S. 271.

7   Michael Grüning: Der Wachsmann-Report, Berlin (Verlag der Nation) 1986, S. 574 bzw. 471.

8   Konrad Wachsmann: Wendepunkt im Bauen, Wiesbaden (Krausskopf-Verlag) 1959, S. 232.

9   Sigfried Giedion: Bauen in Frankreich – Bauen in Eisen – Bauen in Eisenbeton, Leipzig/Berlin (Klinkhardt & Biermann) 1928, S. 6.

10 Antonio Sant'Elia: Futuristische Architektur, in: Ulrich Conrads: Programme und Manifeste zur Architektur des 20. Jahrhunderts, Bauwelt Fundamente 1, Basel (Birkhäuser Verlag) 2013 (2. Nachdruck), S. 32.

11 El Lissitzky: Proun und Wolkenbügel, Fundus Bücher 46, Dresden (VEB Verlag der Kunst) 1977, S. 82.

12 Otto Maier: Die räumliche Syntax. Konrad Wachsmanns Beitrag zum Bauen in unserer Zeit, Dissertation bei Fritz Haller, Universität Karlsruhe 1989, S. 324.

13 Hans Poelzig: »Der Architekt« (1931), in: Bauwelt 27–28, 2009, S. 9.

14 Julius Posener: Neuere Aufsätze, Basel (Birkhäuser Verlag) 1995, S. 55 f.

15 Wachsmann 1959 (zit. Anm. 8).

16 Arthur Schopenhauer: Metaphysik des Schönen, München/Zürich (Serie Piper) 1985, S. 138 f.

17 K. F. Schinkel in: J. Posener: Vorlesungen zur Geschichte der neueren Architektur V, ARCH+ 69/70, S. 42.

18 Michael Grüning: Der Wachsmann-Report, Berlin (Verlag der Nation) 1986, S. 534.

19 C. G. W. Boetticher in: J. Posener, Fröhlich und Kaufmann (Hg.): Schinkel zu Ehren, o. J., S. 19.

20 Ebd., S. 24.

21 H. P. Berlage, zit. nach Werner Oechslin: Eugène Emmanuel Viollet-le-Duc, Zürich (gta Verlag) 2010, S. 11.

22 Gottfried Semper: Eisenkonstruktionen (1849), in: Wissenschaft, Industrie und Kunst, Mainz (Florian Kupferberg Verlag) 1966, S. 22.

23 Gottfried Semper: Wissenschaft, Industrie und Kunst – Vorschläge zur Anregung nationalen Kunstgefühls (1851), in: Wissenschaft, Industrie und Kunst, Mainz (Florian Kupferberg Verlag) 1966, S. 68.

24 In: ARCH+ 159/160, Formfindungen, Mai 2002, S. 27.

25 Richard Lucae nach Sokratis Georgiadis: Nachwort zu S. Giedion: Bauen in Frankreich […], Berlin (Gebrüder Mann Verlag) 2000, S. 10.

26 Sokratis Georgiadis: Nachwort zu S. Giedion: Bauen in Frankreich […], Berlin (Gebrüder Mann Verlag) 2000, S. 2.

27 Le Corbusier: 1922 – Ausblick auf eine Architektur, Bauwelt Fundamente 2, Braunschweig/Wiesbaden (Vieweg) 1982, 4. Auflage, S. 31.

28 Giedion 1928 (zit. Anm. 9), S. 120.

29 Peter Smithson: Heroic Period of Modern Architecture, London (Thames & Hudson) 1981.

30 Leonardo Benevolo: Geschichte der Architektur des 19. und 20. Jahrhunderts, München (Callwey Verlag) 1964, 2. Band, S. 328.

31 Curt Siegel: Strukturformen der modernen Architektur, München (Callwey Verlag) 1960, S. 189.

32 Wachsmann 1959 (zit. Anm. 8), S. 230 f.

33 Slavoj Žižek: Was ist ein Ereignis?, Frankfurt a. M. (S. Fischer) 2014, S. 11 f.

34 Reyner Banham, Hiroyuki Suzuki: Modernes Bauen in Japan, Stuttgart (DVA) 1987, S. 6 f. Siehe auch Martino Peña Fernández-Serrano: El seminaro de Wachsmann en Japón, rita_08, Noviembre 2017, S. 86 f. unter: https://www.academia.edu/36075613/The_Wachsmann_s_Seminar._Sharing_influences (Stand: 5.2.2019).

35 Rem Koolhaas, Hans Ulrich Obrist: Project Japan, Köln (Taschen Verlag) 2011, S. 20.

36 Ebd.

37 Hans Hollein: Schriften & Manifeste, Hg. von F. Burkhardt und P. Manker, Wien (di:angewandte) 2002, S. 53 f.

Wissenschaft und Technik ermöglichen Aufgaben, deren Lösung genaue Studien erfordert, bevor Endresultate formuliert werden können.

Die Maschine ist das Werkzeug unserer Zeit. Sie ist Ursache jener Wirkungen, durch die sich die Gesellschaftsordnung manifestiert.

Neue Materialien, Methoden, Prozesse, statische und dynamische Erkenntnisse, Planungen, soziologische Verhältnisse müssen akzeptiert werden.

Den Bedingungen der Industrialisierung folgend, durch Multiplikation von Zelle und Element, soll sich das Bauwerk indirekt entwickeln.

Modulare Koordinationssysteme, wissenschaftliche Versuchsmethoden, Automationsgesetze, Präzision beeinflussen das schöpferische Denken.

Sehr komplexe statische und mechanische Probleme fordern engste Zusammenarbeit mit Industrie und Spezialisten in idealen Meisterteams.

Humane und ästhetische Vorstellungen werden neue Impulse erhalten durch kompromisslose Anwendung zeitgenössischen Wissens und Könnens.

Vom Bauen in unserer Zeit

Konrad Wachsmann,
Vortrag Ulm, Dezember 1956

(Unkorrigiertes Transkript des Vortragstextes)

Diese sieben Leitsätze dienen als eine grundsätzliche Erklärung meiner Arbeiten, die zur Zeit mit Hilfe der amerikanischen Regierung in einer Wanderausstellung durch Deutschland geschickt werden. In kurzer und improvisierter Fassung versuche ich die Notwendigkeit einer neuen Interpretation des Details des Gesamtgebietes des Bauens anzudeuten.

Wenn ich mich seit meiner frühesten Jugend ausschliesslich für die Analyse der Methoden und den Einfluss von Wissenschaft und Technik, die in der praktischen Auswirkung den Begriff der Industrialisierung zur Folge haben, interessiere, dann tue ich das gewiss nicht um der Sache selbst willen oder um als ein perpetueller Erfinder zu gelten. Ich habe früh einsehen müssen, dass es die richtigen Werkzeuge noch nicht gibt, um mich als Bauender meiner Zeit, dem Standard unseres Wissens und Könnens entsprechend, auszudrücken. Gewiss würde ich mich lieber nur mit dem tätigen Bauen beschäftigen, so wie ich das schon in einer früheren Periode getan habe, aber indem ich die Möglichkeiten ahne, die noch nicht für einen generellen Zweck befreit sind, kann ich die Wirkungen den

Ursachen nicht vorwegnehmen und muss alle verfügbare Zeit der Forschung widmen.

Dass Wissenschaft und Technik Aufgaben ermöglichen, sollte so verstanden werden, dass wir nicht nur vor Aufgaben gestellt werden, die wir zu akzeptieren hätten, gleichgültig ob sie gut sind oder nicht, sondern mit dem Wort »ermöglichen« versuche ich zu erklären, dass neue Kenntnisse als hart erarbeitete Vorteile und Geschenke dem Menschen erscheinen müssen, die Tore öffnen in eine neue mögliche Welt, die nicht von vorgefassten Meinungen, geboren aus dem Sicherinnern, kontrolliert wird. Diese Dinge sollten zu unserem eigenen Nutzen genau studiert werden. Man kann sie nicht ignorieren. Darum sehe ich ein gewisses Hindernis, ein Bauwerk zu konzipieren, bevor wir nicht möglichst exakte Kenntnisse, dessen besitzen, von dem was wir nun wirklich tun können.

Die Maschine als das Werkzeug unserer Zeit erscheint mir nicht ein vergrössertes Handwerkszeug, sondern in ihr sehe ich eine neue Annäherung an den Begriff des Originals. Während ein Objekt, von einem Handwerker gemacht, eine originale Schöpfung repräsentiert, wie oft auch immer an sich identische Teile wiederholt werden, produziert die Maschine nur Kopien. Das Original ist der Teil der Maschine, der das endgütlige Objekt formt. Wenn wir uns also Profilmesser, Vorrichtetische, Stanz-, Press- oder Gesenkformen etc. vorstellen, so müssen wir, ähnlich vielleicht wie in der Photographie, uns mit den Begriffen des Negativs und Positivs beschäftigen.

Auch ist es von Wichtigkeit zu erkennen, dass der qualifizierte Handwerker unserer Zeit der Werkzeugmacher ist. Es würde mir schwerfallen, über solche Tatsachen einfach hinwegzusehen, so als ob sie keinen Einfluss auf das schöpferische Denken hätten! Ich wünschte, dass der genaue Platz des Planers unserer Zeit in der Reihe jenes Teams vorgeschrieben wäre, in das gehört: Wissenschaftler, die die fundamentalen Prinzipien formulieren, Ingenieure, die diese Ergebnisse benutzen und auf aktuelle Aufgaben anwenden, Techniker, die Zeichnungen und Informationen an die Werkzeugmacher weiterleiten, und schliesslich der Werkzeugmacher mit seinen Erfahrungen, der die Originale, die Werkzeuge, schafft, sie alle stellen die Ordnung der heutigen schöpferischen Aktivität dar, in der der Planende nun seinen Platz finden muss.

Die neuen synthetischen Materialien und ihre Eigenschaften, Methoden und Prozesse, sind die im Gegensatz zur Kenntniss von den klassischen Materialien heute für den Planer meist kaum mehr als vage Begriffe, aber sie müssen auf das genaueste und mit der gleichen Exaktheit bekannt sein wie als dem Wissenschaftler selbst. Dasselbe gilt auch für die vollkommen neue Konzeption der Planung, die den Funktionen unserer und einer vorgeahnten kommenden Zeit untergeordnet sein sollte.

Wenn wir wissen, dass der Ziegelstein und die Mörtelfuge, der
Holzdübel oder der Nagel, die Niete oder die Schweissnaht, fundamentale Ursachen sind, die das Bauwerk bestimmen, genau so wie
die Ziegelbau-, Holzbau- oder Steinbautechnik der dominierende
Faktor der endgültigen Erscheinung solcher Bauten ist, dann sollte
man sich mit den neuen Elementen und deren kleinsten Zellen und
ihren Beziehungen zueinander genau auseinandersetzen.

Unterwirft man sich einem Ordnungssystem, so bedeutet das
keineswegs eine Einschränkung unseres schöpferischen Denkens
zum Nachteil der Phantasie und des Gefühls, die wir in einer freien
Arbeit eventuell entwickeln könnten. Im Gegenteil, die modularen
Koordinationssysteme werden unseren Sinn für die kleinen Diffe-
renzen schärfen, sie werden helfen, den Menschen kritisch zu machen und ihm die Möglichkeiten wiedergeben, durch ein immer tie-
feres Hineingehen in eine Struktur die Qualitäten solch eines Werkes zu erkennen. Er braucht sich nicht mehr mit der Oberflächen-
sensation des Neuen abzufinden, die nicht gestattet, näher hinzu-
sehen. wissenschaftliche Versuchsmethoden sollen nicht mehr dem
Bauenden vorweglaufen, sondern sie sollen *sein* Instrument sein,
mit dem er erst den Gedanken zur Wirklichkeit umformt. Die Automationsgesetze, die ein weiteres Instrument der Zusammenfassung
von Funktion, Menge, Zeit und Distanz sind, müssen verstanden
werden, Mit ihrer Hilfe wird das Kleinste höchst bedeutend werden
und durch sie wird der Entwerfende gezwungen, jedem Teil die
grösste Beachtung zu schenken. Aber über all dem steht der neue
Gedanke der Präzision. Es kann doch nicht so sein, dass Rustikale
oder die Zollstockungenauigkeit das Ideal menschlichen Wohlbeha-
gens darstellt. Ich glaube, dass der Begriff der Präzision vielleicht
etwas leichter verstanden wird, wenn wir uns die Bautechnik der
Griechen vorstellen.

Da wir uns nun vor solchen und unendlich viel mehr Problemen
von gleicher Wichtigkeit in fast hilfloser Unkenntnis befinden und
nicht wissen, was wir zuerst tun sollten, und selbst dann, wenn wir
es wissen, nicht als Individuum fähig wären, für alle diese Dinge
eine entsprechende Formulierung und Antwort zu finden, glaube
ich, dass die Arbeit des Bauenden, wenn sie überhaupt eine tiefere
Bedeutung haben sollte, hinauswächst aus dem Studio des individuellen fühlenden, träumenden Baukünstlers und aufgeht in der starken aktiven Tätigkeit des anonymen Teams der arbeitenden Gruppen, die durch Kenntnisse und Vorstellungen und vorbereitet zum
Risiko des Experiments schliesslich im Wechselspiel, ohne durch
vorgefasste Meinungen beeinflusst zu sein, Lösungen entwickelt, in
denen die fertige Erscheinung des Ganzen nun eigentlich ein Ne-
benprodukt der gesamten Anstrengungen ist. Über dieses Zusam-
menspiel der Gruppen und über das Training selbst möchte ich bei
späterer Gelegenheit noch einmal etwas sagen.

Die Kräfte, die in dem Denken, Wissen und Handeln unserer Zeit zu erkennen sind, werden uns neue Impulse geben, aus denen sich das Weltbild der Gegenwart und Zukunft entwickeln mag. Der Mensch, der sich solche Umwelt schafft, braucht nicht zu fürchten, erdrückt zu werden. Er wird plötzlich erkennen, dass dieses seine lebendige Umwelt ist, in Einklang mit dem, was er weiss, darum in Einklang mit dem, was er fühlt. Seine Begriffe dessen, was er als schön empfindet, seine ästhetischen Vorstellungen, entwickelt aus rationellen Notwendigkeiten und übertragen in den abstrakten Begriff des Symbols, werden ihm eine neue Umgebung formen, für die er arbeiten muss. Erst an diesem Punkt könnte ich mir vorstellen, dass der wahre Meister, der Künstler, das Werk weiterbauen könnte, bis er durch das, was die Natur ihm gegeben hat, es zum Kunstwerk erhebt.

Wohin mögen nun all diese Dinge führen? Ist es möglich, irgendwelche Voraussagungen zu machen? Wäre nicht jede Voraussagung schon wieder eine vorgefasste Meinung? Ich glaube, man sollte so etwas nicht versuchen, und trotzdem möchte ich hier, nur zur Erläuterung dessen, wovon ich eigentlich spreche, sagen, wie ich mir selbst die Entwicklung des Bauens in der Zukunft vorstelle.

Die Vorbereitungen werden komplizierter sein, aber die Bauideen der Designer werden viel einfacher werden, als sie es heute sind. Ich kann mich nicht entsinnen, jemals ein Bauwerk gesehen zu haben, das *zu* einfach war. Ich sah fast nur Bauten, die nicht einfach genug waren. Aber wenn ich ein wirklich einfaches Bauwerk sah, erschien es mir immer als ein sehr schönes. Ich zögere, einen Unterschied zwischen einfach und naiv zu machen. Naiv-sein ist eine Tugend. Und ich glaube, dass wirklich moderne Bauten in Zukunft weniger raffiniert sein werden, dafür aber naiver.

Der Gebrauch von Balken wird mehr und mehr verschwinden. Sie werden durch die horizontalen Platten ersetzt werden. Auch die Stützen wird man in Zukunft wohl anders als heute beurteilen. Sie werden fast völlig verschwinden, so dass wir sie schliesslich gar nicht mehr bemerken, selbst wenn sie da sind. Ebenso wird sich das, was wir uns unter Wänden, Fenstern, Türen vorstellen, beachtlich ändern. Ich könnte mir denken, dass nur Flächen existieren werden, undurchsichtige, durchsichtige und bewegliche. Und es werden Öffnungen und es wird dynamischer Raum da sein, und die mechanischen Installationen unserer Strukturen werden sich ausdehnen in unglaublich komplizierten Systemen, hauptsächlich in den horizontalen Flächen. Diese Platten werden aber auch die wesentlichsten Kräfte tragen. Man wird vielleicht unterdrücken, was oft in der Vertikalen betont wird.

Was die Struktur betrifft, so wird möglicherweise die Tendenz herrschen, den entspannten Kräften zu folgen. Es könnte auch zu Systemen der Konzentrierung von Kräften in Punkten führen.

Mehr und mehr werden sich die Massen in kleinste Glieder, die im Raum verteilt werden, auflösen. Sie werden sich in Gelenken treffen und so die Idee von Punkten im Raum schaffen, die durch imaginäre Linien verbunden sind. Um diese imaginären Linien mag dann das Material verteilt werden, das durch seine eigene Krümmung und in sich selbst verformt wiederum Kraft produziert. Gekrümmte und zusammengesetzte Elemente und Auskragungen werden die heute immer noch akzeptierten horizontalen Balken ersetzen. Wir sind bereits zu der allgemeinen Überzeugung gekommen, dass die Sprache der klassischen Architektur nicht präzise genug ist, um sie auf heutige schöpferische Aufgaben anzuwenden. Genau so ist es schwer vorstellbar, dass irgendeine Idee eines wirklich modernen Gebäudes existieren könnte, die sich mit Hilfe konventioneller oder klassischer Konstruktionsmethoden realisieren liesse. In solcher Überzeugung mag auch einer der Gründe liegen, weshalb wir heute im allgemeinen geneigt sind, die grossen, reinen Konstruktionen der Technik und die dynamischen mechanischen Maschinen als wirklich zeitgemäss und modern zu akzeptieren.

Die Oberflächenprofilierung wird in einem ersten Stadium so gut wie verschwinden, und es werden glatte Flächen vorherrschen. Wir nähern uns einer Periode, in der der Mensch die Linien wiedererkennen wird, das Spiel der Linien, durch Fugen und Oberflächen bedingt. Solche gewicht- und masselosen Flächen werden die zukünftigen Strukturen dominieren. Mehr als jemals wird Leichtigkeit vorherrschen, Kraft und Schwere werden aufgehoben sein. Eine der Hauptideen zukünftiger Architektur wird die klare Unterscheidung und Trennung jedes Objekts und jeder Funktion, im Detail und im Ganzen, sein.

Ich möchte nicht davon sprechen, wie die Menschen einmal zusammenleben werden, nicht über Stadt- oder Landesplanung und über Verkehrsprobleme. Aber ich weiss, dass einmal eine Ordnung existieren wird, aufgebaut auf dem Prinzip der Wiederholung des Nucleus, des strukturellen Kerns der Verbindungen, eine Ordnung, die die Fugen, die Oberflächen, die Strukturen, den Raum, die Bauten, Strassen, Plätze und Parks, die die Städte schafft und schliesslich die ganze Landschaft der zivilisierten Welt. Und hier könnte man hoffen, dass der Künstler entstehen möge, der durch seinen Genius und seine Vision fähig ist, Tatsachen und Funktionen in die abstrakte Sprache der Kunst zu übertragen: die Geschichte der Baukunst würde dann von neuem beginnen.

Unter den Umständen aber, unter denen wir gleichsam als Pioniere leben, diesen zukünftigen Zustand vorbereitend, wollen wir uns damit begnügen, den Funktionen zu folgen und in unseren Aktionen unpersönlich, objektiv und bescheiden sein.

Die Wirkung folgt der Ursache, »die Form folgt der Funktion«. So lange sich die Menschen neuen Einsichten und wissenschaftlichen Entdeckungen anzupassen haben und sich mit dem Studium und der Analyse praktischer Erfahrungen beschäftigen müssen, so lange wird eine dynamische Bedingung existieren, die diesen Satz Sullivans rechtfertigt. Wenn aber der Mensch die Begrenzungen erkennt, die auf seinen Fähigkeiten zu begreifen basieren, und so in der Lage ist, alle umfassenden Faktoren nicht nur im technischen Sinne sondern auch in Bezug auf die sozialen Rückwirkungen und ihre symbolischen und gefühlsmässigen Werte zu meistern, dann kann man einen Idealzustand voraussehen, in der die Funktion der Form folgen und die Ursache den Effekten untergeordnet sein mag.

Ich kann mir kein höheres Ziel vorstellen, nach dem der Mensch streben sollte.

Konrad Wachsmanns Werk ist untrennbar mit einem zentralen Ideal der modernen Architektur verbunden: Die vollständige Industrialisierung des Bauens sollte endgültig alle ökonomischen, sozialen und technischen Probleme der Infrastruktur sowie der Behausung der Massengesellschaft lösen. Unter anderem sollte jedem Menschen durch die Abdeckung seines grundlegenden Wohnbedarfs mittels standardisierten Wohnbaus auch eine individuell sinnstiftende Lebenspraxis ermöglicht werden.

Hundert Jahre nach ihrer Entstehung wissen wir heute, dass diese Vision weder im Kapitalismus noch im Sozialismus in einem umfassenden, gesellschaftsprägenden Sinn realisiert werden konnte. Jene Bauaufgaben des 20. Jahrhunderts, die am weitestgehenden von industriellen Herstellungsprozessen durchdrungen waren – der Plattenwohnbau in Osteuropa, die hochgradig vorgefertigten Eigenheime in den USA, der Siedlungsbau in Westeuropa, die technisch-militärischen Anwendungen und teilweise auch der Hochhausbau – waren entweder zeiträumlich begrenzt oder auf spezielle Sparten beschränkt. Eine umfassende Mechanisierung (heute: Digitalisierung) sämtlicher Bauprozesse aller Sparten – von der Bedarfserhebung über die Planung bis zur Produktion – ist auch im frühen digitalen Zeitalter noch nicht in Sicht: Weltweit wird der überwiegende Großteil aller Bauten immer noch intuitiv geplant und handwerklich hergestellt – angepasst an lokale Ressourcen, Mentalitäten und Bauvorschriften.[1]

Im Nachkriegs-Europa der 1950er Jahre sah man die Chancen für eine profunde Rationalisierung des Bauens noch optimistisch. Der Wiederaufbau und das beginnende Wirtschaftswachstum hatten enorme Nachfrage geschaffen. Viele junge Architekten erkannten – wie schon ihre Vorgänger in der ersten Nachkriegszeit der 1920er Jahre – in der weitestgehenden Mechanisierung, Standardisierung und Industrialisierung die alternativenlose Zukunft des noch größtenteils handwerklich geprägten Baugewerbes. In Österreich war diese Rückbesinnung auf Ideale der heroischen Moderne zusätzlich von der Abgrenzung der jungen, um 1930 geborenen Generation gegen ihre Lehrer motiviert, die das Zeitalter der Diktaturen mithilfe einer »moderaten«, unverdächtigen Modernität überlebt hatten – und natürlich auch gegen die Nachwirkungen der NS-Architektur durch einige ihrer auch in den 1950er Jahren noch aktiven Vertreter.[2] Konrad Wachsmann repräsentierte das Gegenteil: Aus dem US-Exil, in das er als deutscher Jude vom NS-Regime gezwungen worden war, kam er 1954 zu seinen folgenreichen Vortragsreisen in Europa als Avantgarde-Held der Moderne und als exemplarischer Vertreter ihrer Industrialisierungs-Euphorie.

Bilanz vorweg: ein Stimulator der europäischen Nachkriegsarchitektur

Wachsmann übernahm 1956 auf Empfehlung von Egon Eier-

Eine neue Anonymität des Bauens auf technischer Grundlage

Konrad Wachsmann, die Rationalisierungsvision der Moderne und ihre Folgen in Österreich

Matthias Boeckl; Abb.: 62–78

mann[3] und als Nachfolger des Züricher Architekten Hans Hofmann den Architekturkurs der von Oskar Kokoschka mitbegründeten Internationalen Sommerakademie in Salzburg. Für die Verhältnisse im Österreich der Wiederaufbauzeit – beim ersten Wachsmann-Kurs lag die Nachkriegs-Besatzung Österreichs durch die Alliierten gerade erst ein Jahr zurück – war die Teilnehmerschaft bemerkenswert international. Neben den österreichischen Kursbesuchern gab es auch Fortbildungswillige aus der Schweiz, aus Deutschland, den USA, Finnland, Italien und anderen Ländern. Die meisten von ihnen waren junge Absolventen, die sich in diesem Postgraduate-Kurs über den Stand der Industrialisierung des Bauens informieren wollten. Wachsmanns Seminar wirkte aber auch als wahres Initiationserlebnis einer Gruppe von rund 20 jungen österreichischen Architekten um Friedrich Achleitner, Erich Boltenstern junior, Hermann Czech, Roland Ertl, Johann Georg Gsteu, Hans Hollein, Franz Kiener, Friedrich Kurrent, Bernhard Leitner, Otto Leitner, Wolfgang Mistelbauer, Gustav Peichl, Johannes Spalt, Ottokar Uhl, Michael Untertrifaller senior und Gunther Wawrik.[4] Hier konnten sie erstmals ein altes Ideal der internationalen Moderne in authentischem Kontakt mit einem seiner wichtigsten Vertreter entdecken. Denn die österreichische Moderne, in deren Geist diese hoffnungsfrohen Baukünstler von Clemens Holzmeister, Lois Welzenbacher, Erich Boltenstern senior, Oswald Haerdtl und anderen Protagonisten der Zwischenkriegs- und teilweise auch der NS-Zeit ausgebildet worden waren, hatte – im Gegensatz zur deutschen Avantgarde – das traditionelle handwerkliche Bauen nie grundsätzlich hinterfragt. Soziale Sinnstiftung war selbst von der fortschrittlichsten sozialreformerischen Wiener Gruppe um Josef Frank eher dem kollektiv ausgeübten Handwerk zugetraut worden.[5]

Ging es aber Wachsmann tatsächlich nur um den technischen Aspekt der Rationalisierung, also um eine bloße Mechanisierung des Bauens, mit der man die »Industrialisierung« gemeinhin verband?[6] Die Erinnerungen seiner Schüler vermitteln ein breiteres Bild der Wachsmann-Botschaft, die sonst oft – stark verkürzend – nur auf der formalen Ebene rezipiert wurde, vor allem in plakativen Stab- und Knotenkonstruktionen.[7] Aber nur wenige österreichische Architekten unter den Salzburger Wachsmann-Schülern konnten die prägende Erfahrung des Kurses langfristig zu einer konsequent praktizierten Planungsmethode weiterentwickeln, etwa in der Partizipationsbewegung: Schon an der Sommerakademie wurde das Planen im (Fachleute-)Kollektiv trainiert, das Ottokar Uhl dann konsequent um die Nutzer erweiterte. Beide Lager der Wachsmann-Rezeption in Österreich werden weiter unten ausführlich beschrieben.

Rückblick: Avantgarde und industrielle Bauproduktion

Wie kam es zu diesem folgenreichen »Impact« auf die europäische Nachkriegsarchitektur? Gemeinsam mit Walter Gropius,

Hannes Meyer, Martin Wagner, Ernst May, Georg Muche und anderen zählt Wachsmann zu den Pionieren einer umfassend gedachten Rationalisierung des Bauens, die letztlich auch zu einer neuen Ästhetik führen sollte.[8] Diese Ideologie steht in Gegensatz zur pragmatischen Tradition der Moderne, die industrielle Produktionsweisen nur dort in den bestehenden Baubetrieb einführen wollte, wo sie ohne technische Schwierigkeiten und marktgerecht integriert werden konnten.[9]

Die weitgehend industrielle Produktion von Gebäuden mittels verschiedenster Vorfertigungs-Technologien ihrer (auf der Baustelle handwerklich zusammengebauten) Elemente existierte indes schon lange vor ihrer »Entdeckung« durch die Avantgarde des 20. Jahrhunderts. Beispielsweise wurde nicht einmal der von Wachsmann stets als Beginn der Bau-Industrialisierung präsentierte *Crystal Palace* in London 1851 zu seiner Entstehungszeit als »Architektur« rezipiert.[10] Beim Holzbau hatte die Vorfertigung von Holzelementen für großangelegte Kolonisierungskonzepte sogar schon Jahrzehnte vorher begonnen: Das Londoner Unternehmen *Manning* lieferte ab 1820 derartige Systeme für 5000 englische Siedler in der südafrikanischen Kap-Provinz und in den 1830er Jahren auch für Australien.[11] Die zügige Besiedelung des amerikanischen Westens wurde – hundert Jahre vor den Aktivitäten von Wachsmanns *General Panel Corporation* – ebenfalls wesentlich von vorfabrizierten Holz- und Eisenpaneel-Systemen ermöglicht. So werden in der Literatur vorwiegend englische und amerikanische Beispiele für eine frühe und auf Siedlungen beschränkte Bau-Industrialisierung vor 1900 genannt. Einige Systeme dieser Ära – wie etwa jene des englischen Unternehmens *Calway and Co.*, des Liverpooler Ingenieurs J. A. Brodie und des New Yorker Architekten Grosvenor Atterbury – basierten bereits auf Betonpaneelen, während das norddeutsche Unternehmen *Christoph & Unmack* – in dem der 25-jährige Konrad Wachsmann 1926 nach seinem Architekturstudium bei Heinrich Tessenow in Dresden seine Laufbahn begann – seit 1882 Holzelemente für die Baracken des preußischen Militärs produzierte.[12]

Die Avantgarde entdeckte diese Systeme erst kurz vor dem Ersten Weltkrieg für sich. In den 1920er Jahren steigerte sie diese Euphorie zu einem dogmatischen, nun durchaus weltanschaulich gemeinten Begriff industriellen Bauens als ideologisches System – analog zu den politischen Systemen jener Zeit, die ebenfalls absolut und alternativlos konzipiert waren: »Wir akzeptieren die Maschine als das Werkzeug unserer Zeit. Das bedeutet, dass wir damit auch eine Gesellschaftsordnung anerkennen, die sich in ihrer Grundstruktur völlig den Folgen der Industrialisierung angepasst hat.«[13]

Dieses umfassend lebensreformatorische Bauverständnis war jedoch – im Gegensatz zu pragmatischen Konzepten, die sich auf leicht integrierbare neue Bauweisen beschränkten – unter freien

Verhältnissen der Marktwirtschaft schon wegen des grundlegenden menschlichen Distinktionsbedürfnisses zum Scheitern verurteilt. Nur unter den besonderen Bedingungen von Diktaturen oder jenen der us-Kriegswirtschaft konnte es durch staatlich subventionierte Projekte in abgegrenzten Teilbereichen implementiert werden.

Konrad Wachsmanns späterer Partner Walter Gropius war der Pionier dieser »weltanschaulichen« Betrachtungsweise der Industrialisierung. Paradoxerweise entstand diese aber just unter *künstlerischen* Vorzeichen: Während seiner Mitarbeit bei Peter Behrens verfasste Gropius gemeinsam mit diesem 1909/10 ein »Programm zur Gründung einer allgemeinen Hausbaugesellschaft auf künstlerisch einheitlicher Grundlage m.b.H.«. Dieses Manifest war an die Führung des AEG-Konzerns gerichtet und basierte auf Behrens' Erfahrungen im Siedlungsbau für das Unternehmen. Seinem ambitionierten Titel wird es jedoch kaum gerecht, da es, so Winfried Nerdinger, »außer Anregungen zur Normierung von Bauteilen keinerlei Ideen zur Fertigung und Produktion [enthält] – und im Übrigen waren standardisierte Fertigbausysteme in den USA, England und auch Deutschland schon längst entwickelt.«[14] Das allgemeine Ziel der Herstellung von Gebrauchsgegenständen auf »künstlerisch einheitlicher Grundlage« stammt vom industriekritischen Gesamtkunstwerk-Ideal der *Art-Nouveau-* und der *Arts-and-Crafts*-Bewegungen um 1900. Es findet sich auch im Programm des 1907 von Peter Behrens, Josef Hoffmann, Joseph Maria Olbrich, Paul Schultze-Naumburg und anderen gegründeten Deutschen Werkbundes.

Ein latenter Widerspruch, der die Geschichte der Werkbünde auch weiterhin begleiten sollte, liegt in der scheinbar paradoxen Verbindung der Adjektive »einheitlich« und »künstlerisch«: Kann Individualität (des Nutzers) just durch Normierung (seiner Gebrauchsobjekte) ermöglicht werden? Durch das Einfallstor einer »künstlerischen Anleitung« der Wirtschaft wollte Gropius offenbar etwas »Unkünstlerisches« bewirken: nämlich eine standardisierte Bauproduktion, die mit ihrer radikalen Normierung des Produkts – eventuell auch der Nutzungsweisen – bei der Realisierung einer selbstverwirklichenden Lebenspraxis durch den Konsumenten definitiv einen emanzipatorischen Aufwand des Letzteren erfordert, den nicht jeder leisten kann oder will. So gesehen handelt es sich durchaus um ein elitäres Konzept.

Europäische Prototypen der 1920er und 1930er Jahre: Gropius und Wachsmann

Anfangs lieferte die Rationalisierungsobsession der Avantgarde auch irrationale Planungsergebnisse. Ein erstes Beispiel derartiger Konflikte von technischen Standardisierungen mit realen Nutzerbedürfnissen bot die Siedlung in Dessau-Törten 1926–28, wo Gropius identische Häuser – nur um eine »rationale Fließbandherstellung« zu demonstrieren – wegen der gewählten Produktionsmethode entlang zweier paralleler Reihen in *verschiedene* Himmelsrichtungen orientieren musste: Damit opferte er eine wesentliche funktionale Anforderung bewusst einem »höheren Ziel«[15].

In praktisch allen derartigen frühen »Industrialisierungs«-Projekten waren die Baukosten wegen der neuen Technologie und der geringen Anzahl an Produktionseinheiten höher als bei etablierten handwerklichen Bautechniken, da diese längst keine Entwicklungskosten mehr verursachten: Die enorme Anfangsinvestition für die neue Produktionstechnik hätte erst in ferner Zukunft durch den Absatz großer Produktionsmengen zurückverdient werden können. Dieses klassische Problem der Finanzierung hoher Entwicklungskosten einer neuen industriellen Produktionsweise begleitet seither alle einschlägigen Baukonzepte. Es konnte im Bauwesen – im Gegensatz zur vorbildlichen Autoindustrie – niemals gänzlich gelöst werden, da vorgefertigte Wohnhäuser in einer konkurrenzfähigen Qualität kaum je die für eine Amortisierung der Anfangsinvestition erforderlichen Absatzzahlen erreichten.[16]

Ein zweiter Fall, in dem Gropius' Ambition der Durchbruch zum Massenmarkt verwehrt blieb, war sein Beitrag zur Werkbund-Ausstellung von Modellhäusern in Stuttgart 1927. Das Haus Nr. 17, das dort buchstäblich im Schatten der Häuser von Le Corbusier stand, war als Stahlgerüst mit Füllwänden aus 8 cm starken Expansitkorkplatten und Asbestschieferplatten konstruiert. Winfried Nerdinger zieht auch für diesen Prototyp eine ernüchternde Bilanz: »Nicht nur Kritiker sprachen vom Barackenmäßigen der Bauten, sondern auch die Bauhausstudenten waren enttäuscht über ihren Direktor und meinten, so etwas wie Le Corbusiers Bauten hätte aus Dessau kommen müssen. In ihrem Tagebuch notierte Ise Gropius darauf, dass Gropius die Häuser Le Corbusiers als rückständig kritisierte, denn die Zukunft läge in der Mechanisierung der Bauproduktion.«[17]

Eine dritte Episode ist das Projekt einer »Häuserbaufabrik«, die der Bauhaus-Gründer 1928 mit dem Berliner Bauunternehmer Adolf Sommerfeld aufziehen wollte. Dafür unternahm Gropius eine ausgedehnte Studienreise in die USA und inszenierte nach seiner Rückkehr gemeinsam mit László Moholy-Nagy eine Ausstellung, die »amerikanische« Bausysteme propagierte. »Aber die Häuserbaufabrik«, resümiert Nerdinger erneut, »zerschlug sich und die beschworene amerikanische Bauwirtschaft blieb auch weiterhin ein etwas nebulöser, meist nur statistisch gebrauchter Begriff«.[18]

Metallkonstruktionen begannen sich zu dieser Zeit als bevorzugte industrielle Serienhausbautechnik sowohl am Markt als auch bei den von Architekten ersonnenen Prototypen zu etablieren: Schon 1924 hatte Friedrich Förster (1930 mit Robert Krafft verbessert für die *Hirsch Kupfer- und Messingwerke* in Eberswalde) ein innovatives Wandelemente-System aus Holzrahmen mit

Kupferpaneelen für vorgefertigte Häuser entwickelt: »Dieses Konzept hatte keine konstruktiven Vorbilder am deutschen Hausbaumarkt und nicht einmal unter früheren, vielbewunderten britischen Modellen.«[19] Nach Präsentationen von traditionalistisch gestalteten Prototypen auf Bauausstellungen analysierte Walter Gropius das *Hirsch-System* 1931 für die Zeitschrift *Bauwelt* und begann danach das Unternehmen bei der experimentellen systematischen Verbesserung anhand von Modellbauten umfassend zu beraten. Letztlich wurden aber – trotz vieler Verhandlungen mit Entwicklern in Europa, Amerika und in der Sowjetunion über eine Serienproduktion – nur einige Dutzend dieser Häuser hergestellt, meist als Prototypen, einige wenige auch für private Endkunden.

Auch österreichische Architekten und Unternehmen starteten um 1930 Versuche in Richtung Serienproduktion vorgefertigter Metallhäuser. Der Stahlhersteller *Böhler* – dessen Besitzerfamilie eng mit den Wiener-Moderne-Pionieren um Josef Hoffmann verbunden war[20] – entwickelte ein Wandsystem mit Stahlrahmen, Stahlpaneelen und innerer Heraklith-Dämmung. Prototypen aus diesem System wurden, teilweise nach Architektenentwurf, auf deutschen Bauausstellungen präsentiert. Das Konzept konnte sich jedoch nie am Markt etablieren – genauso wenig wie das Stahlhaus, das Josef Hoffmann für den steirischen Hersteller *Vogel & Noot* entworfen hatte.[21]

Gleichzeitig entwickelte Richard Buckminster Fuller in den USA sein *Dymaxion*-Konzept für ein industriell produziertes Aluminium-Fertighaus, das 1928–30 nur in zwei Prototypen hergestellt wurde. Seine geodätischen Kuppeln aus industriell produzierten Leichtbauelementen folgten ab 1948. Einer der Erfolgsfaktoren dieses Systems war seine Adaptierbarkeit für zahlreiche Kontexte und Funktionen – mit der großen Ausnahme des Wohnens.

Konrad Wachsmann, der mit Gropius ab 1941 im gemeinsamen US-Exil zusammenarbeitete, hatte seine Erfahrungen mit rationellen Produktionstechnologien zunächst im Holzbau erworben. Nach einer Lehre als Möbel- und Bauschreiner und dem Besuch der Kunstgewerbeschule in Berlin studierte er 1923 an der Dresdner Akademie bei Heinrich Tessenow und 1924 an der Berliner Kunstakademie bei Hans Poelzig. 1926 trat er in das Holz- und Stahlbauunternehmen *Christoph & Unmack* in der ostdeutschen Stadt Niesky ein. 1929 eröffnete er ein Architekturbüro in Berlin, das mit dem Ferien-Holzhaus für Albert Einstein in Caputh bei Potsdam schlagartig bekannt wurde. 1930 publizierte er ein Fachbuch über Holzbautechnik.[22] Von der »Machtübernahme« der Nationalsozialisten 1933 bis zu seiner von Einstein ermöglichten Emigration in die USA 1941 lebte und arbeitete Wachsmann unter anderem in Italien, Spanien und Frankreich. Auch in dieser unruhigen Zeit hielt er stets intensiven Kontakt mit den wichtigsten Persönlichkeiten der deutschen und europäischen Architekturavantgarde von Tessenow über Poelzig und Gropius bis zu Le Corbusier.[23] Aber schon beim Einstein-Projekt hatte er seine Lebensaufgabe erkannt: »Einstein als Auftraggeber zu haben, das war eine ungeheure Reputation. Obwohl es eigentlich leichtsinnig war, gab ich meinen Posten als Chefarchitekt (bei *Christoph & Unmack*, Anm. d. Verf.) auf, um in eigener Praxis zu arbeiten. Dabei war ich meiner Zukunft gar nicht so sicher. Entdeckt hatte sich mir lediglich eine universelle, anonyme Aufgabe: die Industrialisierung.«[24]

Jene Projekte, die Wachsmann zwischen seiner Ankunft in Amerika 1941 und dem Beginn seiner Lehrtätigkeit an US-Universitäten 1949 sowie seiner Wanderjahre als Vortragender in direktem und indirektem Auftrag der US-Regierung ab 1954 entwickelte, waren Gegenstand zahlreicher Publikationen[25] und sind auch im vorliegenden Band dokumentiert. Die wichtigsten Hallenbaustudien waren eine *Mobilar Structure* für die *Atlas Aircraft Corporation* und Hangar-Projekte für die *US Air Force*. Bezahlt wurden dabei nur die Forschungskosten. Keines der beiden Systeme erreichte Marktreife und Serienproduktion.

Die General Panel Corporation: Erfolgskriterien des industriellen Wohnbaus

Eine kurzfristige Marktpräsenz konnte Wachsmann jedoch gemeinsam mit Walter Gropius und der *General Panel Corporation* just bei dem in den USA – anders als in Europa – extrem marktgetriebenen Wohnbau entfalten. Das letztliche Scheitern auch dieses 1941 gegründeten und 1951 liquidierten Unternehmens beendete aber viele Hoffnungen der Avantgarde auf einen systematisch-rationellen Wohnbau als Grundlage der vollständigen Industrialisierung des Bauens und eines damit verbundenen gesellschaftlichen und ästhetischen Wandels. Die gründlichste Analyse dieses Scheiterns stammt von Gilbert Herbert.[26] Als Ursache des Misserfolgs identifiziert Herbert eine dramatische ökonomische Diskrepanz: Einerseits verbrauchte das Unternehmen bei der Entwicklung einer perfektionierten Serienproduktion einen stark überhöhten Zeit- und Kapitalaufwand und andererseits hatten sich die Marktbedingungen seit dem Kriegsende 1945 – ohne Großkunden wie das Militär und ohne Regierungssubventionen – gegenüber dem Gründungsjahr 1941 radikal zu einem zivilen Konsumentenmarkt verändert. So standen steigende Entwicklungskosten rasch sinkenden Marktchancen gegenüber. Eine unmittelbare Konsequenz war der geringe Output: In den zehn Jahren ihrer Existenz konnte die *General Panel Corporation* kaum 200 Häuser verkaufen und liefern. Dem ging aber eine Kapitalinvestition (teilweise als öffentliche Subvention) von sechs Millionen Dollar voraus, die fast zur Gänze für die technische Entwicklung und einen neuen Fabriksbau in Kalifornien statt für die eigentliche Produktion verbraucht worden war. Wachsmanns

Perfektionismus, dessen stetiger Verbesserungsdrang eine endgültige Serienfertigung in hohen Stückzahlen ständig verzögerte, sowie kaum vorhandenes Marketing und die mangelnde Konkurrenzfähigkeit der Häuser, die letztlich nicht viel billiger waren als konventionell gebaute, aber trotzdem den »Makel« eines Retortenprodukts trugen, waren weitere Faktoren des Niedergangs. Dazu kamen fehlende Finanzierungsmodelle für die Kunden und regional sehr unterschiedliche Bauordnungen, die eine überregionale und vollständige Standardisierung von Wohnhäusern schon grundsätzlich erschwerten. Das anpassungsfähigere traditionelle Baugewerbe konnte hingegen die große Nachfrage am Markt durch preiswerte, stärker individualisierte, günstig finanzierbare und technisch traditionelle Lösungen überall leicht befriedigen.

Komplett industriell hergestellte Wohnungen wurden bald in einem ganz anderen Kontext erfolgreich realisiert – nämlich im neuen Typ des *Mobile Home*, der in der zunehmend mobilen Konsumgesellschaft immer attraktiver wurde. Ohne große Entwicklungskosten konnte diese Produktion mühelos aus der bestehenden Autoindustrie entwickelt werden. Diese Wendung einer technisch avancierten freien Marktwirtschaft hatte die europäische Avantgarde – obwohl sie den »Taylorismus« der Autoindustrie rhetorisch stets als vorbildlich pries[27] – auch wegen ihrer idealistischen Sozialisierung kaum vorhersehen können.

Für die Idee industriell hergestellter ortsfester Wohnhäuser entstand letztlich in einer Nischensituation der Nachkriegswirtschaft doch noch ein typischer, auch heute noch relevanter Markt samt passender Technologie: die *konventionelle* Fertighausindustrie ohne die hohen technologischen Ansprüche der *General Panel Corporation*. Abseits aller weltanschaulichen Visionen und um den Preis des Verzichts auf sozialreformerische Ansprüche, radikale technische Innovation sowie einen »ästhetischen Wandel« konnte sich eine pragmatische Auffassung industrieller Vorfertigung etablieren: In Märkten von Schwellenländern und weniger anspruchsvollen Marktsegmenten von Industrieländern war und ist diese Strategie unter Nutzung und Weiterentwicklung vorhandener Vorfertigungstechnologien sowie mit dem Antrieb großer Kapitalreserven durchaus erfolgreich.

Das bewiesen nicht nur die staatlich geförderten Plattenbaukonzepte im sozialistischen Ostblock und im sozialdemokratischen Westeuropa, sondern auch einige US-Beispiele, unter denen etwa Nelson Rockefellers *International Basic Economy Corporation (IBEC)* besonders erfolgreich war. Dieses Unternehmen baute in großem Stil vorgefertigte Wohnhäuser auf Puerto Rico. Die ersten Entwürfe auf Basis von Betonfertigteilen wurden vom österreichischen Exilarchitekten Simon Schmiderer in Zusammenarbeit mit dem Ingenieur Armando Vivoni entwickelt. Eine zweite Phase

brachte dann Ortbetonhäuser, die komplett in eine einzige wieder-
verwendbare Schalung gegossen wurden.[28] Da für diese Methode
kaum Entwicklungskosten anfielen und da vom Bauträger auch äu-
ßerst günstige Finanzierungsmodelle für die Kunden angeboten
sowie die Häuser nur stückweise auf Bestellung eines hungrigen
Marktes gebaut wurden, entwickelte sich das Projekt zum wirt-
schaftlichen Erfolg: Im Gegensatz zur *General Panel Corporation*
konnte die IBEC mit guter Marktkenntnis, bewährten Finanzie-
rungsinstrumenten und pragmatischen Technologien reüssieren.

Der späte Wachsmann: ideale Theorie statt ernüchternder
Praxis

Welche Konsequenzen zog Wachsmann, als das Scheitern der
General Panel Corporation absehbar wurde? Seine Reaktion war der
Rückzug ins Akademische. Bereits 1949, also zwei Jahre vor der
endgültigen Löschung des Unternehmens, nahm Wachsmann einen
Ruf nach Chicago an das *Institute of Design* des *Illinois Institute of
Technology* (IIT) an. In diesem Jahr war das vom Bauhäusler László
Moholy-Nagy fünf Jahre zuvor gegründete Designinstitut dem
IIT inkorporiert worden, an dem seit 1938 der ehemalige Bauhaus-
Direktor Ludwig Mies van der Rohe lehrte und einen neuen Campus
mit mehreren Gebäuden errichtete. Auch andere Exilkünstler wie
der aus Paris gekommene Maler und Bildhauer Hugo Weber lehrten
am IIT. So war Wachsmann 16 Jahre nach seiner Flucht aus Deutschland für sieben Jahre in ein vertrautes Ambiente der ehemaligen
europäischen Avantgarde zurückgekehrt. Nun hatte aber mit dem
Kalten Krieg eine geopolitische Entwicklung eingesetzt, in der sich
für die führenden Köpfe der deutschen Moderne, die in den 1930er
Jahren in die USA emigriert waren, strategisch wichtige neue Aufgaben ergaben. Neben der militärischen Präsenz in Westeuropa unterstützte die US-Administration mit dem *Marshall-Plan* intensiv den
Wiederaufbau in den kriegsgeschädigten Ländern und lancierte mit
zahlreichen *Amerika-Häusern* vor Ort sowie Reisestipendien für
europäische Studierende an US-Universitäten ein breit angelegtes
Bildungsprogramm (u. a. durch die *Fulbright-Stipendien*), das westliche Werte fest in der zukünftigen europäischen Elite verankern
sollte.[29] Zu dieser Strategie gehörte auch die Förderung von Studi-
en, Ausstellungen, Seminaren, Forschungs- und Vortragsreisen von
amerikanischen Künstlern und Akademikern in ganz Europa.

Eine besondere Stellung in diesen Programmen genossen naturgemäß jene Künstler und Intellektuellen, die nach ihrer Flucht
vor dem Nationalsozialismus von den USA großzügig aufgenommen
und erfolgreich in deren kulturelles Leben integriert worden waren.
Als glaubwürdige und überzeugende Botschafter des *American Way
of Life* konnten sie durch ihre ursprüngliche Sozialisierung in Europa nun eine perfekte Kommunikation mit jungen europäischen
Künstlern, Wissenschaftlern und Politikern herstellen. Das zeigte

sich nicht nur an Leuchtturm-Projekten wie der Berliner *National-galerie* von Mies van der Rohe (1962–68) und der *Gropiussiedlung* (Großsiedlung Britz-Buckow-Rudow, 1960–73), sondern auch an Konrad Wachsmanns großer Wirkung in Österreich ab 1956. Von 1954 bis zu seinem Tod 1980 reiste er unermüdlich zu Vorträgen, Seminaren und Ausstellungen vorwiegend in Deutschland, Italien und Österreich. 1954 unterrichtete Wachsmann als Lektor am Lehrstuhl von Egon Eiermann in Karlsruhe, 1955–56 unternahm er für die US-Administration eine Vortragstournee nach Japan, Israel, Deutschland und Österreich, die zum Engagement an der Salzburger Sommerakademie führte, 1959 hielt er ein Seminar in Lausanne, 1962–64 plante er für die Stadt Genua, 1969 besuchte er die Bauakademie in Ostberlin und das Bauhausarchiv in Westberlin, 1970 die Sowjetunion, 1971 schickte er eine Wanderausstellung über seine Arbeit auf Reisen, 1973 bereiste er die DDR und Polen, 1978 und 1979 erneut Ostdeutschland. Daneben erfüllte er Professuren und erfuhr zahlreiche Ehrungen in den USA.

Wachsmann in Wien

Im Zuge der obgenannten globalen Tournee kam Wachsmann auch nach Österreich. Hier nahm er an einem »Interdisziplinären Managerseminar« am Semmering teil[30] und hielt in Wien einen folgenreichen Vortrag unter dem Titel *Erziehung – Planung – Industrialisierung*. Am 24. April 1956 bat die *Zentralvereinigung der Architekten (ZVA)* unter Präsident Erich Boltenstern in Zusammenarbeit mit der *United States Information Agency (USIA)* zu dieser folgenreichen Präsentation in den Vortragssaal des *MAK*.[31] Für die etablierten Wiener Architekten brachte das eine erneute Konfrontation mit jener technikbegeisterten Avantgarde, die in Österreich – trotz punktueller, aber folgenloser Versuche einiger Architekten und Industrieunternehmen in der Zeit um 1930 – keine Tradition hatte, nun aber über das US-Exil scheinbar zu weltweitem Einfluss gekommen war. Man bemühte sich daher um eine ehrliche Auseinandersetzung mit dieser Strategie. Roland Rainer, dessen Wiener Stadthalle sich damals gerade im Bau befand, und ZVA-Chef Erich Boltenstern referierten ihre Eindrücke von Wachsmanns Vortrag in der vereinseigenen Zeitschrift *Der Bau*.[32] Rainer kommentierte die eher akademische denn marktfähige Fixierung Wachsmanns auf das wichtigste konstruktive Detail industrieller Bausysteme – den Knoten: »Das mit der Gründlichkeit und Präzision durchdachte Detail – nicht irgendeines, sondern das *eine*, charakteristische Detail der besten Zusammenfügung der Elemente – hat Wachsmann zu jener ›Kunst der Fuge‹ entwickelt, das ihm Ausgangspunkt für die gesamte Konstruktion, ja darüber hinaus Ausgangspunkt in unerforschtes Neuland der Gestaltung ist«. Zur Diskussion der Architektenausbildung bemerkte Rainer, dass die Idee von »Elementarklassen zur Entfaltung von Materialverständnis und Konstruktionsgefühl« zwar im Bauhaus kultiviert worden sei, aber das »soll es auch in Wien, z. B. unter Strnad, gegeben haben – das ist allerdings lange her. Gerade diesbezüglich könnten Wachsmanns Ausführungen unmittelbar Anregung für die Weiterführung unserer eigenen modernen Tradition geben.«

Erich Boltenstern, der 1929 bis 1934 an der damaligen Kunstgewerbeschule als Assistent des von Rainer angesprochenen Oskar Strnad gewirkt hatte, konnte Wachsmanns Ideen aus der Perspektive einer Sozialisierung in der Wiener Moderne betrachten – und sogleich auch relativieren: »Sie gelten in erster Linie für Amerika, wo die Verhältnisse in konstruktiver und technischer Hinsicht noch weit mehr auf die Maschine abgestellt sind als in Europa, aber wahrscheinlich wird diese Entwicklung auch hier immer mehr diese Richtung nehmen.« Nach der Schilderung von Wachsmanns kollektivistischem Seminarsystem der Architektenausbildung in Teams mit einer jeweils ungeraden Anzahl an Teilnehmern zieht auch Boltenstern den – nicht näher differenzierten – Vergleich mit der Wiener Moderne: »Ich erinnere nur an einen Lehrer, wie es Strnad war, der aus tiefster Erkenntnis der Grundlagen unseres Lebens und der daraus entspringenden Formenwelt schon ähnliche Wege wie Wachsmann gegangen ist.«

Auf die junge Architektengeneration, die nach viel traditionelleren Modellen ausgebildet worden war und nach Alternativen zum wenig innovativen Wiederaufbaubetrieb dürstete, wirkte Wachsmanns Vortrag allerdings wie ein Erweckungserlebnis: »Für uns war das ein unglaublicher Eindruck. Wachsmann schien vieles von dem einzulösen, was wir vergeblich in Wien versucht haben«, erinnert sich Friedrich Kurrent.[33]

Wachsmanns rationale Planungsmethode in Salzburg:
»Das Ergebnis entsteht zwingend logisch von selbst«

Die fünf Sommerseminare, die Konrad Wachsmann in den Jahren 1956 bis 1960 in Salzburg gab, sind in der Fachliteratur gründlich beschrieben worden.[34] Schon zwei Jahre nach Beginn der Kurse wurden die ersten Arbeitsergebnisse dokumentiert und in der Wiener *Galerie Würthle* mit Ausstellung und Katalog präsentiert.[35] Im letzten Jahr der Kurse, 1960, erschien ein Artikel, der bereits die Ergebnisse der »Teamarbeit« der ersten vier Jahre präsentierte.[36] Wachsmann selbst zog 18 Jahre nach dem letzten Kurs eine abschließende Bilanz über sein Salzburger Engagement.[37]

Im Mittelpunkt der faszinierten Erinnerungen der Kursteilnehmer stehen meist Wachsmanns innovative Arbeitsmethoden, weniger die konkreten Bauentwürfe, die sich daraus ergaben. Vor dem gewohnten Hintergrund der traditionellen Meisterschulen und der technischen Fakultäten der österreichischen Architektenausbildung wirkten die offene Diskussionsatmosphäre, die Teambildung und der systematisch in der Gruppe geplante Ablauf der Studien

völlig neuartig. Obwohl deren Ergebnisse vorerst offen bleiben sollten, steuerte die Arbeit aber letztlich doch auf bestimmte Ziele zu,
wie sich Friedrich Achleitner, Teilnehmer der ersten beiden Seminare 1956 und 1957, erinnert: »Wer die souverän ›dirigierten‹ Wachs-
mann-Seminare miterlebte, konnte schon damals den Eindruck gewinnen, dass er selbst, bewusst oder unbewusst, kalkuliert oder
instinktiv, auf ein bestimmtes Ziel, auf eine konkrete Formvorstel-
lung zusteuerte, obwohl er die Illusion der totalen Offenheit des
Ablaufes bis zur letzten Minute aufrechterhielt.«[38]

Die kollektivistische Lehrmethode war darauf angelegt, individuelle »Handschriften« und Sichtweisen möglichst auszuschließen
sowie Objektivität herzustellen. Die gesamte lange Vorgeschichte
der Avantgarde-Auffassung industrialisierten Bauens, das in einer
idealen Zukunft die »Architektur« ablösen sollte, hatte ja stets die
Überwindung der künstlerisch-individuellen Bauplanung durch ra-
tional-kollektive Methoden verfolgt – letztlich den vollständigen
Ersatz der Künstlersubjektivität durch »objektive« Planungsme-
thoden. »Industrialisierung« war nur der Ausdruck dieser angestreb-
ten totalen Rationalisierung, die Maschine ihr Werkzeug, nicht ihr
Zweck.

Bei der Premiere 1956 teilte Wachsmann die 21 Seminarteilnehmer in sieben Dreiergruppen. In den ersten beiden Jahren fand die
achtwöchige praktische Arbeit der Studierenden in den *Dombögen*
statt, einer Raumflucht über den Arkaden, die das Spätrenaissance-
Ensemble am Salzburger Domplatz rahmen und die fürsterzbischöf-
liche Residenz mit der Domkirche verbinden.[39] Friedrich Kurrent
und Johannes Spalt unterstützten Wachsmann als Assistenten und
hatten sich auf diese Aufgabe durch einen Besuch beim Meister an
der *Hochschule für Gestaltung* in Ulm vorbereitet.[40] Am Beginn
wurden konkrete Entwurfsaufgaben vermieden, die Teams sollten
zunächst allgemein recherchieren: »Die Aufgabenkreise umfassten
Themen wie Material/Produktion, Konstruktion, Elemente, Modul,
Installation, Planung und Begriffe«[41], aber auch »Fügen und Verbinden«, wie sich Kurrent erinnert: »Das Ziel war stets, auf Basis dieser
Vorstudien am Ende gemeinsam ein Projekt zu erarbeiten, von dem
auch ein Modell gebaut wurde.«[42] Das gemeinsam geplante Baupro-
jekt war etwa 1958 eine multifunktionale Veranstaltungshalle, der
schon 1956 und 1957 variable Hallenprojekte als Anwendungsbeispiele der vorher erarbeiteten modularen Technik vorangegangen
waren.[43]

Am Weg zum finalen Gemeinschaftsprojekt sorgte Wachsmann
durch Expertenvorträge, vor allem aber durch planmäßige innere
Kommunikation der Gruppe nicht nur für inhaltlichen Austausch,
sondern auch für die Anonymisierung der einzelnen gestalterischen
Ideen: »Da wochenweise geplant wurde (6 Tage), und an jedem
Wochenende eine zusammenfassende Diskussion vorgesehen war,

musste auch der ›Stoff‹ in 6 Teile zerlegt werden. Am Ende eines
jeden Tages tauschten die Teams das von ihnen zum Thema Erarbeitete untereinander aus, reichten es also weiter, denn am Schluss
der Woche musste ja jeder Seminarteilnehmer vollständig und voll-
inhaltlich über alle Problemkreise informiert sein. Das ging mehrere
Wochen so und brachte eine derartige Fülle von schriftlichen Aufzeichnungen und Zwischenresultaten, dass wir uns nicht vorstellen konnten, wie ein mögliches Endresultat aussehen würde. Wachsmann schaffte dies – aus uns – in einer abschließenden auch rhetorisch glänzend entwickelten Zusammenschau. Das Ergebnis war
für uns einzigartig, zudem höchst überraschend, da es zwingend
logisch – quasi von selbst – zu entstehen schien.«[44]

Diese Magie, mit der Wachsmann seinen verblüfften Schülern
und einer verwirrenden Materialfülle am Ende des Seminars eine
konkrete Bauplanung entlockte, steht in einem gewissen Gegensatz
zum rationalistischen Anspruch seiner Methode. Manifestartig beschrieb er diese im Ausstellungskatalog von 1958: »Die Existenz der
Maschinen bestimmt das Bauen unserer Zeit. Die Maschine erlaubt
keine willkürliche, individuelle Entscheidung über irgendein Thema. Im Gegensatz zu einer handwerklichen Ausführung ist das industriell hergestellte Produkt Teil einer umfassenden Ordnung.«
Daran müsse sich auch eine zeitgemäße Architektenausbildung orientieren: »Der Studienplan basiert auf einer direkten Zusammenarbeit aller Beteiligten und der aktiven Mitarbeit an der Analyse
gestellter Probleme. So werden Resultate erzielt, die nicht mehr auf
Begabung und Talent oder Anpassung an die individuelle Hand-
schrift eines Meisters beruhen, sondern die objektive Sprache des
zeitgenössischen, organisatorisch technisch Möglichen sprechen
mit dem Ziel, unter Vermeidung vorgefasster Meinungen, das Bild
unserer Umwelt aus gegenwärtigen Bedingungen herauszuformen.«
Eine gründliche Reform der Ausbildung von Planern fordere letztlich sogar die Abschaffung des Architekturentwurfs als zentrales
Lehrfach: »Während der Studien sollten die Aufgabenbereiche und
die Methodik der Entwicklung eines Problems als *Ersatz der Ent-
wurfslehre* in engster Zusammenarbeit mit Wissenschaft, Technik,
Industrie, Wirtschaft und Politik formuliert werden.«[45]

Im Ausstellungskatalog von 1958 druckte man auch Stichwor-
te *Zur Industrialisierung des Bauens* ab, die gesellschaftspolitische
Fragen stellen: »Die Maschine ist das Werkzeug unserer Zeit. Sie
ist Ursache jener Wirkungen, durch die sich die Gesellschaftsordnung manifestiert.« Wachsmann interpretiert hier allerdings die
Möglichkeiten der Industrie, die schon damals konsumentenorien-
tierte *Customization*-Strategien kannte, noch auf eine strikt mecha-
nistische Weise: »Den Bedingungen der Industrialisierung folgend,
durch Multiplikation von Zelle und Element, soll sich das Bauwerk
indirekt entwickeln.«

In diese Kerbe schlägt auch der 1957 in Paris geschriebene Katalogbeitrag des Schweizer Malers und Bildhauers Hugo Weber, mit dem Wachsmann am *Institute of Design* des IIT in Chicago zusammengearbeitet hatte. Weber hatte in der US-Emigration als Autor und Filmemacher mit Moholy-Nagy am *New Bauhaus Chicago* gelehrt, war eng mit Mies van der Rohe befreundet und modellierte 1961 eine Porträtbüste des berühmten Architekten. Wachsmanns Bemühungen um eine Ent-Individualisierung des Bauens fasst er plakativ zusammen: »Das Bauen ist belastet durch Gewohnheiten, Vorurteile, Berufsinteressen, wie kaum ein anderes Gebiet unserer Zivilisation. Die besten Möglichkeiten der maschinellen Technik dem Bauen zukommen zu lassen, verlangt prinzipielleres Denken und radikaleres Vorgehen. Die Arbeiten Konrad Wachsmanns stehen zur Diskussion als Gegenpol zu einer Architekturbewegung, die im plastischen Spiel: Kubus, Raum, Fassade, Dekoration, ihren Ausdruck findet. Der Mode steht die Konstante struktureller Wesentlichkeit entgegen. Eine neue Anonymität des Bauens auf technischer Grundlage ist das Ziel, die Erwartung und Hoffnung.«[46]

Wirkung in Österreich: neue Planungsmethoden, neue Berufsbilder

Die fast hundert Teilnehmer und zwei Teilnehmerinnen an den Salzburger Sommerkursen, die von einigen Architekten zweimal und von zwei Begeisterten[47] sogar dreimal besucht wurden, verarbeiteten die in zwei kurzen Monaten vermittelte Botschaft Wachsmanns auf sehr unterschiedliche Weise. Zwar musste das oben erwähnte »radikale Vorgehen« in der österreichischen Baurealität ebenso Illusion bleiben wie die Etablierung eines Forschungsinstituts zum industriellen Bauen, dessen Gründung einige der rund 20 österreichischen Wachsmannschüler erfolglos anstrebten.[48] Seit der Wiener Ausstellung und dem Katalog von 1958 sowie dem Erscheinen seiner programmatischen Schrift *Wendepunkt im Bauen* 1959[49] entfaltete sich in Österreich jedoch eine deutlich wahrnehmbare allgemeinere Wirkung Wachsmanns auf den Gebieten der Architekturtheorie und der Planungsmethodik.

Am konsequentesten implementierte Ottokar Uhl, der den Wachsmann-Kurs 1957 besuchte, die Vorstellung einer umfassenden Planbarkeit sämtlicher in das Bauen involvierter Prozesse. Unter den österreichischen Architekten kam er damit dem Avantgarde-Ideal der Wachsmann-Generation – rationelle Planung als Instrument gesellschaftlichen Wandels – am nächsten. Auch für Uhl machte »Technik« keineswegs vor den gesellschaftlichen Prozessen halt, sollte ihnen jedoch dienstbar gemacht werden – und nicht umgekehrt. Geprägt und aktiv im katholischen Milieu verstand er menschliche Bedürfnisse nicht als Ballast für »übergeordnete« technoide Planungsideen, sondern als Grundbedingung sozial orientierten Bauens. Andere als gemeinschaftsdienliche Funktionen des Bauens – von der Kirche bis zum sozialen Wohnbau – waren für ihn undenkbar. In einem Brückenschlag von materiellen zu immateriellen Kategorien definierte er so das Soziale als geeignetes Aktionsfeld von »Technik« im Allgemeinen und des rationellen Planens im Besonderen: Nutzerbedürfnisse sollten nun genauso wie die technisch-industriellen Voraussetzungen des Bauens als Parameter erfasst und systematisch in die Planung integriert werden. So entstanden Uhls Partizipationsmodelle, die individuelle Nutzerwünsche in ein rationelles Planungs- *und* Bausystem fügten. Umgesetzt in weitgehend industrialisierten, aber modular anpassbaren Bauweisen verschaffte er der Idee Wachsmanns im Begriff eines »prozesshaften Planens«[50] erstmals eine solide soziale Basis. Uhl realisierte diese Kombination aus partizipativer Planung und industrialisierter Bauweise erfolgreich in vielen Wohnbauten. Im Sakralbau nutzte er mit seinem Montagekirchensystem ab 1962 die Grundprinzipien der Wachsmann-Konstruktionen aus Stäben und Knoten konsequenter als die meisten anderen österreichischen Architekten.[51]

Im vielgestaltigen Œuvre von Hans Hollein, der schon am ersten Salzburger Kurs teilgenommen hatte, präsentieren sich mögliche Inspirationen davon facettenreich, da Wachsmann »die Dinge auf einer höheren Ebene als der einer allgemeinverbindlichen Modernität angegangen« ist.[52] Schon vor dem ersten Sommerakademie-Kurs zeigte Hollein 1956 in seinem Diplomarbeitsprojekt eines Weltausstellungspavillons in einem Fachwerkdach aus räumlich angeordneten Stäben seinen Kenntnisstand zeitgenössisch-avancierter Konstruktionen. Bald nach der Sommerakademie-Teilnahme studierte er 1958–59 am *Illinois Institute of Technology*, wo Wachsmann 1949–54 gelehrt hatte und Ludwig Mies van der Rohe gerade emeritierte. Aber schon 1959–60, während seiner Studienzeit an der *University of California, Berkeley*, arbeitete Hollein in einer organoid-archaisierenden Ausdrucksweise, die sichtlich auch den späten Surrealismus und die frühe Pop-Art rezipierte. Die Individualisierungsstrategien der postmodernen Konsumgesellschaft inspirierten ihn schließlich zur Entwicklung einer systematischen *Design Research*, die man im weitesten Sinne auch als Weiterentwicklung der forschenden Planungsstrategien Wachsmanns deuten könnte. Sichtbaren Ausdruck fand diese Arbeitsweise in der Ausstellung MAN transFORMS, die Hollein mit Lisa Taylor anlässlich der Eröffnung des *Cooper Hewitt Museum of Design* 1976 in New York konzipierte.

Als Assistent an Holleins *Institut für Design* an der *Hochschule für angewandte Kunst Wien* arbeitete an dieser Ausstellung auch Hermann Czech mit, der 1958 und 1959 die Sommerakademie-Kurse besucht und dort im zweiten Jahr als Assistent mitgewirkt hatte. Wie Ottokar Uhl und Hans Hollein interpretierte auch Czech die Lehre Wachsmanns eher grundsätzlich als auf einer formalen Ebene: Sie bestehe »darin, dass Planungsentscheidungen nicht auf ›Einfällen‹ beruhen könnten, sondern auf einem methodischen Weg erarbeitet werden müssten; und zwar unter anderem deshalb, weil jede dieser Entscheidungen im Maßstab der industriellen Produktion unbegrenzt vervielfältigbar sein musste. Wachsmanns Lehre war getragen vom Glauben an die Technologie der Vorfabrikation; aber dahinter stand die geistige Dimension der Planungsverantwortung und der architektonischen Qualität. Von den modularen Problemen der Vorfabrikation aus konnte Wachsmann die Augen für die Struktur einer gotischen Halle oder für die Ecklösung eines Renaissance-Palastes öffnen. In dieser Gedankenwelt steht die formale Vorstellung nicht am Anfang, sondern am Schluss des Entwurfsprozesses.«[53] Schon 1959 hatte Czech im Salzburger Kurs nach Wegen gesucht, modulare Bauprinzipien geistreich und in größter Freiheit zu interpretieren, indem er vorschlug, »die beiden zentralen Begriffe der modularen Addition – *Element* und *Verbindung* – gleichzusetzen, die Verbindung als Element zu betrachten, und damit den orthogonalen Raster verlassen zu können«[54].

Modulare und serielle Bauweisen in Österreich seit 1956

In der Baupraxis modularer Konstruktionsweisen mit industriell vorgefertigten Elementen fanden Wachsmanns Ideen in Österreich bei vielen Projekten seiner Sommerakademie-Schüler Gerhard Garstenauer, Johann Georg Gsteu, Franz Kiener, Friedrich Kurrent, Johannes Spalt und Gunther Wawrik breite Anwendung: Stahlkonstruktionen aus Stäben und Knoten, Betonfertigteile als Stützen und Träger, Wandsysteme aus Stahl- und Kunststoffpaneelen sowie eine grundsätzlich modulare Ordnung der Entwürfe waren jedoch in den 1960er Jahren – gespeist aus verschiedensten Quellen[55] – im Grunde schon zum Mainstream der internationalen Moderne avanciert. So bauten in Österreich bei weitem nicht nur Wachsmann-Schüler, auf die sich unsere Darstellung beschränken muss, eine konstruktive, leichte und modulare Moderne – stellvertretend sei hier nur auf die wegweisende Arbeit von Traude und Wolfgang Windbrechtinger sowie die Projekte von Josef Lackner verwiesen. In den Wunderjahren scheinbar unbegrenzten Wirtschaftswachstums repräsentierten diese Bauweisen einen unverwässerten Fortschrittsoptimismus wie kaum eine andere kulturelle Praxis. Zudem standen sie – wie die gleichzeitige Malerei des abstrakten Expressionismus, der man in vielen Ausstattungen dieser Bauten begegnen konnte – auch klar für eine westliche Orientierung der österreichischen Gesellschaft im Kalten Krieg. Mit Wachsmann konnte die konstruktive Moderne ja auf eine US-amerikanische Provenienz verweisen. Die zweite Wurzel – nämlich jene in der deutschen Architekturavantgarde der 1920er Jahre – passte hingegen gut in den frühen Wohlfahrtsstaat zunehmend sozialdemokratischer Prägung.

Die Bandbreite der Wachsmann-Rezeption in Österreich er-
streckt sich über mehrere Bauaufgaben, unter denen jedoch die
öffentlichen, und hier insbesondere jene der katholischen Kirche
dominierten. Diese steuerte damals einen bemerkenswerten Wachs-
tums- und Öffnungskurs mit zahlreichen innovativen Sakral- und
Gemeindebauten. Die Kirche hatte damals in Österreich nahezu als
einziger Bauherr den Willen und das Potential, avancierte zeitgenössische Architektur in großem Maßstab zu realisieren. Wie in diesem
Bereich modulare und vorgefertigte Konstruktionsweisen angewendet werden konnten, zeigt beispielhaft das *Kolleg St. Josef* in Salzburg-Aigen, das die Wachsmann-Schüler Friedrich Kurrent und
Johannes Spalt 1961–64 gemeinsam mit Wilhelm Holzbauer nach
dessen Rückkehr aus Amerika als Arbeitsgruppe 4 realisierten:
Auf Basis eines 2,5 × 2,5 m-Rasters wurde der 40 × 40 m messende
Wohn- und Sakralbau mit zentral gelegener Arena-Kapelle als modular strukturierter Stahlbau mit v-förmigen Dachträgern errichtet,
die in freier Untersicht auch den Innenraum prägen. Ein Besuch
Wachsmanns nach seiner Lehrtätigkeit in Salzburg brachte seinen
ehemaligen Schülern Anerkennung des Meisters für diesen Entwurf ein.[56]

Ähnliche Konzepte hatte die Arbeitsgruppe 4 schon 1958–61
gemeinsam mit Johann Georg Gsteu beim Projekt des *Seelsorgezen-
trums Steyr-Ennsleiten* verfolgt. Hier wurde die Wachsmann-Idee,
modulare Konstruktionen aus möglichst wenigen vorgefertigten
Elementen zu entwickeln, in Form von x-förmigen Betonstützen
eingelöst, die – gestapelt und verbunden mit großen Betonrahmen
– für die verschiedenen Funktionen der Kirche, des Gemeindezen-
trums und des Glockenturms zu verschiedenen Baukörper-Dimen-
sionen und -Proportionen rekombiniert werden konnten. Gsteu
realisierte zudem 1960–65 beim *Seelsorgezentrum Baumgartner
Spitz* in Wien eine ähnlich radikale Modulkonstruktion aus Beton
im Stützenraster von 1,80 m, die über auskragende Dachrippen einen beeindruckenden stützenfreien Innenraum in der kristallinen
Proportion von 1:1:1 bot.

Gerhard Garstenauer demonstrierte ab 1968 mit seinen Projekten für Bad Gastein, wie Wachsmann-Prinzipien im Tourismus
Anwendung finden können. Im *Kongresshaus* und im *Felsenbad* realisierte er große modulare Betonskelettkonstruktionen aus vorgefertigten Elementen. Das Dach des Kongresshauses wurde mit vier
großen Lichtkuppeln in geodätischer Konstruktion aus Stahlstäben
und -knoten versehen. Einige dieser Leichtkonstruktionen wurden
auch im lokalen Skigebiet – eingeflogen per Helikopter – als Liftsta-
tionen verwendet.[57]

Franz Kiener, der bereits den ersten Wachsmann-Kurs 1956
besucht hatte, zeigte schon im gleichen Jahr mit dem Entwurf seines eigenen bemerkenswerten Wohnhauses in Salzburg-Gneis die

Möglichkeiten auf, in kleinem privatem Maßstab aus vorgefertigten Elementen modular konzipierte Bauten zu realisieren.[58] Auch Gunther Wawrik hatte an der Premiere 1956 teilgenommen und realisierte gemeinsam mit seinem Partner Hans Puchhammer seit 1961 mit dem *Einfamilienhaus Markart* in Perchtoldsdorf, dem *Bürohaus Grothusen* in Wien sowie dem *Landesmuseum Eisenstadt* eine Reihe von strikt konstruktiven, auf modularen Konzepten und Vorfertigungselementen basierenden exemplarischen Entwürfen.

Die obgenannten Teilnehmer an den Salzburger Kursen und die angesprochenen Projekte illustrieren stellvertretend eine relativ breite Wachsmann-Rezeption im Österreich der 1960er Jahre, wobei diese Auswahl keine Vollständigkeit beanspruchen kann. Denn die fundamentale und systemische Natur der damals bereits weithin publizierten Wachsmann-Lehre[59] brachte es mit sich, dass sich in fast allen innovativen Architekturtheorien jener Zeit einige ihrer (auch von anderen Denkern bearbeitete) Elemente wiederfinden – sei es die Überzeugung von einer grundsätzlich modular-additiven Struktur des Bauens (im Gegensatz zu einer skulpturalen Auffassung), das Rationalisierungsideal der Moderne oder der allgemeine Zweifel an der Relevanz intuitiv-individueller Entwurfsstrategien im Industriezeitalter.

Perspektiven: Schaffen Architekten sich selbst ab?

Diese *rationalistische* Strömung der späten Moderne kann als eine Art Revival gesellschaftsreformerisch-idealistischer Ideologien der klassischen Moderne bezeichnet werden. Schon deshalb war sie keineswegs in allen Aspekten tatsächlich *rational*, etwa bezüglich der Effizienz der eingesetzten Mittel – die Performance bestimmter Wachsmann-Konstruktionen ließe sich durch »konventionelle« Bauweisen wohl mit geringerem Zeit- und Entwicklungsaufwand erreichen oder gar übertreffen. Das galt auch für das wichtigste Kriterium der Konsumgesellschaft, die ja zu Zeiten des Wachsmann-Revivals in den 1960er Jahren im Westen schon volle Fahrt aufgenommen hatte – nämlich die Individualisierung und Distinktion des Konsumenten auf allen Ebenen. Diese individuellen Identitätskonstruktionen konnten durch einen stetig ausdifferenzierten Mix an industriellen und handwerklichen, »modernen« und traditionellen Fertigangeboten der explodierenden Bau- und Einrichtungs-, Konsum- und Gebrauchsgüterindustrie mit wesentlich geringerem materiellen und intellektuellen Aufwand realisiert werden, als das mit Baukasten-Elementen je möglich wäre: Denn die Elemente von Systembauweisen können zwar durch Standardisierung unaufwändig hergestellt werden, erfordern aber in ihrer konkreten Anwendung stets eine zeitintensive Rekombination. Wachsmanns erneute Überlegungen zu basalen Standardisierungen, die ja eigentlich schon in der frühen Industrialisierung etabliert worden waren, kamen so gesehen um Jahrzehnte zu spät, griffen zu kurz und hatten jeden Anschluss an die technische und wirtschaftliche Realität der Konsumgesellschaft verloren.

Die glückliche und naive, im Wortsinn weltvergessene Phase der Wiederaufbau-Konsumgesellschaft währte jedoch nur kurz: Schon die erste Ressourcenkrise zu Beginn der 1970er Jahre zeigte klar ihre Grenzen auf. Nun wiederholte sich die (Architektur-)Geschichte einmal mehr: Wie schon in der ersten Industrialisierung des 19. Jahrhunderts reagierte der wissenschaftlich-technische Sektor viel rascher auf die neue Situation als der ästhetisch-kreative. Die grundlegenden Antriebskräfte der Industrialisierung sind die permanente Produktivitäts- und die davon ermöglichte Qualitätssteigerung. Sie widmeten sich nun vorrangig dem explodierenden Bedarf der Konsumgesellschaft an Informationsverarbeitung: Die wachsende Datenflut musste für eine effiziente maschinelle Verarbeitung wesentlich einfacher kodiert werden als das mit Sprache oder Bildern in der nicht-elektronischen Kommunikation der menschlichen Physis möglich ist – so griff man auf die schon in den 1930er Jahren von Claude Shannon erfundene binäre Datencodierung zurück. Als elektrische Schaltungen konnten diese Daten in Rechenmaschinen (Prozessoren) extrem schnell verarbeitet werden, die wiederum mit der Erfindung der Transistoren und der integrierten Schaltkreise seit den 1960er Jahren zu immer effizienteren Computern ausgebaut wurden.

Die von Nerdinger und anderen[60] vermutete Analogie von Industrialisierung und Digitalisierung würde für die seither entstandene Situation einen ernüchternden Befund ergeben: Wie schon beim *Crystal Palace* in London 1851, als der revolutionäre Bau aus vorgefertigten Eisen- und Glaselementen von keinem einzigen Fachmann als »Architektur« erkannt und der reale Baubetrieb stattdessen für ein weiteres halbes Jahrhundert aus historischen Materialien und Formen gestaltet wurde, begann gleichzeitig mit der Digitalisierung als mehr oder weniger bewusste Gegenreaktion die intensivste Blütezeit der postmodernen Architektur. Und so wie bei dem um 1920 bereits weit fortgeschrittenen Raffinement der Industrieproduktion, als die Architekturavantgarde endlich deren Potential erkannte, aber es mit ihrem Standardisierungsdogma bloß auf eine romantisierend-archaisierende, viel zu kurz gegriffene Weise interpretierte, nutzt die kreative Branche heute die Digitalisierung oft auf eine unkritische, rückwärtsgewandte und ästhetisierende Art.

Wachsmann hatte die pragmatische Natur der Industrie verkannt, die keineswegs nach technischer Perfektion strebt, sondern nur nach Produktivität im Sinne der effizienten Befriedigung einer Nachfrage – mit welchen Mitteln auch immer. Mit seinem ästhetisierenden Perfektionsdrang *über*forderte Wachsmann die Industrie, während er mit der übertriebenen Standardisierung ihre Anpassungsfähigkeit *unter*forderte – beides beispielhaft in der *General*

Panel Corporation. Ähnliches konstatiert heute Mario Carpo in seiner Analyse der aktuellen digitalen Planungspraktiken: Wegen dem verbreiteten Unverständnis heutiger Designer von der Natur der *Artificial Intelligence (AI),* die letztlich auf einer »neuen, post-wissenschaftlichen Logik« basiere, »we are likely to make a terrible mess of it, and of what remains of our own scientific logic at the same time«[61].

So wie einst Wachsmann und die Avantgarde seiner Zeit das komplexe System »Industrie« unter Missachtung des zugrunde lie-genden Referenzsystems »Markt« ästhetisierend auf »Standardisie-rung« und »Maschine« reduzierten, so nutzen wir heute laut Carpo die sturen Trial-and-Error-Methoden der *AI* auf eine irrational-handwerkliche, ja sogar vorindustrielle Weise: »today's computa-tional tools work like artisans, not like engineers«. So wie einst die Avantgarde an die gesellschaftliche Heilkraft des ästhetisch Stan-dardisierten und konstruktiv Schönen glaubte, so glauben wir heute wie im Mittelalter erneut an Magie, nämlich jene der digitalen Robotik: »[...] the magical virtue of computational trial and error. Making is a matter of feeling, not thinking: *just do it.* Does it break? Try again ... and again ... and again. Or even better, let the computer try them all (optimize). The idiotic stupor (literally) and ecstatic silence that are often the primary pedagogical tools in many of today's advanced computational studios rightly apprehend the incantatory appeal of the whole process: whether something works, or not, no one can or cares to tell why.«[62]

Neben der neuen, *AI*-getragenen Anti-Rationalität, die Carpo als zivilisatorische Gefahr beschreibt (»Why waste time to argue? Ask the crowds. Why waste time on a theory? Just try it and see if it works.«) stellen sich auch auf der praktischen Ebene zahlreiche kri-tische Fragen an die aktuelle *AI*-Euphorie in der Planungsbranche. In verschiedener Form begleiten sie schon seit jeher die Geschichte der Moderne. Dazu zählt der weltentrückte Ästhetizismus ebenso wie die Marktferne avantgardistischer Konzepte oder die (davon mitverursachte?) Marginalisierung des Architekten als potenter Umweltgestalter. All diesen Phänomenen liegt der generelle Spezia-lisierungsprozess der Evolution zugrunde. Seit Beginn der Neuzeit trieb er die Entwicklung eines Kunstbegriffs voran, der sich immer mehr auf reine Ästhetik spezialisierte und selbst neue gesellschaft-liche und technische Entwicklungen ausschließlich aus dieser Per-spektive betrachtete. Das hat legitime Gründe: Weil sich geordnete formale Strukturen in der Menschheitsgeschichte stets als Anzei-chen positiver Funktionalität und daher als evolutionär günstig er-wiesen, wurden sie als »schön« interpretiert.[63] So entfaltete der künstlerische Ästhetizismus als Idealisierung des Mensch-Gemach-ten, Human(istisch)en eine lange, sozial wirksame Tradition, die von der schönen Kathedrale über den perfekten Renaissance-Stadt-plan bis zur sinnstiftenden handwerklichen Schönheit der *Arts-and-Crafts*-Bewegungen reicht. Doch während dieser Entwicklung erodierte die Potenz des Schönen: Von der Gesamtkompetenz für jede Umweltgestaltung, die es als Gottesgabe noch im Mittelalter besaß, hat es sich heute als eines unter vielen Verkaufsargumenten spezialisiert.

Die logische Reaktion darauf wäre eine Ent-Spezialisierung der Architekten, die sich von der bloßen robotischen Produktion von Schönheit (in Form, Konstruktion und Produktion) emanzipieren und sich den letztlich politischen Fragen der Ressourcenverteilung zuwenden müssten. Der Mangel an Pragmatismus, der schon Wachsmanns konstruktiv-technoiden Ästhetizismus scheitern ließ, ist auch heute lebensbedrohlich für die gesellschaftliche Rolle der Architekten. Die baulichen Probleme der Welt sind nämlich keineswegs technisch-schönheitlicher Natur, sondern meist politisch-wirtschaftlicher. Für die basale Infrastruktur in Entwicklungsländern und die bauliche Anpassung entwickelter Länder an den Klimawandel stehen längst praktikable, effiziente und nachhaltige Hybridtechnologien zur Verfügung. Deren massenhafte Implementierung bedarf grundsätzlich genauso wenig der AI, wie es in den 1960er Jahren des perfekten industriell gefertigten Knotens bedurfte, um massenhaft akzeptablen und preiswerten Wohnbau zu schaffen. Wenn Architekten diese gesellschaftliche Verantwortung ablehnen und es bevorzugen, ihre Kreativität exklusiv in virtuelle Technologien zu investieren, dann ändert sich das Berufsbild fundamental. Architekten könnten letztlich durch IT-Experten ersetzt werden, die ja als eigentliche Spezialisten für die Entwicklung digitaler Tools ausgebildet sind.

1 Zur Analogie von Industrialisierung und Digitalisierung des Bauens vgl. Winfried Nerdinger, Rainer Barthel, Richard Junge, Roland Krippner und Frank Petzold (Hg.): *Wendepunk|te im Bauen. Von der seriellen zur digitalen Architektur*, München (Detail, Institut für internationale Architektur-Dokumentation) 2010.

2 Profilierte NS-Architekten wie Friedrich Tamms, Wilhelm Kreis und Herbert Rimpl prägten auch den Wiederaufbau kriegszerstörter deutscher Städte.

3 Friedrich Kurrent berichtet, dass der Salzburger Kunsthändler und Sommerakademie-Mitbegründer Friedrich Welz 1956 als Nachfolger für Hans Hofmann auf Spalts und Kurrents Vorschlag den deutschen Wiederaufbau-Pionier Egon Eiermann kontaktierte, der wiederum Wachsmann vorschlug, da dieser an der Technischen Hochschule in Karlsruhe »mir ohnehin nur meine Schüler verdirbt«. Diesen Vorschlag unterstützten Kurrent und Spalt, da sie kurz zuvor im Wiener Vortrag Wachsmanns vom 24.4.1956 dessen Planungs- und Ausbildungstheorien mit Begeisterung kennengelernt hatten (Gespräch mit dem Autor, 2.12.2017). – Dank an Friedrich Kurrent für zahlreiche weiterführende Informationen und Perspektivenkorrekturen.

4 Insgesamt nahmen rund 100 Architekten an den fünf Sommerakademiekursen 1956–60 teil, davon rund ein Viertel aus Österreich. Die publizierten Teilnehmerlisten

(Barbara Wally: *Die Ära Kokoschka. Internationale Sommerakademie für bildende Kunst Salzburg 1953–63*, Salzburg 1993, S. 191–198) sind jedoch unvollständig. Wachsmann wählte seine Schüler nicht nach Qualifikation aus, sondern streng in der Reihenfolge ihrer Anmeldung – die ersten 21 Kandidaten eines Jahrgangs durften teilnehmen (Auskunft von Hermann Czech, 18.4.2018). – Dank an Hermann Czech für zahlreiche weiterführende Informationen und Perspektivenkorrekturen.

5   Gerhard Garstenauers Erinnerungen zeigen, dass diese konträren Orientierungen der deutschen und österreichischen Moderne den jungen Architekten der 1950er Jahre klar bewusst waren: »Damals haben die Deutschen ihre besondere Beziehung zur Industrie zum Ausdruck gebracht, während die Österreicher ihren ›Nerv für das Handwerk‹ bewiesen haben (vgl. Max Eisler im Band *Österreichische Werkkultur*, 1916)«. – Gerhard Garstenauer: *Begegnung mit Konrad Wachsmann*, in: Ina Stegen (Hg.): *Das schönste Atelier der Welt. 25 Jahre Internationale Sommerakademie für bildende Kunst*, Salzburg 1978, S. 54.

6   Zur Begriffsbildung vgl. Sigfried Giedion: *Mechanization Takes Command. A Contribution to Anonymous History*, New York 1948 sowie Carlo Testa: *Die Industrialisierung des Bauens*, Zürich (Artemis) 1972. – Zur »Philosophie« Wachsmanns vgl. Barbara Dafft: *Autopoiesis. Die Genese des »Grape Vine Project« (1953) von Konrad Wachsmann*, Masterarbeit, ETH, Zürich 2009. – Zu den Parallelen in der Konkreten Kunst vgl. Richard Paul Lohse: *Normung als Strukturprinzip*, in: werk/œuvre 3/1974, S. 348–354.

7   Hermann Czech nennt als Beispiel für eine oberflächliche Wachsmann-Rezeption das ehemalige Casino und Café Winkler am Salzburger Mönchsberg von Cziharz-Lenk-Meixner, errichtet 1974 und 2002–04 ersetzt durch den Neubau des Museums der Moderne von Friedrich-Hoff-Zwink (Gespräch mit dem Autor, 18.4.2018).

8   Zur Konvergenz ästhetischer

und politischer Konzepte vgl. Boris Groys: *Gesamtkunstwerk Stalin*, München 1988. – Mit den ästhetischen Konsequenzen von Rationalisierung und Partizipation befasste sich auch der Wachsmann-Schüler Ottokar Uhl: *Thesen zu einer Aneignung einer eigenen Gestaltungskultur (Ästhetik) für Betroffene*, in: Ders.: *Gegen-Sätze. Architektur als Dialog. Ausgewählte Texte aus vier Jahrzehnten*, Wien (Picus) 2003, S. 180–181. – Untersuchungen zur ästhetischen Dimension des Industrialisierungsideals im Allgemeinen und im Œuvre Wachsmanns im Besonderen stehen m. W. noch aus.

9   Gilbert Herbert: *The Dream of the Factory-Made House, Walter Gropius und Konrad Wachsmann*, Cambridge, MA (MIT) 1984, S. 67 ff.

10   Nicht einmal nach seinen Vor-Ort-Analysen der Weltausstellung in London 1851 und dem Erlebnis des Crystal Palace nahm Gottfried Semper, der führende deutsche Architekturtheoretiker des 19. Jahrhunderts, die Eisen-Glas-Konstruktion in seine fundamentalen Materialkategorien des Bauens auf.

11   Herbert 1984 (zit. Anm. 9), S. 12.

12   Ebd., S. 13 u. 89.

13   Konrad Wachsmann: *Einführung*, Manuskript für einen Ausstellungskatalog, Akademie der Künste, Berlin, Konrad-Wachsmann-Archiv. – Zum »Systemcharakter« der Industrialisierungs-Vision der Moderne vgl. Herbert 1984 (zit. Anm. 9), S. 7 ff. sowie Steeve Sabatto: *Totipotenz und Automation bei Konrad Wachsmann*, in: Laurent Stalder und Georg Vrachliotis: *Fritz Haller. Architekt und Forscher*, Zürich (gta Verlag) 2015, o. S.

14   Winfried Nerdinger: *Walter Gropius*, Ausstellungskatalog, Berlin (Gebrüder Mann) 1985, S. 12.

15   Ebd., S. 82–89.

16   Herbert 1984 (zit. Anm. 9).

17   Nerdinger 1985 (zit. Anm. 14), S. 19.

18   Ebd., S. 22.

19   Herbert 1984 (zit. Anm. 9), S. 106.

20   Josef Hoffmann baute für Heinrich Böhler Wohnhäuser um und vermittelte ihm Heinrich Tessenow als Planer seiner Villa in St. Moritz. Hans Böhler war ein wichtiger expressionistischer Maler der Secession und der Neukunstgruppe.

21   Eduard F. Sekler: *Josef Hoffmann. Das Werk des Architekten*, Salzburg (Residenz) 1982, S. 412. – *Standardhäuser – Die Häuslbauer*, Ausstellungskatalog, Architekturzentrum Wien, 1997.

22   Konrad Wachsmann: *Holzhausbau – Technik und Gestaltung*, Berlin (Wasmuth) 1930.

23   Überblick über Wachsmanns persönliches Netzwerk in Michael Grüning: *Der Architekt Konrad Wachsmann. Erinnerungen und Selbstauskünfte*, Wien (Löcker) 1986 (= *Der Wachsmann-Report*, Berlin, Verlag der Nation, 1986).

24   Ebd., S. 223.

25   Dietmar Strauch und Bärbel Högner: *Konrad Wachsmann. Stationen eines Architekten*, Berlin (Progris) 2013. – Claudia Klinkenbusch: *Das Konrad Wachsmann-Haus in Niesky. Ein Holzbau der Moderne*, Bautzen (Lusatia) 2014. – Steeve Sabatto: *Innovation technique et programmation technologique dans le contexte nord-américain de l'après seconde guerre mondiale et de la Guerre Froide. L'œuvre architecturale de Konrad Wachsmann (1942–72) comme étude de cas*, Dissertation, EHESS Centre Alexandre Koyré, Paris 2017. – Marianne Burkhalter und Christian Sumi (Hg.): *Konrad Wachsmann and the Grapevine Structure*, Zürich (Park Books) 2018.

26   Herbert 1984 (zit. Anm. 9), S. 299 ff.

27   »Nachdem man fabrikmäßig so viele Kanonen, Flugzeuge, Lastwagen, Eisenbahnwagen hergestellt hat, fragt man sich: Könnte man nicht auch Häuser fabrizieren?« – Le Corbusier: *Kommende Baukunst*, Berlin und Leipzig (DVA) 1926, S. 197.

28   Matthias Boeckl: *Villen in Los Angeles – Siedlungen in Puerto Rico*, in: Ders.: *Visionäre & Vertriebene. Österreichische Spuren in der modernen amerikanischen Architektur*, Berlin (Ernst & Sohn) 1995, S. 320 ff.

29   Solche Stipendien hatten u. a. auch die Studienaufenthalte von Hans Hollein und Wilhelm Holzbauer in den USA ermöglicht, die später zu Pionieren der postmodernen Architektur wurden.

30   Grüning 1986 (zit. Anm. 23), S. 549. – In der Erinnerung von Friedrich

Kurrent könnte bei diesem Seminar ein Kontakt zu Karl Schwanzer und damit zur *Zentralvereinigung der Architekten* entstanden sein, die Wachsmann schließlich auch nach Wien holte.

31 Kostenabrechnung vom 27.4.1956, Zl. 337–56, MAK, Wien.

32 *Konrad Wachsmann – Planung und Erziehung*, in: Der Bau 5-6/1956, S. 120–121.

33 Kurrent (zit. Anm. 3).

34 U.a. in: Gerhard Garstenauer: *Begegnung mit Konrad Wachsmann*, in: Stegen 1978 (zit. Anm. 5), S. 52–55. – Friedrich Kurrent: *Konrad Wachsmann*, in: Ders.: Texte zur Architektur, Salzburg (Müry) 2006, S. 194–199. – Bernhard Steger: *Das utopische Potential des Bauens. Konrad Wachsmann und die österreichische Nachkriegs-avantgarde*, in: Elisabeth Großegger und Sabine Müller (Hg.): *Teststrecke Kunst. Wiener Avantgarden nach 1945*, Wien (Sonderzahl) 2012, S. 250–259. – Marko Pogacnik: *Konrad Wachsmann and the Team-work Concept in Salzburg. A Conversation with Friedrich Kurrent and Hermann Czech*, in: Burkhalter und Sumi 2018 (zit. Anm. 25), S. 134–139.

35 Konrad Wachsmann: *Bauen in unserer Zeit*, Katalog zur Ausstellung, veranstaltet von der Internationalen Sommerakademie für bildende Kunst, Salzburg, und der Zentralver-einigung der Architekten, Galerie Würthle, Wien, 20.1.–22.2.1958.

36 *Teamarbeit an der Salzburger Som-merakademie*, in: Bauen + Wohnen 10/1960, S. 368–381.

37 Konrad Wachsmann: *Teamarbeit im Seminar*, in: Stegen 1978 (zit. Anm. 5), S. 48–51. – Seine Erin-nerungen auch in: Grüning 1986 (zit. Anm. 23), S. 549–51.

38 Friedrich Achleitner: *Vorbemerkung*, in: Grüning 1986 (zit. Anm. 23), S. 6.

39 Kurrent (zit. Anm. 3).

40 Pogacnik (zit. Anm. 34), S. 134.

41 Steger (zit. Anm. 34), S. 253.

42 Kurrent (zit. Anm. 3).

43 *Teamarbeit* (zit. Anm. 36).

44 Garstenauer (zit. Anm. 34), S. 53.

45 Wachsmann 1958 (zit. Anm. 35), S. 18–20, Hervorhebung Matthias Boeckl.

46 Hugo Weber: *Bau und Maschine*, in: Wachsmann 1958 (zit. Anm. 35), S. 9.

47 Andrew Rothe und Peter Schmid.

48 Kurrent (zit. Anm. 3).

49 Die Erstausgabe dieses Werks erschien im Krausskopf-Verlag, Wiesbaden.

50 Ottokar Uhl: *Prozesshaftes Planen* (1993 ff.), in: Bernhard Steger: *Vom Bauen. Zu Leben und Werk von Ottokar Uhl*, Dissertation, Techni-sche Universität Wien, 2005, S. 185 ff.

51 Uhl war auch Pionier der Verbreitung der aus Holland stammenden parti-zipativen SAR-Planungsmethode unter Voraussetzungen industrialisierten Bauens – daran knüpften jüngere Architekten wie Georg Reinberg an und praktizieren bis heute ihre Planungsstrategien für gesellschaft-liche und bautechnische Prozesse in diesem Sinne, vgl. Georg W. Reinberg, Matthias Boeckl (Hg.): *Reinberg. Ökologische Architektur. Entwurf – Planung – Ausführung*, Wien/New York (Springer) 2008, S. 10–16.

52 Zitiert nach Bernhard Steger (zit. Anm. 34), S. 255.

53 Hermann Czech: *Über Konrad Wachsmann, Karl Kraus und Adolf Loos*, Beitrag zur Ausstellung *ex libris*, Architekturforum Tirol (aut), Innsbruck 2002. – In Bezug auf die architekturhistorischen Interessen Wachsmanns weist Czech auf dessen Dokumentationen alter Bauten in einem Fotoband eigener Aufnahmen hin: Konrad Wachsmann: *Aspekte*, Wiesbaden (Krausskopf-Verlag) 1961.

54 Hermann Czech: *Architektur, von der Produktion her gedacht*, in: Hintergrund, Nr. 41, Architektur-zentrum Wien 2009, S. 25.

55 Dazu zählt auch Frei Otto, der – seinerseits von Mies van der Rohe und der US-Ingenieurtradi-tion geprägt – seit den 1950er Jahren leichte Flächentragwerke und modulare Konstruktionssys-teme realisierte.

56 Kurrent (zit. Anm. 3).

57 Gerhard Garstenauer: *Interven-tionen*, Salzburg (Pustet) 2002.

58 Ingrid Holzschuh (Hg.): *Franz Kiener. Eine Ordnung als Anfang*, Zürich (Park Books) 2016, S. 48–49.

59 Wachsmanns Bestseller *Wendepunkt im Bauen* war 1959 erschienen.

60 Nerdinger 2010 (zit. Anm. 1).

61 Mario Carpo: *The Second Digital Turn. Design Beyond Intelligence*, London/Cambridge, MA (MIT Press) 2017, S. 162.

62 Ebd., S. 164.

63 Zur evolutionären Funktion des Schönen vgl. Wolfgang Welsch: *Blickwechsel. Neue Wege der Ästhetik*, Stuttgart (Reclam) 2012.

WF   Lieber Eckhard, ich freue mich wie immer sehr, bei dir in Bregenz auf Besuch zu sein! Wie bereits am Telefon besprochen, haben wir heute die Aufgabe, über Person und Werk von Konrad Wachsmann und deine persönliche Verbindung zu ihm zu sprechen. Wie bist du auf ihn gestoßen, was hat dich an ihm fasziniert und angezogen?

ES-F   Kenntnis von Wachsmann nahm ich von der ersten deutschsprachigen Publikation des Hangars in Baukunst und Werkform.[1]

WF   Wann war diese Publikation?

ES-F   Daran kann ich mich nicht mehr genau erinnern, es muss Mitte der 50er Jahre gewesen sein. Zu dieser Zeit kam Wachsmann auch für einige Tage nach Aachen zu einem Symposion. Ich habe damals gemeinsam mit meinen Partnern Altenstadt und Rudloff an den Plänen zum Landeshaus in Köln[2] gearbeitet, ein Projekt, das in der Tradition von Mies stand. Kurz nach dessen Fertigstellung ist unser Team zerbrochen, was mir die Möglichkeit gab, mich intensiver mit strukturellen Fragen zu beschäftigen. Diese Neuorientierung hat mich schlussendlich zur Raumstadt gebracht.

WF   Wann hast du begonnen, an der Raumstadt zu arbeiten?

ES-F   Schon 1958 würde ich sagen. Meine Ideen zu Raumstrukturen konnte ich nicht in das Team einbringen. Ich hatte das Gefühl, das ist meine Sache.

WF   Wie ging es nach der Trennung des Teams weiter?

ES-F   Ich habe mich, wenn man so will, an die Arbeit mit den Raumstrukturen gewöhnt und viel theoretisch gearbeitet, was natürlich kein Geld einbrachte (*lacht*). Mit dem Bau des Landeshauses hatten wir zum Glück keine wirtschaftliche Flaute.

WF   Gab es zum damaligen Zeitpunkt Vorbilder, die für dich wichtig waren?

ES-F   Die erste Figur, die mich interessiert hat und mit der ich mich auseinandergesetzt habe, war Mies van der Rohe. Ganz ähnlich wie bei Wachsmann bin ich auf ihn auch durch eine Publikation aufmerksam geworden, konkret der auf einem strikten Flächenraster basierende Masterplan für den *IIT*-Campus in Chicago.

WF   Wie steht Mies im Verhältnis zu Wachsmann, was deine Arbeiten mit den Raumstrukturen betrifft?

ES-F   Nun, Wachsmanns Hangar schlug damals ein wie eine Bombe. Wachsmann hat ja dann auch lange in Österreich gewirkt, an der Sommerakademie in Salzburg.[3]

WF   Was hat dich am Hangar angesprochen?

ES-F   Diese exemplarische Vorfertigung, die einen gewissen universellen Anspruch hat, auch wenn ich heute noch der Meinung bin, dass der Hangar dafür ein zu kleines Thema war. Ich entsinne mich noch genau, dass ich zuerst anhand der Modellfotos die Geschosshöhe vom Hangar rausgemessen habe, die etwa drei Meter beträgt. Ich dachte mir dann, da kann man alles Mögliche reinpacken!

Eckhard Schulze-Fielitz im Gespräch mit Wolfgang Fiel

Bregenz, 13. März 2018

Eckhard Schulze-Fielitz, Wolfgang Fiel; Abb.: 79–83

WF   Also dich hat nicht nur die Struktur und dessen universeller Vorfertigungsanspruch, sondern auch die Frage interessiert, wie man sie füllen kann?

ES-F   Genau, das war und ist bis heute eine kardinale Frage für mich!

WF   Wir können davon ausgehen, dass sich Wachsmann diese Frage nicht gestellt hat. Das Tragwerk sollte einen möglichst großen Raum stützenfrei, elegant und so effizient wie möglich überdachen.

ES-F   Das habe ich ihm auch damals bei aller Hochachtung vorgeworfen, dass er all die potenziellen Nutzräume in seiner Struktur ungenutzt lässt. Dafür hätte es eigentlich andere Möglichkeiten gegeben, Pneus oder was weiß ich.

WF   Kannst du den Aspekt der Nutzräume im Verhältnis zur Struktur näher erläutern?

ES-F   Mich hat damals ähnlich wie Yona[4] die Struktur als raumbildender Rahmen interessiert, den wir von der bestehenden städtischen Bebauung abgekoppelt und damit Nutzräume geschaffen haben, die sich gewissermaßen als zusätzlicher Layer über die bestehende Topografie legen. Yona hat diese Topografie meist städtisch interpretiert, was in meinem Fall nicht notwendigerweise der Fall war. Was Wachsmann mit dem Hangar vorgeschlagen hat, war – wie du schon gesagt hast – die Schaffung eines möglichst großen stützenfreien Raumes unter der Struktur, die in seinem Fall die Funktion eines Daches übernommen hat.

WF   Warum denkst du hat er sich den Hangar für die exemplarische Entwicklung eines räumlichen Tragwerks vorgenommen?

ES-F   Nun, es gab einen Auftrag der US Air Force. Wie er den gekriegt hat, entzieht sich meiner Kenntnis. Kurz vor seiner Publikation[5] kam er zurück von einer Weltreise, die er auf Kosten der Air Force gemacht und während der er überall auf der Welt Vorträge gehalten hatte. Er war ein brillanter Erzähler, des Wortes mächtig. Seine Vorträge waren mit tollen Fotos gespickt, die er auf seinen Reisen gemacht hat. Mit Seitenhieben auf die Konkurrenz hat er nicht gespart. Ich kann mich beispielsweise erinnern, dass er über Le Corbusiers Ronchamp gesagt hat, die Welt nicht mehr zu verstehen.

WF   Das ist umso erstaunlicher, da Wachsmann selber eine kurze Zeit lang in Le Corbusiers Büro gearbeitet und in ihm grundsätzlich einen Mitstreiter bei der Propagierung industriellen Bauens gesehen hat. Sind deiner Erinnerung nach in diesen Vorträgen auch Kollegen genannt worden, die ihm Vorbild waren? Buckminster Fuller würde mir spontan einfallen.

ES-F   Er war wohl eher egoman veranlagt (lacht), obwohl er mit Walter Gropius zusammen ein Fertighaus entwickelt hat, das auf mich allerdings keinen nachhaltigen Eindruck machte.[6] Für mich waren vielmehr die Bezüge zur Raumstadt wichtig, die auf der Hand lagen.

WF   Hast du mit Friedman über diese Bezüge geredet, hat er sich mit Wachsmann beschäftigt?

ES-F   Ich kann mich nicht entsinnen, dass sich Friedman auf Wachsmann bezogen oder sich mit ihm beschäftigt hätte. Es war ja damals nicht so, dass alles, was in den USA entstanden ist, in Europa sofort verbreitet und rezipiert wurde.

WF   Hattest du irgendwann das Bedürfnis, dich mit Wachsmann persönlich auszutauschen oder ihn kennen zu lernen?

ES-F   Nun, das ergab sich einfach so! Ende der 50er Jahre wurde von der Stadt Essen die sogenannte Deutsche Bauausstellung[7] geplant, bei der es auch einen Kongress geben sollte. Weil ich damals aufgrund des Landeshauses, der Raumstadt und der Kirche in Eller, die sich damals im Bau befand, schon ein gewisses Renommee hatte, wurde ich gefragt, wen man einladen könnte. Auf meiner Liste standen aber nicht Heroen wie Mies oder Le Corbusier, sondern zum großen Teil jüngere und zum damaligen Zeitpunkt in Deutschland noch wenig bekannte Namen wie Frei Otto, Buckminster Fuller, Yona Friedman, der damals überhaupt nicht bekannt war, Kenzo Tange oder eben Konrad Wachsmann.[8] Friedman hat irgendwann später geschrieben, dass die Stadt Essen die Leute angeschrieben hat und alle sind gekommen. Das war ein hervorragender Kongress aus meiner Sicht.

WF   Und als derjenige, der die Liste zusammengestellt hat, hast du alle persönlich kennengelernt?

ES-F   Jedenfalls sind alle nach Essen gekommen. Es war sehr interessant, die damals am Horizont auftauchenden Großen neben sich zu erleben!

WF   Du hast auf dieser *DEUBAU* ja auch einen eigenen Pavillon errichtet, den die Teilnehmer des Kongresses auch gesehen haben, wie ich annehme. Hast du unmittelbare Reaktionen darauf bekommen?

ES-F   Den müssen sie gesehen haben, der stand ja mitten auf dem Gelände.[9] Er hat auf die Leute mehr Eindruck gemacht als auf mich. Ich hatte nicht das Gefühl, dass die Besucher bemerkt haben, dass es sich eigentlich um ein expansionsfähiges und daher unfertiges Gebilde handelte. Dass es darin noch eine Ausstellung gab, war damals für mich nebensächlich.

WF   Hast du mit Wachsmann über deine Raumstadt gesprochen?

ES-F   Ja, nach dem Kongress. Wir haben einige Tassen Kaffee zusammen getrunken und er hat im Prinzip positiv auf die Raumstadt reagiert, ich denke auch deshalb, weil meine ersten Überlegungen dazu noch stärker von strukturellen Fragen und weniger von der möglichen Nutzung bestimmt waren.

WF   Deine spätere Entwicklung war ja vor allem von der Auseinandersetzung mit urbanen Fragen geprägt.

ES-F   Genau. Dieses Interesse hat es bei Wachsmann meiner Einschätzung nach nicht so gegeben.

WF   Was für ihn vielleicht auch einer der Gründe war, die Möglichkeit der Ausfüllung nicht in Erwägung zu ziehen.

ES-F   Ja, das habe ich ihm auch vorgeworfen, dass er diesen kleinen weiteren Schritt nicht getan hat.

WF   Hat er die technischen und ingenieurmäßigen Lösungen alleine entwickelt oder dafür im Team mit Spezialisten gearbeitet?

ES-F   Ich weiß, dass er brillante japanische Zeichner im Büro hatte. Darüber hinaus hat ihm seine Lehrtätigkeit an der UCLA sicherlich wertvolle Kontakte zu Kollegen und talentierten Studenten eingebracht. Was mich an Wachsmann immer fasziniert hat, war die suggestive Kraft seiner Darstellungen. Auch der Umstand, dass er quasi mit einem Knoten das ganze Ding gelöst hat, ist sehr beeindruckend! Schuldgefühle hatte ich ihm gegenüber trotzdem keine.

WF   Wie meinst du das, Eckhard? Wollte er dich zum Komplizen machen und du hast nein gesagt?

ES-F   Da ich meine Raumstadt Ende der 50er Jahre zu entwickeln begonnen habe, bestand durchaus die Gefahr, in den Geruch des Plagiats zu geraten. Es gab zwischen unseren Ansätzen aber wesentliche Unterschiede. Ich habe ja mein Modell der Raumstadt so konzipiert, dass sich das Raumgitter in vier verschiedene Positionen drehen lässt, die ich als *alpha-, beta-, gamma-* und *delta-Position* bezeichnet habe. Nach meiner Definition ist der Hangar auf Basis eines Quadratprismas in *alpha*, also eine Tetraeder-Oktaeder-Packung einzuordnen,[10] weshalb ich ihn immer als potenzielle Raumstadt gesehen habe.

WF   Hat diese Sichtweise damit zu tun, dass sich im Gegensatz zum ersten Raumstadtmodell die späteren konkreten Anwendungsbeispiele intensiver mit der Frage der Umsetzbarkeit beschäftigt haben?

ES-F   Durchaus, wenngleich ich auch in dieser Hinsicht von der unglaublich detaillierten Ausarbeitung der Wachsmann'schen Entwürfe extrem angetan war, die mir damals das Gefühl gaben, das auch Architektur eine Manifestation des technischen Fortschritts sein kann. Obwohl Wachsmann eigentlich nicht viel gebaut hat, hat er nie einen Zweifel daran gelassen, dass ihm die Umsetzung oder Realisierung seiner Projekte sehr wichtig war. Da es auch mir nicht gelungen ist, meine Raumstadt umzusetzen, habe ich Wachsmann in diesem Sinn immer als einen Seelenverwandten gesehen, der Zeit seines Lebens nicht aufgehört hat, den technologischen Fortschritt im Bauen zu propagieren und mit hohen formalen Ansprüchen zu verbinden.

WF   Ich finde, das ist ein wunderbares Schlusswort und Ansporn für die kommende Generation. Lieber Eckhard, ich bedanke mich ganz herzlich für das aufschlussreiche Gespräch!

ES-F   Sehr gerne (*lacht*).

1   *Hangar für die us Air Force*,
     publiziert in Baukunst und Werk-
     form, 1954. Siehe auch *Hans Ulrich*
     Obrist and Wolfgang Fiel in
     conversation with Eckhard Schulze-
     Fielitz, in Wolfgang Fiel (Hg.):
     Eckhard Schulze-Fielitz: Meta-
     sprache des Raums/Metalanguage
     of Space, Wien/New York (Springer)
     2010, S. 408.
2   Landeshaus Köln (1955–59), Eckhard
     Schulze-Fielitz mit Ulrich von
     Altenstadt und Ernst von Rudloff.
3   Meisterklasse Wachsmann von
     1956–60.
4   Yona Friedman und Eckhard
     Schulze-Fielitz verbindet seit ihrer
     ersten Begegnung 1959 eine
     enge Freundschaft, die mit einem
     gemeinsamen Entwurf für eine
     Brückenstadt über den Ärmelkanal
     (1963) auch architektonisch Aus-
     druck fand. Diese spezielle Verbin-
     dung würdigend, hat das Kunsthaus
     Bregenz 2011 eine von Wolfgang
     Fiel und Eva Birkenstock kuratierte
     dialogische Präsentation ihrer
     Arbeiten gezeigt.
5   Konrad Wachsmann: *Wendepunkt*
     im Bauen, Wiesbaden (Krausskopf-
     Verlag) 1959.
6   *General Panel Corporation*, in:
     Konrad Wachsmann: *Timebridge,*
     Konrad Wachsmann: An Autobio-
     graphy (1981). Unveröffentlichte
     Autobiografie, AdK, Konrad-
     Wachsmann-Archiv, Wachsmann
     2128, S. 158 ff.
7   *DEUBAU 62*, Deutsche Bauausstel-
     lung in Essen. Die Generalthemen
     des Kongresses lauteten »Archi-
     tektur und Städtebau. Standortbe-
     stimmung und Zielsetzung« sowie
     »Gestaltung und Technik moderner
     Raumstrukturen«. Außerdem
     wurde auf Kernschauen u. a. auf
     die Bereiche Städtebau, Wohnungs-
     bau, Raumstrukturen und Schulbau
     eingegangen.
8   Neben Eckhard Schulze-Fielitz
     haben Felix Candela, Yona Friedman,
     Richard Buckminster Fuller,
     Z. S. Makowski, Ernst May, Frei Otto,
     Hans Bernhard Reichow, Zygmunt
     Stanislaw, Kenzo Tange und Konrad
     Wachsmann Vorträge gehalten.
9   *DEUBAU Pavillon, Essen*, in: Fiel 2010
     (zit. Anm. 1), S. 110 f.
10   *Metaeder*, in: Ebd., S. 358–395.

»Während meines Aufenthalts in Los Angeles im Frühjahr 1963 erzählte ich dem Präsidenten der USC und allen Beteiligten meine Idee, ein Bauinstitut zu schaffen. Ich erhielt ihr Einverständnis sowie ihr Versprechen, eine solche Institution zu unterstützen. Sie boten mir das gegenüber vom Campus gelegene Armory Building an, direkt oberhalb des Space Museum.

Ein Jahr später wurde die Einrichtung eines Bauinstituts, mit der im Herbst 1964 begonnen werden sollte, durch die Leitung der USC und die Fakultät für Architektur genehmigt.«[1]

Die oben zitierte Darstellung der Ereignisse findet man in Wachsmanns unveröffentlichter Autobiografie *Timebridge 1901– 2001*, an der er ab Mitte der 1970er Jahre bis zu seinem Tod im Jahre 1980 in unregelmäßigen Abständen schrieb. Wie dies oft der Fall ist, war die tatsächliche Sachlage jedoch weitaus komplexer.

Vor Wachsmann übersiedelte dessen früherer Kollege in Chicago, Crombie Taylor, nach Los Angeles. Dieser war 1962 als stellvertretender Dekan der *USC School of Architecture* eingesetzt worden. Taylor, der zwischen 1951 und 1954 nach Serge Chermayeffs Rücktritt als amtierender Leiter des *Institute of Design* tätig war, kam mit dem Auftrag an die *USC*, die »graduate education programs« (an einen ersten Hochschulabschluss anschließende Studienprogramme; Anm. d. Übers.) der Schule zu erweitern.[2] Eine der ersten Handlungen Taylors als stellvertretender Dekan bestand in Wachsmanns Ernennung zum Professor und Leiter der *Division of Building Research* an der Fakultät; ab Herbst 1964 unterrichtete der deutsche Architekt an der *USC*.

Anders als aus den Schilderungen des Architekten hervorgeht, gab es jedoch bis Mai 1968, als Wachsmanns Vorschlag für das »Bauinstitut an der USC« vom Dekan für Architektur Sam T. Hurst und dem damaligen Vizepräsidenten für akademische Angelegenheiten Dr. Milton Kloetzel angenommen wurde, kein »Bauinstitut« an der *USC*.[3] Vielmehr war Wachsmann 1964 zuerst mit der Leitung der »Building Research Division« betraut worden. Dabei handelte es sich um einen Vorgänger-Fachbereich des Bauinstituts, aber eine dennoch völlig anders geartete Einrichtung. Tatsächlich hatte Wachsmann schon vor seiner Ankunft auf dem Campus damit begonnen, Pläne für etwas weitaus Ambitionierteres als nur eine Abteilung für Graduate-Studienprogramme an der Schule für Architektur zu schmieden.

Wachsmann hatte bereits 1963 in Italien mit der Planung des späteren Bauinstituts begonnen, bevor er von Crombie Taylor an die Fakultät der *USC* berufen wurde.[4] Mehrere Jahre zuvor hatten die beiden einander in Chicago kennengelernt, als sie dort an der kurzzeitig als *New Bauhaus* bezeichneten Fakultät des *Institute of Design* tätig waren. Zu diesem Zeitpunkt arbeitete Wachsmann gerade an seinem berühmten Hangar für die *US Air Force*. Zehn

Bauwissenschaften: Konrad Wachsmanns Bauinstitut an der University of Southern California (USC), 1964–74

Phillip Denny; Abb.: 84–92

Jahre später war Wachsmann nun als nicht mehr ganz junger
Architekt in Genua mit einem letztendlich zum Scheitern verur-
teilten Projekt zur Sanierung des Stadthafens beschäftigt. Ohne
lang zu zögern, brach er nach Los Angeles auf.[5]

An der USC ordnete Taylor die Neukonzeption der von der
Schule angebotenen *Graduate*-Programme an. Aus diesem Grund
widmete sich Wachsmann ein Jahr lang der Studie eines möglichen
Lehrplans. Diese Vorarbeit wurde aus Mitteln der Stiftung *Graham
Foundation* finanziert und umfasste eine Reihe von im Jahre 1964
veröffentlichten Diagrammen. Die von Wachsmann vorgeschlagene
Lösung war ein Bauinstitut, ein Forschungszentrum, das es Studierenden mit einem ersten Hochschulabschluss ermöglichen sollte,
unter der Leitung der Fakultät und mit dem Ziel, den Titel *Master of Building Science* zu erwerben, gemeinsam finanzierte Forschungsarbeit zu leisten.[6]

Am Institut wurde gewissermaßen ein Modell für staatlich ge-
förderte Forschungsarbeit nachgebildet, das Wachsmann zehn Jahre zuvor am *Institute of Design* entwickelt hatte. In Chicago hatte
ein mit der Regierung abgeschlossener Vertrag zur Herstellung eines vorgefertigten Bausystems für Flugzeughangars Wachsmann
und mehreren Studierenden im Verlauf von fünf Jahren die Entwicklung von aus Stahlrohren zusammengesetzten Raumfachwerk-
strukturen ermöglicht. Wenngleich aus diesem ersten Einstieg in
den Bereich der staatlich geförderten Forschung im akademischen
Kontext einige der bekanntesten Arbeiten Wachsmanns hervorgin-
gen, war diese Arbeit nicht ganz unproblematisch.

Kurze Zeit nach Wachsmanns Berufung an die Fakultät des
Institute of Design im Januar 1950 – er wurde mit der Leitung eines
»Fachbereichs für fortgeschrittene Bauforschung und -gestaltung«
beauftragt – entbrannte ein Konflikt mit dem Institutsleiter Serge
Chermayeff. Nach Erhalt des Forschungsvertrags mit der *US Air
Force* schlug Wachsmann vor, Studierende am *Institute of Design*
mit einem ersten Hochschulabschluss gegen Bezahlung und auch
Anrechnung ihrer Arbeit für das Studium zur Mithilfe bei den
Arbeiten anzuwerben. Chermayeff lehnte den Vorschlag ab mit der
Begründung, dass dieser unlauteren Berufswettbewerb darstelle.
In einem Brief an den Dekan des *Illinois Institute of Technology*
äußerte Chermayeff seine Bedenken, dass »durch die kostengünsti-
ge Ausführung von Arbeiten, die als Entwicklung eines Privat-
projekts eines einzelnen Unterrichtenden interpretiert werden
könnten, durch studentische Hilfskräfte, ein sehr gefährlicher Prä-
zedenzfall für eine Schule gesetzt« werde.[7]

Zugleich gab es einen Briefwechsel zwischen Chermayeff
und Bauhausgründer Walter Gropius, einem glühenden Verfechter
des sogenannten *New Bauhaus* in Chicago. In seiner Beschreibung
Wachsmanns, eines engen Freundes und ehemaligen Mitarbeiters

in der *General Panel Corporation* (von Gropius und Wachsmann gegründete erste vollautomatische Fabrik zur Produktion vorfabrizierter Bauelemente, Anm. d. Übers.), nahm sich Gropius kein Blatt vor den Mund: »Wachsmann ist mir mit all seinem Charme als solch egozentrischer Mann bekannt, dass er meines Erachtens nicht als Lehrer tätig sein sollte; seine egoistischen Ambitionen werden in Gemeinschaft mit anderen stets eine sprengstoffartige Wirkung entfalten. [...] Ich habe Wachsmann direkt angeschrieben und ihn ersucht zurückzutreten.«[8] Wachsmann befolgte den Rat seines berühmten Mentors und legte sein Amt am 15. Mai 1951 nieder. Dies bedeutete jedoch nicht für Wachsmann das Ende, sondern für Chermayeff, der nur wenige Wochen später zurücktrat.[9] Bald darauf kam Wachsmann zurück an die Fakultät und wurde unter dem amtierenden Dekan des *Institute of Design* Crombie Taylor mit einem befristeten verlängerbaren Vertrag eingestellt. Wachsmanns Posten in Chicago war an den Zugang zu Forschungsgeldern, vor allem an den bis 1955 laufenden Vertrag mit der *US Air Force*, gebunden. Am 31. März 1955 erhielt er sein Kündigungsschreiben.[10]

Das Bauinstitut an der *USC* stützte sich später auch auf gesponserte Forschung, doch das Finden von Sponsoren erwies sich zunächst als problematisch. Wachsmanns Berufung erfolgte zwar im Jahre 1964, doch erst drei Jahre später – im Jahre 1967 – erhielt das Institut sein erstes gefördertes Forschungsstipendium. Unterdessen unternahm das Institut technische Studien im Rahmen von Wachsmanns architektonischer Praxis, die dann bei der Gestaltung eines Rathauses für California City zum Einsatz kamen. Obwohl dieses Projekt das Institut und dessen Forscher unterstützte, bildete es nur einen kleinen Aspekt der erklärten Mission der Einrichtung, die darin bestand, ein »Zentrum für Studium, Forschung, Entwicklung und mit allen Aspekten der Industrialisierung und deren Auswirkung auf Planung und Architektur verbundenen Information zu sein«[11].

Der Gründer des Bauinstituts stellte sich dieses als Kern eines sich stetig erweiternden Netzwerks verwandter naturwissenschaftlicher und künstlerischer Disziplinen vor. In einer Mitteilung an den Universitätspräsidenten skizzierte Wachsmann sechs Grundbestandteile des Programms: Grundlagenforschung, angewandte Forschung, studentische Ausbildung, die Ausbildung Lehrender, ein Doktoratsstudium in Gebäudewissenschaften und ein Informationszentrum. Das Institut sollte als Sammelbecken für die Kompetenzen der Universität mit dem Ziel der Transformation der gebauten Umgebung fungieren. Tragweite und Auftrag der Einrichtung waren in einer Reihe von Diagrammen festgelegt worden, die Wachsmann bald nach seiner Ankunft in Kalifornien skizziert hatte. Der Gestaltung der Räumlichkeiten des Instituts sollte jedoch die Aufgabe zukommen, diese Konzepte in den konkreten Raum umzusetzen.

Als die Proteste gegen den Vietnam-Krieg auf dem Campus Ende der 1960er Jahre einen Höhepunkt erreichten, errichtete Wachsmann, der während des Zweiten Weltkriegs und danach für das US-
Militär gearbeitet hatte, das Institut am Rande des USC-Campus in
der ehemaligen Waffenkammer des 160. Infanterie-Regiments. Das
Gebäude wurde den Erfordernissen des Instituts gerecht: Mit der
riesigen Garnisonshalle im Zentrum des Gebäudes erhielten die Forscher ausreichend Platz für die Inszenierung von Prototypen und
Ausstellungen, und Bürotrakte auf beiden Seiten der Halle wurden
renoviert, um der Vision eines »interdisziplinären Forschungskör-
pers« des Instituts Raum zu geben. Die nachfolgenden Entwürfe
des Grundrisses des Instituts passten das Gebäude schrittweise an
die strukturelle Klarheit des institutionellen Diagramms an. Jeder
Raum wurde unter Berücksichtigung der wesentlichen Tätigkei-
ten des Instituts entwickelt. Beispielsweise sollte das »Laboratorium« dem Urheber zufolge eine Maschinenhalle für die Herstellung
von Forschungsprototypen sein und das »Informationszentrum«
sollte eine festverdrahtete Verbindung zum Zentralrechner der USC
sicherstellen sowie »jedes mögliche Kommunikationsmedium« mit
einschließen.

Das Herzstück des Instituts bildete jedoch der Konferenzraum.
Im Anschluss an die von Wachsmann in den 1950er Jahren ausge-
arbeiteten Seminarprotokolle wurden strukturierte Diskussionen
aufgezeichnet und für zukünftige Referenzzwecke in die Datenbank
des Instituts eingegeben. Die Möglichkeit, Informationen zu erfassen sobald diese übertragen wurden, ermöglichte es dem Institut,
die Feedbackschleife durch Rückbezug auf sich selbst zu schließen
und Informationen zugunsten künftiger Forschungsarbeiten zu-
rückzugewinnen. Die soziale Funktion des Raums war in Wachsmanns Lehrplandiagrammen genau vorgesehen. Diese enthalten
einen Sitzplan für die Entfaltung eines optimalen Gedankenaustau-
sches zwischen den einzelnen Teams. Wie die anderen Räume des
Bauinstituts sollte der Konferenzraum die Produktion und Infor-
mationsübertragung begünstigen. Ob dies in Form von Modellen,
Zeichnungen, Vorlesungen, Fotografien, Filmen oder Prototypen
zum Ausdruck kam – das Hauptanliegen des Instituts galt der Verbreitung von Informationen.

Die Erhöhung der Anzahl der in das Netzwerk des Instituts
eingebundenen Produktionsknoten war eine Strategie zur Erhöhung des Ansehens der Forschung. Sowohl Bauhausgründer Walter
Gropius als auch Designtheoretiker Horst Rittel besuchten das
Institut und Buckminster Fuller kam bei Besuchen in Los Angeles
während der Entwicklung des *World Game* in den späten 1960er
Jahren häufig vorbei. Auch Ludwig Mies van der Rohe stattete dem
Institut einen Besuch ab und Wachsmanns Erinnerung zufolge
musste der gesundheitlich angeschlagene Meister mit Hilfe eines

Gabelstaplers in der Halle der Waffenkammer in das Obergeschoss
zum Institut befördert werden.[12] Von 1966–71 war auch Fritz Haller
ein Mitarbeiter des Instituts. Er entwickelte Gitterstrukturen, die
seine späteren Entwürfe für Gebäudesysteme vorwegnahmen.

Das einzige Projekt, dessen Realisierung nachweislich in vol-
lem Umfang durch das Institut erfolgte, war jedoch der *Location
Orientation Manipulator, l.o.m.*, ein von den beiden Doktoranden
John Bollinger und Xavier Mendoza entworfener Roboterarm. Die
Apparatur sollte der Untersuchung der »Kinematik vorgefertigter
Gebäude« dienen, d.h. der Manipulation von Objekten im Raum.
Der *l.o.m.* wurde durch einen Zuschuss des holzverarbeitenden Unternehmens *Weyerhaeuser* über eine Laufzeit von drei Jahren finan-
ziert und markierte den endgültigen Einstieg des Instituts in die
»Grundlagenforschung«. Dieser von Vannevar Bush im Jahr 1945
als »ohne ein Nachdenken über praktische Ziele durchgeführte«
Untersuchung definierte Arbeitsansatz brachte keine Lösungen
hervor, sondern »Allgemeinwissen und ein Verständnis der Natur
und ihrer Gesetze«[13]. Während die Untersuchung von Struktur-
systemen für das Rathaus von California City im Kontext eines
Architekturprojektes entwickelt wurde, hatte die *l.o.m.*-Apparatur
keine so unmittelbaren Anwendungsmöglichkeiten. Vielmehr war
die Entwicklung dieser Apparatur zwecks Untersuchung von Bau-
themen die eigentliche Forschungsagenda.

Tatsächlich hatte der *l.o.m.* außerhalb des Instituts keinen
sinnvollen Zweck. Die Apparatur war nicht genügend ausgereift,
um von der Bauindustrie aufgegriffen zu werden, und somit konnte
sie von den Sponsoren nicht für die Produktion eingesetzt werden.
Letztendlich wurde die imposante Apparatur demontiert, verpackt
und ging verloren. Zwischen 1967 und 1971 erwies sich der *l.o.m.*
jedoch als unschätzbar nützlich für die am Institut Mitwirkenden.
Für Wachsmann bot die Apparatur die *Daseinsberechtigung* des Instituts, ein hochkarätiges Projekt, das den Fortbestand seiner Einrichtung rechtfertigte. Die Sponsoren sahen darin eine Gelegenheit,
an einer angesehenen Universität eine Allianz zwischen ihrem Unternehmen und dem neuesten Stand der Forschung im Bereich der
Bauwissenschaft zu bilden. Für die Doktoranden Bollinger und
Mendoza war die Apparatur im Hinblick auf ihre Doktortitel nützlich. All diesen Zwecken gemeinsam war allerdings die Fähigkeit
der Apparatur, bestechende Bilder zu liefern.

Ob er nun auf Fotos im Werbematerial des Unternehmens *Weyerhaeuser*, in Bollingers und Mendozas gemeinsamer Dissertation
oder im Rahmen von Wachsmanns Lichtbildvorträgen erschien – der
l.o.m. war ein Objekt von ausgeprägter ästhetischer Präsenz und
hatte eine größere Ähnlichkeit mit László Moholy-Nagys *Licht-
Raum-Modulator* als mit einer Versuchsapparatur. Dem *l.o.m.* als
Objekt, das zwar über eine beachtliche ästhetische Qualität verfügte,

jedoch von geringem Wert für weitere Forschungen oder die praktische Anwendung war, ist die Verkörperung des zentralen Para-
doxons des Instituts zu bescheinigen. Als Wachsmanns Forschungsagenda einen zunehmend theoretisch-spekulativen Charakter an-
nahm, verringerte sich sowohl für staatliche als auch gewerbliche
Sponsoren gleichermaßen der Nutzen seiner Forschung.

Nach Abschluss des *L.O.M.*-Projekts im Jahre 1971 kämpfte das
Institut unentwegt für die Rechtfertigung seiner Existenz als Standort für experimentelle Arbeit in den Bereichen Bauwissenschaft
und Technologie. Das Institut hatte sich in Konflikt mit der vorherrschenden Dynamik der Forschungsökonomie des Kalten Krieges
gebracht. Durch die Vermeidung der angewandten Forschung konnte das Institut zunächst keine überzeugenden Argumente liefern,
um Unternehmen als Sponsoren für neue Projekte zu gewinnen. In
zweiter Hinsicht distanzierte sich Wachsmann angesichts seines
»hypothesefreien« Ethos von öffentlichen Finanzierungsquellen für
wissenschaftliche Forschungsarbeiten. Auf die Frage, welcher Nutzen aus der Durchführung von Projekten wie dem *L.O.M.* gewonnen
werden könne, erwiderte Wachsmann: »[...] Meine Antwort lautete
stets, dass ich es nicht weiß. Aber diese Antwort gab ich jedes Mal,
wenn ich mich mit einer Aufgabe befasste. Wenn mir die Lösung
oder der Zweck bekannt wären, würde ich gar nicht beginnen.«[14]

Im Jahre 1974 wurde das Bauinstitut wegen mangelnder Finanzierung geschlossen. Zuvor hatte Wachsmann jedoch ein auf die
Standardisierung der Wissensgenerierung ausgerichtetes Unter-
richtssystem entwickelt und eine Schule zur Umsetzung desselben
errichtet. Im Zusammenhang mit der lebenslangen Beschäftigung
mit der Industrialisierung des Architekten stellt das Institut Wachsmanns ehrgeizigste Anregung für eine Angleichung der Architektur
an die Wissenschaft und die Industrie dar. Der Umstand, dass sich
diese Zusammenführung auf dem Gelände einer Schule ereignete,
stand sowohl mit dem Programm des Bauhauses als auch mit der
von Präsident Eisenhower 1961 als »militärischer-industrieller-aka-
demischer Komplex« bezeichneten aufkommenden Transformation
der Universität im Einklang.

Verglichen mit anderen Einrichtungen für Bauwissenschaft aus
dieser Zeit ist das Bauinstitut ein Ausnahmefall. Es ist insofern ungewöhnlich, als es den Anliegen der Forschungsökonomie nicht zu
entsprechen vermochte, zugleich aber dem Modell der wissenschaftlichen Forschungslaboratorien an der Universität nachgebildet war.
Vielmehr strebte das Institut die Schaffung eines pädagogischen
Systems an, dessen Parallelfunktionen als didaktisches Umfeld und
Versuchslaboratorium koproduktiv sein sollten. Ob dies nun im Konferenzraum oder im Laboratorium stattfand – als Produkt gespon-
serter Forschung sollten neue Informationen generiert, erfasst und
profitabel eingesetzt werden. Die Studierenden sollten zu Teilneh-

mern an dieser zirkulären Erzeugung wertvollen Wissens werden und ihr akademisches Laboratorium wurde dabei zum Produkt des Institutes.

Wachsmanns unbeirrbarer Glaube an den Wert der Gestaltung entsprach jedoch nicht dem evaluativen Kalkül seiner intendierten Sponsoren. Dennoch deuteten Wachsmanns systematische Transformation der pädagogischen Aktivitäten in einen ökonomisch produktiven Prozess in die Richtung, die die gebäudewissenschaftlichen Laboratorien und die akademische Wissenschaft im Allgemeinen nach den 1970er Jahren einschlagen sollten. Wie im Falle des Bauinstituts und anderer Universitätslaboratorien organisierte der konkrete Raum die – materiellen und personellen – Ressourcen der Universität, um verkaufsfähige Forschung zu produzieren. In dieser Hinsicht wurde das Institut genau zu jenem kritischen historischen Zeitpunkt errichtet, der den Übergang von industriellen Produktionsformen zur postindustriellen Wissensökonomie kennzeichnet. Während die von Wachsmann in seiner frühen Karriere unternommenen Anstrengungen, vorgefertigte Gebäudesysteme zu entwickeln, nach einer Einbeziehung der Architektur in die Industrie zielten, unternahm das Bauinstitut den Versuch, die *Architektur an sich* als ein durch wissenschaftliche Arbeit konstruiertes technologisches Produkt neu zu konstituieren.

1   Konrad Wachsmann: *Timebridge, Konrad Wachsmann: An Autobiography* (1981). Unveröffentlichte Autobiografie. Akademie der Künste, Berlin [kurz: AdK], Konrad-Wachsmann-Archiv, Wachsmann 2128, S. 260.
2   Taylor hat sich während seiner Amtszeit von 1962–1985 um die Erhöhung des Ansehens der Schule verdient gemacht. James Lytle: *Crombie Taylor, Architect-Historian, Dies at 85*, USC News, 30. August 1999.
3   Konrad Wachsmann: *Memo to Dr. Milton C. Kloetzel, Proposal to Authorize the Creation of a Building Institute, May 22, 1968*, in: *Crombie Taylor Papers*, Ryerson and Burnham Libraries des Art Institute of Chicago. Box 5, Serie 19, Mitteilungen, Wachsmann USC.
4   Die erste Skizze des Grundrisses des »Department of Building Research« ist mit »KW« signiert und datiert mit »Genova«, Italien. AdK, Konrad-Wachsmann-Archiv, Wachsmann 350.
5   Im Allgemeinen wurden die biografischen Details aus Wachsmanns Leben aus der im Archiv der Akademie der Künste in Berlin aufbewahrten unveröffentlichten Autobiografie *Timebridge 1901–2001* des Architekten zusammengefügt. In den meisten Fällen wurden die biografischen Details und Daten vom Autor durch die Einfügung anderer Materialien und wissenschaftlicher Veröffentlichungen verifiziert. Beispielsweise wird diese Beschreibung von Wachsmanns Umzug nach Los Angeles durch den Briefwechsel zwischen Crombie Taylor und Konrad Wachsmann aus dem Jahre 1963 bestätigt.
6   Nachdem die ersten Studierenden das Curriculum für das Masterstudium absolviert, sich jedoch zu einem Verbleib an Wachsmanns Forschungsinstitut entschlossen hatten, kam später der Titel »Doctor of Building Science« hinzu. Die ersten Promotionsausschüsse wurden 1967 auf Ad-hoc-Basis gegründet und die Verleihung des ersten Titels erfolgte im Jahre 1969. Siehe

Konrad Wachsmann: *Memo,
Subject: Doctoral Program*, in:
Crombie Taylor Papers, Ryerson and
Burnham Libraries des Art Institute
of Chicago, Box 5, Serie 19, Mittei-
lungen Wachsmann usc.

7   Serge Chermayeff: *Letter to Dean
William A. Lewis, Illinois Institute
of Technology, May 15, 1951*, Illinois
Institute of Technology Archives,
Institute of Design Records. Box 5,
Institute of Design – General
(1949–1970).

8   Siehe Walter Gropius: *Letter to
Serge Chermayeff, Director of the
Institute of Design, May 21, 1951,
Confidential*, Illinois Institute of
Technology Archives, Institute
of Design Records. Box 5, Institute
of Design – General (1949–1970).

9   Chermayeff stand seit seiner
Berufung im Jahre 1946 unter dem
Druck, die finanzielle Schieflage des
Instituts zu korrigieren; es gelang
ihm nicht. Serge Chermayeff: *Letter
to Walter P. Paepcke, June 5,
1951*, Illinois Institute of Technology
Archives, Institute of Design
Records. Box 5, Institute of Design –
General (1949–1970).

10   J. T. Rettaliata: *Letter to Professor
Konrad Wachsmann, Institute
of Design, March 31, 1955*, Illinois
Institute of Technology Archives,
Institute of Design Records. Box 5,
Institute of Design – General
(1949–1970).

11   Wachsmann 1968 (zit. Anm. 3).

12   Interview mit John Bollinger,
Absolvent des Bauinstituts und
Inhaber des Doctor of Building
Science Degree, 1. Juli 2018.

13   Vannevar Bush war während des
Zweiten Weltkriegs Leiter des
us Office of Scientific Research and
Development. Vannevar Bush:
Science, the Endless Frontier,
Washington (United States
Government Printing Office) 1945.

14   Konrad Wachsmann: *The Future
is Everything*, in: Wachsmann 2128
(zit. Anm. 1), S. 341.

Ein Beitrag zu Huxley's *Brave New World*[1]: *Wendepunkt im Bauen*[2].

Die Bemühungen Konrad Wachmanns, neue Baumethoden zu entwickeln, die der modernen Technik entsprechen, sollen nicht unterschätzt werden. Zum größten Teil handelt es sich um weitgespannte Konstruktionen. Vom Stand dieser Arbeiten ist die Öffentlichkeit immer ausreichend unterrichtet worden, bis endlich ein zusammenfassendes Buch »Wendepunkt im Bauen« erschien und auch denen, die ein Seminar in Salzburg, Karlsruhe, Oslo oder Tokio nicht miterlebt haben, klar wurde – was übrigens nach den Publikationen bereits zu ahnen war –, daß man es hier mit einer Art baulicher »Religion« zu tun hat: Wir begegnen nicht nur dogmatischen Feststellungen, sondern auch der Prophezeiung (die trotz aller Beteuerungen eine »vorgefaßte Meinung« bedeutet!), daß der vorgeschlagene und beschrittene Weg der einzig richtige sei.

Dieses Dogmatische mit all seinen Merkmalen braucht keinesfalls negativ gewertet zu werden, es soll lediglich auf die Gefahren hingewiesen werden, die bei solcher Darbietung der Lehre aus einigen übertriebenen Formulierungen und falschen Folgerungen entstehen können.

Die Feststellung, »das empirische Wissen wurde durch die exakte Wissenschaft abgelöst«, scheint übertrieben. Da im Bauen die Mathematik angewandt wird, ist unter »exakt« selbstverständlich der mathematische Begriff zu verstehen. Die angewandte Mathematik ist aber approximativ. Mit ihr sind nur die idealisierten Modellfälle zu erfassen. Bei der Bemessung wird mit willkürlich festgelegten Werten gerechnet. Legt man weiterhin noch Wert auf diesen Satz, so kann er höchstens lauten: »Das empirische Wissen wurde durch die empirische Wissenschaft abgelöst.« Diese Ablösung geschah anscheinend, als »[...] Bedingungen, die nichts mehr mit den Ursachen bisheriger Wechselerscheinungen zu tun haben, einen Wendepunkt des Bauens auslösten«. Als dieser Wendepunkt soll, wie das auch Fred Hochstrasser, Ulm und Winterhur, in der Bauwelt 16/1960 bestätigt, das Jahr 1850 betrachtet werden, in dem Paxton den Kristallpalast erbaute. Ohne die Leistungen von Paxton zu schmälern, muß erwähnt werden, daß in England bereits Ende des 18. Jahrhunderts Brücken aus Gußeisen gebaut wurden.[3] Weiterhin müssen auch die Konstruktionen von J. B. Papworth (1821) und Rouhault (1833) sowie die erste Kabelbrücke von Marc Seguin über die Rhône bei Tournon (1824) erwähnt werden. So wird klar, daß man ebensowenig von einem Wende*punkt* sprechen kann wie beim Bauen vom Knoten*punkt* als dem zentralen Problem. Es kann nur von einer Entwicklungsperiode die Rede sein.

Nach der Ankündigung »einer generellen Zusammenfassung der Gegenwartsprobleme des Bauens« als einführende Arbeit, »in deren Folge dann vielleicht jene komplexen Probleme im einzelnen in weiteren Publikationen von Berufenen behandelt werden

Zwei Rezensionen – Konstruktionsspiele

Stefan Polónyi

Rezension *Wendepunkt im Bauen,* aus: *Bauwelt* Heft 29/1961

(Unkorrigiertes Transkript des Originaltextes)

könnten«, sind die Beispiele interessant, aber einseitig. Die Entwicklung der Stahlbetonkonstruktionen fehlt fast völlig, obwohl dieses Material im Bauen der letzten hundert Jahre eine nicht ganz unwesentliche Rolle gespielt hat.[4]

Wenig Trost geben die Bilder von dem großartigen Youtz-Lift-Slab-System, wenn auf den nächsten Seiten Zimmermannkonstruktionen aus Stahlbeton von Felix Samuely zu sehen sind. Zwar steht dabei eine Bemerkung, die auf die nicht ganz stoffgerechte Gestaltung hinweist, aber wozu dann dieses Beispiel?

Die Konstruktionen Wachsmanns sind bis zur Montage einer vollautomatischen Herstellung angepaßt, wobei noch Bedingungen erfüllt werden, die meist nur für militärische und schaustellerische Zwecke erforderlich sind, nämlich:

1. Kombinationsmöglichkeit,
2. Abbaumöglichkeit und Wiederverwendung in anderer Kombination,
3. Austauschbarkeit der Einzelelemente in gewissen Grenzen.

Dazu kommt, daß Wachsmann immer erst ein Skelett sucht und die statische Konstruktion von den raumbegrenzenden Flächen getrennt behandelt, im Gegensatz zu Buckminster Fuller, der bei seiner Leichtbaudomkonstruktion aus Aluminiumstandardelementen die Flächen in die Tragwirkung einbezieht. Daraus folgt, daß er auf kleine Grundelemente zurückgehen muß, daß die Anschlüsse (Knotenpunkte) sich unzählig vermehren und daß bei der Montage moderne Hilfsmittel meist nicht angewendet werden können.

So erscheinen die Wachsmannschen Konstruktionen eher als Rückschritt gegenüber den Paxtonschen: in London wurde 1850 mit Kränen montiert; bei Wachsmann laufen die Leute mit Rohren unter dem Arm und Knotenpunkten in der Tasche herum. Anscheinend fiel der Unterschied zwischen einer Montage auf der Baustelle und einer Montage am Band nicht auf. Es ist klar, daß Wachsmanns Grundbedingungen auch zu materialverschwenderischen Konstruktionen führen. Die Knotenpunkte beschränken die Auswahl der verwendbaren Rohre. Die Variationsmöglichkeit besteht meist lediglich in der Wandstärke und in der Anzahl. Schon bei Zugstäben ist die Anpassungsfähigkeit zu gering. Bei Druckstäben spielt auch die Knickung eine Rolle. Die Aneinanderreihung von unabhängigen Rohren verringert nicht die Knickzahl.

Rechenbeispiel:

A   Es soll 50 t Druckkraft aufgenommen werden bei einer
Stablänge von 3,00 m. Material: St 55.29, nach DIN gerechnet[5].

Erforderlich:	1 Rohr
Außendurchmesser:	191 mm
Wandstärke:	5,25 mm
Gewicht:	24 kg/m

B   Festlegung des Außendurchmessers

auf	89 mm
Erforderlich:	4 Rohre
Wandstärke je:	8 mm
Gewicht:	64 kg/m

Der Materialbedarf beträgt im Fall B das 2,67fache des normal
gerechneten Falles A.

Durch die bei den Knotenpunkten in einem Querschnitt angeordneten Schweißnähte entsteht ebenfalls ein Materialverlust, oder
es sind ein Spezialschweißverfahren und das Durchleuchten aller
Nähte erforderlich. Bei Rohren ist das schwer durchzuführen, besonders bei der Konstruktion für die amerikanische Luftwaffe, wo
auf der Baustelle geschweißt wird. Die bestehende »dynamische
Struktur« ist, von statischen Kenntnissen unbelastet, entwickelt
worden. Um einen Knotenpunkt, in dem viele Elemente zusammen-
treffen, zu vermeiden und das Skelett auf ein oder zwei Grundelemente zurückzuführen, sind die Anschlüsse nicht bei dem Stützen-
kopf, sondern im Feld bzw. in der Stützenmitte angeordnet. So entstand das dreischenklige Bumerangelement, das beträchtliche Bie-
gemomente aufnehmen muß, besonders wenn die Stützen auf den
einzelnen Etagen verschoben angeordnet sind. Eine Bemessung
würde bei dem skizzierten fünfetagigen Bauwerk zu einem erschüt-
ternden Ergebnis führen. Ein Teil der Anschlüsse muß biegesteif
ausgebildet werden. Alle diese komplizierten Knotenpunktprobleme
können vermieden werden, wenn man, statt nach einem Skelett zu
suchen, die Aufgabe anders formulieren würde: Es sind Flächen zu
schaffen, die die Räume trennen bzw. abschließen und gewisse statische und andere Bedingungen erfüllen. Die Frage wäre also: Wie
sind diese Flächen zu gestalten bzw. womit sind sie auszustatten,
damit die Bedingungen erfüllt werden? Dadurch gelangt man zu
Flächentragwerken, bei denen die Anschlüsse nicht in einzelnen
Punkten konzentriert, sondern an Linien verteilt sind.

Das Material für die »dynamische Struktur« soll später bestimmt werden. Die stoffgerechte Gestaltung wird durch die vorher
festgelegte Konstruktion gehemmt.

Es ist weiterhin charakteristisch, daß Wachsmann und seine Teams dieselben Konstruktionen oder Konstruktionsteile für grundverschiedene Zwecke und Beanspruchungen verwenden.

Dieser falsche konstruktivistische Formalismus wird durch Addition weitgespannte Konstruktionen schaffen, »wie sie vorher nie konzipiert werden konnten«, und entwickelt »nicht nur eine neue Ästhetik und eigene Sprache bisher unbekannter Schönheitsbegriffe«, »sondern darüber hinaus eine neue Ethik der Kunstanschauung überhaupt als Symbol einer neuen Epoche«.

Die Konstruktionen werden in Teamarbeit entworfen. Da es »nicht in der Absicht des Teamtrainings liegt, das Talent zu züchten«, ist es klar, daß in dem Team Leute vom Beta-Typ[1] arbeiten, die Maschinen werden von Gammas[1] angefertigt, die Montage führen Deltas[1] aus.

1   Aldous Huxley: *Brave New World*, 1932 u. 1949. Deutsche Ausgabe: *Schöne Neue Welt*, Fischer Verlag (Frankfurt a. M.) 1953, o. S.

2   Konrad Wachsmann: *Wendepunkt im Bauen*, Krausskopf-Verlag (Wiesbaden) 1959, o. S.

3   Eric de Maré: *The Bridges of Britain*, B. T. Batsford LTD (London) 1954, o. S.

4   Sigfried Giedion: *Space, Time and Architecture*, Oxford University Press (London) 1952, 9. Auflage, o. S.

5   Verein deutscher Eisenhüttenleute (Hg.): *Stahl im Hochbau*, Verlag Stahleisen mbH. (Düsseldorf) 1959, 12. Auflage, o. S.

Vorwort

Dank einer großzügigen Förderung, die mir die *University of Southern California* über die Initiative *Advancing Scholarship in the Humanities and Social Sciences* gewährte, konnte ich mich im Jahr 2009 einer Studie des Schaffens von Konrad Wachsmann widmen. Den Höhepunkt dieser Beschäftigung bildete die im August 2010 im *Los Angeles Forum for Architecture and Urban Design* gezeigte Ausstellung *Connection Points: Konrad Wachsmann Reconsidered*. Diese Schau umfasste analytische Zeichnungen, 3-D-Druckmodelle und Animationen. Schwerpunkt meiner Forschungsarbeit waren drei Projekte Wachsmanns: das *General Panel House* (1941–1949), der *US Air Force Hangar* (1951) und die *Study of a Dynamic Structure* (1953). Der folgende Text geht auf die während dieser Zeit durchgeführte Forschungsarbeit insbesondere zur *Study of a Dynamic Structure* zurück.

Study of a Dynamic Structure, 1953 →93–95

Die auch als »Grapevine Structure« (Weinstock-Struktur) bekannte *Study of a Dynamic Structure* blieb zwar im Vergleich zu Wachsmanns früherem Werk unbefriedigend gelöst, ist aber die erste Arbeit, in der Wachsmann den Begriff eines durchgängigen einzelnen Bauelements untersuchte, bzw. bestand das Problem – wie er es selbst ausdrückte – im Entwurf eines für jeden denkbaren Zweck einsetzbaren universellen Strukturelements.[1] Diese Suche nach dem »universellen« Einsatz von Bauteilen sollte einen Großteil seiner beruflichen Laufbahn in Anspruch nehmen. Mit dem Projekt *Study of a Dynamic Structure* zeigt sich aber ein anderer Ansatz zu diesem Problem. Dem Knoten bzw. dem Verbindungsteil wird hier nicht in gleicher Weise Rechnung getragen. Tatsächlich wird der Knoten solcherart negiert, dass sich an der vermeintlichen Verbindungsstelle von Elementen faktisch ein Hohlraum befindet. Diese theoretische Struktur manifestiert sich dann im Verlauf einer Reihe von Linien, die einander nie berühren. Während Wachsmann Zeichnungen von einem Gehäusesystem vorlegte, das vermutlich die Herstellung von praxistauglichen Bodenplatten und Decken zuließ und die vertikalen Säulen ummantelte, gab dieses Projekt in seiner konzeptuellen Form seiner Forschung eine neue Richtung. Für einen Architekten, der den größten Teil seines beruflichen Werdegangs dem Versuch widmete, die Verbindung von Werkstoff- und Baukomponenten zu lösen, ist die Vorlage einer theoretischen Struktur, in der der Knoten faktisch vollkommen negiert wird, durchaus ungewöhnlich. Damit allerdings begann Wachsmann zu erforschen, wie ein repetitives Konstruktionssystem eine »dynamische« Form hervorbringen konnte, die sich jedoch »[...] bedingt durch Spannungszustände« verändern würde.[2]

Der Grundbaustein des Systems basiert auf einem kubusförmigen Modul mit einer Kantenlänge von ca. 3,7 m. Die geometrischen

Verbindungspunkte: Konrad Wachsmann — eine Neubetrachtung

John A. Enright; Abb.: 93–97

Prinzipien wurden von Wachsmann anhand einer Reihe von Zeichnungen schematisiert. Diese beginnen mit einem Doppelkreuz im Plan. Durch Rotationsvorgänge bildete sich ein Windrad heraus, aus dem acht balkenartige Teile entstanden, die durch einen kleineren, um 45 Grad gedrehten Kubus mit dem Zentrum des Moduls verbunden waren. Der zentrale Kubus bildete vier vertikale säulenartige Teile, die sich im Plan so aus dem 45°-Winkel drehen, dass sich oben ein orthogonales Verhältnis ergibt. Dieser zentrale gedrehte Kubus wurde weiter in sechzehn Quadrate auf jeder Seite aufgegliedert, und genau da vermittelte das System zwischen den sechzehn Balken des Windrads und den acht Säulen; vier nach oben und vier nach unten. Von entscheidender Bedeutung in diesem geometrischen Spiel ist der Diagonalschnitt durch den zentralen Kubus, basierend auf der Rotationsgeometrie, die zu dem Hohlraum führte. Das eigentümlichste Element der Geometrie ist die Negation des eigentlichen Verbindungsknotens und dessen Ersatz durch Baustoffe und Vektoren, die das Zentrum umgeben aber niemals erreichen. Das daraus entstehende »Element« ist dann eine Einheit, die zwei horizontale balkenartige Teile enthielt, die ein »V« bilden und mit der Basis des als »Querlenker« bezeichneten sich drehenden Vertikalelements verbunden waren. Das fertige Teil bestand aus acht zwischen der Horizontalen und der Vertikalen vermittelnden Querlenkern, die im Raum schweben und einander nie berühren. Wachsmanns Vorstellung zufolge umfasste dieses System ein Modul für einen generischen Gebäudetyp, dem ein Tragwerksraster in der Größe von 7,3 × 7,3 m zugrunde lag. Dies erforderte die Verbindung der paarweise zwischen den oberen und unteren Elementen und vermutlich zwischen und unterhalb der Bodenstruktur vermittelnden »v«-förmigen Querlenkerelemente mit einem anderen wiederkehrenden Strukturträger.[→96, 97]

Vor dem Hintergrund der Tatsache, dass die erstellten zweidimensionalen Diagramme auf einer bestimmten Ebene von unzureichender Genauigkeit waren bzw. eine Verzerrung in der planimetrischen und sektionalen Darstellung aufwiesen, erforderte die von uns vorgenommene Modellierung des Systems ein gewisses Maß an Interpretation. Ferner nahmen wir insofern die »Abwickelbarkeit« der daraus entstehenden verdrillten Flächen an, insofern man sich diese als ebene Flächen vorstellen konnte, die sich in die gewünschte Geometrie biegen ließen. Dies erforderte viel Herumexperimentieren und ständigen Rückbezug auf die Originaldiagramme. Unsere gedruckten physikalischen Modelle zeigen sowohl die primäre doppelpilzförmige Struktur, einen »Baum« der primären Lastaufzeichnung eines Teils des Systems, und ein größeres Systemmodell der Struktur. Festzuhalten ist, dass aufgrund der Tatsache, dass sich die nachgezeichneten Kraftlinien und die Elemente selbst tatsächlich nicht wie von Wachsmann konzipiert verbinden, die Hinzufügung kleiner Einsätze bzw. von »Schweißnähten« in den 3-D-Druck-modellen notwendig war, um das System zu Vorführungszwecken auszustellen.

In Wachsmanns Zeichnungen wurde auch die Basiseinheit verändert und ein ausgewogenes Verhältnis für die Struktur vorge-sehen. Durch die Verwendung der genau gleichen Elemente wird die durchgehende Vertikalität der Säulen negiert und stattdessen ein alternierender verschobener Verlauf der Vertikalelemente ge-schaffen. Dies zeigt, dass Wachsmann mit der Erforschung von Variation innerhalb des Systems begann, die gezielt ein anpassungs-fähiges Verhältnis zwischen sich verschiebenden Vertikalelementen erzeugen konnte. Diese von den pragmatischeren Zwängen seiner sonstigen Forschungsarbeit befreite theoretische Struktur, bei der es sich eher um ein Raumdiagramm als um eine ernsthaft ausgearbei-tete strukturelle Lösung handelte, machte es Wachsmann möglich, sich einen weitaus plastischeren und dynamischeren Ausdruck des Raumes vorzustellen.

Dieser neue Ansatz war möglicherweise eine Antwort auf die Kritik, dass der repetitive Charakter strukturbasierter Lösungen die poetischeren Aspekte der Architektur außer Acht lässt. Wie Itohan Osayimwese aufgezeigt hat, wurde Wachsmann von dem Kritiker Serge Chimayeff [sic] »[...] eine nur auf ein mythisches Uni-versalgelenk fokussierte kurzsichtige Suche nach der Panazee«[3] vorgehalten. In seiner Beschreibung des Projekts spielte Wachsmann nahezu eine defensive Haltung hoch:

»Nur auf der Basis einer oberflächlichen Einschätzung könnte man die Auffassung teilen, dass der technisch-wissenschaftliche An-satz, die konsequente Anwendung automatisch gesteuerter, indus-trieller Produktionsprozesse und die systematische modulare Koor-dination aller Konstruktionselemente, -teile und -produkte unwei-gerlich zu Monotonie bzw. – wie ich immer wieder zu hören erstaunt bin – zur völligen Auslöschung jedes geistigen und emotionalen Im-pulses führe. Neben vielen anderen gewährt die folgende struktu-relle Untersuchung einen Einblick in die Zukunft, die solche Metho-den tatsächlich ermöglichen können.«[4]

Wachsmanns Verweis auf die Zukunft ist angesichts der aktu-ellen Aspekte der geometrischen Komplexität des Systems treffend. Die von uns entwickelten digitalen Modelle erbringen den Nach-weis für die geometrische Genauigkeit und den Detailreichtum sei-ner Untersuchungsskizzen. Nach der Übertragung aus zwei Dimen-sionen in den dreidimensionalen Raum offenbart sich das Projekt dank der dynamischen Navigierbarkeit als ein noch interessanteres Konstrukt. Dieses Projekt kann in dem Sinne, dass das System von Kontinuität und Kraftlinien abhängig ist und unweigerlich eine vollkommene Negation »des Verbindungsgliedes« darstellt, als ge-bührender Abschluss von Wachsmanns Forschungen zu Knoten-

und Verbindungselementen angesehen werden. Andererseits ist es ebenso Ausgangspunkt für ein anderes Verständnis komplexer Strukturen. In diesem Sinne war Wachsmann möglicherweise seiner Zeit voraus, da es neue digitale Werkzeuge Architekten und Bauingenieuren ermöglichen, sich mit immer komplexeren Systemen auseinanderzusetzen.

Nachtrag

Im Juni 2018 hatte ich im Rahmen meines Besuchs der Architekturbiennale in Venedig (Italien) die Gelegenheit, Marianne Burkhalters und Christian Sumis Arbeit zu besichtigen und in die zugehörige Publikation *Konrad Wachsmann and The Grapevine Structure* Einsicht zu nehmen. Während jede neue Interpretation von Wachsmanns Schaffen zu begrüßen ist, unterscheiden sich unsere Auffassungen von der *Study of a Dynamic Structure* in Bezug auf die Herangehensweise jedoch in einigen Punkten, die es hervorzuheben gilt. Sowohl in den Zeichnungen als auch in der großformatigen Holzskulptur von Burkhalter und Sumi erfolgt eine übermäßige Vereinfachung der Basisgeometrie der Struktur auf gerade Linien sowie die Schaffung einander schneidender Teile, wo Wachsmann dies ursprünglich sicher nicht beabsichtigte. Dies mag zwar einem natürlichen Impuls zur Rationalisierung der Struktur entspringen, geht aber meines Erachtens an Wachsmanns Zielsetzung vorbei. Ich nehme an, dass die durch Wachsmann konzipierte Struktur faktisch eine Kritik an der Tyrannei des tektonischen Problems des Knotens darstellte. Die Nichtberücksichtigung der Verbindung an sich war sowohl das Anliegen als auch das Ergebnis der Untersuchung. Wie aus unserer Forschungsarbeit hervorgeht, ist die Struktur auch in entfaltbaren gekrümmten Flächen rationalisierbar. Daher ließe sich die Struktur tatsächlich aus Stahlplatten fertigen und in die Form der ebenen Flächen jedes Teils biegen, ohne dass die Querlenker grob geschnitten werden müssten. Letztendlich ist der Appell der *Study of a Dynamic Structure* an uns alle in der Hintergründigkeit der in ihr vorgebrachten Ideen enthalten. In diesem Sinne bleibt sie auch auf wunderbare Weise ungelöst.

1   Konrad Wachsmann: *The Turning Point of Building: Structure and Design.* Übersetzt von Thomas E. Burton, New York (Reinhold Pub. Corp.) 1961, S. 194.

2   Ebd.

3   Itohan Osayimwese: *Konrad Wachsmann: Prefab Pioneer*, in: Dwell Magazine, Februar 2009, S. 100.

4   Wachsmann 1961 (zit. Anm. 1).

Im ersten Teil seines Buchs *Wendepunkt im Bauen*[1] trifft Konrad Wachsmann die Feststellung, dass »Grundsätze, die sich von den bisher vorherrschenden grundlegend unterscheiden, eine vollständige Überarbeitung aller komplexen Fragestellungen erfordern, die nicht nur einzelne Instanzen oder Teile, sondern den gesamten Bausektor umfassen.« Zu seinen Lebzeiten eröffnete die Industrialisierung des Bauprozesses neue Möglichkeiten und verlangte daher nach neuen Wegen der Annäherung an die Tragwerksgestaltung.

Die Serienfertigung ermöglichte die Herstellung großer Mengen von Gleichteilen bei geringen Grenzkosten. Das nun zu lösende Problem bestand darin, Bauwerke und Bauteile so zu konzipieren, dass die Gestaltungsabsicht mit einer begrenzten Anzahl verschiedener Arten von Strukturelementen zum Ausdruck kommen konnte. Exemplarisch zeigt sich dies in Abb. 1b[→99], in der eines der Modelle des USAF-Hangars veranschaulicht wird. In dem Bauwerk kommen eine Strukturknotenart, eine Trägerlänge und ein konstruktives System in rhythmischer Wiederholung innerhalb einer dreidimensionalen modularen hierarchischen Organisationsstruktur zum Einsatz.[2] Die Wachsmanns Bauwerken eigene neue Qualität beruht auf der Quantität. In deutlichem Gegensatz dazu waren präindustrielle Bauwerke in der Tradition, in der Handwerkskunst und in der Intuition verwurzelt. Als Beispiel ist in Abb. 1a[→98] die *Old Walton Bridge* zu sehen. Diese weist zahlreiche unterschiedlich große lasttragende Elemente auf, die nicht seriell herstellbar, sondern für die stückweise erfolgende manuelle Fertigung und Montage vorgesehen sind. Aus der inhärenten Komplexität des Konstruktionsprinzips der *Old Walton Bridge* ergibt sich ein facettenreiches Erscheinungsbild, während die mögliche Bauwerksdimension dadurch allerdings auf ein für eine Truppe qualifizierter Zimmerer zu bewältigendes Ausmaß begrenzt wird.

Heute ist die Bauindustrie mit einem ähnlichen Paradigmenwechsel wie zu Lebzeiten Konrad Wachsmanns konfrontiert: Durch digitale Planungs- und Fertigungsmethoden wird die Herangehensweise an die Baukonstruktion grundlegend verändert. Das seit den 1970er Jahren existierende computergestützte Design (CAD; Computer-Aided Design) diente zunächst als Ersatz für die Zeichenbretter. Obwohl die CAD-Methodik jener zur Erstellung einer manuellen Zeichnung anfangs sehr ähnlich war, wurden Tinte und Papier aufgrund der von CAD gebotenen Genauigkeit und Flexibilität bei der Vervielfältigung von oder Änderungen an einer vorhandenen Zeichnung allmählich von dieser Technologie verdrängt. Damit CAD jedoch die Spielregeln auf dem Gebiet der digitalen Gestaltung ändern konnte, war ein weiterer Schritt erforderlich: das Aufkommen parametrischer Geometriewerkzeuge. Diese versetzten den Benutzer in die Lage, über Algorithmen Geometrie zu generieren. Mithilfe visueller Geometrie-Skripting-Umgebungen wie *Generative*

Parametrische Tragwerksgestaltung als Inspirationswerkzeug für ein Wiederaufgreifen des USAF-Hangars von Konrad Wachsmann

Clemens Preisinger,
Andrei Gheorghe,
Moritz Heimrath,
Adam Orlinski; Abb.: 98–138

Components[3] oder *Grasshopper*[4] können die Benutzer durch die Verbindung von auf einem Datenstrom Operationen ausführenden Funktionsbausteinen (siehe Abb. 2[→100]) eine beliebige Geometrie konzipieren. Dies hebt das Kommunikationsniveau zwischen Benutzer und Computer von den im traditionellen CAD-Ansatz verankerten *Point-and-Click*-Methoden auf eine sprachliche Ebene. Abb. 2[→100] zeigt beispielhaft eine gekrümmte Oberfläche, die einem unter der Figur abgebildeten visuellen Skript zugrunde liegt: Eingaberegler auf der linken Seite bestimmen die Steuerpunkte der Oberfläche. Die grauen Blöcke stellen zu einem gegebenen Zeitpunkt jeweils eine Operation für die Umsetzung der Eingabe auf der linken Seite in die sich rechts von der Definition ergebende endgültige Form dar.

Die Auswirkung des Skripting auf die Geometriegenerierung ist jener der Serienfertigung ähnlich: Die Erstellung der parametrischen Konfiguration für eine bestimmte Art von Geometrie oder geometrischer Vorstellung ist oft zeitintensiv und kompliziert. Einmal erarbeitet, kann eine Definition jedoch mehrfach und fast kostenfrei wiederverwendet werden.

Derzeit erfreut sich die auf dem CAD-Programm *Rhinoceros* basierende visuelle Skripting-Umgebung *Grasshopper* (*GH*)[5] in der Geometrie-Skripting-Community weit verbreiteter Beliebtheit. Dieser Erfolg ist zum Teil auf dessen offene Programmgestaltung zurückzuführen, die Drittentwicklern das Erstellen von Plug-ins ermöglicht, die die Fähigkeiten von *GH* verbessern.

Einer dieser Plug-ins ist *Karamba3D*[6]. Dieser ergänzt *GH* um Strukturanalysefunktionen. Bei *Karamba3D* handelt es sich um eines jener Werkzeuge, das Studierende der im Jahr 2017 an der *Universität für angewandte Kunst Wien* abgehaltenen Lehrveranstaltung »Advanced Structures« mit dem Ziel verwendeten, eine zeitgenössische Neuinterpretation der Arbeit Konrad Wachsmanns vorzunehmen. Abb. 3a[→101] zeigt eine *Grasshopper*-Definition, die zur Bestimmung der Dicke einer Schalenstruktur das Bild eines Blattes als Ausgangspunkt verwendet (siehe Abb. 3b[→102]). *Karamba3D* integriert sich nahtlos in *GH* und stellt Objekte wie Lasten, Stützen, finite Elemente, Querschnitte und Lösungsverfahren zur Verfügung, die eine Strukturmodellanalyse ausmachen.

Ein Merkmal, das *Karamba3D* von den traditionellen Strukturberechnungsprogrammen unterscheidet, ist dessen Interaktivität: Änderungen der Geometrie führen unmittelbar zu einer aktualisierten Strukturantwort. Dies scheint auf den ersten Blick von geringer Bedeutung zu sein, hat jedoch einen großen Einfluss auf das Verständnis von Ursache und Wirkung des Benutzers in Bezug auf die Struktur: Anstatt die Ergebnisse wie im Falle der traditionellen Finite-Elemente-Programme nur nacheinander zu erhalten, kann der Benutzer eine Vielzahl alternativer Geometrien durchblättern und dadurch eine Filmsequenz von Ergebnisbildern erstellen.

Karamba3D verfügt über Komponenten für die automatische Querschnittsgestaltung und Topologieoptimierung, die den Benutzer von Routinetätigkeiten entlasten. Als Teil des Ökosystems der *Grasshopper* Plug-ins ist *Karamba3D* mit anderen Werkzeugen wie Optimierungs-Engines kombinierbar, die mit jeder parametrischen Definition verbunden werden können, um eine Geometrie zu beliebigen Leistungskriterien hin zu entwickeln.

Im Rahmen des im Jahr 2017 an der *Universität für angewandte Kunst Wien* abgehaltenen Seminars »Advanced Structures« wurde vier Gruppen von Studierenden die Aufgabe gestellt, Konrad Wachsmanns USAF-Hangar-Entwurf zu analysieren und sich ihn neu vorzustellen.

Nach einer intensiven Literaturstudie zum Werk Konrad Wachsmanns verwendeten die Studierenden die Geometrie des USAF-Hangars als Ausgangspunkt für ihre Reise in das Gebiet der parametrischen Geometrie. Einige von ihnen begannen, mit Algorithmen zur Querschnittsoptimierung zu experimentieren: Auf Basis des von äußeren Lasten hervorgerufenen Kraftflusses wird jeder Strahlquerschnitt auf das absolute Minimum reduziert. Aus Abb. 4[→103] wird ersichtlich, wie ein solcher Algorithmus Strukturmuster hervorbringt, die auf Kraftkonzentrationen an den Auflagern reagieren.

Alle Gruppen von Studierenden experimentierten mit unterschiedlichen Parametrisierungsstrategien in Kombination mit der Finite-Elemente-Analyse. Dies führte oft zu höchst unregelmäßigen Strukturen wie in Abb. 5.[→104] Dabei kam ein Topologieoptimierungsverfahren auf Basis der Evolutionären Strukturoptimierung[7] zum Einsatz, um die strukturell ineffizienten Bestandteile einer anfangs dichten Geometrie auszusortieren.

Obwohl Struktur in der Klasse »Advanced Structural Design« eine wichtige Rolle spielt, liegt der Schwerpunkt auf dem Experimentieren und einer ganzheitlichen Betrachtung der Bauplanung. In dieser Hinsicht eignet sich die parametrische Gestaltung besonders gut für die Anpassung von Strukturgeometrien an verschiedene Anwendungsszenarien und Kontexte. Abb. 6[→105] und 7[→106] illustrieren, wie eine parametrische Definition ein bestimmtes Anwendungsprogramm unterstützt, indem zwei Haupt-Stützbereiche im Zentrum angesiedelt sind und die Decke an den gegenüberliegenden Eckpunkten den Boden berührt.

Im Laufe der Jahre hat sich die Klasse »Advanced Structural Design« als erfolgreiches Format erwiesen. Studierenden wird dabei die Möglichkeit einer Reflexion über Beispiele der klassischen modernen Architektur geboten, indem diese als Ausgangspunkte für ihre eigenen Gestaltungsvisionen herangezogen werden. Insofern eröffnete die schrittweise Einführung parametrischer Werkzeuge wie *Grasshopper* und *Karamba3D* neue Möglichkeiten.

Gerade für einen Bereich wie Tragwerksgestaltung, der von Architekturstudierenden manchmal als trocken und abstrakt betrachtet wird, ist eine motivierende und spielerische Herangehensweise an die Thematik wesentlich. In diesem Zusammenhang können parametrische Werkzeuge im Lehrplan der Architekturschulen eine wichtige Rolle spielen.

1   Konrad Wachsmann: *Wendepunkt im Bauen*, Stuttgart (Deutsche Verlags-Anstalt) 1989 (ND der in Wiesbaden im Krausskopf-Verlag erschienen Ausgabe von 1959), o. S.

2   Ebd.

3   Robert Aish: *SmartGeometry* Workshop ACADIA 2004, Konferenzbeitrag.

4   David Rutten: *Galapagos: On the Logic and Limitations of Generic Solvers*, in: Sonderausgabe der Zeitschrift Architectural Design: Brady Peters/Xavier De Kestelier:

    Computation Works: The Building of Algorithmic Thought, 83(2)/2013, S. 132–135.

5   Ebd., o. S.

6   Clemens Preisinger/Moritz Heimrath: *Karamba – A Toolkit for Parametric Structural Design*, in: Structural Engineering International, Bd. 24, 02/2014, S. 217–221.

7   Y. M. Xie, G. P. Steven: *A simple evolutionary procedure for structural optimization*, in: Computers & Structures, 49/1993, S. 885–896.

Biografien

GERALD BAST

Gerald Bast wurde 1955 geboren. Seit 2000 ist er Rektor der Universität für angewandte Kunst Wien. Nach dem Studium der Rechts- und Wirtschaftswissenschaften an der Universität Linz, wo er 1979 zum Doktor der Rechtswissenschaften promovierte, war er im Bundesministerium für Wissenschaft und Forschung und an der Ludwig Boltzmann Gesellschaft beschäftigt. Er ist Mitglied des Representative Board der European League of Institutes of the Arts und Herausgeber der Publikationsreihen »Edition Angewandte« und »ARIS – Art, Research, Innovation and Society«.

Als Rektor der Universität hat Gerald Bast einige neue Programme initiiert, die sich mit den Themen der Transdisziplinarität und der Wechselbeziehungen zwischen Kunst und Gesellschaft beschäftigen. Er gründete das Angewandte Innovation Lab mit Schwerpunkt auf der Rolle der Künste in innovativen Prozessen durch die Förderung der Kommunikation zwischen Kunst, Wissenschaft und Technologie, Wirtschaft und Politik.

Gerald Bast ist Herausgeber zahlreicher Publikationen zum Thema Universitätsrecht, Universitätsmanagement sowie Bildungs- und Kulturpolitik und hat an mehreren internationalen Institutionen Gastvorträge zur Rolle von Kunst, Kreativität, Innovation und höherer Bildung gehalten, unter anderem an der John Hopkins University Washington D.C., Columbia University New York, Tsing Hua University Beijing, Tongji University Shanghai, City University of Hong Kong, University of Auckland, Lalit Kala Akademi New Delhi, University of Porto, NTU Singapore, beim European Forum Alpbach und beim Europäischen Kulturforum in Brüssel.

KLAUS BOLLINGER

Klaus Bollinger studierte Bauingenieurwesen an der Technischen Universität Darmstadt und lehrte an der Universität Dortmund. Seit 1994 ist er Professor für Tragkonstruktion an der Universität für angewandte Kunst Wien und auch Dekan des Institutes seit 1999.

Im Jahr 1983 gründeten Klaus Bollinger und Manfred Grohmann das Ingenieurbüro Bollinger + Grohmann Ingenieure. Heute ist die Firma in zehn Städten und sieben Ländern mit rund 200 MitarbeiterInnen aktiv und bietet internationalen Bauherren und Projekten ein komplettes Leistungspaket, unter anderem Tragwerks- und Fassadenkonstruktion, Geometrie, Bauphysik und Brandschutz, an.

FLORIAN MEDICUS

Florian Medicus studierte Architektur an der Universität für angewandte Kunst Wien unter Wilhelm Holzbauer, Zvi Hecker und Zaha Hadid. Im Jahr 2002 nahm er an der Berlage Institute Master Class in Rotterdam unter Rem Koolhaas teil. Florian Medicus erhielt sein Diplom 2005 unter der Professur von Wolf D. Prix und der Angewandten. Im selben Jahr begann er das Fach Tragkonstruktion an der Universität für angewandte Kunst Wien gemeinsam mit Klaus Bollinger zu unterrichten. Weitere Lehrverpflichtungen zum Thema Architekturtheorie führten ihn zusammen mit Bart Lootsma an die Akademie der bildenden Künste Wien und die Leopold-Franzens-Universität Innsbruck sowie an die Internationale Sommerakademie für Bildende Kunst Salzburg, wo er Itsuko Hasegawa assistierte. Florian Medicus publiziert regelmäßig zum Thema Architektur, Urban Design und bildende Kunst und veranstaltete die Ausstellung New Frontiers mit Schwerpunkt »junger experimenteller Architektur« und »Zeichnen«, die auch in Bratislava, Berlin, Krems, Paris und Wien stattfand.

Er ist Mitherausgeber von Unbuildable Tatlin?! (Springer, 2012) und Endless Kiesler (Birkhäuser, 2015). Florian Medicus wohnt und arbeitet in Salzburg, Wien und München.

EVA-MARIA BARKHOFEN

Eva-Maria Barkhofen wurde 1956 in Essen geboren. Staatlich geprüfte Berufsreiterin; Studium der Kunstgeschichte, der Klassischen Archäologie und der Europäischen Ethnologie an der Westfälischen Wilhelms-Universität Münster;

Promotion 1990; 1990–91 Volontariat bei den Staatlichen Museen zu Berlin, Preußischer Kulturbesitz, 1991–94 Referentin für Inventarisation und Dokumentation am Brandenburgischen Landesamt für Denkmalpflege; 1994–2006 Leiterin der Architektursammlung an der Berlinischen Galerie, Landesmuseum für Moderne Kunst, Fotografie und Architektur; 2006–2020 Leiterin des Baukunstarchivs an der Akademie der Künste, Berlin. 1998–2019 Sprecherin der Föderation deutschsprachiger Architektursammlungen und seit 2014 von der Industrie- und Handelskammer öffentlich bestellte und vereidigte Sachverständige für architekturbezogene Kunst und Archivobjekte.

PARSA KHALILI

Parsa Khalili ist Architekt und Gründer von WAZEONE, einem Architekturbüro in Brooklyn. Zurzeit ist er Gastvortragender an der Princeton School of Architecture und hat bereits mit Elizabeth Diller, Richard Meier, Peter Eisenman und Coop Himmelb(l)au zusammengearbeitet. Er studierte an der École Nationale Supérieure d'Architecture de Versailles, University of Illinois at Urbana-Champaign sowie an der Yale School of Architecture. Khalili hat zahlreiche Preise für seine Gestaltungs- und Forschungsarbeiten gewonnen und vielfältige Publikationen verfasst. Seine Interessen gelten der Gestaltungskritik, nichtwestlichen Formen von Modernismus, visuellen und diagrammatischen Repräsentationen sowie neuen digitalen Medien.

MARK WIGLEY

Mark Wigley ist Professor für Architektur an der Columbia University. Als Historiker und Theoretiker untersucht er die Schnittstelle zwischen Architektur, Kunst, Philosophie, Kultur und Technologie. Er ist Autor von Büchern wie Derrida's Haunt: The Architecture of Deconstruction; White Walls, Designer Dresses: The Fashioning of Modern Architecture; Constant's New Babylon: The HyperArchitecture of Desire; Buckminster Fuller Inc. Architecture in the Age of Radio; Are We Human? Notes on an Archaeology of Design (zusammen

mit Beatriz Colomina) und Cutting Matta-Clark: The Anarchitecture Investigation. Seine aktuelle Ausstellung und Publikation ist Passing Through Architecture: The 10 Years of Gordon Matta-Clark, Shanghai, Power Station of Art, 2019.

ANGELA LAMMERT

Angela Lammert ist Leiterin interdisziplinärer Sonderprojekte an der Akademie der Künste, Berlin und PD am Institut für Kunst- und Bildgeschichte der Humboldt-Universität zu Berlin. Sie veröffentlichte und kuratierte zahlreiche Publikationen und Ausstellungen zur Kunst des 19. bis 21. Jahrhunderts: u. a. »Filme ausstellen«, in: Display und Dispositiv. Ästhetische Ordnungen (München, 2018), Bildung und Bildlichkeit von Notation. Von der frühen Wissenschaftsfotografie zu den Künsten des 20. Jahrhunderts (München, 2016), Gordon MattaClark. Moment to Moment. Space. Hg. mit Hubertus von Amelunxen und Philip Ursprung (Nürnberg, 2012)

MATTHIAS BOECKL

Matthias Boeckl promovierte in Kunstgeschichte 1988 an der Universität Wien; Professor für Geschichte der Architektur an der Universität für angewandte Kunst Wien; Chefredakteur von architektur. aktuell; Autor und Gestalter von zahlreichen Essays, Büchern und Ausstellungen zum Thema moderne und zeitgenössische Kunst und Architektur.

WOLFGANG FIEL

Wolfgang Fiel ist Senior Lecturer an der Universität für angewandte Kunst Wien und arbeitet in diversen Funktionen und organisatorischen Rahmen als Architekt, Künstler, Gestalter, Kurator, Forscher und Schriftsteller. Er ist gründender Leiter des in Wien beheimateten ICP Institute for cultural policy, Gründungsmitglied der gemeinschaftlichen künstlerischen Praxis tat ort, Berater der UNIDO, Mitglied des Beirates für Kunst und Kultur des österreichischen Bundeskanzleramtes sowie Mitglied des Beirates für politische Theorie des Verlages Cambridge Scholars Publishing, UK.

Als Autor hat er umfangreiche Werke verfasst und publiziert. Seine

neuesten Bücher sind, u. a. Getting Things Done, erschienen im Birkhäuser Verlag, und Emancipating the Many: A Practice Led Investigation into Emergent Paradigms of Immediate Political Action, erschienen bei Cambridge Scholars Publishing.

PHILLIP DENNY

Phillip Denny ist Doktorand der Architektur und Theorie an der Harvard University. Seine Arbeit beschäftigt sich mit dem Austausch zwischen Gestaltung, Medien und Technologie im 20. Jahrhundert. Seine Schriften sind unter anderem in der New York Times, in Volume, Metropolis und im Harvard Design Magazine erschienen. Zurzeit arbeitet an der ersten englischen Übersetzung des urbanen Manifests La ville cybernétique (Die kybernetische Stadt) des kybernetischen Künstlers Nicolas Schöffer. Er hat bereits Masterabschlüsse in Architektur und der Geschichte der Architektur in Princeton und Harvard erworben.

STEFAN POLÓNYI

Stefan Polónyi (geboren 1930 in Gyula, Ungarn) gilt als einer der renommiertesten deutschen Bauingenieure und Hochschullehrer. Nach seinem Diplom in Budapest (1952) war Polónyi ab 1957 als beratender Ingenieur in Köln tätig und von 1965 bis 1972 Professor für Tragwerkslehre an der TU Berlin. Von 1973 bis 1995 war Stefan Polónyi Professor für Tragkonstruktionen an der Universität Dortmund und Mitbegründer der Abteilung Bauwesen.

Neben vielen herausragenden Projekten mit Architekten wie etwa Kurt Ackermann, Norman Foster, Frei Otto, Gustav Peichl oder auch Oswald Mathias Ungers veröffentlichte Polónyi eine Vielzahl von wegweisenden Büchern und Beiträgen zum besseren Verständnis von Architektur und Tragkonstruktion; zuletzt Wie man die Architektur zum Tragen bringt, Essen, Klartext Verlag, Essen, 2016.

JOHN A. ENRIGHT

John A. Enright, FAIA, ist stellvertretender Direktor/leitender wissenschaftlicher Mitarbeiter an der sci-Arc und Mitbegründer des Architekturbüros Griffin Enright Architects, Los Angeles, zusammen mit Margaret Griffin, FAIA. Ihre Arbeit wurde auf lokaler, nationaler und internationaler Ebene publiziert und bereits mit mehr als vierzig Preisen für herausragendes Gestalten ausgezeichnet, darunter AIA-Preise auf allen Ebenen sowie The American Architecture Award des Chicago Athenaeum. John Enright lehrte Gestaltung und hielt Technologieseminare an der sci-Arc, Syracuse University, University of Houston und University of Southern California. Seine wissenschaftliche Forschung beschäftigt sich sowohl mit Gestaltung und Bautechnologie, als auch mit neuen digitalen Paradigmen bezüglich der Herstellung und Konstruktion.

CLEMENS PREISINGER

Clemens Preisinger ist Bauingenieur und Forscher. Er begann seine Laufbahn als Forscher am Institut für Tragkonstruktion an der Technischen Universität Wien. Seit 2008 arbeitet er für Bollinger + Grohmann Ingenieure in Wien und gleichzeitig an einigen Forschungsprojekten an der Universität für angewandte Kunst Wien. Dort ist er aktuell Leiter der Abteilung Digital Simulation, wo die Möglichkeiten zur Anwendung computergestützter Modellierungsverfahren in der frühen Phase der Architekturplanung untersucht werden. Seit 2010 entwickelt Clemens Preisinger freiberuflich das parametrische, interaktive Finite Element Program *Karamba3D*. Er schloss das Studium des Bauingenieurwesens mit der Promotion an der Technischen Universität Wien ab.

ANDREI GHEORGHE

Andrei Gheorghe ist Architekt und unterrichtet an der Universität für angewandte Kunst Wien. Er studierte an der Akademie der bildenden Künste Wien und, nach der Verleihung des Fulbright-Stipendiums, auch an der Harvard University, wo er mit Auszeichnung diplomierte. Andrei Gheorghe hat an der Akademie der bildenden Künste Wien, sci-Arc Los Angeles, Portland State University und Harvard Graduate School of Design

(Career Discovery Program) unterrichtet. Zuvor arbeitete er als Architekt für Jakob + MacFarlane, dECOi Paris und Foreign Office Architects (FOA) in London. Sein Forschungsschwerpunkt liegt disziplinübergreifend an der Schnittstelle von Design & Technologie in Architektur, Konstruktion und Digitalen Medien; ein Thema, wofür er mit dem Harvard Digital Design Award 2009 und dem internationalen AZ Award 2015 ausgezeichnet wurde. 2019 hat Andrei seine Dissertation an der Universität für angewandte Kunst Wien unter der Leitung von Hani Rashid und Klaus Bollinger abgeschlossen.

MORITZ HEIMRATH

Moritz Heimrath hat an der Staatlichen Akademie der Bildenden Künste Stuttgart studiert und sein Studium an der Universität für angewandte Kunst Wien im Jahr 2010 abgeschlossen. Derzeit ist er Partner bei Bollinger + Grohmann Ingenieure in Wien und arbeitet auch im Entwicklungsteam von *Karamba3D*, einem interaktiven parametrischen Finite Element Plug-in für *Grasshopper*. Sein wissenschaftlicher Schwerpunkt beschäftigt sich mit dem Verhältnis zwischen Struktur, rechnergestützten Strategien und ästhetischen architektonischen Konzepten. Zudem hat er sich auf parametrische Entwurfsmethoden spezialisiert und verwendet digitale Tools für die Evaluierung, generative Berechnung und Optimierung in seiner alltäglichen beruflichen Praxis. Moritz Heimrath lehrt die Umsetzung von digitalen Entwurfsstrategien am Institut für Technologie GSO in Nürnberg, Deutschland, sowie digitale Analysen und Simulationen an der Akademie der bildenden Künste Wien. Im Jahr 2012 erhielt er das MAK-Schindler-Stipendium vom Bundesministerium für Unterricht, Kunst und Kultur.

ADAM ORLINSKI

Adam Orlinski hat Architektur an der Universität für angewandte Kunst Wien studiert, wo er zum Abschluss seines Studiums mit dem Würdigungspreis des Bundesministeriums

für Bildung, Wissenschaft und Forschung für herausragende Leistungen ausgezeichnet wurde. Derzeit arbeitet er bei Bollinger + Grohmann Ingenieure Wien sowie im Entwicklungsteam des *Karamba3D*, eines interaktiven parametrischen Finite-Element Plug-In für *Grasshopper*. Er hat sich auf parametrische Tools wie *Rhino 3D + Grasshopper*, *Karamba3D* und *Kangaroo 2* spezialisiert, und wird oft von verschiedenen europäischen Universitäten eingeladen, Workshops zum Thema rechnergestützter Entwurfsstrategien zu veranstalten. Er ist Mitverfasser des künstlerischen Forschungsprojekts »n.formations und »fluid bodies« (FWF-PEEK), das sich mit dem komplexen ästhetischen Potential von fortgeschrittenen strukturellen Algorithmen beschäftigte.

DANKSAGUNG

Diese Publikation wäre ohne die groß-
zügige Unterstützung der Universität für
angewandte Kunst Wien und die frucht-
bare Zusammenarbeit mit dem Baukunstarchiv der Akademie der Künste in Berlin
nicht möglich gewesen.

Den Herausgebern ist es ein
besonderes Anliegen, Roswitha Janowski-
Fritsch für ihren unermüdlichen Einsatz
und Paulus M. Dreibholz für seine Geduld
und einfühlsame grafische Gestaltung
großen Dank auszusprechen.

Vielen herzlichen Dank an unsere
Autorinnen und Autoren: Gerald Bast,
Eva-Maria Barkhofen, Parsa Khalili,
Mark Wigley, Angela Lammert, Matthias
Boeckl, Wolfgang Fiel und Eckhard
Schulze-Fielitz, Phillip Denny, John A.
Enright, Stefan Polónyi, Clemens Preisinger,
Andrei Gheorghe, Moritz Heimrath und
Adam Orlinski. Großer Dank gebührt auch
den Studierenden von 2012 und 2016 und
den Künstlerinnen und Künstlern Andreas
Zybach, Tomás Saraceno, Han Koning,
Gego, Antony Gormley, Lilah Fowler, Tae
Eun Ahn, Peter Smithson, Peter Jellitsch,
Olafur Eliasson, Michal Bartosik, Mark
Hagen und Jürgen Mayer H.. Sie alle haben
zum Gelingen dieses Werks beigetragen.

Unser besonderer Dank gilt Ray
Wachsmann, Eva-Maria Barkhofen und
Tanja Morgenstern, außerdem Raffael
Strasser, Camilla Nielsen, Roderick
O'Donovan, Irina Pálffy-Daun-Seiler und
Marina Brandtner für ihre wertvolle
Unterstützung.

Auch wenn die Arbeit an dieser
Publikation langwierig und mitunter auch
anstrengend war, sind wir überzeugt,
dass wir damit nun dem Leben und herausragenden Werk Konrad Wachsmanns in
gebührender Weise Tribut zollen.

Nochmals ein herzliches Dankeschön
an alle!

Klaus Bollinger, Florian Medicus

IMPRINT

Editors: Klaus Bollinger and Florian
Medicus, Institute of Architecture
at the University of Applied Arts Vienna
and the Akademie der Künste, Berlin

Editorial Team: Roswitha Janowski-
Fritsch, Florian Medicus

Library of Congress Control Number:
2019954419

Bibliographic information published
by the German National Library;
The German National Library lists this
publication in the Deutsche National-
bibliografie; detailed bibliographic
data are available on the Internet at
http://dnb.dnb.de.

Project Management "Edition Angewandte"
on behalf of the University of Applied Arts
Vienna: Roswitha Janowski-Fritsch,
A-Vienna

Content and Production Editor on behalf
of the Publisher: Katharina Holas, A-Vienna

Translation: Camilla Nielsen, Roderick
O'Donovan, A-Vienna

Copy Editing: Irina Pálffy-Daun-Seiler (GE),
Marina Brandtner (EN)

Graphic Design: Atelier Dreibholz,
Paulus M. Dreibholz and Raffael Strasser,
A-Vienna

Printing: Holzhausen, die Buchmarke der
Gerin Druck GmbH, A-Wolkersdorf

Cover Photo: © Christoph Opperer

© 2020 Birkhäuser Verlag GmbH, Basel
P.O. Box 44, 4009 Basel, Switzerland
Part of Walter de Gruyter GmbH, Berlin/
Boston

ISSN 1866-248X
ISBN 978-3-0356-1962-1

987654321
www.birkhauser.com

edition:'ʌŋgewʌndtə
Universität für angewandte Kunst Wien
University of Applied Arts Vienna

IOʌ INSTITUTE OF
ARCHITECTURE

AKADEMIE DER KÜNSTE

Gefördert durch / Funded by

Die Beauftragte der Bundesregierung
für Kultur und Medien